MUSINGS OF A
LIPSTICK LESBIAN

A True Story of

Blind Love and Betrayal

Susan Isabella Sheehan

This book is dedicated to my beloved children and grandchildren, who believed in me when I no longer believed in myself and found me when I was lost beyond hope.

Table of Contents

Introduction

Our stories are who we are. This is the true story of the five and a half years I spent in an unstable and violent Lesbian relationship. During that time, I learned that there is a distinct difference between loving the idea of someone and loving who they actually are, and I almost lost my life in the midst of this discovery.

Writing about personal experiences while remaining objective is difficult at best. In this narrative I have done my absolute best to do just that. It has taken me more than a year to write this. Many of the events were extremely painful to recall, and as I wrote, it was as if I were reliving the moments.

I am certain that many of my readers will be able to closely relate to the turn of events that took place from January 2008 to March 2014. If not, then perhaps this will help you to appreciate a better understanding of the fragility of being human, being in love, and the sudden painful realization of what truly is.

My decisions created the perfect combination of events that formed a storm that nearly destroyed my life. I had a beautiful family and an amazing job from which I planned to retire. I traveled extensively, especially to Ireland, spending weeks at a time there. Then one morning, in a moment of dark despair, all of that changed.

This is the true story of what happened during the strangest five and a half years of my life. A story of hope and hopelessness, joy and despair, love and absolute cruel abuse and pain that I endured during that relatively brief period of time, and finally finding home and hearth once again.

Chapter One: The Breakdown

In January of 2008, I filed for divorce from my second husband. Tom was a bit of an eccentric and had somewhat odd and unusual thoughts about life and how to manage it. He was, as I discovered, conducting DNA testing on one of our residents on the property that we managed together by inserting his tongue into her mouth and probing.

She was blissfully ignorant, her boyfriend was completely unaware, and it was the second time this had happened in as many years. The first time that I was made aware of his activity I sat him down and had a long conversation with him. I told him that I loved and forgave him, but that if it ever happened again that I would file for divorce.

Fool me once shame on you, fool me twice shame on me, as the saying goes. He was gone from my life by the end of January, and I assumed most of the responsibility for our one hundred and fifty-four unit property, with the exclusion of maintenance. I had his former assistant took care of all of the residents maintenance issues.

Of course, my heart was broken. I did love Tom very much, and he was a wonderful companion. I missed him yet I was so incredibly angry with him for what he had done. I shed so many tears over the following month and a half that I developed an infection in my right eye and had to seek medical help from my ophthalmologist.

The Spring and Summer passed very smoothly. I was not in the least bit overwhelmed with my position. My residents loved me. My youngest daughter was my assistant manager. My home life was wonderful, even though I was a bit lonely from time to time. In June, my oldest daughter Stephanie and her family moved in with me.

Of course, I did have people whom I loved to talk to on a daily basis, and not just over the phone, but having my daughter and her family actually living with me was special. I thoroughly enjoyed my grandchildren there, along with the time I was given to spend sharing love with them.

My morning coffee and meals were no longer solitary events. Stephanie joined me on the patio every morning and was there to prepare our lunches and dinners every day. Stephanie, the children and I went out to lunch many times, and Landon joined us a couple of those times.

One of our favorite spots was Daphne's Greek Family Style restaurant in Sunnyvale. Home life was wonderful. My youngest child, Maggie, would stop by with my granddaughter Caitie in the mornings before work, and my son David came by when he was able to, sometimes by himself, sometimes with Rachel and the children.

Stephanie and I went shopping together often, and even took the Caltrain to San Francisco once with her children Zacc and Corryn. It was the first time either of them had been on a train, and I watched them as they looked out of the windows in amazement as we moved swiftly past all of the cities and towns.

Life was wonderful at home, my workdays were productive, and everything was going simply fine. At that time, I was a member of an online group to save the Hill of Tara in Ireland, which was being threatened by the M-3 Motorway which was being planned for construction.

One day in late August while I was visiting our online group, I noticed that they were canvassing for protestors to join them in the fight against the construction of the motorway. I made a rash decision, one that was almost regretful, that I would travel to Ireland alone for two weeks to aid the protestors.

One of my greatest passions was, and still is, the preservation of the integrity of the ancient sites in Ireland. Honoring my Ancestors and the land from which my family came was important to me. So, I made my plane reservations and was offered accommodation while I was there by a woman I had met online in the Save Tara group.

My children didn't want to me to travel by myself, but I was not afraid to do so. I have always been quite adventurous and had traveled alone many times in the past. It is just that I had never traveled over five thousand miles alone, so this concerned them. I tried to put their minds at ease by saying that I would be just fine.

I returned from Ireland on September 26th, 2008. Although I was exhausted and defeated from my trip, I was still scheduled to return to work on the 28th. I had one day to recover from the plane ride and accompanying jet lag. Saturday was spent getting my home affairs in order and trying to rest up for Sunday's work.

Even though Stephanie and Landon had kept the house stocked while I was away I found that I needed to purchase a few personal toiletries, so I decided to drive to one of the local stores. I told Stephanie that I would be right back, but when I tried to start my car, I discovered that the battery had died while I was away.

I went back inside the apartment and told Landon. He removed my old battery and drove me to the auto parts store to purchase a new one. He took the time to install the new battery for me, which I was grateful for. When he was finished installing it I ran my errands and drove back home to get some much needed rest.

After being away for two weeks I was actually looking forward to being in my office again. I awoke early on the morning of the 28th and prepared for the day ahead of me. Even though I was still a bit travel fatigued I was anxious to see what condition my office was in. I had coffee and cigarettes with Stephanie before setting out for my office.

Stephanie and I sat together on one of my patios enjoying one another's company. She had done a rather spectacular job of taking care of all my plants, both inside the apartment and on both patios. I had roses, hibiscus, herbs and other beautiful plants filling both of my patios, and many beautiful potted plants inside.

My office was less than one hundred yards from my apartment, and my walk there was always enjoyable. I got along well with all of my residents, treating them as if they were a part of my own family, making them feel comfortable, welcome and at ease. I loved my job and was blessed to have it.

I opened the door to my office and was extremely pleased to see that it was in perfect condition, thanks to Maggie, who was my assistant manager two days a week, and who had taken over my position while I was away in Ireland. There was literally nothing for me to do other than to answer the phone. I was incredibly delighted.

That evening was spent with Stephanie, Landon, and the grandchildren. Stephanie had prepared a delicious dinner, something that I had missed while in Ireland. We spent hours after dinner visiting and catching up on life. Before going to bed, I sat outside by myself, breathing in the fresh air and feeling extremely grateful to be home.

My apartment was beautiful, richly furnished and thoughtfully decorated with items that Tom and I had collected during the years that we had been together. There was a master bedroom, a middle bedroom that was converted into an office, and a large guest bedroom, where Stephanie, Landon and the two grandchildren stayed.

Monday morning came, and it was back to the office for me. The day went smoothly. There were a few resident issues which I handled with ease, along with several early rental payments to be entered into the computer. I took my lunch break at the normal time, and Stephanie had a lovely repast prepared for me.

We visited while I ate, then went out onto the patio to smoke and have coffee. When my lunchbreak was over I went back to the office to finish my day. I spent the rest of the afternoon putting together brochure packets and tidying the office. I made sure that my computer was backed up to the main office computer and took out the trash.

When I arrived home, the apartment was darkened and empty. There was no one home. I was deeply disappointed. I had been so lonely while in Ireland, and I needed my family to be nearby. I waited for the children and grandchildren to return, but the time passed by without anyone coming home.

For whatever reason I decided to open a bottle of red wine. I sat outside on my patio drinking wine and smoking cigarettes, and before I knew it the bottle was empty. I opened yet another bottle. I should have known better, but I had not realized yet the state my psyche was in. Fragile, bruised, and ready to collapse.

I drank the second bottle and decided to just go to bed. The next morning, September 30th, I awoke as usual, but not very bright eyed or bushy tailed. Stephanie was already up and about and greeted me with a smile. She poured me a cup of fresh hot coffee, and I took it out to the patio to drink it, have a cigarette, and think.

But deep thought was something that I should have avoided. As I sat there, I began to ruminate on my recent journey to Ireland, as well as the lonely night before. I was overcome with dark and depressive thoughts and couldn't control myself. I simply couldn't stop the emotions that I were brewing.

What I didn't realize is that I was falling into a deep despair accompanied by complete and utter hopelessness. I abruptly got up from my chair and went to my bedroom. I took two large, dry Sacred Datura pods from my altar. I went into the kitchen, placed the pods into my coffee cup, crushed them into miniscule fragments.

I poured hot coffee onto them, and placed the cup into the microwave. I had ingested Datura several times in the past, exceedingly small amounts though, and only for the perceptual and mood altering effects, more like a DMT Spiritual journeying. But this time I was hellbent on finishing myself.

I never once considered the ramifications if I were to survive suicide. All that I could think was that I was finished with life and the pain that it brought with it. The microwave dinged, I pulled my cup out, and began sipping on the concoction. I could taste the toxins in the liquid and feel the burn as it flowed down my throat.

Then I put my head back and forced myself to drink the entire contents of the cup. Stephanie was exercising in my home office and I went in there to tell her what I had done. I tried to tell her how lonely I had been in Ireland, and how empty I felt when she, Landon, and the grandchildren had gone out the night before.

I tried to tell her that it was as if I had been abandoned by them, and that all that I wanted to do was die. But the words just didn't come out. The Datura had already taken hold of my mind and body. Somehow, though, I managed to tell her that I felt all of this was her fault, when none of it actually was.

I was unable to say anything else. My thoughts were jumbled, and my body began feeling like a rubbery substance. I couldn't walk on my own. Stephanie saw what was happening and quickly moved to help me get into my bed. As she walked me down the hallway my legs felt like they were fifty feet long and made of elastic.

I was hopelessly melting into the carpet and hallucinating wildly. My perceptions were altered to the point that I didn't know where or when I was. Keep in mind that Datura, when taken in small amounts, is beneficial, but the amount that I had taken it is considered extremely dangerous and deadly.

She phoned the EMT's immediately, who in turn contacted the Mountain View police department. I remember conversing with my deceased aunt, brother, and parents, all of whom stood in the corner of my bedroom. I vaguely remember asking Stephanie if she could see them. I can only imagine the severity of her distress.

I was told that the EMT's and police arrived quickly. I really do not remember them being there, but I was told that I was promptly taken by ambulance to a local hospital. The next hours are vague and foggy. A gastric lavage was performed in the emergency room and I was placed on a seventy-two hour psychiatric hold and suicide watch.

I faintly recall being in the hospital, and have the vaguest memory of being restrained, my wrists chained above my head, apparently to protect myself and others. I have a dreamlike memory of being given several different drugs, one of them injected directly into my abdomen repeatedly by a demon-like nurse.

I was disoriented, confused, and the medications they were giving me only magnified those effects. I remember David and Maggie visiting me the evening of my hospitalization. I vividly recall seeing David and Maggie standing at the foot of the bed. They were talking to me, but I couldn't understand what they were saying.

I recall looking at them and saying, "You both look like the Simpsons. Your skin is bright yellow". I honestly don't know how they reacted as I was slipping in and out of consciousness, heavily drugged with anti-psychotics and the remnants of the Datura. Maggie later told me that I was smoking an imaginary cigarette.

I had caused deep distress for my children and most likely my grandchildren as well, and I didn't even realize it. I spent only one night and part of the next morning hospitalized. When Maggie stopped by to check up on me the next morning I told her that I was going to leave the hospital and go home.

She said emphatically that it was not a good idea, and that I really needed to stay in the hospital until I was fully recovered, both physically and mentally. I didn't listen to her. I called for a nurse and I demanded that I be discharged immediately. The nurse told me that was impossible, as I was on a mandatory 72-hour hold.

I was obstinate and not going to take no for an answer. I located the catheter that they had inserted into my bladder, and looking at the nurse, told her that I was going to rip it out of my body if she didn't take it out. This must have shocked her because she came to my bed immediately and removed the catheter.

I was spinning wildly, completely drained and still feeling the effects from the Datura and the anti-psychotic drugs that I had been given, but I got out of the bed anyway, almost falling to the floor. Maggie held onto me to keep me from injuring myself. I asked her to take me to her van.

With Maggie's help I managed to walk out of the hospital and get into her van. She drove to my apartment, all the while watching me out of the corner of her eye. She pulled into the parking space next to my car and came around to the passenger side to help me with getting out of my seat. She walked me to the door of my apartment and knocked.

The Downward Spiral

Stephanie opened the door, her eyes wide with surprise. I could hear the grandchildren in the living room. Maggie said, somewhat apologetically, "Mama refused to stay in the hospital." Stephanie sighed, and together they walked me down the hallway and helped me into my bed making me as comfortable as was possible.

Still under the influence of the anti-psychotic drugs and Datura, I spun as I lay back on my pillow. I felt dirty, and my hair was hopelessly knotted and tangled. I asked Maggie to help me brush it out, but the back of it was wadded into a tightly tangled ball. Try as she might, Maggie couldn't manage to get a brush through it.

She asked if she could wash and condition it, and I weakly replied yes. Since I was not able to stand for long she placed a plastic patio chair in the shower. She turned on the water, allowing it to warm up so that it would be warm and soothing. She helped me undress, get into the shower, and guided me into the chair.

Maggie washed my hair, gently massaged conditioner into it, and secured it on top of my head with a clip. Nest, she lathered my body and then rinsed the body wash off with warm water. Taking the clip from my hair she massaged the conditioner into my scalp for what seemed like hours.

After rinsing the conditioner out, she began brushing my hair while I was still seated in the shower. Even though my hair was clean and conditioned the brush could barely move through the tightly wound knots. It took her over an hour to brush my hair, and when she was finished, a ball of hair at least five inches in diameter had come out.

My long, beautiful waist length hair, which I had grown in honor of my two grandmothers, was damaged, possibly beyond repair. I couldn't believe it, but there was nothing that I could do about it. Plus, I was in no state to do anything. My mind was trying to recover, my body was weakened, and my thoughts were almost nonexistent.

My children were embarrassed by what I had done, and in retrospect I do not blame them. Rather than admit to our employer Regan that I had attempted suicide, Maggie told him that I caught a stomach virus while in Ireland, had been hospitalized, and was now on bedrest for the next two weeks.

He told her to have me rest and check in with him when I was feeling better. I was grateful to her, because even though I was still not in the right frame of mind, and my body was weakened, I didn't want to lose my job. I had come too far and worked too hard to get to where I was in the company.

Throughout the ensuing two weeks, as the impact of the Datura and anti-psychotic medications receded, I redeveloped a penchant for alcohol. I had struggled in the past with it. During a particularly difficult time in my early forties, I used it as a coping mechanism, which I knew was maladaptive, but it seduced me and I fell in love with it.

I had kept a stock of liquor in the apartment, half gallon handles of gin, vodka and rum, and I began drinking small amounts at first, then as the days progressed I consumed it in larger and larger quantities, usually in the afternoon. In the evenings I drank wine, plus liquor. I was saturating my body, keeping myself hopelessly inebriated.

Stephanie was my strength and support through this dark time. She asked if I would care to write, and she placed a notebook and pen on my nightstand, suggesting that I write down my thoughts and feelings. I made an attempt at it but grew tired very quickly of trying to remember things that only conjured distress and depression.

Suicide was often in my thoughts. I was both happy and sad that I had failed in my attempt. I wondered why exactly I hadn't been successful. Frequently, when I closed my eyes, I wished to never awaken again, just to go blissfully to sleep and never wake up. But I always did return to the reality of life.

Michael, a friend from work, called one evening to see how I was doing. I invited him over and he brought a bottle of vodka with him. We drank in my bedroom, me lying on the bed, him sitting on it. I was comfortable enough with him that I was perfectly frank about what I had done. He was not in the least bit surprise, but he was concerned.

He asked if there was anything at all that he could do for me, and I told him that being my friend, listening to me, and supporting me through this period of time was enough. Before he left he told me that he would be available anytime that I needed to talk, but as it turned out we didn't speak again for several years.

I had moments of pure, crystalline rationale, when I felt inspired to write or create art. Those moments never lasted long, and I would lose my momentum, falling into depressing and melancholy declines for days at a time. I never considered connecting with a therapist or psychiatrist because that would suggest a type of failure on my part.

The days passed slowly, feeling like years instead of hours, crawling along at a snail's pace. In the second week after my suicide attempt Regan, the owner of the company I worked for, called to inquire how I was doing. Although I was not close to recovering I fibbed and told him in a cheerful voice that I could start back anytime.

He was thrilled. He said that I would need to get a medical release from a doctor before returning to work. I replied that I would make an appointment as soon as we finished talking and I hung up the phone. I didn't have my own doctor, but I was part of the Camino Group of medical providers and didn't have a problem connecting with one.

I was able to make an appointment for the very next day. I was undeniably not ready to assume my responsibilities for the property, but I didn't want to lose my job as a result of not being able to attend to my normal duties as property manager. I was conflicted but decided to move forward and attempt an acceptable level of normalcy.

The next morning, I drove myself to the clinic which was located only a few blocks away from my apartment. I checked in with the receptionist, was handed a clipboard with forms attached to it that I was asked to fill out and told that I would be seen shortly. I sat, filled out the forms, and waited.

I was worried that the doctor would have read the report of my recent hospitalization and refuse to give me a work release. But I worried for no reason whatsoever. A nurse called my name and led me into an examination room. The doctor came in soon after, took a cursory look at me, asked how I was feeling, and signed the release.

I felt relieved. He never asked me why I was hospitalized, and even though the clinic was connected with El Camino Hospital, where I had been taken by ambulance, he had not looked at any of my records. I didn't say anything, because I wanted to get back to work. The doctor told me that I could return to work on October 14th.

I hesitated because I didn't actually feel ready to return to work, and I wanted to talk to the doctor more about perhaps getting help, but he left the exam room before I could utter a word. I phoned my employer upon my return home, and he was ecstatic. He told me that he planned on dropping by my office to welcome me back.

I was one of his top performing employees and had done exemplary work for the company for close to five years. I was never late to the office, stayed well past closing time every day, and most of the other managers and all of my residents loved me. The morning of the 14th was upon me before I knew it and I braced myself for the day.

The ever increasing amounts of alcohol that I had begun consuming were beginning to take a toll on me in ways that pointed to a perilous ending. I ignored the warning signs. I told myself that I was a strong woman, reminded myself of all the trauma and ordeals I had survived, and convinced myself that I could power through anything.

Somehow I managed to get through my first day back, but by the time I returned home for lunch I was barely able to walk. Stephanie had a hearty meal prepared for me. She knew that I had lost quite a bit of weight during the past few months. I ate what I could, relaxed on the patio for a while, then returned to my office to finish the day.

Unbeknownst to me, the stage was already set for a devastating disaster. Through some mysterious miracle I was able to make it through the first week without incident, but the following week began a downward spiral that would set in motion events that I would never had dreamed of happening.

I drove to the bank to make a deposit of rental checks. As I was driving back to the office I noticed the liquor store where I always made my purchases from. As if in a trance, I signaled to turn, parked my car, and went inside the store. I began casually browsing the aisles, gazing at the various liquors that were being offered.

I knew better, and could feel my anxiety level rising, but I reached out and got a quart of gin anyway. To make it all seem innocent, I also bought cheese, sausage, olives and crackers. I returned to my office and stashed it all very quickly and discreetly deep beneath my desk where it would be out of view of anyone coming into the office.

I ate some of the sausage and cheese, and when I knew that no one was around, especially the grounds workers, I snuck sips of gin. I heard myself giggle like a mischievous child, felt the alcohol wash over my body with comforting warmth, and I was really quite pleased with myself.

I had just lifted the bottle to my lips to take a drink when I saw Ted, one of the managers from the head office, pulling into the parking lot. I quickly and carefully moved the alcohol deep beneath my desk with one of my feet. I took a breath mint from my purse and put a big, faux smile on my lips.

He walked through the door smiling and told me that he was just checking on me to make sure that I was doing okay. Already feeling the effects from the gin, I smiled back and told him that I was fine and so glad to be back in the office. We engaged in small talk for a few minutes about the property, the main office, and life.

He asked me how my trip to Ireland had been. I replied that it had been delightful, and a wonderful journey. I didn't want to go into detail about a trip gone bad with someone I really didn't know. I somehow managed to have a reasonably intelligent conversation with him. He patted me on the shoulder, said goodbye and left the office.

Even that visit didn't prevent me from continuing to sip on the gin. At that point I really didn't care if anyone else saw me. I wanted relief from the strange and terrible darkness that was slowly descending. I didn't realize that alcohol was the most significant part of the darkness, ruthlessly taking its hold on me.

I continued to drink the gin. I realized that I needed to urinate, so I got up from my chair and stumbled to the door, thinking that I could walk to the commons restroom by the front pool. I didn't make it further than the sidewalk across from the office. The next thing I knew I was lying behind a thatch of thorny bushes, unable to get up.

One of my residents happened to be walking by and saw what happened. He reached through the bushes, helped me back onto my feet and into my office. I was so drunk that I was not in the least bit embarrassed. At that very moment Maggie pulled into the parking lot by the office and saw the entire episode.

She parked her van, came into the office, looked underneath my desk and saw the gin. She realized that I had been drinking. She was livid. She asked me, "Mama, what the hell are you thinking? Get in the van. I'm taking you home right now!" She grabbed my purse and computer, along with the gin, helped me outside and into her van.

She went back to put the phone on answering service, secure the office door, and drove me to my apartment. I was so inebriated that she had to carry me inside. Stephanie was visibly upset, and reasonably so. All of my children were under the impression that I was recovering. But such was not the case.

Stephanie and Maggie put me to bed and I fell into a drunken sleep and didn't awaken until the next morning. I felt hungover but decided to go to the office anyway. I worked the entire day without incident, and I refrained from taking alcohol into my office again. I had not considered the repercussions had I been seen by management.

I loathed the fact that I had lost control of myself. I couldn't think of a reasonable excuse for what I had done by getting drunk in my office. I realized that I was weakened from my suicide attempt, the drugs and the abuse of the alcohol, but I was determined not to allow that to happen ever again.

I even did my best at home to not consume as much alcohol as I had been. I only allowed myself a cocktail after work and a glass of wine with dinner. I thought that I could manage myself this way. What I didn't realize is that I had already fallen into a vortex of enslavement which was taking me into its dark empty chamber.

Somehow I managed to get through the next two weeks without incident, but I was continuing to deteriorate, physically, mentally and spiritually. I had no idea where to find the strength that I used to have. I tried to live and behave as normally as possible, but it was as if it were pointless for me to do so. I was going through the motions of being me without actually being me.

Hitting Rock Bottom

Saturday October 25th was Stephanie's twenty-sixth birthday, and Landon's twenty-eighth birthday was on October 29th, so I decided to treat them to a celebratory dinner. I wanted to try and somehow make up for all of the confusion and chaos that I had unwittingly created. I made reservations at Stuart Anderson's Black Angus in Sunnyvale.

We had a superb celebration, prime rib with all of the accompaniments for the adults, cheeseburgers and fries for the children, and for everyone rich chocolate ganache cake complete with birthday candles for dessert. I almost felt normal, and everyone else, including the babies, seemed to have enjoyed themselves.

I drank way too much wine, though, and Landon drove us home. Back at the apartment I made myself a cup of tea and went outside to sit at the patio to sober up a bit and try to relax before bedtime. I was just beginning to unwind when one of the residents who lived in the apartment above me threw a bucket of dirty water onto the back patio.

This was not the first time it had happened, and the filthy water, which I assumed was mop water, always landed on my beautiful rose bushes. I walked to the back patio and tried to get their attention. One of them popped their head over the balcony railing and I heard sarcastic laughter. I could feel my blood starting to boil.

I regretted ever having rented the apartment to them. They had been a nuisance since they first moved onto the property, thinking that they were above the rules of the property and could do anything that they pleased. They were rude, loud, and obnoxious, and had illegally moved their girlfriends into the apartment.

I went into my apartment and grabbed my property keys. I went up the stairs to their apartment and knocked on the door. No one answered. I was becoming enraged, my blood pressure at a boiling point. I knocked again, louder this time. The next decision that I made was irrational, poorly thought out, and would change the course of my life for years to come.

I listened at the door and could hear them talking and laughing loudly. Knowing better than to do so I used my property key and unlocked their front door. I peered into the apartment and asked them why they had thrown the bucket of water onto my patio. They continued to laugh at me, which only served to infuriate me further.

I noticed the girlfriends inside, and not being quite sober said, "Please, do not throw your water over the balcony, and you girls have one day to complete a change of occupancy or I will have you all evicted from this apartment." I opened the door a bit further and the tip of my toe went over the threshold.

I was, for all intents and purposes, inside their apartment. They didn't respond. They looked at me and laughed. I pulled the door shut, turned away, still hearing their laughter, and walked back down the stairs. I went into my apartment and hung up my keys. I didn't think about the impact my toe going past their threshold would have.

The next morning, I woke up ready to start my work week. I was just finishing my first cup of coffee when there was a knock on my front door. I couldn't imagine who it could be. I answered the door, and there stood Regan, his executive assistant Jean, and Sherry, the manager of managers.

Sherry looked at me with contempt and told me that I had breached my contract with them by entering an apartment without permission from the resident. She demanded that I turn in my property keys. She informed me that I was terminated effective immediately. My knees buckled and my body began to go numb. I heard buzzing in my ears.

I tried to explain what had actually happened, but Sherry refused to listen to me. Regan didn't look at me, but Jean, an old and decrepit woman who had been with the company since the dawn of time, pursed her lips, shook her head disapprovingly, and stared at me. Sherry told me that I had five days to vacate the premises.

Jean spoke up and told me that I was to never step foot on one of their properties again. She went on to tell me that if I attempted to try to stay with either my son David or my daughter Maggie, both of whom worked for the same company and lived on their properties, that she would have me arrested for trespassing and thrown in jail.

She had a smug look on her old, grizzled face as she spoke. Sherry had her hand out, waiting for the property keys. Jean continued to stare at me, but Regan never looked my way. Sherry and Jean seemed to be relishing what was happening. I was breaking down inside the entire time and felt as if I were going to faint.

In the close to five years that I had been with the company there had never been even a smidgen of love lost between Sherry and myself. From day one there was always animosity, a silent hatred, which emanated from her towards me. Perhaps she was intimidated by my strength or perhaps she was afraid that I would take her job.

Regan continued nervously looking away, never meeting my gaze. I felt that this was not his idea, but I was never able to prove that. How I wished that he had known my about my attempted suicide and that I was still not recovered. I know that things would have gone in a vastly different direction.

But he didn't know because I had not told him, and the doctor who had released me to return to work had not even glanced at my records. Regan was a kind and compassionate man and given my condition and state of mind following my suicide attempt, he would have sought help for me had he known.

Sherry didn't say another word. Instead, she held her hand out, tapping her foot on the cement, waiting for me to give her the property keys. Reluctantly, and with tears in my eyes, I went into the kitchen and took the keys off the hanger they were on. I went back to the opened door and handed them to her.

They all turned and left without saying another word. I was speechless. I was immediately stricken with a sense of dread and fear. This was the company that I had planned to retire from. I had given my all to them, outperformed all the other managers, and received awards based on my accomplishments.

What was I going to do? I slowly closed the door and collapsed onto the carpet in the hallway. I was sobbing uncontrollably. Stephanie came out of her room and found me there. She asked if I was okay and between sobs I told her what had happened. She couldn't believe it. She helped me up and took me outside to the patio.

She poured me a fresh cup of coffee brought it out to the patio and went back inside to call David. He told her not to worry, that he would call the owner the next day to get everything sorted out. She then phoned Maggie who said she would stop by the apartment on her way to Hillsborough Plaza in San Mateo.

Rather than wait for Maggie, and while Stephanie was busy with the children I got dressed, put on some makeup, got my car keys and purse and went outside. I got into my car and started it. I didn't know what I was doing or where I was going, but I put my car in reverse and backed out of the parking space.

I put the car gear and drove away, heading towards El Camino Real, which was the main street closest to the property. At the stop light I saw a bar on the corner across the street, so I drove there and parked my car. I was not one to frequent bars, so I sat for a minute thinking. The next thing I knew it I was inside and seated at the bar.

I ordered a Hennessy's brandy. It was down in one gulp, then I ordered another, then another, and on and on it went, until I was close to becoming drunk. Hours had passed since I walked in the door. The bartender was happy to keep serving me. Why not, at twenty-five dollars a pour?

I was beyond devastated. I was destroyed. Once again, all that I could think of was suicide. And I sunk even deeper into darkness, wishing that I had been successful the first time. I decided to go home and got in my car but I didn't make it home. I ended up passing out in my car in the parking lot of a shopping center across the street from the bar.

I was awakened by a police officer knocking on the driver's side window. He asked me if I was okay, and I told him that I was only tired and had dozed off. I didn't want him to know that I had been drinking and be arrested for DUI. I had never even had a traffic ticket. He was satisfied with that and left.

I eventually managed to drive myself home and went inside my apartment, only to start drinking more. I was trying to drown out this new, and dreadful, reality. I don't even know if anyone else was in the apartment. Stephanie and her family moved out a few days later, and I was left to wallow in my miserable failures alone.

David phoned me the next day and told me that he had spoken with Regan. He had agreed to give me until December 2nd to vacate the apartment, but I no longer worked for him. Maggie checked in on me from time to time trying to get my out of my slump, but it didn't work. I knew, deep down in my heart, what a bitter disappointment I had become.

I continued to spiral downwards, alcohol consuming everything around me. I didn't leave the apartment, ordering my food and alcohol online. One day I did have to leave my apartment to walk to the store and buy cigarettes. I had been drinking and I knew better than to try and drive.

As I was walking down an exceptionally long set of cement steps I suddenly missed a step and fell onto the pavement below. I was barely aware of having fallen as I was highly inebriated. One of my elderly residents saw me fall and came running. She was much older than myself, but she ran down the steps and helped me up anyway.

She ended up walking me to my apartment and helping me into bed. I know that she knew that I was drunk, but she didn't say a word about it. She simply tucked me into bed and quietly left to return to her own apartment. I waited until she was gone and got out of bed. I ended up walking to the store anyway.

This time I avoided walking by her apartment, choosing rather to walk the long way around the property and out the back. I bought cigarettes and even more alcohol. I managed to return home in one piece and drank myself into a corpselike numbness, eventually falling onto the bed and passing out.

During those confusing and befuddled days my children phoned the Mountain View police to come to my apartment and conduct 'welfare checks' on me. Twice I was taken to psychiatric units for evaluation. Once was to Gateway, a behavioral health facility, the other to the psychiatric unit at Valley Medical Center, both located in San Jose.

On the first such occasion I had been sitting at my dining room table smoking a cigarette and drinking hot tea. There was a knock at the door and when I answered it I saw four police officers standing there. They asked if they could come in for a few minutes and I invited them in.

Two of them followed me into the dining room while the other two wandered throughout the apartment, looking from room to room. I sat back down at the dining room table and lit a cigarette. One of the officers ordered me to put my cigarette out and I refused. I told him that he was in my home, and that I would smoke if I wanted to.

The next thing I knew he was violently jerking me up from my chair, slapping handcuffs on me, dragging me out the front door to his cruiser, and shoving me into the back seat. I saw two police cruisers in the parking lot. He and another officer got into the cruiser I was in and the other officer began driving.

They drove me to Gateway to have me admitted and to be evaluated. While they were talking to the intake staff, with their backs turned towards me, I simply walked out the door and called a taxi. I stood on the street corner smoking a cigarette while I waited for the taxi. I knew that my children were worried about me, but this was ridiculous.

I really didn't blame them, however I did wonder why they didn't come to check on me themselves. In fact, I don't recall any of them phoning me during this period of time. I was sure that there was confusion, disappointment and anger melded together in their minds. I was hurt and baffled and decided to address this with them.

When I arrived at my apartment Stephanie and Maggie were removing and disposing all of the liquor that was in the apartment. I watched as they carried bag after bag of bottles to the dumpster. I didn't try to fight or stop them. I knew that as soon as they were gone that I would simply go online and place another order for more liquor.

During the following days I consumed volumes of alcohol, mostly cognac, and I ate extraordinarily little. I occasionally ordered delivery food which sat on my counter mostly untouched. I just wanted to drown out the misery that I found myself in, escape to an alternate reality where things were once again normal and good.

On the second occasion I was sitting at my patio table trying to relax. There was a knock at the door. I got up to answer it, hoping that it was one of my children. Instead, it was another 'welfare check'. There was a female police officer and her partner standing there. The female officer kindly asked if she and her partner could come in and speak with me.

I opened the door and invited them in. We sat at my dining room table for about a half hour talking, and through gentle persuasion and engaging charm she somehow convinced me that I needed to go for another psychiatric evaluation. I willingly agreed to this, realizing that I really did need some type of help, but I was handcuffed yet again.

I was driven to the Valley Medical Center psychiatric unit which is located next to the hospital in San Jose, California. The officers stayed long enough to make sure that I was admitted this time. After being admitted, I was taken to the adult unit and told to sit until I was called by a nurse.

It was late evening by this time, and most of the patients were already down for the night. A nurse finally walked over to where I was seated and told me that I would be there for the rest of the night and possibly the next day, and that I was going to have to be evaluated by a psychiatrist before a decision for my discharge was made.

I asked her when that would be and she said that the evaluation would be the next morning. She led me to a room filled with large, dirty chaise lounges where people were sleeping and told me that I should lie down and try to get some rest. I replied that I wasn't tired, and asked if I could sit in the commons and watch some television.

She told me that would be fine. My body was vibrating with a strange and insistent energy. I could feel my blood pressure rising. I tried to watch television, but I couldn't sit for more than a few minutes. I got up from my chair and began pacing the room. There were a few other patients in the commons, very disturbed people.

Some were staring off into the distance, one was arguing violently with himself, another was forcing herself to vomit. I didn't belong here. Yes, I was having problems, but I was not mentally ill. I paced down the hallways and back to the commons area. As I paced one of my feet crossed a line of yellow tape on the floor.

A police officer was sitting at a desk just beyond the line reading a book. He looked up and curtly ordered me to stay on my side of the tape. I asked him why and he replied that the patients had to stay on their own side. Now what in the world could a line of tape do? It certainly couldn't keep anyone out.

Rather than following his orders, I stood directly on top of the tape and walked on it, as if I were on a tightrope. He abruptly stood up and again ordered me to stop. I asked him what would happen if I didn't. He caressed his firearm and said in a loud voice "Do it again and you'll find out!" He was actually threatening me with his gun!

That was enough for me to stop at once and go to the other side of the room, as far away from him as possible. I decided that I would try to lie down, so I went to the room with the dirty chaise lounges. I was fortunate enough to find an empty one. There were no sheets or blankets, and I wondered if the chair was even sanitary.

I tried to close my eyes, tried to will myself to sleep, but sleep didn't come. I was cold and uncomfortable. I lay there for a while but couldn't get to sleep and mentioned this to one of the nurses who had come to check on the patients. She told me that she had something that might help me and she left the room.

When she returned, she had two Ativans with a plastic cup of water. I had never taken a sleep aid before but felt that it couldn't hurt. Somehow, I managed to sleep for a few hours, but it was not a restful sleep. I was in a strange place, surrounded by very strange people, and those in charge didn't seem to really care about any of the patients.

There were about ten other people in the room, all of them asleep but me. I didn't belong in this place and could hardly wait to see the psychiatrist. After a couple of hours in the chair I got up and asked if there was coffee. A medical aide directed me to a table set up with coffee service.

I took a Styrofoam cup, put some powdered creamer in it, and opened the spigot on the coffee urn. There was no sweetener, so the brew was really quite bitter. I was told that someone would be bringing breakfast shortly, but I was not in the least bit hungry. I wandered aimlessly around the unit for a while, searching for a way out.

I was feeling trapped, panicking, almost as if I had been buried alive. I needed to find a way out. When I was finished with my coffee, I broke the styrofoam cup into small pieces. Every time one of the aides or nurses would go out the exit door I would run and try to put pieces of the cup between the door and the jamb, but to no avail.

I soon tired of this futile attempt at freedom as it was not actually working, so I sat down to watch television with some of the other patients, keeping a close eye on them the entire time. I was not in the mood for any confrontations. Not long after that a cart was pushed

43

through the door filled with trays that our breakfasts were on.

The trays were set up on a table in the same hallway as the coffee service. I walked over and looked at the offering, all of which made me nauseous. Watery eggs with the whites still gelatinous, under-toasted bread with no butter, and pink sausages that appeared to be mostly raw, swimming in cold grease. I was disgusted.

The room was crowded with people at this point, milling about, and while I was trying to make my way to the commons, someone walked up behind me and silently vomited on my back. I don't know if it was intentional, but when I turned around there was a younger woman with a big grin on her face with fresh vomit dribbling down her chin.

I was speechless! I walked as quickly as I could to the commons area. An aide saw what had happened and rushed over, apologizing, and tried to wipe the vomit off me, but to no avail, and most certainly he couldn't get rid of the foul stench. I went back into the commons room. I was, as you can imagine, very unhappy.

I stopped at the nurse's window long enough to ask when I was going to be able to speak with a psychiatrist. She told me that my appointment was for ten a.m. It was only seven-thirty, so I had more than a couple of hours to wait. I began pacing the floor again. I was nervous and disquieted.

I had no idea what was going to happen. For all I knew the psychiatrist was going to have me committed to an asylum. I thought about how I had come to this very unpredictable and regrettable place. How in the world was I going to mend the broken relationships and solve the dilemma that I found myself in?

I heard one the nurses call my name, telling me that I had a phone call. It was Maggie and my heart leapt with joy. She must have called the police department to find out where I had been taken. I spoke with her for a while, told her that I was doing okay, and about my experiences overnight and that morning.

My joy soon turned to ashes when she told me that they, the children, had decided that I needed to go to a rehabilitation center, and that they had chosen one that they all felt would be a good fit for me. I didn't know what to say. Maggie didn't give me a chance to speak. She told me that they all loved me and said goodbye.

As I hung up the phone I began to panic. Rehab! I didn't know anything about rehabilitation centers beyond a few movies that I had seen, and I didn't think that I was a suitable candidate for one. I wanted to speak with the psychiatrist to see what he thought. I was willing to do anything else but that.

A nurse interrupted my thoughts and told me that it was almost time for my appointment. She told me to sit in the commons area until I was called. Just then I saw an older man in a white jacket coming through the door. He was an attractive and kind looking man. I wondered if he was the psychiatrist.

Around fifteen minutes later my name was called and I was told that the doctor would see me now. A woman opened a door for me and I went in. The doctor was seated behind a desk looking over my file. He glanced up at me and asked how he could help. Somehow I felt immediately comfortable and was able to speak with him.

I recounted everything, from my journey to Ireland to the present, including my attempted suicide. He wrote some notes in my file and then we talked some more. During our conversation I mentioned that my children were recommending that I sign myself into a rehab in order to process and heal from the breakdown and trauma.

I told him adamantly that I didn't want to do this. But he agreed with my children and told me that I did need some help to get through the issues that I was experiencing. He said that he could recommend a couple of exceptional rehabs, but I told him that my children had already decided on one.

The one thing that he was very emphatic about was that I needed, at all costs, to avoid any program that was based on the '12 steps', in other words, AA, NA, and all the other A's. He told me that he was going to discharge me immediately and asked if I had a ride home. I told him no, and I could see that he was thinking.

He said not to worry, that he would make arrangements for a taxi voucher for my ride back to my apartment. I thanked him for his time, advice and being so kind. I got my personal belongings together and waited at the nurse's station to be officially discharged. Soon, one of the nurses told me that I was free to go.

I practically ran out of the door and into the fresh air. I stood by the curb and waited for the taxi to arrive and drive me home. I wondered what was awaiting me when I got there. I was so very worried about what my future was going to be, or if I was even going to have a future.

Chapter Two: Camp Recovery

Returning to an empty apartment felt peculiar and knowing that this was no longer my home brought with it such a feeling of despondency and emptiness. I made myself a cup of hot tea and was just getting ready to sit down with it and smoke a cigarette when there was a knock at the front door.

I was reluctant to open it, afraid that it might be one of the managers from the main office, or maybe another visit by the police, but I opened it anyway and was relieved to see that it was Maggie. She gave me a warm hug. She said that she was taking me to the rehabilitation center that she had told me about later that evening,

She said that she would be back when she got off work, and that I needed to pack enough clothing and toiletries for a month's stay. I felt lightheaded, shaky, and terribly confused. Maggie was on her lunch break and needed to get back to work, but she stayed just a bit longer to make sure that I did as she requested.

She told me a little about the rehabilitation center, that it was situated in the Santa Cruz mountains in a lovely, forested setting, and that I would have my own private bedroom with bath. She told me that there were daily group sessions, its own staff psychiatrist for face to face therapy, and professionally trained addiction specialists.

I didn't want to go, but I went into my bedroom anyway, got my large suitcase out from the closet, placed it on my bed, and started packing random items. In my heart of hearts, I was hoping that something would miraculously happen to reinstate my employment and everything would go back to what I knew as normal.

But the wheels of fate were already set in motion and there was no going back. Maggie had told me not to bother packing any spray items, such as perfume, hairspray or deodorant. There were certain things that the rehabilitation center didn't allow and those items were amongst them.

I continued tossing just any piece of clothing that I found into the suitcase, not caring what it was. My bedroom soon became a disaster area, something that in the past I would never have allowed. But now I really didn't care. This was no longer my home, and when everything was moved out I wouldn't even be there.

I was despondent, and my mind was so fractured that I was willing to let the responsibility of moving my belongings fall on the shoulders of whomever was willing to do the job, if indeed that ever happened. For all I knew everything that I owned, my precious possessions, was going to be donated to a second-hand store.

I sat outside on the patio and waited. Suddenly, I felt the urge for liquor, and I remembered that I had a bottle of cognac hidden in my bedroom. I went inside, got the bottle and poured a large amount into my teacup. I sipped it slowly as I sat on the patio, waiting for Maggie to come and drive me to the rehabilitation center.

My suitcase was already in the hallway. I had no idea what I had packed and I really didn't care what was in it. This was all surreal to me. I smoked, I drank cognac, and I waited. The cognac began washing over me, bringing with it the familiar warmth and comfort that I had become used to.

At six o'clock Maggie came through the front door and told me that it was time to go, that someone was waiting for me at the rehab to process my intake. A violent storm was brewing, and I asked Maggie if she thought it would be safe for us to drive up the mountain. She replied, "I had a good teacher Mama", and touched my hand.

I knew that she was a competent driver because I had taught her myself, but I was looking for any excuse to get out of actually going. She assured me that it would be fine. We sat at the dining room table and talked for a while. I was exhausted, worn down, depleted. The effects of the Datura and anti-psychotic drugs were mostly gone, fortunately.

But the amount of alcohol that I had consumed during that month lingered. Maggie said that it was time to go, so, with a very heavy heart, and slightly inebriated, I grabbed ahold of my suitcase, sullenly dragged it behind me out to Maggie's van. During our ride, Maggie told me more of what she knew about the rehab.

She said that I was going receive one-on-one counseling from all of the professionals on their team. She had been told that there were group meetings five days a week, and the center offered recreation for the patients. The families of the clients were allowed to visit on the weekends, and she promised that she would come.

The drive up the mountain to Scott's Valley was terrifying. There was lightning and thunder, and the road, which had sharp corners every few miles, was slippery from the torrential rain. I tried to make light of it, telling Maggie that perhaps we would see 'Large Marge', a character from a PeeWee Herman movie, which lightened the mood.

Maggie carefully maneuvered through the storm, and we arrived at the rehab unharmed. I told her that maybe I would be able to do this, to get through the month. She told me that I had to, that they all believed in me and my strength, that I would heal and regain my former self, and that I would be able to start over again.

I was uncertain about that last part. She parked the van in the large parking lot and helped me with my suitcase, leading the way through the pouring rain to the intake office. We were met by a man who introduced himself as Jeff. He opened the door and welcomed us in. I had an immediate distaste for the man.

He walked with an arrogant strut, almost as if he were pimping this place. I had promised the children that I would at least try this, do something to heal my broken soul, so we followed him inside. He told Maggie to wait in the reception area while he took me into his office to do the intake.

Taking hold of my arm, he steered me into his office. I sat across the desk from him and waited for him to begin. I was already feeling extremely uncomfortable. Jeff had a sinister, creepy kind of charm, something that he must have thought was enticing. But it felt slippery to me and set my teeth on edge. I watched him suspiciously from where I sat.

He smiled smugly and asked me about myself. I spoke about the past month or so, leaving out the Datura episode. He handed me a clipboard with some forms on it, along with a pen, and asked me to fill it out while he checked for availability. I busied myself with the forms, all the while listening to him aimless and witless chatter.

When he came to the part about how much it was going to cost for me to be accepted into the rehab I stopped filling out the forms and handed him the clipboard. $10,000.00!!! I no longer had health insurance to cover the amount. I had plenty of money saved, but that was not the point. I told him, quite frankly, no thank you.

I rushed out of his office, grabbed my suitcase, and ran out the front door. Maggie followed closely behind me. She asked me what had happened, and I told her what it was going to cost me. She was stunned. They had not told her how much the price of the stay was when she had inquired about Camp Recovery.

Already stressed out, the drive home in the continuing onslaught of rain, thunder and lightning only served to further accentuate the tension. I worried that we might get into an accident. As a result of the storm Maggie took the wrong exit off of the freeway, and we ended up in downtown San Jose, not even close to where we were supposed to be.

Of course, we both ended up laughing at the seemingly hopeless situation. We finally arrived back at the apartment, after what felt like hours. Maggie helped me into the apartment and made sure that I was comfortable. I was grateful that I had been left the key to my apartment by Sherry.

Maggie placed my suitcase in the master bedroom, then told me that she needed to get home as she was working in San Mateo the next morning. I gave her a hug and kiss and wished her goodnight. The next day was November 1st, David's twenty-ninth birthday, as well as the first day of our Irish new year.

In times past I had always celebrated Samhain, which is on October 31st, but this time I didn't even bother observing it. Instead, I went online and ordered more Hennessey's cognac. I spent that night drinking and drowning in my misery. I wanted to forget the confusion and pain that I had created for myself and others.

The next morning David phoned me. He asked if I would like to come to his home to celebrate his birthday that evening. He told me that he would pick me up and bring me home afterwards. I asked him to give me a couple of hours and that I would be incredibly happy to come to the celebration.

This would give me a chance to sober up a bit before he got to my apartment. My apartment. Not any longer. I had destroyed everything, all of my hopes and plans dashed, and for what? Because I had been lonely in Ireland, or because I was newly divorced? Was it because I had been left alone in my apartment on that one night?

None of it made any sense to me. I had always been such a powerhouse. Where had my strength gone to? The hours passed and David arrived to drive me to his home for the celebration. I was reasonably sober. All of the children and grandchildren were there. I hoped that the grandchildren were unaware of what had happened.

I visited with everyone, trying to put on a semblance of normalcy. We had dinner and visited some more. During dinner David mentioned that he and Stephanie were planning to drive me back to Camp Recovery the next morning. I was crushed. I had hoped that plan had been placed on a backburner permanently.

But such was not the case. I felt that I had no other choice but to agree. He said that while I was in the rehab that they would work together to move all of my belongings into a storage facility, but that he wouldn't be able to pay for it. I gave him my bankcard without batting an eye because I knew that I could trust him.

When we were finished with the celebration I gave everyone a hug and kiss, told them that I loved them and goodbye for then, and David drove me back to my apartment. He couldn't stay long but assured me that everything was going to be fine as long as I worked with the program that

Camp Recovery offered.

I spent a mostly sleepless night, tossing and turning, worrying and wondering. At four in the morning, I got out of bed and made a pot of coffee. It was not doing me any good to stay in bed any longer. I sat on my patio in the dark, long before the birds had awakened, long before there was traffic on the freeway next to the property.

I drank my coffee, smoked countless cigarettes, and tried to keep my rising anxiety under control. Before I knew it David and Stephanie were at my front door ready to pick me up and drive me into the Santa Cruz Mountains. I got my suitcase from my bedroom, and slowly, dolefully walked to the door.

David took my suitcase from me and placed it in the trunk of his car. We all got in and, unbeknownst to any of us, the journey to five and a half years of suffering and hell began. This time the drive up the mountain was uneventful. The skies were clear, no rain, no lightning and no thunder.

As we drove up the mountain I felt my blood pressure begin to rise and my ears began ringing. David and Stephanie were talking but I couldn't hear what they were saying. I sat silently in the back seat of the car in an exceptionally elevated level of anxiety. They both noticed and told me to just relax, that everything was going to be fine.

The drive seemed to be over almost as soon as it began. I found myself back in the same parking lot that Maggie and I had been to two nights previous. I felt as if my heart was going to stop beating. David pulled my suitcase out of the trunk and I slowly, almost begrudgingly, followed him and Stephanie to the intake office.

I was relieved to see that smarmy Jeff was not the intake person. Instead, it was a woman whom I believed to be around the same age as myself. The atmosphere was quite informal and the woman was unpretentious. She greeted us and shook my hand. She asked David and Stephanie to have a seat while I was processed.

I was invited into the intake office where she helped me to go through the forms that they needed me to initial and sign. When I was finished I had entered into a legally binding one month contract with them for the sum of ten thousand dollars, equaling three hundred and thirty three dollars per day! I could have rented a luxury suite for that price.

I had left my bankcard with David so that he could pay for a storage facility for my belongings, and he had left it at his home, so my only alternative was to divide the amount between two of my credit cards. I quickly made a plan to cash in a certificate of deposit that I owned and pay those amounts off in full once I had completed this program.

When I was finished with the intake process I went out into the waiting area to let David and Stephanie know that I would be staying this time. We hugged, and I gave them kisses, and very sadly watched them as they walked out the door. I felt utterly defeated and doomed. I couldn't imagine how this was going to help, but I was willing to try.

A short, heavy set, grey haired woman by the name of Charlotte approached me and ordered me to grab my suitcase and follow her. She escorted me up a long flight of concrete stairs, fairly flying up them ahead of me, to the room to which I had been assigned. It was all that I could do to pull my heavy suitcase behind me.

It's Not The Hilton

On the landing I saw a large balcony with several tables that had umbrellas, and plenty of chairs. The balcony was dirty, with trash and cigarette butts lying about under the tables and along the railings. The building on the landing was long, with eight doors. I was to learn that each door led into separate rooms.

It was similar to a small apartment complex. Charlotte opened one of the doors of and we walked in together. What I observed stunned me. Directly in front of me was a dark, dank and dingy bathroom. I walked into the main room and saw four very narrow single beds with old quilts on them positioned along the walls.

There were two desks positioned side by side under a dirty window, a couple of old metal chairs and a large walk-in closet. Small metal wall lamps were installed above the head of each of the beds for reading. The room itself was grimy and smelled like old sweaty bodies that had not been washed for months.

I said "Charlotte, this is some kind of mistake! This cannot be my room. My children were told that I was to have a private room with ensuite bath." She looked at me and laughed. She said "Susan, this is your room.

It's not the Hilton for crying out loud!" I replied that for the price that I had paid that it should have been. I was thoroughly disappointed.

She said that I needed to get my bed made and unpack my belongings and try to make myself at home. I realized that I had to accept this for what it was. After all, I had already paid ten thousand dollars for this pigsty. I was sharing the room and bathroom with four other women that I didn't even know, but I would make the best of it.

After Charlotte left I set about making the bed that was to be mine for the next thirty days and nights. The sheets were thin and worn, and the quilt was threadbare. The pillow that she had given me was old and stained, and smelled like soured saliva from who goodness knows how many other mouths.

I looked around the room. One of the three other beds had clothing folded on it, so I figured that it belonged to someone. The other two beds had folded sheets, a pillow and quilt on them, so they were likely vacant beds. I looked out of the filmy window and could see what I came to know as the commons area below.

I began unpacking my clothing that needed to be hung. Thankfully, I was able to find enough hangers to place them on, but even so I was hesitant to hang my clean clothes in the dirty closet. I found that I had to move items on the floor aside just so that I could get everything hung up.

Before she left the room Charlotte told me that once I was done that I was to report to the nurses station at the base of the stairs. Having acrophobia, stairs have always been a challenge for me, so I held tightly onto the rail and walked carefully down them, counting them as I went.

There were twenty-eight steps in all, and the pitch was quite steep, which I found quite dizzying. At the bottom of the stairs I looked around, found the nurses station and knocked on the window. There was a nurse inside typing on a computer. She saw me and directed me to a door on the side and opened it for me.

Once inside she asked me to take a seat and told me that she would be with me in a few minutes. It was not even eleven in the morning and already I had developed a deep-seated aversion to this place. From what I could see the entire property appeared to be rundown, decrepit, and dilapidated.

The nurse finished inputting her notes into the computer and she turned her attention to me. She asked how I was feeling and I told her that I was fine. She told me to hold my arms out level to my chest with my palms down, which I did. What she was doing was checking for delirium tremens, which I didn't have.

I know that if had exhibited signs of delirium tremens that they would have quarantined me in what I was to learn was the detox unit. She took my blood pressure and temperature, noting everything down in my file. She told me that I should be glad that I had arrived on a Sunday as there were no group sessions for me to attend.

She suggested that I take the time to familiarize myself with my new surroundings, which is exactly what I did. As soon as I left the nurses station I began walking. I walked past the intake center, and towards the parking lot at the entrance to the property. A male employee appeared out of nowhere, startling me.

He raised his voice and abruptly told me that I had to turn around immediately, that this area was off limits to the clients. I did so, but reluctantly. I was not used to being told what to do. I headed back towards the intake center and decided to walk up one of the many trails that were on the property.

There were huge tree roots, ruts and rocks in the middle of the trail that I walked. I was glad that I had my boots on, which provided me with stability. There were quite a few cabins along the way, each one numbered, and I was soon to discover that these were where most of the group sessions were held Monday through Friday.

Not seeing anything else of note or interest I returned to the commons area to see what else I could find. On the weekends, the rehab was open to visitors, and I could see several families, some with children, gathered on a grass covered hill, sitting on blankets and enjoying picnics and each other's company.

I wondered if anyone was going to visit me the next weekend, but I doubted it. I missed my children and grandchildren sorely, but I had done a rather good job in alienating them, plus I knew that it was going to take time for me to work on mending our relationships. I walked in front of what I would learn was the dining hall.

There were several vending machines in front of the building filled with candy, chips and soft drinks. The machines wouldn't do me any good though as I had not brought any cash with me. I saw that there was a large, circular building in the center of the commons so I walked over and went inside.

There was an enormous, meeting room inside the building, along with a media room where a few of the clients were watching television. There was also a room where clients could go to listen to music. There were locked doors with placards on them, one being the office of the staff psychiatrist, Dr. Steven Michael Stein.

A stairway led to the upstairs. There were closed doors which opened into what I later learned were the offices of administrative staff. There were no computers or cellphones allowed on the property. We were, for all intents and purposes, cut off from the outside world and its influences.

There were several public pay phones located next to the nurses station where clients were allowed to speak for ten minutes each evening with family and friends. I sat at one of the many small tables in the commons and lit a cigarette. A younger man asked if he could join me and I told him that I would be glad for the company.

I introduced myself and he told me that his name was Victor. I asked him when meals were served and he pointed towards the building that I had seen earlier. He told me that breakfast was served at seven a.m., lunch at noon, and five p.m. for dinner. He also told me that there was a coffee service set up every morning at six a.m.

I replied that was a little later that I usually had my coffee, but I certainly planned to make use of it. I did love my coffee in the mornings! I looked at my watch and noticed that it was close to noon, so Victor and I decided to share lunch together. There was a lengthy line of people already formed waiting for the doors to open.

We got in line and waited. It was not long before the doors opened and the line began moving forward. Once inside I could see that the dining hall was older, but good sized, and with plenty of tables and chairs, and I saw that the employees kept it clean. There was a counter where the clients ordered their meals.

The kitchen was situated right behind the counter, with employees moving about preparing the food. When it was my turn I told the older gentleman behind the counter that I was an ovo-vegetarian, and he said that he could definitely help me out with that. He suggested a veggie burger with a side salad for my lunch.

I replied that it sounded fine to me. He asked me to move forward so that the next person behind me could place their order and told me that someone would call me when my food was ready. Just past the counter was the beverage service table. There were two urns of coffee, several types of tea in bags, and hot water dispenser.

There was also milk and a variety of juices offered. I chose a cup of hot tea. I was incredibly happy to see that they also had the sweetener that I always used. I looked around the dining hall for a vacant table and saw that Victor had already found one, so I walked over and joined him.

We chatted while we waited for our orders to be prepared. It was not long before I heard 'veggie burger'. That was my cue to return to the counter and pick up my meal. There was a fairly nice side salad to go with it, but unfortunately someone had doused it with a creamy dressing, which I definitely do not like.

I took the sandwich and salad and returned to the table. After all, I really didn't have to eat the salad, or I could scrape off the dressing. I could see from where I was standing that a woman had seated at the table Victor had chosen. I was happy to meet more people here, and I hoped that Victor didn't mind more company.

I placed my food on the table and sat down. I introduced myself to the woman, who smiled and took my hand in hers, shaking it vigorously. She told me that her name was Ann, and that she had been at the Camp for two weeks. Her skin was dry and calloused and her hands were as cold as ice, but she had kind eyes and a nice smile.

She immediately began to regale both Victor and me with her entire life story, what her addiction was, which was alcohol, and that she had been a client at the Camp three other times. I nodded my head sympathetically. I felt sorry for her, but I also felt as if she were divulging too much personal information.

I would soon learn that the clients were encouraged to share their stories as often as possible as part of their rehabilitation. Not wanting to share much of myself with either she or Victor, I told them that I was from the Bay Area, that I had lived there for quite a few years, and that all of my children and grandchildren lived there also.

That was it, all that I had to share with them. I finished my meal, minus the salad, and stood up. I thanked both Ann and Victor for their company and told them that I was sure that I would see them again soon. I took my dishes and placed them in a tub on a rack by the beverage service. I left to walk around the property some more.

I noticed ping-pong tables set up outside on the commons, and some of the clients were enjoying themselves by playing. There were more tables with chairs in various locations throughout the property. I found the laundry center, the cost of which was included in the exorbitant price of the Camp.

I looked down towards the lawn where I had seen the visiting families earlier, but no one was in sight. I was not sure what the visiting hours were, but I couldn't imagine that they were already over. The clients and their families must have moved indoors, or perhaps they had been in the dining hall and I failed to see them.

I returned to my room to try to and relax until dinner time. The only other occupant of the room was sitting on her bed. I introduced myself and she told me that her name was Barbara. She said that she was fifty-four years old, which was exactly my age. She said that her other roommate had 'graduated' the Camp and had already gone home.

That meant that there were only two of us in the room and that, at least, made me a bit more comfortable. I asked her how long she had been at the Camp. She said that she had been there for less than a week. She had crashed her car while drunk and part of her sentence was to sign herself into rehab.

I inquired as to why the room was in such deplorable condition, and she told me that because of physical disabilities she was unable to keep the room clean, and the last roommate simply ignored it. She said that there was a weekly cleaning service that came by, but they didn't do a particularly good job of it.

I told her that I planned on changing that, and I would take on the initial responsibility of bringing the room, bathroom, closet and everything else up to common standards and then if we were to have more roommates they could help me keep it organized and clean. She said, "Good luck with that", with a big smile on her face.

She was a handsome looking woman, with long, wavy brown hair and a deep, raspy voice, kind of like Miss Kitty on the old western series

'Gunsmoke', and really quite pleasant. I was incredibly happy to have someone like her as a roommate. Truly genuine and solid, and very down to earth.

She told me that the Camp gave out weekly awards to the room that was the most organized ad cleanest, and I determined at once to make sure that the room I was in received that award every single week that I was there. The time passed quickly as we talked, and soon it was time to go to the dining hall for dinner.

We walked down the stairs together. I was not very hungry, but I knew that I needed to eat something to keep my strength up. Once again, there was a lengthy line formed with a large crowd of people waiting for the doors to open. The offering for dinner was either meatloaf with mashed potatoes and a vegetable or macaroni and cheese with a vegetable.

I chose macaroni and cheese for my dinner, and a side salad with balsamic. There was a variety of small desserts, puddings, a gelatin dessert and cookies, so I also took a pudding and a few of the cookies. The head cook told me when I ordered that there were no other clients who were vegetarians, so they didn't always have great choices.

He also told me that he had spoken with the director and together they had decided that they were going to add more vegetarian options so that those who wished to have their meals meatless would have more choices in what they ate. I thanked him and told him that I did eat the occasional egg and loved cheese.

I joked with him about serving tofurkey for Thanksgiving dinner, which was coming up in just a few weeks. He looked at me oddly, but he took me seriously and said that he would see what he could do. I thanked him, and with my meal in hand, walked over to the beverage table to get some coffee.

Barbara took me by the arm and warned me that they only served decaffeinated coffee in the evenings so that the sleep of the clients was not disturbed. They didn't want clients wandering around at night. I decided to have a cup of tea instead. Barbara and I sat together and were joined by two younger men, Jason and Ben.

They were extremely interested in my jewelry. I patiently told them that every piece symbolized an aspect of my spirituality, and that no, I was not a Christian, I was not a Wiccan, but instead I followed an Ancient Irish path. That didn't seem to cause alarm in either one of them. I began to relax and feel a bit more comfortable.

We chatted and laughed while we ate our dinners, and I opened up with more about myself. Still, I was reluctant to discuss my failed suicide. I am not sure if I was embarrassed, or maybe I was afraid of what they might think of me. Perhaps in time I might divulge more of why I was there at the Camp.

They asked if I had ever been to Ireland, to which I replied that yes, indeed I had, three different times. I regaled my new friends with tales of my journeys, in Ireland and Europe, touching briefly on my most recent one which didn't turn out so well. They shared a bit about themselves. It actually was quite a pleasant mealtime.

Dinner was soon over, so I excused myself and got up from the table. I placed my dishes in one of the tubs provided and walked outside. Barbara followed behind me. The sun was just beginning to set and a chill was setting in. I could see dark clouds forming in the sky above me.

I realized that I had not brought a jacket nor an umbrella with me to the Camp. Even so, I felt that I would be fine. I had packed several warm sweaters, slacks, and my boots. I also had my old wool shawl with me. That should be enough to keep me warm and cozy. Barbara and I walked back to the room together.

She went right into the room and I followed after, not to stay, but to get a pack of cigarettes. I had decided to spend some time out on the balcony reflecting on my first day at the Camp. I was still not sure about this place. I didn't feel that I belonged there. I looked up into the heavens and put everything into the hands of my Deities.

I began to tire. Night was setting in, it had been a long day, and I wanted to just go to sleep. I went inside the room and told Barbara that I was going to get ready for bed. Falling asleep proved to be somewhat of a problem as Barbara was a heavy snorer, loud enough to raise the roof, but I finally drifted into a dreamless slumber.

I was rudely awakened from my sleep by one of the counselors flashing an extremely bright flashlight into my face. I sat up, and in a loud voice demanded to know what was going on. Her reply was that she was doing the nightly 'bed check' to make sure that none of us had absconded from the Camp.

Needless to say, I was very annoyed and asked that she not do that again. She told me that she was sorry, but it was her job, and that she would try not to shine the flashlight in my face again. I grumbled and told her that I hoped not. I felt that it was needlessly rude of her. It made it seem like a prison setting rather than a rehab.

Barbara was also awake, and I told her that I was going to rig the door so that it couldn't be opened from the outside. That gave her a good laugh, but I was serious. I was not sure how I would do it, but I would find a way to keep the midnight invasions to a minimum. This was a strange place filled with even stranger people.

My life had not always been a bed of roses, but it certainly had never been as peculiar as the situation that I now found myself in. I turned my face to the wall and despite the snores coming from Barbara's side of the room I finally managed to get back to sleep, but it was a troubled one that didn't allow me to rest well.

She's Poison!

I awoke fairly early as was my custom. I used the toilet, washed my face, and went out onto the balcony to smoke a cigarette before taking a shower. One of the other clients was already sitting at a table and I joined her. I introduced myself and she told me that her name was Nicci 6. We chatted for a while, just small talk.

She told me that she was an oxycodone addict. She was close to her graduation day, and she said that she could hardly wait to get out of here, that her clan was waiting for her back in Los Angeles. I wondered why she come such a long distance to attend rehab. I also wondered what 'clan' meant to her.

I asked Nicci if the morning coffee was real or decaffeinated and she laughed. She told me that they only served decaffeinated coffee in the evenings, and that I should be pleased with what they had to offer in the mornings. I looked at my watch and saw that it was five-thirty, so I went back inside the room to take a shower.

The stall was scummy, moldy and musty, and I actually didn't feel clean even after showering. I got dressed and went down the twenty-eight steps of the stairs to get some coffee. I took my towels with me so that I could stop off at the laundry center to put them in a dryer. This would become my morning ritual for the entirety of my stay.

The doors to the dining hall were still locked, so I lit a cigarette, leaned against the wall, and waited. It was not long before a young man opened them. I went inside. He told me that coffee would be ready shortly, so I waited. Soon there were two large urns filled with steaming hot fully caffeinated coffee.

There were a variety of creamers, along with my favorite sweetener. There were also several choices of tea. The only drawback was the size of the styrofoam cups. The cups only held eight ounces, and my mug at home held about sixteen ounces. Going up and down the stairs for more coffee didn't sound very appealing to me.

Instead of making multiple trips I decided to get four of the cups, put creamer and sweetener in them, and fill each one with the brew. I carefully balanced the cups, cradled in my arms, carrying them across the commons and to the stairs. I set two of the cups down at the base of the stairs and carried the other two up the stairs and to a table.

I went back down the long flight of stairs for the others. Now I could sit back and enjoy my coffee and cigarettes without having to worry about all of the difficulties of the stairs until it was time for breakfast. But I had forgotten that I still had to go down to the laundry center to get my towels.

My calves and thighs were already getting a workout. I was grateful that I had spent so much time walking when I was last in Ireland as the exercise had kept the muscles in my legs strong. I set my coffee aside and went back down the stairs. My towels were nice and dry.

I had brought my own with me when I packed for the Camp as I didn't care to use others towels. I took them into the room and folded them, placing them at the foot of my bed, which I had already neatly made. I still had a half hour before breakfast, so I decided to try and tidy the unkempt room.

I found an old rag in the closet and got it wet, wringing out the excess water. I wiped down the railings on my bed, the light that was hanging on the wall behind it, and the two desks. Next I went into the bathroom and tried to wipe the muck off of the counters. They were caked with old makeup and dried soap foam.

Barbara was sitting on her bed watching me. She reminded me that there was a cleaning service that came in once a week. I replied that they didn't seem to be doing a particularly respectable job. The uncarpeted floors were dingy and had small particles of debris everywhere, and all of the woodwork was dull and lacked luster.

I couldn't seem to be able to get all of the ground in dirt off of the desks. It was hopeless. I told Barbara that I was going to get a broom and cleaning supplies from the intake office before doing too much more cleaning. Laughingly she wished me luck in my endeavors. She got up off of her bed and left the room to get her breakfast.

I was still busy trying to put a shine on the interior of the room when two younger women suddenly appeared, giggling as they walked through the door. They told me that they were my new roommates. One was named Tiffany and the other one Kelly. So much for me thinking that Barbara and I were going to be alone in the room.

Tiffany was an attractive young woman, rather plumpish, with short brown hair and a fair complexion. Kelly was also attractive. She had short black hair and golden amber colored eyes. Her demeanor was mannish, and Tiffany referred to her as 'my dyke'. I assumed that she was Gay, and that perhaps Tiffany was as well.

Tiffany told me she and Kelly had been in detox together for several days, but that they were recovering and could now be in a regular room. I told them that I was happy to meet them, introduced myself briefly, then I returned to my frustrated cleaning. I went into the bathroom to see what else I could do about all of the grime.

It was impossible to disinfect without actual cleaning products, so I gave up trying. When I walked out of the bathroom I saw Kelly with a mattress over her head. Tiffany was nowhere to be seen. Kelly was trying to flip the mattress on her bed, which was directly across from mine. She yelled, "Are you just going to stand there, or are you going to fucking to help me?"

I helped her situate the mattress, but I really didn't care for her tone of voice. I had done all that I could in sprucing up the room with no supplies so I decided to go out on the balcony for a cigarette before going for my breakfast, as well as to escape Kelly. My coffee was cold by then, so I poured it out and put the styrofoam cups in a trash can.

I sat down at one of the tables and lit a cigarette, wondering what the day would bring. When I was finished I went back down the stairs, walked across the commons, and went into the dining hall. The older cook greeted me as I walked in. There were the usual choices for breakfast. Eggs, bacon, sausage, potatoes, toast, and cereal.

I decided on two eggs, potatoes and toast. I poured myself a large cup of orange juice, along with another coffee, and looked for Barbara, who happened to be sitting with two other women. They all greeted me with smiles. I pulled out a chair and sat down. The dining hall was filled with people, and the loud incessant chatter was somewhat overwhelming.

I was suddenly experiencing sensory overload. I was quiet as I ate, listening to the other three women at the table talk amongst themselves. One was named Jean and the other one Carol. They were roommates at the Camp and had actually checked in on the same day. Both were alcoholics, and both had some pretty wild stories to tell.

It was a fairly pleasant breakfast, but I was finished before anyone else at the table. I cleared my plates and went outside to get some air and enjoy the relative quiet. I looked around the commons and saw that only a couple of people were walking about. Today I would begin my group sessions, six of them each and every weekday.

Barbara had told me that all of the sessions were close to an hour long, and that was fine with me. I returned to the room to get a notebook and pen so that I could take notes during the group sessions that I would be attending. While I was in the room one of the counselors stopped by to inspect the room.

She had a checklist on a clipboard. She started in the bathroom, walked through the main room and into the closet. She shook her head and told me that this room was at the bottom of her list. I told her that I could guarantee that would be changing very soon, and it would be an entirely different room the next day. She looked at me and smiled.

"Well, good luck with that." I told her that luck had nothing to do with it, just some good old fashioned hard and honest work, which I was not in the least bit afraid to put forth. I asked her when the next inspection was and she replied that they were conducted every weekday. I smiled and told her that I would see her in the morning.

I had no idea where my first group session was being held, so I went down the stairs and into the intake center to ask someone. There was a younger woman seated at the reception desk. She looked up as I walked in. She appeared to be little more than a teenager and I wondered why she was not in school.

I told her my name and what I needed and she looked at a sheet of paper. She instructed me to walk up the main path and find cabin number three, where I would be taking part in a group therapy session. She gave me rather vague directions and told me that I needed to be there by nine a.m., and to be sure to be on time.

The property where the Camp was located was fairly large, and as I noted earlier, the trails were filled with tree roots, ruts and rocks, so I had to walk carefully to avoid twisting an ankle or falling. The cabin was quite a distance away from the intake center, but I finally found it and knocked on the closed door.

A middle aged man whom everyone called Captain Ron opened the door for me and invited me in. There were about fifteen other people, men and women alike, of all ages and backgrounds, seated in chairs that were arranged in a semi-circle. Captain Ron sat in a chair where he could see everyone.

He was an interesting looking fellow, affable and kind. He had longish white hair, a full beard, and a good sized paunch. If he had been wearing a red suit and with a tousled cap he might have been mistaken for Santa Claus. He welcomed me to the group and asked me to introduce myself, which I did.

Almost everyone greeted me, with the exception of a few who kept their heads either down, covered with a hoodie or turned away. The group session lasted about an hour. As I walked through the door to go outside I was met by yet another counselor by the name of Cynthia. She instructed me to go to cabin number six for my next session.

I lit a cigarette and started walking in the direction she had pointed. It was not even ten a.m. as I headed for my second group session. I smoked as I walked, wondering what this group would be like. Along the way I met up with a few of the people from the last group who were walking in the same direction.

I was to discover that the sessions were similar in that they focused on addictions of all kinds. Some of the sessions were for retrospection, some were for sharing, and others were for instruction. After walking for what seemed a mile I finally found the right cabin. There were a few people standing outside.

The counselor had not arrived yet, so we just stood there, smoking cigarettes and making small talk. A young woman noticed the jewelry that I was wearing and asked me what it represented. My jewelry was becoming quite popular. Not going into great detail, I told her that it stood for my spirituality.

I certainly didn't want anyone becoming suspicious or superstitious about me, and I most definitely didn't want any problems with anyone. I was, and still am not, a Christian, and down through the years I learned to keep that essentially to myself to prevent unwarranted harassment from others.

The counselor finally arrived and unlocked the door. We all went inside and sat down. There were plenty of chairs to accommodate this group of around twenty people. The chairs were again placed in a semi-circle with the counselor's chair facing everyone. This counselor was female, and she seemed to be pleasant enough.

She looked to be about thirty-five years old and was wearing old jeans and an old sweatshirt. I do not recall her name, but that really does not matter. She began by asking everyone in the room to introduce themselves and talk about their addiction, exactly as it was in the first group.

I really didn't believe that I had one, but when my turn came I talked a bit about alcohol and how it had affected my life over the past month. I chose not to mention my suicide attempt. There was no 'cross-talking' allowed in any of the group sessions, so no one commented on what I had said.

Some nodded their heads in agreement, showing that they understood and empathized with the problems that I had been experiencing. The session lasted an hour, and then we were free to go to our next session. The counselor pointed me in the right direction, and some of the people that had been in this recent session walked with me.

My third session was not much different from the first two. The counselors who led the sessions were rather pedestrian at best, with the exception of Captain Ron. Most of them appeared to have perhaps a high school education. The counselor for this session was a male and his name was Mike.

He had a shaved head, a long goatee, both arms were tattooed, and he was wearing a tank top, hoodie and cargo shorts with sandals on his feet. He looked like a beach bum. I suspected in that moment that most of the counselors were former addicts, or maybe still actively using drugs or alcohol. I wondered if the Camp did drug testing on them.

None of them seemed to be well educated. And they most certainly didn't involve themselves with the sessions to a remarkably high degree. As I have said, I had seen movies and read about rehabs and group therapy sessions in the past, just out of curiosity, and those that I was attending appeared to be stereotypical of those.

But of course, my experience was not firsthand. The sessions I had been in so far were led by the clients for the most part, with the counselor on the sidelines in case of an argument or disagreement. I was delighted when the counselor told everyone that we were dismissed for lunch. But something was bothering me.

At the end of each session the counselors had everyone stand in a circle, arms around each other's waists, and stomp their feet on the ground shouting "Keep coming back! It works!" It sounded almost cult-like to me. I had never heard anything like it before.

With this thought playing in my mind, I walked to the dining hall to get in line, which was already moving by the time I arrived. I saw a few of the people that I had met earlier in the sessions ahead of me in line. I finally made it to the door and soon I was at the counter where I could order my lunch.

The dining hall was crowded and everyone appeared to be shouting. The head cook had prepared a special salad for me, complete with field greens, beets, sprouts and diced eggs. He asked me what kind of dressing I would like and I told him that I preferred balsamic. He said that they would call me when it was ready.

I had not seen Barbara all morning, but easily located the table at which she was seated. There were three other women seated with her, and there was plenty of room for me to join them. We chatted for a while. Once again I was regaled with their life stories and addictions, but I veered the conversation to other topics when it came to myself.

Soon my name was called and I went to the counter to pick up my salad. I had already gotten a cup of hot tea, so I returned to the table to eat my lunch and listen to more about the lives of the other women. One told the story of how she used to jog along a canal bank close to her house.

She would always take a large water bottle along, but rather than filling it with water she would fill it with vodka. One day she fell in the canal and that is how she ended up here. Another told about her drunken escapades while shopping, and that in her inebriated state shoplifted as many items as she could. She was never caught.

The clients all had an hour long break for lunch, and I wanted to return to the room to decompress from the morning's group sessions, so I finished my salad and excused myself. I told the two other women that it was pleasant having met and visited with them, and that I appreciated them sharing their stories.

Upon my return to the room, I saw that Kelly was lying on her bed with her hoodie pulled closely around her face. I said hello to her but she didn't reply. I believed that she was feigning sleep in order to avoid any conversation. I was to learn that she habitually avoided going to the group sessions. Why was she even at the Camp?

For the price I had paid I had decided to take full advantage of every single opportunity that the Camp offered and utilize the time that I was afforded for deep retrospection. What I came to find out was that many of the clients stays were paid in full by their health insurance, and a few were given full grants to take part in the rehab.

During my breakdown I had neglected my Spiritual devotional readings, but when I packed before leaving for the Camp, my books were one of the items that I made sure that I brought with me. I sat on my bed reading my devotionals and thought about the morning's sessions. I wondered what the afternoon sessions would bring.

I went out onto the balcony to smoke a cigarette and wait for the time to pass. Around twelve forty-five I went down the stairs to find a counselor who could direct me to my next session. I was told to go to cabin number five. I located the cabin, and since the door was open I went inside. This would be my first session of the afternoon.

There was no one inside yet. I found a seat and made myself as comfortable as possible and waited. Soon more people came in, and finally the counselor made an appearance. This counselor was another male by the name of Brian, but he seemed a bit different from the Mike the beach bum.

Rather than dressing casually, he had made an attempt to at least dress somewhat professionally. There was more retelling of life stories, addictions, troubles and woes. Some had encouraging tales to tell, and others were only able to recount horror stories. When it came to me I again shied away from my failed suicide attempt.

I spoke only about alcohol and how I felt it had recently affected my life. Brian listened but didn't respond. The other clients in the room nodded their heads, indicating that they could relate to what I had gone through. When I was finished speaking everyone clapped their hands, which, as I was to learn, was a sign of respect.

The session was over before I knew it and I asked where I needed to go next. The counselor said that I didn't have another group just then. He said that an appointment had been made for me with the staff psychiatrist, Dr. Steven Michael Stein, and I would need to go to the large circular building by the commons to check in.

I sauntered along the dirt path to the commons area, smoking a cigarette as I walked. I was in no hurry to meet with the psychiatrist. When I finally arrived at the building I went inside and saw an older woman sitting at a table just inside the door. She asked my name, checked her list, and told me to have a seat.

She stood up and walked through a door across the room, closing it behind her. A few minutes later she came out and told me that the doctor would call me when he was ready. He opened the door about a half hour later and invited me into his office, which was little more than a room with a desk, a chair and a cart filled with books.

There was, of course, a computer and landline phone on the desk, along with a pile of folders which I assumed held client files. He was younger than me, perhaps in his mid-forties. He was dressed casually, wore glasses and had a distinguished looking goatee. Dr. Stein invited me to sit on the couch, which I did.

He had a file in front of him, which I assumed was mine. He looked it over and then spoke. "I see that you are dealing with both suicide ideation and alcoholism." I replied that I did attempt suicide, and that I consumed vast quantities of alcohol after the fact that did an excellent job numbing my mind.

"You have a disability, and we are going to take care of you here. Would you like me to prescribe any medications?" I said no thank you, I had made it thus far simply fine without any. It was just a bit strange that he didn't suggest a medication, especially since he must have known that I was not familiar with psychotropic medications.

He had me sign some forms, one for disability and another for releasing him of liability, then he reached behind himself to the cart that was stacked with books. He turned to me and said "I want you to start reading this book. Try to get through the first nine chapters, and on our next appointment we can discuss it."

I looked at the book cover and saw "Alcoholics Anonymous" emblazoned across it. No! The psychiatrist at Valley Medical had warned me against this. He had told me not to have anything to do with AA, NA or any of the A's. I was astonished. This was all wrong. I thanked him anyway, took the book, and walked out of his office.

I asked the woman at the table if she knew where I was supposed to go next. She told me to go to the intake office and speak to one of the counselors, which is what I did. The same young girl from earlier told me that I didn't need to go to any further group sessions that day, and that I was free to go to my room or for a walk around the grounds.

That made sense to me as it was already past three p.m. Before I left I inquired about a broom, dustpan and cleaning supplies. Charlotte, the older woman who had taken me to my room the day before, was listening. She asked me what I needed I talked to her about the condition of the room, and in particular the bathroom, and told her that I needed industrial strength everything.

She said that she would see to it that supplies were brought to the room that afternoon. I went up the long flight of stairs and into the room. There was no one inside, which I was grateful for as I needed time to myself, to think about, assess and process my meeting with Dr. Stein, which had only lasted about fifteen minutes.

I heard a knock at the door, and when I opened it I saw Charlotte standing there with all of the tools and cleaning supplies that I needed. I was delighted! Now I would be able to clean everything. I thanked her, and she laughed. I told her my plan to win the weekly award for the cleanest room while I was at this rehab, and she laughed again.

I joined in on the laughter and told her that everyone would soon see. Since I had plenty of time before dinner, and I could always reflect on the meeting with Dr. Stein later on in the evening, I decided to deeply clean the entire room. So, with tools and cleaning supplies in hand, I set to work on the room.

The first room that I cleaned was the bathroom, which smelled worse than any old and mucky locker room that you could imagine. I had spray foam and glass cleaners for this job. I sprayed the counters and the two shower stalls with the foam cleaner first. While that did its job I put toilet bowl cleaner into both toilets and scrubbed them.

I then swept the bathroom, sweeping all of the dust and debris out into the main room. I had always been a firm believer in taking matters into hand, being initiative-taking and not waiting for someone else to change things that I do not like. Being disorganized and messy had never been one of my attributes.

I was determined to polish and shine this place and make it clean and comfortable, at least myself. I didn't even mind if my three roommates appreciated my efforts. The foam cleaner had done its job on the shower stalls, and all that I had to do was rinse the foam off of the walls and floors of the showers.

Next, I scrubbed the toilet bowls again, dried the seats, and wiped the counters down. The counters were so caked with old makeup and dried soap that I had to spray them twice. While the foam was working I sprayed the mirrors, which were chipped and marred with age, and polished them the best that I able.

While I was in the bathroom Barbara came into the room. She was finished with her sessions for the day and needed to rest. I told her that I would be quiet while she rested. I understood how she was feeling. I was finally able to get all of the makeup and soap off of the counters.

The counters were scarred and scratched, and the faucets were deeply pitted from age. I couldn't do anything about that, but at least they were disinfected and clean, and that is really all that I cared about. Barbara was fast asleep and already snoring loudly, so I worked quietly in the room. I sprayed the desks and wiped them down.

The cleaning cloth was black with years of residual dirt. So much for the cleaning crew! I even sprayed and wiped the windowsill, which had a layer of dirt and dust at least an inch thick. I swept the main room, getting under the desks and beds the best that I could. It was difficult for me to believe that anyone could allow such filth to accumulate.

This rehab was certainly poorly managed. For the amount of money that they charged their clients the rooms should have been pristine on a daily basis. Next came the closet. I pushed all of my clothing to one side and began picking up the roommates clothing off of the dirty floor.

I stacked it all as neatly as possible on the suitcases against the wall and hung what I was able to. I hoped that no one would mind me touching their belongings. I swept the closet out, and the amount of dirt and trash that I found was phenomenal. I felt that I was pretty much finished for then.

During one of my walks I had noticed some fragrant wildflowers behind the building where my room was, so I went down the stairs and around the back. I picked a variety of beautiful and colorful flowers. I found an old empty can and took the flowers and it back to the room. I filled the can with water and placed the flowers in it.

I put the bouquet of beautiful wildflowers on one of the desks. It livened the room up significantly. While I was picking the flowers I noticed a long piece of rope lying against the building. I took it with me inside the room and tied one end to the entrance doorknob and the other end to the bathroom doorknob.

I tried opening the entrance door and it wouldn't budge. I was proud of my effort and would definitely use it that night to keep what I considered intruders with flashlights from coming into the room. By the time I was finished it was almost four-thirty, with dinner time right around the corner.

I had not seen Tiffany or Kelly all day, with the exception of Kelly feigning sleep earlier. I gently shook Barbara's shoulder and asked if she wanted to go to dinner with me. She roused ever so slightly, and with her eyes still closed she said in her deep, raspy voice "Yes, of course. Just give me a few more minutes of sleep".

I went out onto the balcony to smoke a cigarette and wait for her. Nicci 6 was sitting at the table with her feet up on one of the chairs. She seemed like a nice enough girl. She was tall and thin, and dressed like a rapper. I knew that she was from Los Angeles and had been around gangs and drug dealing most of her life.

We talked for a while, just casual conversation. I asked her when she was graduating, and she told me that upcoming Thursday. She had friends coming to pick her up then. She was excited to be going home to her 'crib'. She told me that she missed everyone there, even though she spoke with someone from her 'clan' every single day.

It was getting closer to dinner time, so I went back into the room to check on Barbara. She was in the bathroom washing her hands. She said that she was impressed with how clean everything had turned out in the room, and I thanked her for noticing. I planned to talk to all three roommates about helping me keep all of it up.

She told me that she had left a book of matches in one of the stalls, just in case I needed to light a match. Now, that was really old school. I had not heard of that technique for years! We walked down the stairs and headed towards the dining hall. For some reason there was not a line of people waiting to get in.

I wondered if we were late, but once we were in the door I could see that we were actually a bit earlier than most. The offerings for that evening were baked chicken, mashed potatoes and vegetables, or the vegetarian choice of meatless Chow Mein, which is what I had. Barbara had the baked chicken. I saw Kelly and Tiffany sitting at a table in the back of the room.

I asked Barbara if she would like to go and sit with them to get to know them better, especially since they were our new roommates and she replied that would be fine. I got a cup of tea, and Barbara had a cup of decaffeinated coffee. We walked across the room and sat down.

Kelly slouched low in her chair, hoodie pulled low, and frowned when she saw us coming. I wondered if she didn't care for our company. Tiffany, on the other hand, had a big smile on her face and was eager to tell us all about her day. She and Kelly had been assigned to the same groups all day, and they both had a lot of fun.

Fun? Were we supposed to be having fun? I replied that I had only been in four groups that day and talked a bit about my visit with the psychiatrist, Dr. Stein. I mentioned that the visit was very brief, and that I didn't like the fact that he was pedaling the '12-step' programs. They all three looked at me as if I had completely lost my mind.

Barbara said "Honey, the Camp is twelve step based." I sighed and shook my head slowly in disbelief. I told them what the psychiatrist in San Jose had said about avoiding '12-step' programs. I also told them that I had been given a large book about AA by the psychiatrist and instructed to read the first nine chapters before seeing him again.

Tiffany said that she had been a member of AA for several years, owned the book to which I was referring, and that she loved it. I asked her why she was in rehab if the program really worked. All she could say is that she had relapsed, and her husband demanded that she come here, threatening separation.

Kelly was mostly silent, just sitting in her chair listening to us, but she did chime in that she had been an NA member for a long time. I could feel her watching me from under her hoodie. She was a peculiar one. I really didn't know what to think of her. Her eyes were catlike, alluring, and extremely difficult to read.

I supposed that I would discover more about her as time went on, and I planned to make the best of it things and try to be on good terms with her since she was going to be my roommate for the next few weeks. Again, I didn't want any problems with anyone while I was there.

I listened to Barbara and Tiffany while I ate my Chow Mein. It was actually surprisingly good, as was my tea. I finished long before anyone else. While we were eating the dining hall had filled up with even more clients. The din of their conversations was beginning to become abrasive to my ears, so I excused myself from the table.

I cleared my plates and went outside for silence and fresh air. I lit a cigarette and leaned against one of the walls. All of a sudden I heard a loud crashing sound from inside the dining hall, accompanied by shrill, hysterical screaming. I opened the door just a crack and cautiously peered through it to see what was happening.

I saw a massive sized man picking up tables, chairs and anything else that he could get in his hands and throwing them across the room, screaming at the top of his lungs. There were plates, food and shattered fragments of plastic from the tables and chairs everywhere. People were scrambling, frantically trying to get out of his way.

Some of them were hiding behind overturned tables. A few ran past me, through the door and into the commons area. The entire room was in shambles. Two of the male counselors rushed past me into the dining hall and subdued the man. I couldn't believe that this was happening. What kind of place was this?

What if I had not walked out of the dining hall when I did? I could have been hit by one of the chairs, or even hit directly by him. This was terrible! The police came and took the man away in handcuffs. The counselors told us to calm down, and that everything was fine, no one was hurt. The man had experienced a melt-down.

The counselor Mike told everyone that the man wouldn't be coming back to the Camp. I looked around the dining hall. Everyone was wide eyed and on high alert. I could almost feel their anxiety mounting and panic pulsating. I am certain that if there had been alcohol or drugs everyone would have partaken a bit, just to calm their nerves.

I was actually feeling a bit of anxiety myself and decided that I needed to go to my room, but first I got a cup of hot tea to take with me. I needed something to ground myself. My heart was still racing from the violent episode in the dining hall. I thought about my first real day at the rehab. The clientele were truly a mixed bag.

Some looked like they had just been scooped out of a gutter off of a skid row. Others appeared to be upper middle class affluential people, while the rest were average individuals, like me. But we all had one thing in common, which was that we had been caught in the maddening cycle of some form of addiction.

Barbara followed after me, and we sat together on the balcony until the sun was completely set. She said that she had never seen such a thing as what had just happened in the dining hall. Another woman sat down to join us, someone that I would get to know both at the Camp and after our graduations. Her name was Dallas, and she was on her fourth tour of this rehab.

Her 'drug of choice' was alcohol, and the addiction had almost destroyed her marriage. Her mother, whom I came to discover had abused Dallas in perverse ways as a child, would visit on Sunday's and call her every evening. When I got to know her better, she told me that when she was a child her mother forced her to drink drain cleaner.

The caustic chemical destroyed both of her lips. The surgeons had to use a part of her sphincter muscle to rebuild her them. I was appalled. I had not experienced such cruelty as a child. Yes, I had been paddled a couple of times, but nothing that that would come close to this. Her mother must been a truly twisted and hideous woman.

Dallas was a large, attractive robust woman with a commanding presence. Her hair was stylish, bleached blond, and she wore acrylic nails on both her finger and toenails. She always dressed as if she were going out for a night out in town. She wanted herself to be known, and she wanted to know all about everyone else.

She loved to gossip, and regaled Barbara and myself with stories about everyone she knew at the Camp and her acquaintances in town. She didn't smoke cigarettes, or anything else for that matter. Dallas told us that her husband was a businessman in Scotts Valley, owning King Precision, and had owned the business for years.

He was her second husband, her first having died years before. She had two girls and two boys, one in her teens and the rest in their early twenties. We visited for a while longer. More women came up the stairs and were mingling on the balcony. I could barely hear their conversations, not that I was eavesdropping.

It was getting later and I began growing weary, so I excused myself. It was time for me to try and get a good night's rest. I thought that if I could fall asleep before Barbara then I wouldn't have to suffer her deafening snoring. However, I had not accounted for Tiffany and Kelly.

They both came into the room shortly after I had rolled over to go to sleep. They were talking and laughing loudly while they cavorted around the room. I sat up and mumbled hello to them. They laughed more, and Tiffany ran and jumped on her bed. Kelly followed after her, climbing on top of her.

They rolled around on the bed wrestling, screaming and laughing. I asked them if they wouldn't mind toning it down, but they acted as if they didn't hear me. I rolled back over and closed my eyes, pulling my soured pillow tightly over my ears to try and mute their noise. I somehow managed to fall asleep but awoke not long after.

I was in a confused state. Standing beside my bed, I felt as if I was spinning like a Sufi dancer, and completely out of control. I saw flashing strobe lights, and heard what sounded like a freight train, and suddenly became nauseated. It could have been the alcohol receding from my body, or perhaps I was still feeling the effects of the Datura, or both.

It was a very unusual and offsetting experience. Whatever it was, it took me several minutes to realize where and when I was. I looked around the room in the dark. Barbara was still snoring, Tiffany was asleep in her bed, but Kelly was nowhere to be seen. I didn't let myself worry about that though. She was not my problem.

I lay back down and closed my eyes. I managed to get back to sleep, only to be awakened by a flashlight being shone in my eyes. I was beyond annoyed. My rope plan had not worked! I fell asleep thinking about how I could block that door. I was determined to find something to prevent anyone from coming in during the middle of the night.

I awoke much earlier than anyone else, but not very rested. I made my bed, got my towels, toiletries and clothing, and went into the bathroom. I was thrilled that I had cleaned and disinfected the entire bathroom the day before. Now I didn't have to worry about catching a fungus on my feet, or other parts of my body for that matter.

I finished with my shower, got dressed, brushed my hair and put some light makeup on. Barbara and Tiffany were still asleep, and Kelly was still not in her bed. I wondered what had become of her. I went outside to sit and smoke a cigarette in the dark while I waited for the dining hall to open for coffee.

It was deathly quiet, but that was to be expected since the Camp was located in a heavily forested area just outside of Scotts Valley. I could hear the faint calls of birds in the distance and saw the sun slowly creeping over the horizon. I looked at my watch and saw that it was close to six a.m. I went inside the room to get my towels.

I went down the twenty-eight steps of the stairs, into the laundry center, put my towels in a dryer and walked across the commons to the dining hall. The doors were already open, so I went inside and got four cups of coffee. There was no one else inside except for the cooks in the kitchen.

I could detect the smoky scent of bacon and sausage cooking, and my stomach growled. It actually smelled delicious, and I thought that maybe, just maybe I could go off of my vegetarian diet for once. Back on the balcony I reclined in a chair and sipped the hot brew. It was good and strong, and I could feel it warming my insides.

It was chilly out and damp, with Winter just beginning to set in. I once again regretted not having brought a jacket or coat with me. I pulled my wool shawl closer around my thin body and held the cup of coffee close in my hands to keep them warm. I heard someone coming up the stairs and saw Kelly moving cautiously up the steps.

She was on crutches. I asked her what had happened, and she told me that she had slipped and fallen in the middle of the night. Apparently, she had been trying to get candy out of one of the vending machines and somehow ended up falling. She was taken by ambulance to a local hospital. She had sprained her ankle and needed to use the crutches.

I told her that she should be glad it was not fractured. All that I could think is that she was a foolish young woman, especially being out in the commons after lights out. I wondered how she had gotten out of the room without being detected by one of the overzealous counselors. I had thought that we were under lock and key at night.

She hobbled into the room and slammed the door behind her. Well, that should wake Barbara and Tiffany up! It was getting closer to breakfast time, so they needed to be up anyway, but the slamming door would have been a very rude awakening. Barbara peeked through the door and waved at me.

I asked if she wanted me to wait for her to get ready for breakfast and she nodded her head yes. I drank a bit more of my coffee, then went down the stairs to the laundry center for my towels. Back in the room I saw that all the beds were made except for Kelly's. She was huddled deep under her covers with her hoodie pulled tightly over her face.

I shook my head. I found that I was becoming intrigued with Kelly. I folded my towels and placed them on the foot of my bed. The bathroom was neat and tidy, and the entire room still smelled fresh. I went back out onto the balcony to wait for breakfast time. Tiffany walked through the door and sat down at the table with me.

She didn't smoke very often, so didn't have any of her own cigarettes, so she asked if she could have one of mine. I pulled one out of my pack but she declined because I smoked menthols. Well, more for me I guess! She asked me about myself and I told her just a little bit.

Tiffany told me that she had been an exotic dancer until she was diagnosed with breast cancer. She underwent bilateral radical mastectomies the year before and had recently had surgery for breast implants. She pulled her pajama top up and showed me what they looked like.

I was a bit shocked, but I told her that they looked very natural, even though the scars were still visible. Of course, I knew that they would fade in time. Tiffany told me that she enjoyed alcohol, always had, and as she had told me earlier, was already a member of AA, but after the cancer diagnosis she began drinking more frequently.

One day she realized that she was deep in the merciless grips of addiction and spiraling downward. This is why her husband had insisted that she sign herself into rehab. She had three children, two girls and a boy. I said that I had the same and told her their names. She said "Oh! I have a Stephanie!"

I told her my daughter Stephanie's middle name and she gasped. "That is my daughter's middle name! What is your daughter's birthday?" I told her and she jumped out of her seat. "My god! That is my Stephanie's birthday!" I commented that this was quite a coincidence, and perhaps we had more in common than we thought.

Barbara walked out of the room just then, dressed for the day. Tiffany said that she was going to get dressed and would like to join us for breakfast and asked us to please save her a seat. We told her of course we would. Barbara and I went down the stairs and walked across the commons. I thought that we might be early birds.

Alas, there was already a lengthy line formed waiting for the doors to open. Once inside I decided to pass on the bacon and sausage, instead ordering two eggs over medium with toast, accompanied by a bowl of fresh fruit. Barbara ordered eggs, bacon, sausage, potatoes and toast. I figured that she must have been hungry to order all of that.

We got our coffee and found a table in a corner to sit at. I noticed Tiffany come through the doors and waved at her. She saw us and nodded her head. Close behind her was Kelly, hobbling unsteadily on the crutches. They placed their orders and joined us at the table. Kelly had her hoodie pulled tightly around her face again.

I would soon learn that it was something that was a habit of hers. It was as if she were hiding from someone or something. Mine and Barbara's breakfasts were ready, so we went to the counter to pick them up. The bacon and sausage on her plate looked so delicious, and I almost asked her for a piece, but then decided against it.

One of the cooks called out Tiffany and Kelly's orders. Tiffany told Kelly to just sit, that she would pick the food up. Kelly thanked her in a whispered voice. I was struck by that, her voice, which seemed so soft and gentle. There was something about her that I was beginning to find inexplicably intriguing.

Her golden amber colored eyes were beautiful, but they seemed to be filled with mischief, and even perhaps trouble. I seemed to detect a hidden brilliance just under the surface of her gangster persona. She had told us that she was of Puerto Rican/Irish descent. One could see that she was quite obviously a Latina.

I was finished with my breakfast and wanted to return to the room before the counselor came to inspect it. I went outside and lit a cigarette before walking up the stairs. One of the male clients by the name of Tony greeted me, calling me Celtic Goddess. I blushed and told him that I was nothing of the sort.

He said, "Just look at you, with your long, flowing bronze hair and wild, green Irish eyes! You are absolutely a Goddess!" I laughed and thanked him for the compliment and continued walking to the room. Up the twenty-eight steps I walked, my thighs and calves flexing with each and every step.

I was going to be one buff lady by the time I graduated from the Camp. I got up to the balcony and decided to sit at the table closest to the room and wait for the counselor to come for the daily inspection. I didn't have to wait long though. The counselor came running up the stairs without missing a step.

She opened the door to the room and went in, and I followed closely behind her. She had a clipboard in her hand, which she used to assess the condition of the room. She started in the bathroom and moved through the rest of the unit fairly quickly. "Now, this is how a room is supposed to look!"

She continued by saying, "Keep this up and your room will win the award for the week!" I had not put that much time into cleaning, but what time I did was well worth it. I was confident that this room was going to win the award every single week that I was there. But I didn't clean the room just for the award.

I cleaned it because I couldn't stand living in filth and disarray. I was really quite pleased with the outcome. She left and I looked the room over again, making sure that everything was picked up from the floor, that the beds were neatly made, and that the bathroom was clean and orderly.

Barbara came in and I excitedly told her that we had passed the inspection with excellence. She smiled and said, "Good job". It was after eight-thirty, and almost time to head out for my first group session. At least I knew where I was going this time. The day was a repeat of the day before.

I was glad that my next appointment with the staff psychiatrist was a week away. I didn't know what good he was doing anyway. I got my notebook and pen and went outside to wait for the time to pass. The rest of the week was spent getting to know some of the other clients and most of the counselors.

There were quite a few clients and many counselors that I never really got to know. The Camp was separated into two sides: one for adults and one for those who were under eighteen years of age. The young ones had different schedules and different sessions, and they even had different mealtimes.

I actually never did get to meet any of them at that point. After my first week I did make it a habit to greet the new adult clients who were just checking in, greet them with a warm handshake and give them a tour of the grounds so that they could be oriented. I even sat at meals with them so that they wouldn't feel uncomfortable or embarrassed.

I remembered how strange and unsettled I felt when I first arrived at the Camp, and even though I had only been there for a week I felt that it was the least that I could do to make others who were suffering from the effects of addiction feel at home. The counselors noticed this and commended me on my actions.

The room I was in continued to win the award every single week that I was at the Camp. I was delighted with this, knowing that my effort was well worth it. I had put a fair amount of time into the cleanliness and all around tidiness of the room and kept after my roommates with a smile on my face.

The first weekend came, but I knew that I wouldn't have any visitors. My children were either working or too busy with their own lives to make the drive up the hill. I was fine though. I had spoken to all of them a couple of evenings before. They were comfortable with my progress if you could call it that.

As long as I knew that they were doing good, that was all that mattered. On Saturday I washed a small load of laundry and spent time reading the 'Big Book', which is what everyone called the AA book that Dr. Stein had given me. I was anxious to get through the first nine chapters before seeing him again.

My goal in reading it was to become acquainted with the general philosophy in order to have an intelligent conversation with Dr. Stein at my next appointment. There was no one else in the room. Barbara and Tiffany had their families coming to visit, and Kelly was nowhere to be seen.

The other roommates beds were made and the room was neat and orderly and the bathroom was tidy and fresh. I was delighted Barbara and Tiffany were actually stepping up and doing their part to keep the room clean. I finished my laundry, and it didn't take me long to get through those first nine chapters of the 'Big Book'.

There was something about the book that made me feel rather peculiar. It appeared cultish to me, especially after witnessing the almost hypnotic foot stomping and declarations of 'keep coming back it works' at the end of every session that I attended. I planned to read more after my next appointment with Dr. Stein on Monday.

I had eaten a small breakfast earlier, so I was tad bit hungry, and since it was close to noon I decided to head to the dining hall to see what they were offering for lunch. I went down the stairs and across the commons. There were clients playing ping-pong and others passing a football back and forth with their visitors. This made me smile.

Inside the dining hall I could see tables with other clients and their families who were visiting. It made me happy since for me family is everything. Dallas was seated at one of the tables with an older woman who I assumed was her mother. She had been joined by other women and they all seemed to be having an enjoyable time.

I ordered a veggie-burger for my lunch, along with a small side salad. I saw Kelly at a table with a couple of younger men and decided to join them. What could it hurt? I stopped at the beverage table and got a cup of hot tea. As I got closer to the table I saw them whispering behind their hands and laughing.

One of the young men was Victor, whom I had met on my first day at the Camp. The other one was Jason, who had sat with Barbara and me during my first dinner at rehab. They were both quite pleasant. I was to learn that one of them was a methamphetamine addict and the other one was an oxycodone addict.

I asked them all how they were liking the rehab and Kelly said that the only reason she was here was because her employer had insisted that she sign herself in. She told us that she was a meth addict and had been one since she was fourteen years old. I asked her how old she was now and she told me that she was twenty-nine years old.

I was shocked. Fifteen years of hard core addiction! I felt so deeply sorry for her, or anyone else with such an addiction for that matter. I hoped that she would be able to heal from that as a result of the Camp. I noticed that she no longer had crutches, so I supposed that her ankle had healed.

One of the cooks called my name and I went to the counter and picked up my lunch. I was incredibly pleased that they had used Balsamic on my salad. I took some mayonnaise packets for my veggie burger and went back to sit with the other three. I ate while they joked around with each other, sharing drug experiences they all had in the past.

I listened to them talk while I ate and reminisced about my own heavy drug experiences as a fourteen year old runaway in the Haight-Ashbury District of San Francisco. On my first day there, Thanksgiving Day 1968, I was given a hit of LSD, and from that day forward it was pretty much my go to on a daily basis.

Mescaline, Psilocybin, Weed, Speed, you name it I tried it. I had never heard of Cocaine and had only seen others use Heroin. I decided not to share these experiences with my new friends at the table though. I didn't want them to get the wrong idea and thought that it might sound like I was glorifying the use of drugs.

I finished my lunch before anyone else at the table and cleared my plates. I wanted to go back to the room, maybe read for a while, look over my notes, and try to take a nap. It was Saturday, no group sessions, no one looking over my shoulder. I could breathe easy and take a real break.

I walked up the stairs and into the room. I went into the bathroom to freshen up, brush my teeth and rinse my face with cool water. I heard someone come through the door and turned around to see Kelly. She came into the bathroom and sat down to use one of the toilets. I averted my eyes since the toilets didn't have any walls around them.

She finished and walked over to the sink to wash her hands. I hoisted myself onto the counter and watched her. She looked at me out of the corner of her eye. I started to talk about the Camp, and how disappointed I was that it was '12-step' based, but that I would take advantage of what it had to offer otherwise.

What happened next was unexpected, unnerving and amazingly thrilling. She moved closer to me, edging herself quickly and smoothly between my legs. Suddenly her lips were on mine and I jerked away. I was both shocked and entranced. I had never kissed another woman before, at least not in a romantic sense.

She didn't move away. She looked deep into my eyes, put her hands behind my head and kissed me again. This time, and I have no idea why, I kissed her back. A long, lingering kiss. Her hands held me close, pulling me into her. My head was spinning and my heart was racing. Her lips were soft and supple, and very experienced.

I was confused, speechless. She smiled charmingly, flirtatiously, pulled away from me and left the room. I slid off of the counter and went to sit on my bed. I needed to think. My heart was still pounding and I felt dizzy, almost as if I were going to faint. Kelly was twenty-five years my junior. Why would she do this?

Even if I had been younger, or she were my age, I doubted that I would have become involved with her. But fate had another path for me to walk.

I told Tiffany what had happened, and she warmed me to be cautious of Kelly, telling me that she was poison. She had been told stories that would shock even the stoutest of hearts.

In the days that followed Kelly began waking up when I did, taking all of her meals with me, and spending all of her free time with me. She had all of her group sessions changed so that she could attend mine with me. When I sat out on the balcony she would be there, sitting next to me. Mind you, she still spent time with Tiffany, but truly little.

We would go for long walks after dinner, finding secluded spots where we could talk, embrace one another and passionately kiss without interruption. I was slowly becoming infatuated regardless of the warning from Tiffany. One day, I decided to tell Kelly how I felt. Her reply was "I'm flattered", and she walked out of the room.

I could feel my face flush and my blood pressure rising. I was overcome with embarrassment for having said anything, and immediately thought to myself that I was just an old and foolish woman. As they say, obsession and infatuation will kill logic when you need it the most.

I was relieved to see that it was time for dinner. I walked down the stairs and across the commons. Kelly was nowhere to be seen. I ordered my meal and saw Barbara and Tiffany seated at a table close to the back of the room. I was still reeling from my embarrassing moment, but Barbara and Tiffany made jokes and small talk.

Eventually I began to cheer up and put my foolishness behind me. That evening Dallas knocked on the door of my room. She invited me out onto the balcony to join in on her birthday party. Her mother had brought an enormous ganache chocolate cake, along with paper plates, a knife and forks, enough for everyone.

There was a group of us, including Kelly, and we sang happy birthday to her. When we were finished Dallas cut the cake, giving each of us a generous slice. It had been some time since I had eaten anything this sweet, and it was all I could do to finish my piece, but I did it for Dallas. She was actually a sweet person, and I enjoyed her company.

Kelly sat next to me at the table and reached for my hand. I pulled it away slowly, looking at her. I didn't know what she was doing and certainly didn't know if I could trust her. After all, she had done the major part of pursuing, then left me feeling frail and fragmented earlier that day.

Dallas had brought her French coffee press from her room and treated everyone to a small cup of freshly brewed coffee to enjoy. When we were finished with the celebrations, which turned out to be quite fun, I returned to my room alone and got ready for bed. I pulled my quilt back and slid into the bed.

I got as comfortable as was possible on the narrow and lumpy mattress, tucking the thin quilt around my body. I must have fallen asleep immediately because the next thing I knew it was already morning. I had not even awakened to the midnight flashlight, which was still a nightly occurrence.

I got out of bed and went outside for a cigarette. When I was finished I got my clothing and towels and went into the bathroom to shower and get dressed for the day. When I was finished I went to walk out the door and saw Kelly sitting at one of the tables. She stood up and walked over to me.

She took me in her arms and told me that she was sorry for reacting the way she had the day before. She had not really known what to say, but she told me that she felt the same way and that she thought that she was falling in love with me. I melted deeper into her embrace and felt warmth wash over me.

It was already mid-November, and I had become quite accustomed to the rehab. Each weekday was a repeat of the day before. Wake up, shower, get dressed, eat breakfast, lunch and dinner, and of course attend my group sessions. All that, plus making sure that our room was kept up to the standards I had set.

I learned that Kelly and I had become quite the source of gossip amongst the other clients, and a source of worry amongst the staff. I was pulled aside by more than one counselor who warned me against forming any type of romantic relationship with another client, and a couple were quite specific about the other client being Kelly.

During our free time Kelly and I continued to take walks on the property. Sometimes we would talk, but oftentimes we just sat quietly or exchanged loving kisses. She would lie on my lap and I would caress her hair, gently stroking it as she closed her eyes and relaxed. Those moments became precious to me.

She would talk about returning to her hometown of Vacaville after graduating from the Camp and going back to work for the delivery service she had been employed by for several years. She begged with me repeatedly to join her after I graduated, but I was conflicted. I told her that I would have to think about it, which seemed to upset her.

One day, on one of our walks, she opened up to me about her former partner Eleanor. She told me that Eleanor had ended their relationship suddenly and for no apparent reason. They had been together for close to three years. One day, Eleanor kicked her out of the house with only the clothing that she was wearing on her back.

Kelly had an acquaintance across the street, so she moved in with her on a temporary basis. One night they became very drunk and got into a violent brawl. The woman climbed on top of Kelly and began beating her in the face. When Kelly kicked her off the woman opened her mouth and sank her teeth into the flesh just above Kelly's right knee.

She pulled the pantleg of her sweatpants up to show me the scar. Sure enough, it was a large, purple, still inflamed scar clearly showing teeth marks. I gently caressed it, telling her how deeply sorry I was that she had to endure such horrible trauma. She told me it was okay, that it was what she deserved.

Kelly told me that she had a very good friend by the name of Chris who was in the National Guard, who had been deployed to Afghanistan, and he had given a key to his condominium to Kelly, entrusting her to watch over his place and belongings. Rather than honoring his wishes she took her young cat Kudos and moved in after the brawl.

She said that she just wanted to die, so she purchased two 'eight ball's' of methamphetamine from her drug dealer Kale, retuned to Chris's condominium, locked herself in, and spent the next five days binging. She was almost successful in doing what she had set out to do, and that is when she decided she had to go to rehab.

As I came to know her better I realized that she was really quite unrefined and unschooled. Her command of the English language was limited. Although streetwise, as in an addict/gangster sort of way, she didn't have even an iota of the knowledge that most people possessed.

Because of her addiction she had failed miserably in high school, and although she had somehow managed to attend a semester or two at her local junior college, she didn't learn any skill that would enhance her ability to have a career. I excused that away by insisting that it was all due to her meth addiction, and I didn't believe that I was wrong.

Strangely I found this to be a compelling challenge. In addition to being her lover, I could also be a mentor to her, help her to develop language and writing skills, encourage her to take from her life experiences things that could help others. I asked if she had ever considered getting a degree as a drug and alcohol addiction counselor.

She threw her head back and laughed at the very thought. "No, but I would consider being a drug and alcohol addict!", she replied. That should have been a red flag warning for me, but I still was not worried about continuing this bizarre relationship with her. I was slowly falling very deeply in love with her and there was no turning back.

Kelly was sometimes not available to me, but I was always watching for an opening to be near her. On many mornings she would walk out the door of our room with only a t-shirt on and a towel wrapped around her waist and go visit other rooms. Once I found her lying in bed with another girl, but I didn't allow that to bother me.

It seemed as if she could do absolutely anything that she wanted without it causing me alarm. I realized that any relationship could be complicated and potentially confusing, but what I didn't know is that I was being hopelessly drawn into one that was also heartbreaking, brutally abusive, and potentially deadly.

Brainwashing At Its Best

I had reached the midway point of my stay at the Camp. I began to make it my goal to fully participate in all of the group sessions, even going as far as to talk about my suicide attempt. I completed all of the work sheets and essays that I was assigned, and slowly I allowed myself to be seduced by the twelve step program.

It felt right, like I had finally come home to a place where I belonged. There were a few of the group sessions that I especially loved, particularly the one moderated by Captain Ron. He was such a lovable man and had a wealth of wisdom on addiction, as well as other aspects of life, to bestow on anyone who cared to take the time to listen.

One afternoon a counselor announced that all of the sessions were being cancelled the next day so that everyone could participate in a rock painting session, which was not compulsory. Once the rocks were painted we could choose where on the property to place them and were told that they would be left there permanently as inspiration for future clients.

The next morning, I awoke and went through my normal routine long before anyone else opened their eyes. After my shower, I dressed and went down the stairs, put my towels in a dryer, and walked to the dining room for my coffee. It was still dark out, and incredibly quiet, as no one else was up and about.

Back on the balcony, I sat and relaxed, allowing myself to wake up fully. I lit a cigarette and listened to the raucous calls of Bluejays who sat in the giant Redwood trees surrounding the property. Listening closely, I detected gentle coo of an Owl. I reflected on how my life was changing, and wondered what it would bring my way.

I was at the beginning of what I thought was a loving and meaningful relationship. I was starting to appreciate the twelve step program, and I would be graduating from the Camp in just a little over two weeks. I had absolutely no idea what I was going to do after I graduated. I was considering moving to Vacaville to be with Kelly.

That seemed to be the logical choice since I wouldn't be allowed to stay with any of my children, having been threatened by Sherry on the day of my job termination with being arrested and jailed if I set ever foot on one of their properties again. I would have to seriously consider just what it was that I was going to do.

With those thoughts circling in my mind, I went down the stairs and got my towels. Opening the door to my room quietly, I folded the towels and placed them at the foot of my bed. The roommates were all still asleep. I suppose that with group meetings being cancelled they all felt that they could get a bit more sleep.

I looked at my watch and saw that it was only 6:30 a.m.. They all had another half hour before they really needed to get up anyway. Breakfast was served from 7:00 a.m. until 8:00 a.m., so they had plenty of time. I went back out to the balcony and smoked another cigarette and sipped on my coffee.

The sun was just beginning to peek over the horizon, and I could hear songbirds in the forest that surrounded the Camp begin their morning melodies. I could smell the fragrance of the lush growth that surrounded me, and the sounds of the birds filled me with much joy, bringing with them a renewed hope for the future.

Barbara came out of the room ready for the day. She asked if I would join her for breakfast, and of course I said yes. There was no sign of Kelly or Tiffany, so we went down the stairs together and across the commons to the dining hall. Only a few people were in line. It seemed as if the entire Camp was in deep slumber.

After ordering our breakfasts, we got our beverages and found a table. Soon our orders were announced and we went to the counter to pick them up. I looked up and saw Kelly and Tiffany walking through the door and

Kelly said very loudly 'Wus up?'. I laughed and told her that we had a table. Kelly sat next to me and gave me a hug.

Kelly said that she was excited at the thought of decorating rocks but was also glad that there were no group session for the entire day. She was due to graduate on Friday, November 28th, the day after Thanksgiving. She had no visitors coming to join her for the holiday dinner, which made me feel quite sorry for her.

David and Maggie had made arrangements to join me for the Thanksgiving day celebration. I had not seen any of my children since the day that I was dropped off at the rehab, and only spoken on the phone with them a few times each. It would be so wonderful to see the two of them. I had wished that Stephanie was coming.

I invited Kelly to join my children and myself for the dinner, and she shrugged her shoulders, said "Okay", and accepted the invitation. I finished my breakfast first, took my dishes to the tub and headed back to the room. It was a brisk Autumn day, the sun was sparkling in the sky, and everyone I met along the way had a smile on their face.

In the room, I sat on my bed and read my devotionals. Not long after, all three of my roommates walked through the door. Kelly sat on the bed next to me and excitedly asked me if I would like to decorate a rock with her, one that we could both put our mark on, and something that we could both have a memory of.

I told her that I would like that very much. Tiffany said that she was not going to decorate a rock because she didn't want to leave a reminder of herself here at the Camp. I understood what she was saying. For many this place was not the most pleasant of memories or experiences.

I gave Tiffany a hug and told her that I understood. Barbara said that she would meet Kelly and I at the painting station, so Kelly and I went out of the door and down the stairs. As we were walking she took hold of my hand, sending an exhilarating thrill through my body. To me it was an acknowledgement of our budding intimate relationship.

We walked across the commons to the covered patio that adjoined the dining hall. Charlotte and Cynthia were supervising the project and had tables set up, covered with butcher paper. There was an assortment of smooth river rocks on the paper, ranging from three to five inches in diameter.

There were small containers of paint of every color you could imagine, and some was even fluorescent. Different sizes of paintbrushes were standing in large cups of water, ready for us to begin our projects. There were about fifteen other clients participating.

Most of the other clients were simply taking the day off and enjoying their freedom from having to attend the group sessions. Kelly chose one of the larger rocks for us to decorate. We each took an end of the rock, and with paintbrushes in hand, we began to decorate. I painted flowers and hearts, with flourished vines and dots.

Kelly covered her side with red and purple, then painted a large rainbow over the top. When we were finished we signed our names together, 'Kelly And Susan Forever'. We walked to one of the paths leading into the forest and found a lovely outcropping, filled with ferns and wildflowers, and placed our rock there.

That night the Camp held an assembly in the large main building which was mandatory for all clients to attend. The assembly featured former clients who had come to tell us about their addictions and their subsequent success stories. I sat next to Kelly and Tiffanny in one of the middle rows, and Barbara was sitting in the front row.

I listened to the speakers, one by one. They were given fifteen minutes each to tell their stories. I listened intently to each one, ignoring Kelly and Tiffany, who were whispering and giggling, actually making a spectacle of themselves. One of the stories resonated with my own and struck at the core of my heart.

The speaker was a middle aged woman, younger than myself, but her story sounded remarkably similar to my own. She was dressed professionally, her hair nicely styled, and she had a pleasant demeanor. All of the clients had been encouraged to already have a 'sponsor' in place before graduation and I chose her.

I decided to approach her when all of the speakers were finished. We sat through four more speakers and then the assembly was adjourned for the evening. There was a table situated along one of the walls which had been set up with refreshments. Kelly was by my side, and we chose some cookies and coffee for ourselves.

I kept my eye on the woman, wanting to make sure that she didn't leave before I had a chance to talk to her. Tiffany and Barbara were talking to one of the other speakers, most likely both of them trying to find a sponsor. Kelly and I sat together eating the cookies and talking. I asked her if any of the speakers appealed to her as a sponsor.

She told me that she already had a sponsor in her hometown of Vacaville, so she really didn't see the point of having to attend this assembly. I asked if she had not appreciated hearing the stories. She replied, "You heard one, you heard them all", and laughed sarcastically. I shook my head, really not understanding her derision.

I noticed that the woman whom I wanted to speak with was sitting by herself. I approached her and asked if I could sit next to her. She smiled and said yes. I sat down and told her that I was touched by her story, that it was remarkably similar to my own, and that I was looking for a sponsor.

She asked me about myself and my story, so I told her all that I felt was necessary. I always tended to leave out my attempted suicide. It had fast become a source of embarrassment for me, a weak woman who gave up too easily, and I didn't want anyone to think that of me. After listening to me she agreed to be my sponsor.

She wrote her phone number on a piece of paper and instructed me to call her every day and leave a message. I wondered about that, leaving a message. From what I had learned, sponsors were supposed to be, well, sponsors, and be available to their sponsee at all hours, helping them to navigate the twelve steps.

I put the piece of paper in my pocket. I would call her the day of my graduation, wherever I happened to end up. The meeting room was beginning to empty, and it was getting late. I wanted to return to the room and get ready for bed. I needed to wind down after listening to all of the horror and tragedy stories I had just heard.

I told Kelly that I was ready to leave, but she said that she wanted to hang out for a while with Tiffany. I told her that was fine and walked back to my room alone. I sat on the balcony for about half an hour before going in, hoping that I had made the right choice in a sponsor, and wondering why Kelly's had apparently not worked for her.

Kelly and I were practically inseparable. All of our group sessions were together, and we always sat closely together. I found myself thinking about her all of the time. Our mealtimes were spent together, and we shared free moments on the balcony, smoking and talking. We had become lovers without ever having been sexually intimate.

One evening, when I was sitting alone on the balcony, Dallas asked if she could join me. I told her that she was, of course, welcome. She looked at me and began speaking. She began by saying that she didn't believe that I was a lesbian, and I agreed, telling her that I didn't really know, that perhaps I was bisexual, but that I loved Kelly.

Then she told me something that was really quite disturbing. "Kelly is twisted inside Susan. She confided in me that during a meth rage that she shoved a knife up a woman's vagina searching for drugs, and that she had stabbed her own sister over another woman. Kelly was sentenced to a year in the county jail for the stabbing incident."

Dallas insisted that I be careful. She told me that I was in danger if I continued my relationship with Kelly. For some reason what she was telling me didn't sink in. I was in the throes of what I was certain was love. No one could tell me anything about Kelly, no matter the severity, which would change the way that I felt about her.

Every Friday there was a casual get together in a media room located close to the parking lot, and we were all encouraged to attend. It was for connecting current clients with former clients who were there to offer encouragement and advice on how to stay successfully sober once we had graduated from the Camp.

Kelly and I stopped by one evening, just out of curiosity. We met quite a few extraordinarily successful people who had graduated from the Camp and gone on to lead purposeful and productive lives. There were a few of the other current clients there, along with a handful of former clients.

One of them was an older gentleman by the name of Steve. He was short and stout and had a gruff appearance. He told us that he owned a construction company in San Jose, and he wondered if Kelly would be interested in working for him once she had graduated. She told him that she already had a job but he gave her his business card anyway.

I thought that might be a good idea for her, but she was stubborn, and said that she was going to be returning to Vacaville and get herself reinstated as a delivery driver. I knew that I was not going to be able to convince her otherwise so I didn't argue with her. I simply smiled and nodded my head.

The last week of my stay at the Camp was filled with excitement. Not only had I achieved my goal of winning the award for the cleanest cabin every single week, but I was announced co-president of the Camp alongside Tony, the young man who proclaimed me the 'Celtic Goddess'.

Many of the people I had become friends with had already graduated from the Camp. Tomás, Jason and several others had been celebrated and left us behind in pursuit of successful lives, hopefully remaining sober. Each of them gave me their phone numbers and asked me to keep in touch once I had graduated.

The days passed swiftly and before I knew it was Thanksgiving Day. I was exceedingly excited, knowing that David and Maggie would be coming to visit and to join me for dinner. They told me that they would be at the Camp around 10 a.m., so as that time approached I began walking in the direction of the parking lot to greet them.

I was overjoyed to see them. David had brought with him my beautiful cloak which I had bought in Ireland several years before. We hugged and kissed, and I told them that I wanted to take them on a tour of the property. I was not able to show them my room as that was against the Camp's rules, but I could show them many other areas.

The three of us walked up one of the trails so that I could show them the cabins where the group sessions were held. I pointed out the rock that Kelly and I had decorated. They read the inscription and David mumbled "Not likely". I smiled and said that we would see what the future brought.

We returned to the commons area. I showed them the large meeting room and intake center. As we passed one of the ping-pong tables I saw, out of the corner of my eye, a ping-pong ball coming towards me. I instinctively put my hand up, caught it, and threw it back to the players.

One of the young men said, "Wow! Your reflexes are impressive, like a cat!". Some of the other clients applauded me. I laughed and bowed to them. David and Maggie laughed, telling the young man that I had always had a that kind of sense about me, that I was almost always a step ahead of everything in life.

We made our way to the dining hall. The head cook had actually prepared Tofurky for me, which I found delightful. Of course, there was also real turkey, stuffing, potatoes, gravy and cranberry sauce. The children and I had a wonderful time together, and they were pleased with the progress of my recovery.

I introduced them to Kelly, who had joined us at the table. Both of them glanced at her, then at me. David had a stern look on his face, but Maggie smiled at her and shook her hand. They both said hello to her, but I could tell that David didn't approve of her. He had always been quite protective of me.

Together we enjoyed our meals, and when we were finished went outside to have cigarettes and to visit a bit more before it was time for David and Maggie to return to the Bay Area. They brought me up to date with their lives, and I was incredibly sad to see them go but I knew that I would be seeing them again soon.

I only had just a few days left before I graduated and moved on to the next chapter of my life. Of course, Kelly graduated four days before I did, which already had me worried. That evening she reminded me that she would be returning to her job in Vacaville, and that she would give me a call once she was settled.

I begged her not to return to Vacaville. She had talked about an old friend by the name of Kale who was also her meth dealer. That was cause for great concern. I told her that if she stayed in the Santa Cruz area that we could build a life together once I had graduated. She told me that would be impossible.

She wanted to put her own life back together. Her family lived in Vacaville, and she wanted to be near them. I understood that, wishing to be near family, but I was desperate to be with her. Thoroughly convinced that I was in love with her, I would do almost anything to keep her close by.

Kelly, along with Tiffany, graduated the next day. I sat with Barbara while they were applauded and given their certificates. After cake and ice cream, I walked with Kelly to the intake office. She already had her suitcase waiting there. She hugged me and said "I will be back for you next week. I love you Susan."

I watched as she walked past the intake office and headed towards the parking lot. My heart sank, believing that I would never see or hear from her again. But I knew that I really couldn't depend on others to see me through the next phase of my life and accepted this as gracefully as possible.

That same day, Cynthia, one of the counselors, approached me. She told me that I was a perfect candidate for her SLE. SLE stands for sober living environment. I told her that I didn't have a job yet, and she said that was only charging five hundred dollars per month for a shared room, including utilities, so I agreed to try it.

She gave me her name, phone number and address on a piece of paper and told me that she would be expecting me on the day of my graduation. I was a bit uneasy though. I had never been in a roommate situation, other than at the Camp, and even though I had made friends with my roommates it was still a bit of a reach for me.

I knew that I would need a few items before moving into her place and I asked her if it was possible for someone from the Camp to take me to Santa Cruz to shop for bedding and she told me that I should go to the intake office and ask. I did so and Captain Ron happened to be there and offered to give me a ride.

He drove me to Santa Cruz to go shopping at Mervyn's department store. I felt strange being off of the property where I had spent a month of my life but was exhilarated at the same time. I had been completely sober for over a month, didn't have suicidal thoughts, and life was feeling so wonderful and full of endless possibilities.

I purchased a basic, but cozy full size comforter, along with fluffy pillow, a sheet set, and a few throw pillows. While we were in town I asked if we could stop by a branch of my bank. He said yes. I went inside and cashed in the CD that I owned, paying off the credit cards that I had used for the Camp. $10,000.00, gone in a flash.

That evening, I received a phone call from one of Kelly's friends in Vacaville by the name of Drew. He told me that Kelly had gone on a drunken rampage and was completely out of control. He asked if I would be able to do anything at all and I replied that I would see what I could do, which I highly doubted.

I immediately made a phone call to Tiffany, who told me that she couldn't do anything to help. I became distraught and sought out one of the counselors who stayed after work and talked to him about it. He told me that since she was no longer a client there was nothing that he could do for her.

The same night Dallas took Kelly's place as a roommate. I was delighted to have her, even if only for a few days, as she was such an interesting and lovely person. I had fallen asleep when suddenly I awakened to see Dallas at my bedside, completely nude, and peering at me in through the darkness. I asked her what she was doing.

She said, "I wanted to see if you are really a Lesbian." I laughed and told her to go back to bed. She turned away from me and slunk off towards her own side of the room. I watched as she put her pajamas back on and crawled into her bed. Barbara had been watching the entire encounter and snickered out loud.

I spent the next few days worrying about Kelly, but even so I still had to attend all of my group sessions. The day before my graduation we had a group meeting in the large circular building with all of the adult clients from the Camp attending. Mike was the counselor hosting the meeting. He brought a large bucket of ping pong balls into the room and left.

I looked around the room at all of the other clients, then swiftly I got up from my chair, picked up the bucket of ping pong balls, and went around the circle handing one to each of the clients. I then told them that when Mike returned, to throw the ping pong ball that they were holding as hard as they could across the room.

Mike returned to the room and took and sat down in his chair. Suddenly, everyone drew their arms back and let loose with the ping pong balls. The room was filled with chaos and hysterical laughter. People were clapping and stomping their feet. Mike smiled at the revelry and looked straight at me. He knew I had been the culprit.

Tiffany called me that evening to tell me that Kelly had shown up to her job drunk and was fired on the spot, no if's, ands or buts. She had been permanently terminated, and a red flag was placed in her employee file. It seemed like the rehab had not done her any good at all, and I wondered what she would do now.

At that point I gave up all hope of ever seeing her or hearing from her again. I had lived this long without knowing her, and surely I could continue without her in my life. The following day was my graduation, and I was determined to have a fulfilling and successful life, surrounded by my beloved family and friends.

The next morning I woke up in a state of glorious excitement. Today I was to begin the next leg on my journey in life. I immediately took a shower, got dressed, then went down to the dining hall to get my coffee. I sat on the balcony just long enough to drink it and smoke a cigarette, then I went into the room to pack my belongings.

I was too excited to eat breakfast, so I stayed on the balcony with my suitcase until it was time for my graduation ceremony. Barbara joined me and told me how happy she was for me. She advised me to take good care of myself, to watch out for the 'druggies' in Santa Cruz, and told me that she was relieved that Kelly was out of the picture.

She asked if I would be going to meetings, and I replied that from what I understood it was a requirement of Cynthia's for anyone who lived in her SLE. She replied that was a good thing, and that she hoped to see me at some of the meetings and told me that I was welcome to come visit her in Boulder Creek once she graduated.

She left to get breakfast and said that she would see me at the graduation ceremony. My heart skipped a beat when she said that. 10 a.m. came and it was time for me to walk down those twenty-eight steps for the very last time. I would miss my friends at the Camp, but I was ready to get on with my own life.

When I walked into the large meeting room for the ceremony my co-president, Tony, played the song 'Magic Man' by the rock group Heart. I was so thrilled. It was a strange feeling to be leaving behind so many people that I had grown to know and care about. As much as I tried to stay in contact, I lost touch with all but a few.

There were forty or fifty people gathered in the room, many of whom signed my 'Big Book' with wonderful wishes and beautiful words. The ceremony was brief, but the celebration went on for about half an hour. I finally had to tell everyone goodbye, and they gathered around me in a huge group hug, all of them wishing me the absolute best.

Hauling my suitcase behind me, I went to the intake office to be officially discharged. I was extremely excited! David had driven my car up the hill a few days before, followed by Rachel in their car, and he told me that they had packed it with as many of my belongings as would fit. He had left my car keys at the intake office.

He also told me that he and Stephanie would be in the parking lot waiting for me and that they would help me get settled in at Cynthia's place. I left the intake office and walked down the long driveway to the parking lot, all the while craning my head to see if David and Stephanie were there.

I rounded a corner and saw them. I ran to where they were and fell into their arms crying with joy. They held me in their embraces for a few moments, telling me how happy they were to see me. That is when I saw Kelly leaning against a copper colored, full sized Toyota pickup, her arms and legs crossed, and with a big smile on her face.

Here I was, newly 'rehabilitated', and ready to conquer the world, reclaiming the life that I knew before my suicide attempt. Today was first day in new surroundings, and hopefully a fresh start to my life. But fairytales and fantasies rarely come true, and my eyes would be opened, but not wide enough, while living in Santa Cruz.

Chapter Three: Freedom To Live And Love

I looked at Kelly and thought to myself, "So, she has come down after all". As I got nearer to my car she ran to me, putting her arms around me and kissing me. I could smell liquor on her breath. I was apprehensive, but I returned the hug and kiss. I could feel David and Stephanie watching us.

Tiffany was with her and told me that she wanted to take us all to lunch, her treat, before I went to Cynthia's house. I got in my car and started it, the passive restraint closing in on me. Kelly and Tiffany pulled out of the parking lot first, then me, and then David and Stephanie pulled in behind me.

I was not in the least bit familiar with the area, so I stayed close behind Kelly's truck. I could see that she was a wild and careless driver, zooming in and out of traffic, both on the access road and then on the freeway. I was not used to this kind of driving and it was all I could do to keep up with her.

About five miles down the freeway she took the exit to Capitola. She drove down so many side streets that looped and circled that I was completely lost. We finally arrived in Capitola Village, and Kelly parked her vehicle across the street from the Castagnola Deli and Café, which was located next to the beach.

She and Tiffany got out the pickup and walked across the street. I parked my car behind hers, and David parked just beyond me. I waited for David and Stephanie so that we could walk across the street together. The deli was crowded, and it took us a while to find a table to accommodate all five of us.

It was a charming place, and I was delighted that I was able to order a reasonably nice vegetarian sandwich. The other four ordered Reubens, Corned Beef and Roast Beef sandwiches. I felt a little peculiar with Kelly and Tiffany there, but they had insisted that they were going to help me get moved in at Cynthia's.

I asked Kelly to tell me more about what had happened to her in Vacaville and told her about the phone call I had received from her friend Drew. She said that she had 'relapsed', which had been a frequent thing for her in life, had gone to work drunk, and was fired from her job for doing so.

She told me that she had a new plan now. She had already contacted another SLE a few miles from Cynthia's and was going to live there for a while. I knew that she didn't have a job, of course, and I doubted that she had any money saved. I asked her how she was planning to get by.

She smiled and told me that she had it all under control, that everything was going to be just fine. She said that she had enough money saved back to pay for a couple of weeks at the SLE, and by the time she ran out of that money she should have a job. If that didn't work out, she could always go back and live with her mom and dad.

Now, I was not one to judge. My grown children had stayed with me before when they were new to the area or fallen on hard times, but they always moved forward quickly in finding employment and their own places to live. I wondered if Kelly was the same as my children, or if she made it a habit of running home to mommy and daddy.

We finished our lunches and I told the four of them that I needed to get my belongings to Cynthia's house and get settled in. I asked Kelly if she knew where Cynthia's house was and showed her the address. She said that she had a map in her truck and that it wouldn't be a problem finding it.

We finished our lunches and I told the four of them that I needed to get my belongings to Cynthia's house and try to get settled in. I was not sure about the path ahead, but even so I was excited to have graduated from the Camp and have a clear shot at my life. World, get ready, because here

I come!

Life At Cynthia's

I followed close behind Kelly and Tiffany, David and Stephanie followed me, and we drove next to the Pacific Ocean, through several neighborhoods, and up and down winding roads, and we eventually arrived at Cynthia's. Kelly was driving rather maniacally. Fortunately, none of us got into an accident.

I parked my car in the driveway close to the house, got out and walked up to the door. David, Stephanie, Kelly and Tiffany waited for me outside. A young man opened the door and welcomed me into the house. Cynthia came out of her room and greeted me. She gave me a quick tour of the house.

She showed me the small but efficient kitchen, which was stocked with coffee and tea for all of the roommates but told me that I was responsible for my own food. She took me to the laundry area, and the basement where I could store my luggage. Then she took me into the room that was going to be mine.

I followed her inside and was amazed to see a bunkbed on one side of the small room and a very narrow single bed on the other. She pointed to the bottom bunk and told me that was mine. I had not slept in a bunkbed since I was at Summer camp as a child, and I really didn't think that at my age this was appropriate.

I asked about the single bed and she told me that was already taken by someone who would be moving in later that week. I supposed that I was just going to have to accept this until I could find a place of my own. There were two small windows, a dresser, nightstands, and a desk with a chair which was situated in front of a tiny reach-in closet.

I was not in the least bit impressed, but it would do for now. I thanked her and went outside to start unpacking my car. Everyone pitched in, carrying loads into my new room and taking items that I wanted to be stored in the basement down there. Other than the young man who answered the door, and Cynthia, there was no one else at home.

I supposed that I would be meeting everyone else at another time. Cynthia had told me that there were seven others besides me living at the SLE, all of them former clients of the Camp. One big happy family! At five hundred dollars per person each month she was making a pile of money.

It took us about an hour to get all of my things inside the house and ready for me to sort through. David and Stephanie had to return to the Bay Area and Kelly had to drive Tiffany home and check in with her SLE. When they were gone Cynthia said that we needed to sit down together and go over the house rules.

We sat in the living room on one of the three couches. The first thing that she told me was that as a client of her SLE I was required to attend an AA/NA/Any-type-of-A meeting every single day for the next thirty days. She handed me a form and told me that I was to get a signature from the chair of any meeting that I attended.

She then handed me a list of local meetings and told me that the closest one was at the Department of Motor Vehicles, which was about two miles away. The next thing that she told me was that I would be assigned a household chore each week which I alone was responsible for completing every single day, even on the weekends.

Cynthia mentioned that I needed to phone my sponsor every day and speak with her. She let me know that everyone was expected to keep up the kitchen and bathrooms, and to pick up after myself wherever I was in the house. I was also required to apply for work, and I had to check in with Cynthia to let her know when and where I had applied.

The last rule was that no one was to EVER enter her room. She told me that it was her sacred space. She didn't even want anyone to knock on the door. I replied that I respected that, and if I needed anything from her I would wait until I saw her around the house. Other than that, she told me to enjoy my time in her home.

Enjoy myself? Sleeping on the bottom bunk of a bunkbed in a tiny room with two other women, in a house that was unfamiliar to me, in a town that I had never lived in, and with people that I really didn't know? I couldn't imagine actually enjoying myself. But as always, I would make the best of the situation until something else presented itself.

I thanked her and went into my room to unpack my belongings. Cynthia had assigned me two drawers in the small dresser for my folded clothing, and a handful of hangers for the rest. There was barely enough space in the drawers for much of anything, and I found that I needed to store those items in the duffle bags I had in the basement.

I hung what garments I was able to in the miniscule closet, and what didn't fit also went into the duffle bags. I supposed that I really didn't need everything, that I could make do with the small amount that I was able to fit. I was excited though that I finally had my laptop and cellphone, so I set my laptop up on the small desk.

I plugged my cellphone into its charger and set it on the small nightstand next to the bunkbed to charge. Cynthia had given me the access keycode to the internet connection in the house, which of course I was thoroughly pleased with. But I had to wait for my poor old laptop and cell phone to be fully charged before opening it up.

Once my cell phone was charged I phoned my sponsor. The call went directly to voicemail, which is what she had said it would do. I left a message that I had moved into the SLE, and that I was getting settled. I wondered if she would even call me back, but I didn't worry about it too much.

Cynthia gave me the unlock code for the keyless entry to the front door. When I had finished unpacking I stored my luggage downstairs in the basement, which was actually a rather creepy place. I needed to buy some things, food, toiletries, and other items, so I got my purse, cigarettes and cellphone and went outside to my car.

I saw that a few other cars had parked close by me, and thankfully they had not blocked me in. I had not heard anyone come inside so whoever it was must have been in their rooms. I started my car and drove to the end of the driveway. I headed in towards 41st Avenue, where Cynthia had told me the Department of Motor Vehicles was located.

It was almost four in the afternoon, and there was a meeting at that time, so I planned to attend the meeting then go shopping. On my drive there I kept my eyes open, looking for a shopping center where I could find the items that I needed. I saw that there were several, including Capitola Mall which offered a great variety of stores.

The parking lot at the DMV was almost full, and it took me a while to find a parking space. I locked my car and went inside. I asked one of the employees where the AA meeting was and she pointed to a room in the back of the building. I walked through the doors and was happy to see Dallas and Kelly sitting next to each other.

I decided to sit with them. There was a table just inside the door with coffee service and cookies. I got a cup of coffee and went to sit down. The meeting had already started. One by one people were introducing themselves and speaking about their addictions. When it was my turn to introduce myself I told everyone my first name and mentioned alcohol.

That was pretty much all that I had to say. When everyone in the room had their turn the speaker stepped up to the podium. He welcomed everyone and asked if anyone had been sober for a day, a week, a month, or perhaps a year. There were 'chips' for those who had been. I thought this was a wonderful reward for sobriety.

I looked around the room at all of the people. I recognized a few more faces from the Camp. I supposed that most of them were local folks, unlike myself and Kelly. Then, in one of the corners of the room, skulking in the shadows, I saw Jeff from the Camp. He was not participating. Instead, he was listening intently and taking notes.

The very sight of him made me nauseous. What I later discovered is that he frequented several meetings in the area, targeting the most desperate and vulnerable of addicts, enticing them into signing contracts for the Camp, and promising them a future of sobriety and success. He was despicable in my estimation.

The meeting only lasted an hour. Afterwards, I introduced myself to a few of the other attendees, then walked outside to smoke a cigarette. Kelly followed after me. She told me that she had checked in with her SLE, and that so far she liked it. It was only women, something that she could definitely hang with.

She asked me if I would like to have dinner and go for a drive with her that evening. I said that would be fine and told her that I still needed to go shopping for a few personal items, and that I was still getting set up at Cynthia's. She replied that she would come by for me around seven that evening.

She gave me a quick hug and kiss, which thrilled me, and left in her truck. I noticed that Kelly was dressed in cargo pants, a t-shirt, a flannel and men's work boots. She had a baseball cap on her head covering her short, black hair. For all intents and purposes, she looked like a man, and a handsome man at that.

I was still in love with her, but I was a little disappointed that she had not been able to manage herself after graduating from the Camp. I planned to have a heart to heart talk with her about her future and keeping her nose clean. I left the DMV and drove to one of the shopping centers I had seen earlier.

I bought the items that I needed, shampoo, conditioner, lotion, and a variety of fruit and vegetables, along with some naughty snacks for when I had a craving. I returned to Cynthia's house, putting my toiletries in my room and carefully labeled all of the food with my name before I put it away in the kitchen.

It noticed that it was close to six p.m., and Kelly would be by to pick me up at seven, so I went into the bathroom to freshen my makeup. The bathroom was a disaster and I ended up having to clean it before even thinking about makeup. I was not sure how closely Cynthia monitored the house, but it didn't look like she did a very good job.

I didn't bother changing my clothes. I was already dressed in some of my favorite clothing, which was an oversized sweater, leggings, leg warmers and boots. I took my hair out of the braid it was in and brushed it out. I looked at myself in the mirror on the back of the door and was not displeased.

Even though my hair had been damaged during my one night's stay at the hospital after my suicide attempt it was still waist length, fairly healthy and from what I was told, quite beautiful. I went outside to smoke a cigarette and wait for Kelly. I was truly looking forward to spending the evening with her and hearing more about her plans.

I knew that I needed to be focusing on myself and whatever the future held for me. I wondered if Kelly was actually going to be a part of that future. I saw Kelly pull up in the driveway and the passenger door open from inside. I walked over, climbed into the seat, and away we went, with Kelly driving just as crazy as she had earlier that day.

I reached over and gave her a kiss on the lips and asked where we were going to have dinner. She told me that she had heard of a very cool little place in downtown Santa Cruz called the Saturn Café, that only served vegetarian and vegan food. I told her that was absolutely fine with me.

The café was retro, with red upholstery on the seats and the stools, and the tabletops and counters were covered with speckled Formica. The menu offered plenty of vegetarian options, and the prices were really quite reasonable. I ordered a cup of coffee and Kelly ordered a soda. I asked the server to give us a few minutes to peruse the menu.

I decided on the California Burger with sweet potato fries, and Kelly ordered the Chicken Club Sandwich with regular fries. I already had my eye on the desserts and knew that I would be ordering the Strawberry Vegan milkshake. I excused myself to go wash my hands and told Kelly that I would be back shortly.

Kelly was standing outside the front door smoking a cigarette when I returned to the table. I joined her and we talked for a while. I asked her how she was feeling now that she had decided to stay at the SLE, and she replied that she felt fine, and that she knew that she was going to be able to overcome her addictions.

By the time we returned to the table our meals had already been served. We talked as we ate. I told Kelly that I planned on finding another job in property management, something that I actually enjoyed doing, and eventually renting an apartment close to the beach, where I had always wanted to live.

She replied that she would love to join me, and that as soon as she had a job she would be able to help pay the rent, utilities and buy groceries for us. I thought that was a wonderful idea, but I also wanted to make sure that she was ready for a real relationship before setting anything in stone with her.

Kelly knew more about me than I her, so I asked her about her family. She told me that her parent's names were David and Sharon, and that she had two sisters: one older, Brenna, and one younger, Beth. Brenna had four children and Beth had two. They all lived in Vacaville within miles of each other.

I said that I would love to meet them all sometime and she thought that would be a good idea. I suggested that once we had an apartment that perhaps we could invite my family and hers for a barbeque so that everyone could get to know one another. She half-smiled at me but didn't reply.

She began talking about Eleanor, and another woman she had been in a relationship with by the name of Marisol. She told me that she would always be in love with Marisol, but Eleanor was another story. Kelly said that if Eleanor fell off of the face of the earth that she wouldn't give a shit.

I told her that was harsh, but she laughed and said "'Bitches come and bitches go. If I get rid of one, I will have another before the day is over." I found that to be somewhat cavalier, and I told her as much. She laughed again and said, "Whatever Susan. My real friends will always be there for me."

I really didn't know what to say, so I concentrated on eating my burger. The server cleared our plates, poured me a fresh cup of coffee and refreshed Kelly's soda, and asked if we wanted dessert. I declined. What Kelly had said had ruined my appetite. I had snacks at Cynthia's anyway if I really wanted something sweet later.

When we were finished she paid for the meal and we walked outside to her truck. She started the engine and found her way to Highway 1, which is situated next to the Pacific Ocean. The moon was waxing, yet still cast a lovely light upon the glinting waves of the water. I rolled my window down just enough to capture the scent of the ocean.

Kelly said that she needed to buy a pack of cigarettes and stopped at a gas station on the outskirts of Santa Cruz. She asked if I needed anything. I told her that I was still full, and that I had plenty of cigarettes. I waited in the truck, and waited, and waited. Finally, she came out of the store and got into the driver's seat.

She reached over and kissed me. I could smell liquor on her breath. She lit a cigarette, took a deep drag, and looked at me. "You should know that I'm a woman abuser." I asked her what she meant by that, and she told me that she had abused most of the women in her life.

As she drove she recounted some of the experiences she had in the past, and how she had lost every relationship she had because of the abuse. I knew that I should be taking this to heart, but I still was not really listening. I asked her if it was because of her meth addiction and she said yes, that and alcohol.

I asked her why she was drinking now and she told me that it was none of my business. I shrugged my shoulders and turned my head away, looking out of my window. We drove in awkward silence. I didn't know what to say. We had been driving for about an hour when I spoke up and told her that I had to be back at the SLE by ten p.m.

I asked if she didn't also have a curfew, and she replied that no one was going to control her. I insisted that she drive me back to mine though, and reluctantly she found a place to turn around and headed back into town. When we pulled up in front of Cynthia's house Kelly reached across me, opening the passenger door.

She yelled, "Get the fuck out of my truck!". Needless to say, I was confused, but I got out, thanked her for dinner and the drive, and went into the house. I tried to wrap my head around what she had told me about being an abuser. Somehow, it just didn't make sense to me. I went inside, got ready for bed, and fell into a disquieted sleep.

My phone rang around midnight. I sat up slowly, looked at my phone, and saw that it was Kelly calling. When I answered I could hear her sobbing. She told me that she was sorry for how she had treated me and said that she promised to do better. I replied that I was trying to understand but was perplexed by what she had said about abuse.

We ended up talking until she finally fell asleep. Kelly called me almost every night that I lived at Cynthia's, keeping me on the phone for up to five hours at a time, always telling me that she was lonely and just wanted to know that I was there listening to her while she fell asleep.

The next morning, I awoke with great plans for the day that didn't include Kelly. I wanted to check online for job opportunities and drive through the area to familiarize myself. I went into the kitchen to get a cup of coffee and found that none was made. I ground some coffee beans, put them in the coffee maker and made a fresh pot.

There was a patio situated in the center of the house with doors leading from the living room and the hallway closest to my bedroom. When the coffee was brewed I poured a cup and went out onto the patio, which was bare save a small bench. In fact, there were no plants or anything to liven it up. I lit a cigarette and drank some coffee.

When I was finished I returned to my room and got dressed, put some light makeup on and clipped my hair up. I heard a knock at the front door and waited for someone else to open it, but no one did, so I went and opened it. There, standing on the porch, was Tomás, one of my good friends from the Camp.

He had a large suitcase with him, and he excitedly told me that he was officially one of my roommates. I was delighted. He and I got along marvelously. Tomás was Gay and a methamphetamine addict. He was from San Francisco and had checked himself into the Camp just a few days after I arrived.

We had spent many hours at the Camp talking about life and how we had gotten to where we were. He had told me that his older lover had encouraged him to use meth to make him sexier, and that in so doing he almost lost his life. I walked out the door and over to him, giving him a big hug. He was such a teddy bear!

I was glad to have someone that I actually knew fairly well living in the same house that I was. I told him to come on in, but that I didn't know if Cynthia was home or already at work at the Camp. Just then Cynthia's bedroom door opened and she popped her head out. She said, "I will be with you in a few minutes Tomás".

I told Tomás that I would leave him and Cynthia to get him checked into the SLE, and time for him to get settled in his room and suggested that we might grab some lunch and go to a meeting together later that day. He told me that he would like that very much and gave me a hug.

I returned to my room long enough to check for help wanted listings on Craigslist. There was nothing in the immediate area, and certainly nothing else that I was extremely interested in applying to. I had plenty of money, so I was not worried about that part. But I knew that I did need a job eventually, and the sooner the better.

I decided to take a drive to down 41st Avenue towards the Opal Cliffs. I found a small park area with picnic benches that overlooked the beach below where dozens of surfers had assembled. I sat on the table of one of the picnic benches, smoking cigarettes and watching as they swam out past the breakers and surfed seamlessly back to the shore.

I stayed for about an hour, then decided to drive back to Cynthia's to see how Tomás was getting along. While I was driving my cell phone rang. I looked at it and saw that it was Kelly calling. I returned her call as soon as I was parked at the house. She wanted to know if I would like to go to that afternoon's meeting at the DMV with her.

I told her that was planning on attending with Tomás, but I would be happy to sit with her during the meeting. She asked "Is Tomás there?" I told her that he had moved into the SLE that morning, and that I was incredibly happy that he had. She asked sarcastically, "Are you in love with him?" I laughed and reminded her that he was Gay.

On the fifth of December I went for a drive into the Santa Cruz mountains with Kelly. She had been prodding me for sex since we first began our relationship. As we drove she asked me once again if I would have sex with her and I replied "Sure, Kelly. Let us get a motel room and do it!".

She gave me a shocked look, but she immediately drove to the Brookdale Lodge in Boulder Creek where we rented a room. The property was under heavy renovations and we had to walk up a very shaky staircase to get to our room. Once inside I could see that there was not really anything spectacular about it, but it would serve the purpose we had.

Kelly had brought a backpack with her and told me to go into the bathroom. She followed me and told me to undress. I did as she said. She then pulled shaving crème and a shaver out of her backpack and began shaving my genital region. When she was finished she told me to take a shower and when I was done to come to bed.

Kelly had pulled the drapes closed and turned off all of the lights. With a towel wrapped around me, I felt my way to the bed, pulled the covers back and got in. Kelly began kissing me and caressing my body. I returned her kisses, passionately, and even though this was the first time I had ever made love to a woman I allowed myself to be drawn in.

Her lips were always so soft and supple, and kissing her gave me such pleasure. Her skin felt like the softest of velvet as I caressed it. My body instantly responded to hers. She asked me what I liked and I whispered that I didn't know what to say because all of my sexual experiences had been with men.

From what she had told me she was an experienced and thorough Lesbian lover, but her first efforts with me were no more than average. I was disappointed. I had definitely expected fireworks. I sat up, pulled the towel around myself and felt my way through the darkened room back into the bathroom to get dressed.

Kelly asked me if the sex had been okay, and I responded that it was fine. She seemed annoyed. I am sure that she had expected me to fawn over her exquisite skills in bed, but I just couldn't bring myself to lie. Her phone rang while we were talking. It was Dallas. She had graduated that day and was inviting us to join her for dinner.

Kelly put her phone on speaker. I heard Dallas say that we should meet her at Jack O'Neil's restaurant which was close to the Santa Cruz pier. I told Kelly that perhaps we should leave to meet Dallas. Kelly reluctantly got up and dressed and we carefully made our way back down the shaky staircase.

The drive to the restaurant was filled with tension. Kelly was crushed that I had not been more entranced with her lovemaking. I was glad when we pulled up at the curb by the restaurant. Dallas was waiting rather impatiently for us at the entry door. She already had a table for the three of us, so we went inside and sat down.

Even though I had been an ovo-vegetarian for some time, I was in the mood for a rare piece of beef, so I ordered the Prime Rib, complete with baked potato, salad, broccoli and fresh baked bread. Kelly and Dallas ordered the same. We all had iced tea with our meals, being careful to be true to our newly found sobriety.

When Kelly dropped me off at the SLE she once again reached across me, opened the truck door and told me to get the fuck out of her truck. I didn't know if she was just joking, or if she was mad at me and wanted me gone. I was learning that she was extremely capricious in her moods and actions.

Tomás was waiting for me at the kitchen table. It was just past nine-thirty p.m., so I prepared a snack tray for us with cracked pepper crackers, sharp cheddar cheese, grapes and a lovely olive tapenade to spread on the crackers, along with cups of hot herbal tea, and we sat down to visit for a while.

I asked him how his evening had been and he replied that it was fine. I told him about my afternoon and evening, including the short stay at the Brookdale Inn. He laughed and said that it must have been quite an experience for me. I shrugged my shoulders and replied that I thought I had offended Kelly because it was really nothing special.

The next days were filled with meetings, keeping up on my end of the chores at the SLE, and taking long drives with Kelly. When I was not with Kelly I would go out with Tomás and a few of the other roommates from the house. We would have lunch, shop, and hang out at the beach, making memories and having a wonderful time.

Kelly had been living at her SLE for only five days when she was kicked out for coming in drunk and suspected of being high on meth. She didn't have anywhere to stay and asked me to help her. I told her to give me some time to think and that I would let her know. I was extremely concerned, however, of the suspected meth use.

I could afford to get her a room, so I looked online for a local hotel with good rates and found the Capitola Best Western. I phoned them and booked a king size suite for eighty-five dollars per night. I booked it for five nights, which is all that I was willing to put towards it and told the clerk that I would stop by later that day for key-cards.

I phoned Kelly and told her that I had rented a room for her. I heard her catch her breath, and she excitedly thanked me, telling me that she would somehow repay me. I let her know that we could go to the hotel after the meeting at the DMV that afternoon. She replied that she would meet me at the DMV.

I spent the morning completing my assigned chores at the SLE, then went out and did some shopping before going to the meeting. When I returned from the stores Tomás was waiting for me. He said excitedly "You will never guess who moved in!" I asked him who it was and he told me that it was Tassi Rae, from the Camp, and she was going to be one of my roommates.

I had liked Tassi from the moment I met her. She had come to the Camp from Washington State, and she and I had become friends from the start. I walked into my room and there she was, bigger than life, unpacking her belongings and making the top bunk. I asked if she was going to be comfortable up there and she told me she would be fine.

Tassi asked if I were attending a meeting that day, and I told her that I would be, and that I would be meeting Kelly there. Her reaction was priceless. "Are you and Kelly still an item?" she asked. I told her that we were, at least as far as I knew, and that eventually we planned to find a place a move in together.

I also told her about Kelly had been kicked out of her SLE. She sighed and said, "I knew it would happen!" I let her know that I was going to be working on convincing Kelly to seek more help than the meetings or her sponsor were offering. Knowing that she was a diagnosed schizophrenic, I felt that she desperately needed psychiatric care.

I met Kelly at the meeting later that day, and afterwards she followed me to the hotel. We went inside and I introduced myself to the desk clerk, who promptly handed me two key-cards and told me that our room was on the second floor. We had no luggage, so rather than take the elevator we walked up the stairs to the hallway and found the room.

It was a beautiful room, with plenty of space. There was a fireplace and widescreen television, as well as a microwave, small refrigerator and coffee maker. Kelly looked around and said that it would be fine. I thought that it was more than fine. At least she was not going to have to sleep in her truck.

I told Kelly that I had to return to the SLE and gave her a key-card. I trusted that she was going to behave herself while she was in the room. Giving her a hug and kiss I left, hoping for the best, but somehow expecting the worst. When I got back to the SLE Tomás was just getting in his car to leave.

I asked where he was going and he replied that he was stepping out for a bite to eat. He told me that he had heard about Kelly and wondered if she was doing okay. I told him yes, and that I had rented a king suite for five nights so that she would have a safe place to stay while figuring out what she was going to do.

I told him that I was going back to the hotel to take Kelly some dinner and asked if he would like to join us. He replied that he would love to, and wondered if Tassi could join us as well. I told him that would be fine, and maybe we could take some of the board games from the SLE and entertain ourselves after dinner.

The next few days proved to be busy for me. Each day I had to complete my assigned chores, keep my own personal space clean, search for work and go to the hotel to be with Kelly. I also had to find time to go to a meeting every single day and urged Kelly to go with me.

Often I would round up Tomás, Tassi and a couple of other roommates and we would all go to the hotel room just to chill for a couple of hours before having to return to the SLE. We would bring soft drinks, snacks and board games with us, watch television together, and always thoroughly enjoyed ourselves.

I took the time to look up several other SLE's in the area and made phone calls trying to find one that would take a chance on Kelly. I was successful in locating one that was located in Freedom, which was about ten miles South of Capitola. The manager told me that Kelly could move in on the day that she had to check out of the hotel.

I was, of course, extremely excited, and phoned Kelly, telling her that I had wonderful news and that I was coming to the hotel. When I opened the door and walked in, I saw Kelly was sitting slumped over in one of the oversized chairs, holding her head in her hands. She looked at me and said, "You're going to hate me."

I asked her why and with tears in her eyes she told me that she had had sex with the girl that she had bought meth from. I knew that she had used meth! Instead of becoming enraged, which I had a right to be, I told her that I was not upset with her, and that I would forgive her. She got down on her knees and cradled her head in my lap. My heart melted.

I reminded her that I loved her, then we talked about the new SLE, and I told her that she was being given another chance at success. Her face brightened and she hugged me so hard it almost hurt. Just then there was a knock at the door and I walked over and opened it to see a lovely young woman standing there.

"Oh, hi Megan", Kelly said. I didn't know this person, but I invited her inside anyway. She immediately sat on the bed, making herself right at home. I told Kelly that I would like to take a drive to Half Moon Bay and get some dinner to celebrate, and Kelly suggested that we might take Megan along with us. I told her that was fine.

It was a beautiful afternoon as we drove the Pacific Coast Highway to Half Moon Bay. Megan sat in the back seat of Kelly's truck, and I sat in front beside Kelly. We dined on the patio at Sam's Chowder House, with a spectacular view of the ocean. The dinners were reasonably priced, and I paid the entire bill without complaining.

On our way back to the hotel Kelly said that she needed to drop Megan off at the house where she was staying. It was only a few blocks from the hotel, so I didn't have a problem with it. The townhouse where we dropped her was rather run down, and I saw a hefty woman open the door for Megan. I thought she was her mother.

When we returned to the hotel room Kelly said that she more to tell me about the woman she had been intimate with. "It was Megan. I met her at the SLE, and we both got kicked out on the same day." I was speechless! I had just hosted Megan to a wonderful dinner, and she must have been laughing silently the entire time at my foolishness.

But that was not the end of it. Megan was a member of a local meth clan and had enticed Kelly into joining them at their house. This would explain why Kelly was having such a difficult time falling asleep, and why she often didn't answer her phone or reply to my messages. I began to feel a slow rage building up inside of myself.

I went outside to the courtyard and lit a cigarette. I just wanted to leave, let Kelly figure out her future on her own, and put an end to all of the bullshit. I was sorry that I had ever rented the hotel room. I took a few deep breaths, convincing myself that Kelly and I didn't have a serious relationship anyway and I could walk away at any time.

But I didn't walk away. Instead, I walked back to the room to try to sort out the mess that Kelly had created. I had just gone into the room when there was a knock at the door. Opening it I saw Megan standing there, staring at me with a stunned look on her face. I looked at her and felt a quiet fury beginning to burn inside my heart.

I managed to restrain myself from striking her. Instead, I said "Child, you aren't welcome here. You took advantage of my generosity, ate the food that I bought, and knowing full well that you had participated in Kelly's infidelity." Instead of apologizing, Megan began to smile smugly. "All that you are is a child molester!" I laughed at the ludicrous insinuation.

She looked beyond me, trying to get Kelly's attention, a silent pleading in her eyes. Kelly didn't say a word. She knew better than to say anything. Megan reluctantly turned and walked away. It would be months before I saw her face again. She was nothing but trouble, and I should have known that when I met her.

The following days were filled with all of my usual responsibilities, plus getting Kelly settled in the new SLE. She seemed to be reasonably pleased, but I was still very worried that she was going to relapse yet again. I told myself, though, that I was not her babysitter. I gave her a brief kiss and left to go back to my own SLE at Cynthia's house.

That weekend David and my daughter-in-law Rachel drove up the mountain to visit with me. I showed them my room and the rest of the house, and then we drove to Jeffery's Restaurant which was just down Capitola Road. We had a lovely lunch and took our time eating so that we could have a good long visit.

David told me that they had managed to move all of my belongings into a storage unit and handed me my debit card. He said that I could pay the monthly bill over the phone. He asked if they could use my fifty-two inch Bravia television in their apartment and I told him, yes, of course, that I really didn't need it at that moment.

Their visit was not as long as we would have liked, but just seeing them filled my heart with joyfulness. I asked if it would be okay for me to visit with them to celebrate Yule/Christmas and they told me that I was more than welcome, and not to worry in the slightest about Sherry, Jean or Regan.

With Kelly living in Freedom I didn't see her as frequently as I had been. We spoke on the phone every day, and I was fine with that. I was still trying to get over the Megan incident, and with more time on my hands, I often went out to lunch, dinner and shopping with Tomás and a few of the other roommates.

One day we happened upon a small shop that was owned by a former Camp client, and someone that I had met at a few of the meetings. It was a New Age type of shop, with crystals and books, wind chimes and jewelry. As I perused the jewelry case I noticed a sterling silver charm that spelled out 'Screw Guilt'.

I knew that I had to have it and asked the woman to take it out of the case. Then I saw the perfect ring for Kelly. It was a Tiger's Eye gem set in sterling silver. I wanted it as a Yule gift for her, so I purchased both items. I placed the charm on one of the silver chains that I wore around my neck and put the ring away with plans to give it to Kelly.

A few days before the holidays Kelly told me that she was leaving to return to Vacaville to live with her parents and look for a job there. She said that the Santa Cruz area was for losers and she didn't want to stay. I begged her not to go, told her that we could find a place to live locally. She again asked me to move to Vacaville with her.

I offered to find and pay for an apartment or house out of my own pocket in Santa Cruz just so that she would stay. But she was adamant about leaving. My heart was breaking. On Christmas Eve, as I drove to visit my children, I followed her in my car to San Jose to say goodbye. We had dinner together, and I gave her the ring that I had bought for her.

I couldn't believe it when she asked, "Is it even real?" I told her that of course it was. I asked her if she thought I had gotten it out of a Cracker Jack box. She replied "I don't know. No one has ever given me nice things before." She thanked me for it, got up, and left to drive to Vacaville without saying another word. Not even goodbye.

I was incredibly sad and worried, but it was just as well that she was gone. I had my own life to live, and I believed that I was going to be better off without her or her addictive influences in my life. I was doing well at the SLE, and we even had our own little Yule/Christmas celebration there, with Cynthia handing out gifts to everyone.

During the first week of January I received an email from a talk show host from a radio station in Ireland. He inquired if I would be willing to be a guest on the show on January 8th to talk about the M-3 Motorway and the work I had done prior and during the protests. I was honored and told him that of course I would be delighted to.

I was waiting for the trans-Atlantic call from Gay Byrne, the talk show host, when another call came in. I saw that the caller was Kelly. I was reluctant to answer it. All that it would take was for me to hear her hypnotic voice to fall back under her spell. Against my better judgement I answered the call anyway.

She said that she planned on renting a beautiful motel room in Benecia, which was located on the outskirts of Vacaville. She filled my head with visions of a couple in love being reunited. She even promised that she was going to prepare me a wonderful meal. I told her that I would have to think about it and that I would call her back.

As soon as I hung up with Kelly the call from Gay came in. I was finished with the M-3 protests after my return from Ireland, but I able to tell the protestors side of the story to thousands of people in Ireland, letting them know just how much an Irish-American woman could love the history and beauty of the island, and to what lengths I went.

After the interview my mind turned to Kelly. I did and I didn't want to see her, especially since I had not heard from her since Christmas Eve. I knew that Cynthia wouldn't approve of me visiting her. To Cynthia, Kelly was absolute anathema. I decided that I would go anyway, and I fabricated a story that I was going to my son's house for the weekend.

Cynthia said it was a wonderful idea and approved of my visit. I phoned Kelly and told her that I would be coming, and she said that she would rent the motel room for that weekend. I got up the next morning, put a few article of clothing and toiletries in my suitcase, got in my car and drove the one hundred plus miles to Benecia.

She had told me that she needed to buy a few groceries before going to the motel and asked that I meet her at the grocery store and from there I could follow her in my car to the motel. I pulled into the shopping center parking lot and saw Kelly leaning against her truck. I reluctantly got out of my car, not knowing what to expect.

As I walked towards her she ran to me. She exclaimed "You are so beautiful and I have missed you so much!". She wrapped her arms around me and gave me a long, lingering, passion filled kiss. She asked me to follow closely behind her, saying that the motel was just down the access road. Her behavior was peculiar, and she was overly excited.

I parked my car and followed Kelly into the main building, down a hallway and into the room. It was nice, with a king size bed, a wide screen television, and a lovely view of the waterways from one of the windows. There was also a small kitchen. I opened the refrigerator and was shocked to see it stocked with cans of alcoholic cocktails.

It was already late afternoon, and I had not realized how hungry I was. I mentioned to Kelly that I would like to eat, so she began cooking our dinner. She was preparing some sort of pasta dish with Andouille sausage, and the room began to fill with the delicious aroma, causing my mouth to water.

She stopped what she was doing long enough to bring me one of the cocktails I had seen in the refrigerator. Against my better judgement I opened it and sipped on it while she cooked. I turned on the television and watched a travel show while she prepared our dinner. I sipped on the drink some more and soon I was feeling the effects of the alcohol.

I felt the warmth of the spirits coursing throughout my body, which was almost comforting. Kelly had finished cooking and brought the food over to where I was sitting and set a plate in front of me. She sat next to me and we watched television together while we ate. The alcohol was having a strange effect on me and I began feeling nauseous.

I took my plate to the kitchen and placed it in the sink. I told Kelly that I didn't feel well and needed to lie down. She looked disappointed but didn't argue with me. I lay down on the bed, turning to one side, trying to fight the feeling of nausea, not wanting to vomit. I heard Kelly in the kitchen and she sounded like she was grumbling.

I must have fallen asleep because the next thing I knew I was awakened by the voice of a man. He and Kelly were talking about me. He told her that she should teach me a lesson, and that he knew exactly what to do. He came over to the bed and shook me violently. I slowly sat up and looked at them both.

I asked what was going on. Kelly said "What is going on is that we are going for a drive. Get up and get ready to go." I was confused, but I got up, got my purse and cigarettes, and followed them outside to Kelly's truck. She pointed to the man and told me that he was her friend Drew, and that he was going to join us.

I started to sit in the front, but Drew grabbed me by my arm and threw me into the back seat. I was not buckled in, and Kelly began driving wildly, taking the curves so fast that I was thrown against one of the doors, hitting my head. She and Drew laughed, saying that I looked like a rag doll. They didn't even bother to check if I was injured.

I had no idea where we were going, and I was beginning to worry. It seemed like we drove for a long while. I could see a mountainous region ahead, with the full moon casting it's light upon it. Kelly parked her truck and Drew jerked me out of the back seat. I pulled away but he was much stronger than I was and before I knew it I was standing in the roadway.

I could see by the light of the moon that we were in the countryside next to a small, rocky mountain. Drew picked up a stick and began forcing me up a trail, laughing and joking with Kelly that I was like an old cow that needed prodding. I stumbled on the sharp rocks, feeling them rip into my knees, tearing holes in my leggings and cutting into my flesh.

Still, he pushed me, laughing the entire time. Suddenly he stopped, leaving me halfway up the mountain. He and Kelly walked back down the trail to the truck. I could see them down there smoking cigarettes and laughing. I was heartbroken. I managed to get back down by walking carefully down the trail, holding onto branches as I walked.

I finally got to the road. They didn't see me, so I started walking down the road, searching for someone who might be able to help me. Drew finally noticed me and grabbed me from behind, dragging me back to the truck and throwing me into the back seat. Kelly laughed and started the engine, driving us back to the motel.

They walked me through the doors and past the front desk. Kelly told me to keep my mouth shut if I knew what was good for me. As soon as I was in the room I went into the bathroom and locked the door. I looked at my reflection in the mirror and was stunned. I had smudges of dirt on my face and my hair was disheveled and knotted.

I washed my face and tried to brush my hair, but it was too impossibly tangled. I sat on the toilet to take a look at my bloodied knees, cleaning both of them the best that I was able to. My leggings had gaping holes in them, and the rest of my clothes were filthy. Every inch of my body ached. I was sorry that I had ever accepted Kelly's invitation.

I opened the bathroom door slowly and peered into the room. Kelly and Drew were dancing to hip-hop music, throwing each other around the room, and laughing hysterically. I stood watching for a few minutes, then it dawned on me that they were drunk or high, or perhaps both.

I spoke up and asked them why they had treated me with such disrespect and disdain. Kelly replied "Ah, come on. We were just having fun" and went dancing around the room. Drew smirked at me and sat down in one of the chairs. I mentioned my hair and clothing and Kelly said "Here, let me fix your hair for you."

She walked over to me and began pulling my hair into a horribly knotted braid. I asked her to stop and said that I needed to lie down, that I was not feeling well. Kelly said "Go then! We're running to the store. Do not leave the room or call the manager while we are gone or you will be sorry."

I went to bed, pulled the covers over my head, and closed my eyes. I must have dozed off because when I opened my eyes it was morning and they were both gone. I took this as an opportunity to escape the abuse and insanity. I got all of my belongings together and ran out the door, not bothering to shut it behind me.

I hurried to my car, threw my belongings in the trunk, started the engine and drove like a bat out of hell. Had I been kidnapped, and were they on some type of psychotic power trip of abuse? I was in such a state of confusion that I took the wrong freeway entrance and ended up on the wrong freeway. I eventually found my way towards home.

Within two hours I was back in Capitola. The strangest thing is that even though I knew that I had been vilely mistreated, I didn't hold it against

Kelly. I blamed her friend Drew, someone who I would eventually learn to despise. I parked my car in the Capitola Mall parking lot. I was not sure of what my next steps should be.

I looked at myself in the rear view mirror and saw the reflection of an battered woman. "Never again", I told myself. I decided to go to the SLE and check in with Cynthia. No sooner was I through the door than she asked me if had been had any alcohol. I refused to lie so I told her, yes, I had a one small cocktail the day before.

She looked at me sternly and said "You have broken the rules of the house. You have two hours to get your belongings and get out." I was shocked. No leniency, no tolerance, and certainly not one ounce of understanding. Simply get out. I asked about the money I had paid for January and she told me there was no refund. Period.

As I walked through the living room to my room I saw Tomás and Tassi sitting on one of the couches. They asked me what was happening and I told them that I had been kicked out. Tomás stood up and gave me a hug, telling me that everything was going to be fine. I replied that I certainly hoped that it would be. It was the last time that I saw either Tomás or Tassi.

I packed all of my belongings that were in the room and took them outside to my car, then I went into the basement, got my duffle bags and carried them to the front porch. I put my laptop in its carrier, gave the room a cursory glance to make sure that I had everything, and I walked out the door, never to return.

I didn't know what to do. I couldn't go to any of my children's homes because of the threats of being arrested for trespassing if I did. I had once again lost my sense of being and purpose. I had made a simple mistake, but it was a mistake that was to set into motion over five years of chaos, violent abuse and eventual abandonment.

Homemaking 101

I sat in my car for a few minutes hoping that Cynthia would come out and tell me that I could stay after all, but my hopes were futile as she never did. I decided to drive to the Capitola Best Western and rent a room for a few days. I went into the lobby and the manager greeted me by name.

I told him that I needed a suite for two or three nights and he said that he would be happy to accommodate me. I filled out the room registration, gave him my credit card to keep on file, and he gave me a key-card in return. He touched my hand and told me that if I needed anything at all to call him.

I asked if I could get some help with my belongings and he sent a young man outside to help me. He brought a luggage cart with him to carry everything on. I followed the young man to the elevator and up to my room. He waited while I opened the door and I let him go in first. I was happy that the cart had a rack for my hanging clothes.

The room was identical to the one that I had rented for Kelly. It had a living room with fireplace, a table with chairs and wide screen television, a small kitchen area and a separate bedroom. The bathroom was fully stocked and quite accommodating.

I asked the young man if he could leave the cart behind and he told me that he would. I gave him a tip and went into the living room to sit and think for a while. I planned to go to an AA meeting that afternoon, hoping to find someone who either owned or managed another SLE.

I pushed the luggage cart over to the window so that it would be out of the way and sat on the couch to regroup my thoughts. It had been ingrained in my psyche at the Camp that attending meetings and living in an SLE was the only way I could manage myself, and I believed that, so I planned to attend the DMV meeting.

I looked in the bathroom mirror and saw the reflection of a battered woman. No wonder the manager had told me to call if I needed anything. Cynthia had not even allowed me to shower. I was thoroughly embarrassed by my appearance, but even more so, beyond that I was torn apart inside my mind, heart and soul.

I stood in the shower and let the water run over me. I washed and conditioned my hair. Handfuls came out as I ran my hands through it. I was so discouraged. I thought about how Kelly had allowed Drew to abuse me, but still, I didn't hold it against her. I simply couldn't find it in myself to hold her accountable for any wrong doings.

After my shower I got dressed, put fresh makeup on, and looked around the room. I didn't bother putting any of my clothes in the closet or dresser since I was not planning to stay there long. I decided to drive to the store to get a few things. Coffee, creamer, tea, sweetener, some sandwich material, fresh fruit and snacks.

While I was out I saw Dallas with another woman by the name of Mary, who was also from the Camp. They had just come out of a little café in the shopping center. They asked me how I was doing and I told them everything, including what had happened in Benecia with Kelly and Drew. Dallas said "I told you so. She is nothing but trouble".

I said that I felt like perhaps I had done something to cause it to happen, but I blamed all of what happened on Drew. Dallas asked me if I was going to the meeting at the DMV and I told her yes as soon as I picked a few things up at the store. She said that they would save me a seat, and that she wanted to catch up on everything with me.

The hotel offered a nice continental breakfast so I didn't bother buying any food for the morning. I was almost finished shopping when I felt an anxiety attack developing. I had experienced these in the recent past, and they had been coming more frequently lately, so I decided to make an appointment with the Camp psychiatrist, Dr. Stein.

I returned to the hotel and put what I had purchased away. I made sure that the room was neat and tidy for my return, then drove to the DMV. I walked inside the building and headed to the room in the back where the meeting was held. The meeting had not started yet, but Dallas and Mary were already seated.

I got a cup of coffee and joined them. Dallas took my hand in hers and squeezed it. I whispered to her that I needed to find a new SLE, and she told me that she knew someone at that very meeting who managed one and said that she would introduce us. The chairperson called the meeting to order and asked everyone to be seated.

I looked into the dark corner where I had seen Jeff before and there he was, lurking about in the shadows, waiting for someone who had relapsed. He must have been on commission for the Camp. He noticed me looking at him, and before I could turn away he smiled and waved. I really didn't like or trust him at all.

The meeting was over before I knew it. Dallas took me by the arm and guided me over to a younger woman by the name of Freda. Dallas introduced us and I began telling the young woman what had happened. The only thing that I left out was the abuse that I had endured on my nightmarish trip to see Kelly.
She said that she might have a spot for me, but that I would have to

submit to urine tests on a daily basis. I assured her that would be no problem at all, and I gave her my contact information. Freda told me that I would hear from her before the end of the day. I left, but I didn't go to the hotel right away.

Instead, I drove down 41st Avenue to Opal Cliffs. I parked my car and walked to one of the picnic benches. I sat down and lit a cigarette. I really hoped that I would be able to move into Freda's SLE. It would certainly save me some money on the hotel, I would easily be able to afford to pay for the new place.

When it began to grow dark I drove back to the hotel. I was hungry so I decided to make a sandwich, with a cup of tea to accompany it, and sat down to watch some television. I was weary, but my anxiety had leveled off. It had been a very strange couple of days. My mind kept going to thoughts about Kelly. I still had deep feelings for her.

I got my laptop out and wrote her a long email, apologizing for anything wrong that I might have done, and telling her that I didn't blame her. I sent the email and immediately regretted doing so, but for some unknown reason I was compelled. After sending the email I sat down on the couch wondering if I would ever hear from her.

My cellphone rang, interrupting my thoughts. It was Freda. She told me

189

that she did have a spot for me, but that it would not be ready for two more days, and she asked if I would be okay until then. I told her that I would be fine and asked her how much the monthly rent would be. She said four hundred and fifty dollars per month.

I thanked her and said, absolutely, that I would be there on the morning of January 13th with cash in hand. Amazingly, I slept the deepest that I had slept for a while that night. I awoke Sunday morning refreshed. I washed up, got dressed, and went downstairs for a cigarette and to take advantage of the continental breakfast.

When I returned to my room I decided to phone my children. I told them what had happened, leaving out the details of the abuse. I was alive and thought that it was best not to cause them concern. I checked my emails but there was nothing from Kelly. I had not anything else to do immediately but take time to write some thoughts, reflect, and read.

I had my copy of the 'Big Book', as well as my devotional books, so I sat down to read. First my devotionals and then the 'Big Book'. Try as I might I simply couldn't understand the methods and philosophies of AA. I believed that I struggled with it because none of it actually fit who I was. I didn't feel that I was an addict.

I continued to phone my sponsor, but always got her voicemail, even when I called at random times during the day. From what I had been told the sponsor was responsible for making sure that the sponsee worked all of the steps and began to make amends as soon as possible. She was doing me not even one ounce of good.

Regardless, I planned to attend a meeting at the DMV that day, and hopefully I would see some of the people from the Camp that I knew, other than Jeff that is. Suddenly I began feeling overwhelmed and had to leave the room. It was another anxiety attack. I left, but I didn't want to drive. Instead, I went for a long walk to clear my head.

As I walked I could feel my anxiety level receding. I decided to walk to Opal Cliffs, which was only a little over a mile away. As I walked I passed by the shop where I had bought the Tiger's Eye ring for Kelly, and the memories that conjured brought me sadness. I felt my anxiety returning so I pushed those memories to the back of my mind.

I sat at a picnic bench, gazing out upon the Pacific Ocean. It was a cold but sunny day, the rays of the Sun casting sparkling lights upon the cresting waves. I cleared my mind of any thoughts of the past and focused on the immediate future and how I was going to be able to gain momentum and reclaim myself.

I spent over an hour at the park. The walk back to the hotel was serene. I could feel a weight being lifted off of my shoulders. When I returned to my room I got ready for the meeting. I was excited to be able to tell Dallas that I had been approved for a place in Freda's SLE. I knew that she would be relieved that I had somewhere safe to stay.

I arrived at the DMV earlier than I expected. Dallas was standing outside the building with a group of people I didn't know, and even though I didn't feel like meeting new people I walked over to where they were anyway. Dallas was happy to hear my news and said that she had some for me as well that she would tell me after the meeting.

The meeting was a repeat of every single one I had attended so far, everyone introducing themselves and their addiction. There were calls for anyone with a week or more of sobriety so that they could be awarded a 'chip', and Jeff was skulking in the shadows ready to leap on anyone he considered fair game.

It ended as every 12-step meeting did, with everyone standing at their chairs, arms around each other's waists, stomping their feet and yelling "Keep coming back! It works!" My brain screamed cult every single time this happened. Even so, not wishing to look like I didn't belong, I went right along with it.

After the meeting Dallas asked if I would join her at the International

House of Pancakes on 41st Avenue for some coffee so that she could tell me her news. I replied that of course, I would be happy to join her. I followed her to the restaurant, parked my car, and went inside. She was already seated at a booth with Mary.

I ordered a cup of coffee, and Dallas asked if I was hungry. I replied that I was, and she told me to order whatever I wanted to, that she and Mary already had, and that it was her treat. She went on to tell me that her husband had filed for divorce. I told her that I was deeply sorry to hear that, but she said that she was not in the least bit sorry.

"Susan," she said, "I am getting an unusually large divorce settlement. I will have enough money to rent a nice house, and I am going to open a candy shop in Santa Cruz, which has always been a dream of mine." I told her that since this was what she wanted that I was happy for her after all.

I was so glad that Dallas was moving forward with her life, and wished her, as always, the absolute best of luck. We enjoyed a lovely dinner together. Mary regaled us with stories of her husband John's crabbing expeditions off of the shores of Santa Cruz, and promised both Dallas and me that she would bring us fresh crabs.

Two days later, on the morning of January 13th, I packed my car with my belongings and drove to Freda's SLE. It was not too far from where Cynthia's was located, and still in Capitola. I parked in front of the house and walked to the door. A middle-aged woman answered the door and I introduced myself.

She told me that they had been expecting me, that I should go ahead and bring my things in, and wondered if I needed any help. I told her that I would welcome any help she could offer, so she called a couple of more women from inside and we all worked together to bring everything into the house in one fell swoop.

All of the bedrooms were upstairs. We carried all of my belongings up the stairs and into the room, putting it wherever we could find a place. The room was large, much larger than the room at Cynthia's, and there were two twin sized beds. No bunkbeds! I was relieved. I thanked them all and told them that I was going to get things organized.

Freda popped her head into the room and asked if I would come into the bathroom for a urine test. I put down what I had in my hands and followed her across the hallway. The bathroom was rather disorderly, with garments hanging from the shower curtain rod and clothing on the floor.

I took the urine sample container from Freda, squatted over the toilet, placed it between my legs and filled the cup. She watched me like a hawk the entire time. That didn't bother me. I knew that she was simply doing her job. My urine, of course, passed the test. I went to my room afterwards and got money to give to Freda.

I paid for the entire month, even though we were almost halfway through January. There were only women at this SLE, which was fine with me. Dinner was served family style, with everyone pitching in fifty dollars a week each for groceries. We were on our own for breakfast and lunch.

As was the case at Cynthia's SLE, coffee and tea were both supplied liberally to anyone who wanted them. While I was unpacking my belongings my cellphone rang. It was Cynthia. She apologized for reacting in such an irrational way and said that I was welcome to come back to live at her house.

I thanked her but told her that I had already found another SLE, and I would be staying there until I decided exactly what it was that I would be doing. She was extremely disappointed. However, she had brought this on herself by her lack of understanding, and I got the feeling that she was only sorry because she was losing out on money.

I had been at Freda's for a little over two weeks when I received another phone call. This time it was Kelly. I had not heard from her at all since the night of January 10th, and I certainly was not expecting to ever hear from her again. I knew that I must not answer the call, for once I heard her voice I would be doomed.

She didn't ask how or what I was doing, instead, she demanded in a loud voice, "Are you going to get us a place or what?" I was slightly taken aback. Not only was I not planning to get my own place right away, but I also thought that she and I were finished. I took my phone and went out into the backyard to speak with her privately.

I sat down on one of the chairs and lit a cigarette. I asked her what she meant. I listened while she stumbled over her words, trying to rationalize her and Drew's behavior. She said that she loved me and wanted to be with me, and that she had made a mistake in how she had allowed me to be treated earlier that month.

She insisted that none of it was her fault, actually playing on the email that I had sent her. I didn't say anything, choosing rather to listen. She said that she had been drunk when she and Drew had taken me out to the boonies and thought that it would just be a fun thing to do.
I listened as she talked. I began feeling sorry for her.

As unbelievable as it was, I was not able to be angry with her or resist her. I told her that I would think about it, but my mind was already racing with what I needed to do. I immediately went online and searched the classifieds for rentals in the area. It didn't dawn on me that maybe I should be looking elsewhere.

I was able to find three rentals and made appointments to look at them the next day. I didn't tell Freda what I was planning. I was not looking for advice or opposition. But I did talk to one of the other roommates. She was less supportive as I would have liked, but she also knew the backstory to myself and Kelly.

I had so much to learn about Kelly, and as much as I do not like to admit it, I was ignorant. Ignorant of narcissists, gaslighters, abusers, and players. I was ignorant of the life of addicts. I didn't understand to what lengths they would go to appease their addictions, and how much harm they could bring to the lives of others.

I was determined to find a place and make a home for Kelly and myself. I woke up the next morning, got dressed, cleaned the kitchen, which was my chore for that week, and went to my first appointment. The house was just a few blocks from downtown Santa Cruz. I pulled up to the curb and took one look.

I didn't even bother going inside. I could see from my car that it was run down and dilapidated. I drove on to my second appointment. The next choice was a high-end apartment property. I took a tour, but the price of the rent and deposit were more than I wanted to pay. So, it was off to the final appointment that I had that morning.

The apartment was located in Aptos, not far from Cabrillo College. I found the address, drove down the steep driveway, parked my car and got out to look around. A younger woman by the name of Shana came out of one of the apartments and asked if she could help me. I told her that I had an appointment with Lewis, the property manager.

She told me that she was the unofficial manager of the property, and that she was glad to see someone like me looking at the apartment. I wondered who someone like me was. It was not long before Lewis arrived. I introduced myself, shook his hand and he led me to the apartment.

It was located down a short, enclosed corridor just off of the communal area of the property. He opened the door to the apartment and I followed him inside. The unit was freshly painted with brand new carpet. There was an efficiency size kitchen, a small living room and two bedrooms, barely big enough to fit all of my furniture in.

I walked over to the sliding glass doors and opened the blinds. There was a good sized deck, but what struck me most was the yard. I stepped outside and could hear the rushing of water in a forested area just beyond the edge of the yard. I asked him if the yard was for everyone and he said this apartment was the only one with access to it.

I was immediately sold! I told him that I was ready to sign the lease and pay him the first and last month's rents, as well as the deposit, which came to three thousand six hundred dollars. I had to drive to the bank, and asked if he could wait a half hour for me to return with the funds. He agreed and stepped outside to wait for me. I was so excited!

Even if Kelly never made an appearance I was going to have my own place again. A home that I could make my own. I found a local branch of my bank and had a cashiers cheque made out for the amount that I needed. I couldn't wait to get back to the apartment and pick up the key from Lewis. Move in day was only two days away!

I secured the key and drove to Freda's SLE. I was glad to see that she was there. I could hardly wait to tell her that I would be leaving on the first of February. She expressed concern that I was not ready to set out on my own. I thanked her, but I told her that she was not my therapist, and that she really didn't know me as a person.

I went upstairs to my room, got my duffle bag and suitcase out from under the bed and began to pack. I still needed to have the utilities and cable turned on in the apartment and get all of my belongings out of the storage unit in Sunnyvale and situated in the apartment, but those were relatively easy things to do.

I packed everything but my hanging clothes, and when I was finished I phoned all three of my children to give them the good news. They were all thrilled, but worried at the same time. I told them that I had plenty of money in my bank accounts and that I also had over twenty thousand dollars in credit on my cards, so I should be fine.

Then I did the unimaginable. I phoned Kelly. She didn't answer her phone, so I left her a voicemail telling her that I had leased an apartment and that she was welcome to come down anytime. She immediately returned my call, telling me that she would be down on February 1st to help me move in.

She apologized again for what she and Drew had done in early January. She told me that they had taken me to an area around Sulphur Springs Mountain, which was about a half hour from Benecia. She had no idea that Drew was going to be so cruel, and even though she was involved I still did not lay blame on Kelly.

I took the time to get all of the utilities set up and attempted to find someone to help me move my belongings from Sunnyvale to Aptos. My children all worked full time, and I didn't wish to impose on them. I knew that somehow I would be able to manage the move. I was, after all, a grown woman with years of experience behind me.

Needless to say, I was a bit anxious about Kelly coming. I didn't know what to expect, but I was thoroughly convinced that I loved her and that we belonged together. I remembered what Dallas had told me about Kelly's diagnosis of schizophrenia and was determined to talk to her about seeking professional psychiatric help.

I awoke the morning of February 1st, excited with this new start. It was as if new life had been breathed into me. I could start fresh, make a new path, and truly have the life that I knew I deserved. I packed my car and drove to Aptos. Hauling all of my belongings to the apartment took a bit of time, but I finally managed to get everything in.

I went out onto the deck and looked at the yard. I had already begun making plans for gardens and a barbeque area. Now Kelly and I could have the children and grandchildren come to visit, as well as her family, and enjoy barbeques and dinners together. I still had not told my children that Kelly would be moving in with me.

There happened to be a beauty salon next to the driveway that led down to the apartments, and with my hair in such a damaged state, I decided to walk up there and have it cut and styled. The woman who owned the salon told me that it would only be a few minutes, and to have a seat. I watched as she styled an older woman's hair.

When she was done she asked me to come sit in her styling chair. She asked me what I wanted done with my hair and I told her to cut it to my shoulders, all of the damage, all of the ruin. She looked at me and said, 'But your hair is past your waist. Are you sure you want to do this?' I answered yes, please, and give me bangs as well.

With her scissors in hand she began cutting, little by little, and I watched as the long treads of my once beautiful hair landed on the floor beside the chair. Soon there was a huge pile of it and she was finished. She turned my chair around so that I could look in the mirror. I was heartbroken, but I knew that and I could live with it.

I walked slowly back to my new apartment. It would be okay, I would be fine, and my hair would grow back, stronger and healthier than ever, just like myself. I opened the door and went inside the apartment. I was appraising the space, planning on where to place my furniture, when there was a knock on the door.

I opened it I saw Kelly standing there. She came inside and gave me a big hug and kiss as if nothing had happened in January. It felt strange but I went along with it. She walked through the apartment and said it would do. I was not sure what that meant, but I was glad that she at least liked it a little bit.

She looked at me strangely and asked why I had cut my hair. Did she not remember the damage she had done to it? I wondered if there was actually something wrong with her memory. I simply told her that I felt it was time for a change. Moving into a new home, starting a new life together, just a lot of changes and my hair was part of those.

Kelly had brought an air mattress with her and we slept on the floor the first night. The next day, with the help of Kelly and a young man by the name of Jose, whom Kelly had met at the SLE in Freedom, we drove to Sunnyvale, rented a U-Haul moving truck, and loaded it with all of the rest of my possessions from the storage unit in Sunnyvale.

While we were loading the truck Kelly took the liberty of destroying anything that she could find that had to do with my second husband Tom. I watched as she smashed framed artwork after artwork, surreal images that he had worked on for years. I didn't have the courage to stop her. I felt as if she was determined to destroy my entire past.

Jose helped us move everything in, which was difficult for all of us since the walkway to the apartment was only six feet wide. The first things that we set up were the bedrooms. A California King for our bedroom, and a Queen size bed for what we planned to use for a guest bedroom/office. I also had a tiered corner desk that be a perfect fit.

I brought a beautiful dresser and nightstand set for our bedroom from storage, as well as a large chest of drawers for the guest bedroom. The living room was next, with a comfortable sofa and loveseat, as well as a dual leather recliner, which Kelly later convinced me to donate to the SLE in Freedom, stating that there was no room for it.

The children had done a wonderful job packing. All of the boxes were labeled according to the rooms where they needed to be unpacked. I situated several items in the kitchen so that we had the coffee maker and microwave oven ready to go. The refrigerator was empty, but Kelly and I could go grocery shopping the next day.

The first week went fairly smoothly. We were able to rekindle our intimacy, and Lesbian lovemaking became more natural for me, and really quite passionate. Kelly swore to me that she would never harm me again, and I believed her, with all of my heart. I knew that we could make this work if we gave it our all.

The apartment was beginning to look like home. I had plenty of unique and beautiful décor for the walls that I had collected over the years.

Amongst my collections were Fabergé Egg replicas, a stunning collection of angels, and several old world Saint Nicholas's. I brought with me two solid oak bookcases, and plenty of books to stock them.

I had lovely, mature plants for both the interior of the apartment and the back deck. I talked to Kelly about some of my plans for gardens and a barbecue area and she was enthused. I bought a small table and chairs set for the deck and accessorized it with rather quirky statues and decorations that I already had.

Kelly was happy with almost everything in the apartment, with a few exceptions. For instance, I was not a Christian, and I chose to follow an Ancient Irish path. When I attempted to set up my altar she became outraged. She told me that I was a Satan and idol worshiper, and that my altar gave her the heebie-jeebies, so I boxed and stored it.

When I began unpacking my books she reacted the same way. Almost every single book was of Satan as far as she was concerned, and she threatened to take them out to the commons area and burn them. These were books on the Ancient and modern Irish, the Celts, Paganism, philosophy and poetry by some of my favorite authors.

Alarmed, I phoned Stephanie and told her what Kelly was planning to do. She and Landon drove up the hill the very next day and took the books, along with most of my jewelry, back to their apartment in Campbell. It would be several years before I had either the books or jewelry back in my own possession.

There were many things that I didn't understand about Kelly. She would follow me out to the deck when I was phoning my children, demanding to know who I was calling. I caught her going through my phone several times, checking to see who I had called. No one had ever done that to me before.

Kelly refused to allow me to talk about my travels. I had been to Ireland three times, the United Kingdom, France and the Netherlands, and I had so many wonderful stories to share. She didn't want to hear about my first marriage of thirty-two years either, nor my second marriage of five and a half years, yet she often spoke of her past loves.

She began flying into jealous rages if I mentioned either my travels or my marriages, and I had to learn how to keep those memories hidden. It was almost as if she were trying to erase my past. She showed a certain level of affection towards my children and grandchildren but had zero tolerance for anything that she felt might threaten her.

Kelly didn't care for my treasured items that I had collected over the years. The angels, the Fabergé Eggs, the old world Saint Nicholas's, and so many other of my precious possessions were boxed and taken to the Salvation Army. For some inexplicable reason I was not able to argue with her, and just simply allowed it to happen.

I was very confused. I had always been accepting in my relationships, but Kelly was definitely not tolerant as far as I was concerned. I wondered if she actually liked anything about me, and what I was doing in this relationship. I knew that she was fundamental Christian which may have augmented her superstitious ignorance.

Even though Kelly behavior was not one that I was used to I was determined to make our relationship work. I chose not to argue with her, allowing myself to be amiable and agreeable. It could be that her schizophrenia was causing her to act in this way. I planned to discuss her with Dr. Stein at my appointment later that month.

During our second week in the apartment Kelly asked if I would like to go with her to visit her parents in Vacaville the following day. I replied that I would love to meet her parents, but wondered aloud if they would actually enjoy meeting me. She thought for a minute and said, "I think that they will." I guessed that I would soon find out.

It was a two hour drive from Aptos to Vacaville, so when we stopped to put fuel in Kelly's truck, she told me to 'hit the toilet' because she wasn't stopping for anyone or anything. Once we were on the road she turned up the volume on the stereo and blasted hip-hop music the entire way so that it was impossible to have a conversation.

I spent almost the entire drive looking out of my window. The scenery was beautiful once we were past San Jose. The hills were already beginning to turn green, and there were cattle scattered across them grazing. Even though the music grated on my senses I still enjoyed the views.

We arrived at Kelly's parent's house around noon. We got out of the truck and Kelly walked right up and opened the front door without knocking. I heard the loud voice of a woman coming from another room. "Kelly, is that you?", she shouted. Her voice sounded like a booming tuba.

She walked around a corner and came into the living room. Kelly said, "Mom, this is Susan, my friend from Aptos. Susan, this is my mom Sharon." I went over to her, shook her hand, and told her that it was very nice to meet her. She gave me a once over, then told us that there was food in the kitchen if we wanted to eat.

Kelly led the way to the kitchen. Just to the left of the kitchen was a den, which is where her dad was sitting watching television. He stood up when he saw us and came over to give Kelly a hug. He said to me, "Hi, my name is David. It's nice to meet you Susan", then he wrapped his arms around me and gave me a tight bear hug.

I saw that there was a tray of pinwheel sandwiches, some fresh fruit, and paper plates on the counter. I thanked Sharon for preparing such a lovely lunch and she curtly replied that it wasn't her, it was Costco. I asked where the bathroom was and she pointed to a hallway between the den and kitchen. "Just over there" she said.

After I used the toilet I returned to see Kelly and her parents arguing loudly. When they saw me they all fell silent. Then David spoke up. "Good! I'm tired of taking care of him. Be careful. He's hiding in the linen closet in the hallway, and every time I opened it he attacked me, so I attacked him back!"

Kelly had told them that we were picking Kudos up from Chris's condo. I came to find out that while Kelly was at the Camp her dad had been tasked with taking care of the cat, and he hated cats, especially Kudos. I was a bit shocked that he had harmed the cat. I'd been bitten and scratched many times and never struck back.

We visited with Kelly's parents for about two hours. She finally told them that we had to leave, and they walked us out to the truck. I noticed a wooden bench set with three planters sitting by the curb and asked them why they were there. Her mom said, "I don't want them." I asked if I could have them and she told me to feel free.

Kelly didn't want to take them, complaining that it was just more work for her, but I talked her into it, telling her that the set would be perfect for the concrete patio in our backyard. Once we got the bench set loaded we said our goodbyes and began our drive to Chris's condo, which was located in Fairfield, just South-West of Vacaville.

As we were on our way to Chris's Kelly told me that she needed to stop at another friend's house, but that I would have to stay in the truck since he had a Pitbull dog who might be aggressive. I told her that was fine with me. We pulled up in front of an old house that looked nearly abandoned. A grey haired man waved at us.

He was standing inside a garage filled with rusty auto parts, old cans of paint, and loads of junk. I watched as he bent over an old motorcycle, loosening nuts and bolts, and banging on the motorcycle with a hammer. Kelly got out of the truck and walked inside the garage, then they disappeared into the house together.

It was close to an hour before Kelly came out of the house. I didn't mind though. But she had a very peculiar look on her face when she got into the truck, and that I minded. I asked her who the man was and she replied that he was an old family friend, and maybe I could meet him sometime.

We had brought a pet carrier with us, so Kelly pulled it out of the backseat of the truck and brought it with her. She reached under a fake rock and picked up a key for the front door. We went inside and started looking for Kudos, going from room to room. I felt kind of odd looking through someone's home when they were not there.

As I walked down a hallway, I opened the linen closet door, and there he was, hunched up and hissing at me violently, his eyes glowing yellow. Instead of reaching for him I called Kelly, who came immediately and pulled him out of the closet. She cradled him in her arms and gently placed him in the carrier.

His litter box, food and water dishes were in the kitchen, so I got those while Kelly carried Kudos down the stairs and put him into the back seat of the truck. She tried to make him comfortable by talking to him, but it only aggravated him. The entire drive back to our apartment was chaotic, with Kudos yowling and hissing in the back seat

That night, while Kelly and I were making love, Kudos, without provocation, attacked my head. Kelly sat up and started laughing, and I ran into the bathroom to look at myself. There was blood streaming down my face, and I could see several large gouges on my scalp. That was how my relationship with Kudos began.

During the next few days Kudos began to mellow out. He had plenty of comfortable places to sleep, food and water whenever he wanted, and loads of love that both Kelly and I bestowed upon him. Now we had a pet in our home, and it felt as if we were actually becoming a family. But that would soon change.

Fool Me Once, Shame On You

Our third and fourth weeks together in the apartment set the precedent for what was to come in our relationship. Kelly had been staying away from home more frequently, and for hours at a time. I worried, but I thought that she must be visiting Dallas, Mary, or someone else that she might have met at one of the meetings.

I kept myself busy while she was gone. I kept the house neat and organized and began working on the gardens. I planted Calla Lilies along the fence, culinary herbs and flowers in a garden bed, and even potted some pepper and tomato plants. Kelly had helped me arrange the bench set, and I planned to put Elephant Ears in the planters.

One evening, as I was preparing some dinner, Kelly came stumbling through the front door. I thought that she must be drunk. I asked her if she was okay and she yelled "What the fuck do you care?" I told her that I did care, very much, and asked her where she had been. "I was with Megan, at Danielle's house, and it's none of your business."

"So, she's not drunk", I thought to myself. "She's high on meth." I tried to help her to the couch, but she pushed me and I fell into one of my metal and slate end tables with such intensity. I got up, hurting, but still trying to help her, and she pushed me again, harder this time. I flew into the large coffee table and hit my head.

She shoved past me into the kitchen and picked up the phone. I didn't know who she was going to call, thinking that it might be Megan or Danielle, so I unplugged the phone line from the wall. Apparently Dallas was on the other line, and hearing the commotion, called 911 and reported that she was afraid someone was being harmed.

I had no idea that this had happened. I finally managed to maneuver Kelly into the bedroom and onto the bed when I heard a loud knock at the front door. I opened the door and there stood three police officers. Oh my god! I thought that I would never see another policeman at my door. I invited them in.

They saw the ransacked living room, along with the cut on my head that was bleeding. They asked if anyone else was in the apartment and I pointed to the bedroom. One of the officers went into the bedroom and when he came out they he had Kelly in handcuffs. I will never understand what happened next.

One of the officers walked behind me and told me to put my hands behind my back, that she was placing me under arrest. Baffled, I asked her what was going on. She said, "You unplugged the phone line from the wall, which is a domestic violence felony". I was being arrested, and I was dumbfounded.

Kelly and I were taken in different cruisers to the Santa Cruz police department and placed in separate cells. I was left alone to think about what had just happened. I asked an officer if I could see a medic, telling him that I believed that I had either cracked or broken ribs, and maybe even have a concussion from hitting my head.

A medic, if you could call her that, came into the cell to assess me. She felt my left side and looked at the cut on my head. She told me that I should go to the hospital when I was released because she could feel a couple of ribs that were cracked, and she thought that my head should be looked at as well.

About an hour later an officer came to ask me if I wanted to post bail. I didn't know anything about jail, arrest procedure or bail, but I told him yes, I wanted to post bail. He opened the cell door and took me to a desk with a phone and dialed a number. He handed me the phone and on the other end was a bail bonds agent.

The woman on the other line told me that my bail would be $5000.00, and asked if it would it be cash or credit. My god, $5000.00! I didn't want to stay there, so I gave her one of my credit card numbers. She asked if I had a way home and I said "No, I was brought to this jail in a police cruiser." She told me that she would come pick me up.

Then she asked me if I wanted to bail Kelly out, and I didn't even hesitate before saying yes. In that moment I set a mold, and it would take years before I could bring myself to break it. I was giving Kelly free license to abuse me and she would believe that I would never press charges, and that I would always bail her out.

An officer asked me to take a seat on a bench by the door. The agent arrived about half an hour later, signed some paperwork, and told me to follow her. She asked if I was okay, and I told her what the medic had said about suspecting that I had cracked ribs and a concussion. She offered to take me to Dominican Hospital, but I declined.

All that I really wanted to do was get home. I was tired, in pain, and so defeated. I asked the agent if she would be able to pick Kelly up once she was released. She looked at me as if I were crazy and said that she was not willing to do that. I actually didn't know if I wanted Kelly back in the apartment. I was utterly baffled.

The bail bond agent walked me into the apartment. She was startled by the shambles that the living room was in. We sat while she went over my paperwork with me. She said that it was imperative that I show up the next day at the courthouse in Watsonville at 10:00 a.m. for my hearing.

Before she left she told me that it wasn't a good idea to allow Kelly back into the apartment, that she felt that I was in danger, and strongly suggested that I request an emergency protective order against her from the Sheriff's or police department. I thanked her, and told her that I would look into it, knowing that I probably wouldn't.

After she left I plugged the phone cord back into the outlet and looked around the apartment. Kudos was hiding in the guest bedroom under the bed. When I looked under the bed he arched his back and hissed, so I let him be. The living room was in shambles, evidence of Kelly's violent meth and alcohol induced behavior.

I had just finished straightening everything when the phone rang. I heard Kelly's voice. She whispered "Come fucking pick me up now! I'll be walking." As if in a trance, I stopped what I was doing, got my car keys, and drove my car down Soquel Drive. I didn't even know where to look for her and had no idea where the police station was.

It was difficult at best to drive at night since I had extreme night blindness, but I was somehow able to manage. I had driven about two miles when I saw Kelly in the median of the road. I pulled to the side of the road and rolled down my window, calling to her. She ran across the road, not even looking for traffic, and got in the passenger side.

She didn't thank me for bailing her out of jail or for picking her up. Instead, she demanded to know what had taken me so long. I didn't bother to answer her. I drove back to the apartment, both of us silent. I didn't know what to say to her. Not only was she an abuser, but she was also an elder abuser given that I was 54 years old.

Back at the apartment I asked if she had been given any paperwork at the jail. She pulled some wadded papers out of one of her pockets and handed them to me. I flattened them out so that I could read them. She had also been instructed to report to the courthouse in Watsonville at the same time that I had been.

I asked Kelly if she wanted to drive there together and she said "Well, duh. What do you think you dummy!" I told her that the day had been enough for me and that I was going to bed. She slept on the couch that night, which was a great relief to me. I went into the bedroom and locked the door. After what had happened I did not trust her.

The next morning Kelly drove us in her truck to Watsonville, which was about 15 miles South of Aptos. We found the courtroom and sat down together to wait. When our names were called we stood up. The judge glanced at us and said that we were both being charged for domestic violence and abuse.

She looked at the files in front of her, shook her head, and said, "I am dismissing these charges. The district attorney failed to send over the right files and forms. You are both free to go. Case dismissed." And that was that. I had paid $10,000.00 to a bails bonds agent for no reason whatsoever, money I would never get back.

Then and there I vowed that I would never go to jail again, and I would certainly not bail Kelly out of jail, regardless of the repercussions. I was so lucky though. I found out that if charges had been filed for domestic violence that I would have faced one year in a county jail, a $1000.00 fine and summary probation.

Had I been convicted of a felony regarding the phone cord I would have faced two to three years in a county jail, a fine of $10,000.00 and formal probation. I had absolutely no idea that this could have happened when I disconnected the line. In my mind I was only protecting myself against a possible assault by Kelly's meth friends.

Kelly rushed ahead of me, practically running out of the courtroom. I hurried to keep up with her. I didn't want her leaving Watsonville without me. She had already started the truck's engine when I got to it, and I banged on the window, asking her to unlock the door. She seemed almost reluctant to do so.

All of the way home she called me names. Sick, psychotic, alcoholic bitch and dick lover. Old fucking fool. Over and over again. She asked me why I had her arrested, and I told her that I didn't call the police, that it was Dallas who had made the call. She scoffed at me, acting as if she did not believe me.

I asked her why she had even come to Aptos and she told me that she only needed a place to stay, and that she would be better off with Megan or Danielle, or anyone other than me. I replied that there was not one thing holding her back from leaving, and that she was welcome to go anytime she wished.

The rest of the day was filled with a peculiar tension. Kelly rested on the couch, watching television, keeping a close eye on me all the while. The way that she looked at me made me very uncomfortable, like she was possessed by something evil, as if she was ready to pounce on me at any given moment.

The next day was my appointment with Dr. Stein. I was so glad to be able to see him and talk about recent events with him. His office was just off of River Road in Santa Cruz in a small complex that housed a variety of businesses. I found his office and opened the door. There was not a receptionist, only a sign that said, "Ring The Buzzer".

My first appointment lasted for over an hour. He listened as I recounted the events with Kelly since my graduation. He told me that I would be better off without her. He asked me if I was still attending meetings, and I told him that I went when I could. What he didn't need to know was that I was pretty much finished with AA.

I asked him if he would be willing to take Kelly on as a client and told him that she had been diagnosed Schizophrenic. He said that it would be a conflict of interest for him to see her since we were together as a couple, but that he would be happy to recommend another psychiatrist or psychologist who might be able to manage her.

At the end of my appointment, he had diagnosed me with Bipolar I, depression, panic and anxiety disorders, and PTSD. He prescribed a cocktail of drugs to treat those illnesses, most of which I had never even heard of. Lexapro, Abilify, Valium and Depakote. He instructed me to begin taking them that evening, and not to miss a single dose.

Dr. Stein told me that he wanted to see me at least once a month and made my next appointment for me. He encouraged me to attend a meeting at least once a day and said that it would be helpful if I were able to encourage Kelly to join me, that if anyone needed the meetings it was her.

Kelly ended up staying with me, and the ensuing months were filled with both laughter and utter cruelty. There were actual moments where I felt sheer joy, but I knew that I had somehow lost myself in this disastrous relationship. Kelly would spend days away from the apartment without an explanation as to where she had been.

We did a lot of traveling to Vacaville. We visited her parents many times, stayed the night at her younger sister Beth's apartment more than once, and spent time with her older sister Brenna and her family. I even had the opportunity to meet her adoptive grandmother and enjoy time visiting with her. I was always introduced as a friend.

Each time we traveled home from Vacaville she would stop at her friend's house in Fairfield, and she always insisted that I stay in the truck. One day I told her that I refused to stay in the truck. She said that I might be attacked by the Pitbull. I replied that I was willing to take the chance, that it was too hot to sit in the truck and wait for her.

I followed her through the yard, which was filled with dead grass and plants, up a set of broken steps, and onto a small landing. She knocked on a damaged screen door. The grey haired man that I had seen so many times from afar opened the door and invited us in. Kelly turned to me and said "Susan, this is my friend Kale." I was speechless.

Kale, her drug dealer since she was a teenager, who supplied Kelly with meth and goodness knows what other hard, addictive drugs. He walked through a filthy kitchen into an even more filthy living room and sat down in an old, oversized chair. We followed him. I was reluctant to sit but found a wooden chair that looked fairly clean.

He smiled at me, his eyes somewhat glazed. Just then, a large dog walked into the room and came over to me, sniffing the air around me. My heart was beating wildly. I put my hand out in a friendly gesture and she licked it. Suddenly she jumped into my lap and began licking my face and nuzzling me. I laughed and told Kelly that I was fine.

I listened as Kelly and Kale talked. Their conversation was very generalized and somewhat boring. I heard her tell him that I was just a friend from Aptos, and he glanced at me knowingly. I shrugged my shoulders and smiled. It didn't matter to me. Everyone in Kelly's life knew me as the 'friend from Aptos'.

I asked where the bathroom was and Kale pointed down the hallway. I walked through the door and was met with the most foul-smelling stench ever. There were dirty clothes on the floor, the bathtub was stained brown, and the toilet was caked with feces and old urine. I carefully covered the seat with toilet paper and sat down gingerly.

When I returned to the living room I saw Kale holding a clear, glass pipe. He was taking a long drag on it. The room filled with a strange chemical odor, somewhat reminiscent of drain cleaner or battery acid. I thought that he was smoking marijuana, which I had no problem with, but I quickly realized that it must be something else.

He handed the pipe and a lighter to Kelly. She placed the lighter at the bottom of the pipe and heated the glass. When the chamber filled with smoke she took a deep drag on the pipe. She blew out the smoke and asked if I wanted some. I thought about it, and then impulsively decided to go ahead and smoke some of the unknown substance.

Kelly burst out laughing. "You're smoking meth Susan. That's hella funny!". I handed her the pipe and asked why she had given it to me. "Just to see what would happen", was her reply. I told her that I wanted to go home, but she refused. She continued smoking meth with Kale for another half hour or so before she was ready to leave.

I visited Kale's with Kelly only once more and ended up smoking meth with them again. It was not something that I really wanted to do, but I felt compelled to. Perhaps I thought that it would bring Kelly and myself closer together, but it ended up doing exactly the opposite, tearing into our lives with a viciousness that I did not expect.

Oftentimes, Kelly was vexatious. She would start quarrels for no reason whatsoever, talk about my past in derogatory terms, and make fun of how old I was. I would ask her why she was behaving in such a way, and she would reply that was just who she was, take her or leave her, it didn't matter to her.

One day, when she was coming down off of meth and alcohol, she asked me where I saw us in five years. I replied that I would hope that we would still be together, and that we would have worked our way through all of the chaos and turmoil that the beginnings of our relationship had brought with it.

She scoffed and said "I don't see that happening Susan. I've never been in a relationship with anyone longer than three years." I mentioned that my first marriage lasted thirty-two years and she became angry, telling me that I thought that I was so much better that she was, and that I had all of the answers to life.

The month of March brought with it many unexpected events, some wonderful, and others not quite as I would wish. Two weeks before my 55th birthday, Kelly decided to take a trip to Vacaville, purportedly to visit her family. She told me that she would be back well before my birthday, and that she had a surprise for me.

I was worried, not about Kelly, but because I was running out of money. Yes, I had my credit cards, but I was saving those for emergencies only. Rent was paid for that month, but how I was going to pay for the April rent was questionable. I had applied for work at so many different businesses, but to no avail.

The day after Kelly left for Vacaville, I received a phone call. The woman on the line asked if this was Susan Sheehan, to which I replied yes. She introduced herself as a representative of State Disability. She proceeded to tell me that she had been going over my file and saw that I was owed four months backpay for disability.

She told me that I would be qualified for an additional eight months if I continued to be disabled. I asked her how much the award was for and she told me $2468.00 per month. Oh, my goodness! That meant that I would have almost ten thousand dollars in checks coming right away. This was a much needed answer to my worries.

The ongoing monthly checks would be more than enough to pay the rent and utilities every month, and I would still have plenty of money left over to buy enough groceries for Kelly and myself. I was confident that by the time the disability payments ran out I would be able to find full time employment.

I decided not to tell Kelly about the disability payments. I believed that would only serve to give her a reason for not finding employment. She acted as if life was a continual party, not to be taken seriously, and never thinking about the future, especially a future that included me.

Several days before my birthday Kelly phoned me to let me know that she was coming back to Aptos the following day. I was excited. I had actually missed her while she was gone. She reminded me that she was going to be taking me out to celebrate my birthday and mentioned that we might be traveling to Monterey and Big Sur.

I woke up the next morning with a song in my heart. Perhaps the trip to Vacaville had been good for Kelly. She had sounded quite happy when we spoke on the phone. I hoped that she had avoided visiting her drug dealer, Kale, but I knew that might be a little too much for me to hope for.

The apartment was clean and organized, the flowers and herbs that I had planted in the back yard gardens were beginning to flourish, and all of the plants on the deck had matured to the point that they were an enhancement. I wanted everything to be perfect for when she arrived. I even planned a special dinner of steak and Dungeness crab for us.

I was sitting on the deck smoking a cigarette when I heard the front door open. I stood up and opened the sliding door. There stood Kelly, a big smile on her face. I went to give her a hug, and that is when I saw Drew standing behind her. "Surprise!" Kelly said. I turned around and went back outside without saying even a single word.

She must have known that I disliked Drew. He was an abuser and manipulator, an evil person as far as I was concerned. I watched as he swaggered into the apartment as if he owned it, looking around at everything, appraising the furnishings and décor. "Come on, Susan. Come and give me a hug!" She laughed and winked at Drew.

I reluctantly walked back into the living room and gave her a brief hug. I nodded my head at Drew but did not say a word to him. I went into the bedroom and Kelly followed close behind me. Suddenly, she had me pinned by the neck against the wall with her right forearm. "You are NOT going to treat my friends like that!" she whispered.

I began choking, and tears ran down my cheeks. I nodded my head in compliance, but I did not mean it. I began to loathe Drew even more. She dropped her arm and looked hard into my eyes. "I mean it Susan. Bitches come and bitches go, but friends remain forever!" Saying that, she walked out of the bedroom, leaving me there gasping for air.

I sat down on the bed in a state of turmoil. Why had she brought him here, into what was actually my apartment? Kelly wasn't even on the lease. She had no right to do this. I composed myself and went into the living room to see them dancing together to loud hip-hop music. Drew said "Kelly, you are Latina! You can do better than that!"

I ignored them and went into the kitchen. I poured myself a tumbler of iced tea and went out onto the deck, closing the sliding door behind myself. I wanted Drew to go as soon as possible. It was apparent that Kelly would have to drive him back to Vacaville but did that mean that she was going to miss my birthday?

Suddenly they stumbled out the sliding door and onto the deck. Kelly tried to take me by the hand, but I pulled away. "Whatever Susan. You just don't know how to have fun!" Fun? I could see that Drew was drunk, and I suspected that Kelly was either high on meth or drunk. I told them to go back inside and stop being a spectacle.

Drew ended up staying for several days. On my birthday we drove to Monterey and visited the aquarium. The drive was beautiful. I spent most of my time at the aquarium alone since Kelly and Drew decided to frolic from one exhibit to another, making a nuisance of themselves, not even embarrassed by their foolishness.

Drew had a can of energy drink with him, and I knew that he always put alcohol of one kind or another in it, so I suspected that he was already drunk. Kelly seemed sober for once but was behaving like a child anyway. I kept my distance from them. I visited the gift shop and purchased a beautiful paperweight, which I have to this day.

Afterwards, we had lunch at Bubba Gumps on the pier. I tried my best to enjoy myself, but Kelly and Drew continued to behave like children. When the bill came Kelly slid it over to me. I had already paid for our entry to the aquarium, and now it looked like I would be paying for our lunch as well.

When we were finished we walked down Cannery Row. I wanted to decorate the guest bedroom with ocean décor, so I purchased several unique items that I knew would look amazing and add warmth to the room. Kelly mentioned that we should be on our way, that she had the perfect restaurant picked out for my birthday dinner.

On our way out of town we stopped at the Monterey Mission, which was founded by Junipero Serra, a Catholic priest that was well known for his abuses of Native peoples. Rather than wander the grounds, I found a low, rock wall, and sat on it while Kelly and Drew threw rocks at the buildings.

Evening was approaching, so I yelled out to Kelly that maybe it was time to drive South and find the restaurant before it was too dark. I watched the water as we drove, the sun a ball of fire over the ocean, sunrays sparkling off of every crest of the waves. Gulls were diving for dinner, and I could see people walking along the shoreline.

Kelly found the driveway that led out to the restaurant, which was in a breathtaking location overlooking the Pacific Ocean. The restaurant was called Pacific's Edge, appropriately named. She parked the car and we walked along a gravel path and went inside. Once inside, Kelly told the hostess that we were there for my birthday celebration.

The hostess smiled and asked how old I was. Drew chimed in "She's as old as fuck!" Kelly didn't say a word. I was rendered speechless, and so very humiliated. The hostess turned quickly away. I could see that she was embarrassed for me and herself. With menus in hand, she led us to a table with a beautiful view of the Pacific Ocean.

As soon as we were seated Drew and Kelly both placed orders for Long Island Ice Teas. I ordered a single glass of white wine, with a glass of water, just something to sip on as I certainly didn't plan to spoil my birthday by getting drunk. They both downed their drinks immediately and ordered another one each.

They started joking around loudly and punching each other on the shoulders. Drew continued to take verbal jabs at me whenever he was able to. I tried to ignore them both by looking at my menu. I decided to order the Filet Mignon with Lobster Tail and let Kelly know. She and Drew looked at each other and she said, "Us too!".

At $45.00 per plate, I was really hoping that Kelly had enough money to pay the bill. We placed our orders and it was only minutes later that the server brought our salads, with a bowl of freshly baked bread, and told us that our dinner orders would be along soon. I ate my salad in silence while Kelly and Drew tossed lettuce and onions at each other.

I may have been as 'old as fuck', but at least I had the dignity not to act like an irresponsible child. They were ruining my celebration, and I believed that Drew was doing it on purpose. My loathing for him was beginning to become deeper by the minute. I avoided looking at him by gazing out the window.

The server came to take away our salad plates and refill the water glasses. Kelly ordered two more Long Islands for herself and Drew. How were we supposed to get home if Kelly was drunk? I put that worry to the back of my mind, determined to enjoy myself as much as possible. Our dinners arrived and we ate mostly in silence.

Neither one of them knew how to eat a lobster tail, so I showed them how to reach in and pull out the meat. I dipped a large piece in the garlic butter and placed it in my mouth. I watched with amusement as they struggled to imitate me, chuckling to myself. I was with two ill-mannered children who had virtually no life experience.

When we were finished with our main dish, our server removed our plates and brought three pieces of chocolate ganache cake with vanilla ice cream. My piece had a candle on top, and all of the employees gathered around our table and sang happy birthday to me. Drew asked in a loud voice, "What makes you so special, you old hag?".

I looked around and everyone at the tables surrounding us had heard him and had shocked expressions on their faces. I could believe that he had said that to me. How dare he? I didn't want him in my apartment, and I would make sure that he was gone the next day. I had never met anyone so rude.

Our server brought us the check for our meals and drinks, and I discreetly pushed it over to Kelly. She scoffed and asked "Did you really think that I was paying for this? I know that you have plenty of money." I should have known, but I couldn't believe that she would invite me out to dinner and then renege on paying for it.

I gave the server one of my credit cards and paid the bill, which was over

$400.00. I kept my eyes averted from both Kelly and Drew. I was seething inside. Not only had I had paid for my own birthday dinner, but I had also been treated with disdain and animosity by Drew for almost the entire meal. I knew that there was fire in my eyes.

The ride home was frightening. Kelly was quite drunk, and she kept swerving on the notoriously dangerous Highway One that we were driving on. Since I had only drank only one glass of wine I was sober, and offered to drive, but she told me to shut up and mind my own goddamn business.

Drew sat in the back seat. Every so often he would pick something up from the floor of the truck and throw it at Kelly. I asked him to please stop, but he just gave me a smart-alecky smirk and kept throwing things. I was instantly relieved when we finally pulled into the apartment parking lot.

The next day Kelly, at my insistence, drove Drew back to Vacaville. I told her that I never wanted to see him again. She ended up staying for several days, not even bothering to phone me. I suspected that she was visiting Kale and bingeing on meth and alcohol, and I could only imagine what she would be like when she returned home.

I spent the time while she was away regrouping myself. I made the decision to reclaim myself, to strengthen myself mentally and spiritually, and to learn how to assert myself once again. I paid several visits to the beach, watching the horizon, finding peace within, and the determination to be the woman that I once was.

Fool Me Twice And You're Out!

When Kelly arrived home she was unusually cheerful, certainly not what I expected. She took me in her arms and gave me a lingering kiss, holding me longer than was customary for her. She said "Boy, is it ever good to be home!". I returned her embrace, enjoying the moment, and wanting to it last forever.

She told me that she had visited her Grandmother Eva, a lovely woman whom I had met on one of my travels to Vacaville with Kelly. We had shared lunch with her at the retirement home in which she lived. Perhaps Eva had been able to talk some sense into her, make her see the light of day for once.

Kelly asked where Kudos was, and I told her he was in our bedroom asleep. She went in, lay down on the bed, and cuddled with him despite his protests. I went out onto the deck to wait for her, curious to find out why her mood was so elated. She came out to join me, sitting across the table from me.

She said that she would not be visiting Drew anytime soon, and that she had read him the riot act for his behavior. I replied that I appreciated that, that he had caused me such embarrassment at my birthday dinner celebration. I knew that I certainly never wanted to see him again, no matter what.

Unfortunately, Kelly's good mood did not last for long. Within days she was disappearing from the apartment for days at a time, coming home in altered states, which I deeply suspected was from using meth. One day she came home with a woman that I recognized from the day we had dropped Megan off at the run down townhouse in Capitola.

"Hey!" Kelly said, "This is Danielle. I wanted you to meet her, and maybe be friends." Kelly had a weird smile on her face. Danielle was a rather large, tall woman, and looked to be in her mid-twenties. She sat down on the couch and put her feet up on the coffee table. I asked if they wanted some iced tea, and they both said yes.

I went into the kitchen and filled two tumblers with ice and fresh tea, returning to the living room and handing them to Kelly and Danielle. I sat down on the love seat and waited for someone to start a conversation. Kelly spoke up and said "Danielle, show Susan the lipstick you have that makes your lips plump up."

Danielle reached into her backpack and pulled out a tube of liquid. She told me to watch as she applied the liquid to her lips, then handed me to tube and told me to do the same. I took it from her reluctantly. I didn't know where her mouth had been, so I pretended to apply some of the liquid to my lips, then handed the tube back to her.

Kelly said excitedly, "Your lips are already getting plump Susan!" Danielle smiled and put the tube into her backpack. I asked them what their plans were and Danielle replied that their group was going to go for a drive, and she wondered if I would like to join them. I declined, telling her that I had other plans for my day.

For some reason I did not trust Danielle. I knew that Megan lived with her, and Megan was the one who had supplied Kelly with meth, causing her to get kicked out of the first SLE she had lived in after graduating from the Camp. Kelly said that they had to get going, that they had to pick up a few more people, and that she might see me later.

I wondered about that. I told Danielle that it was a pleasure meeting her, gave Kelly a kiss on the cheek, saw them both out of the front door and locked it behind them. I didn't even care where they were going, I had my own things to do. Shopping, gardening, and taking a drive to a beach just South of Aptos.

I still had not told Kelly about the disability payments. I had hoped that she would be looking for employment, but she was otherwise occupied with hanging out with her friends, and I deeply suspected that those friends, including Danielle, were meth addicts, and pulling Kelly down the hole that they dwelt in.

On several of our trips along the coast, Kelly would take me to a secluded beach on the outskirts of Santa Cruz just South of Davenport. To access it we had to park the car, walk a mile down abandoned railroad tracks, and hike down a shoal covered path that was almost vertical. She was amazed at the agility with which I kept up with her.

We went to Wilder State Park along Highway 101. Kelly told me that she had visited there a couple of times in the past. We wandered the grounds and came upon an old barn. There was a ladder that led to the loft above and we climbed it. I was hoping to make some sort of discovery, but that was silly of me.

As we were standing in the loft Kelly let it slip that she, Danielle and Mission, along with several of her other meth friends, had sat up there, drinking and smoking weed. This infuriated me. She had promised that she would no longer have anything to do with them. I climbed back down the ladder and returned to the truck.

Sometimes when Kelly was home it was almost as if we were an old married couple, happy to spend hours together talking, comfortable in silence. There were many times that we would travel to places like Big

Sur, Monterey, Half Moon Bay, and San Francisco, enjoying the drives and each other.

Other times she would flip and put me in chokeholds or pin me against a wall with her forearm. I was so bewildered. I had never been in a relationship such as this, and often wondered what I was doing with her. The only reasonable explanation that I could give myself was that I was in love with her.

We continued to be intimate, not on a regular basis, but frequently enough for myself. Curiously, she began wearing her shirts during our lovemaking. I didn't ask her why. I was simply happy that we were still attracted to each other. Even if I had asked she probably would have told me it was none of my business.

It seemed as if Kelly always had drugs on her mind. One day, after my shower, I was brushing my teeth. I tapped my toothbrush on the side of the sink to dislodge any toothpaste that might have been left behind. Suddenly, there was a frantic knock on the door, and before I could unlock it, Kelly forced the door open.

I was startled. I asked her what was wrong and she demanded to know where the drugs that I had were. I told her that I didn't have any drugs, but she didn't believe me and proceeded to tear the bathroom apart.

Everything from the medicine chest and linen closet ended up on the floor in her frantic search for the non-existent drugs.

One day in early June, Kelly had been gone from the apartment for several days. I was getting ready to drive to downtown Santa Cruz to attend the Gay Pride parade and festival when the phone rang. It was Danielle on the other end. She told me that she was outside my apartment with Kelly, and that I needed to come outside to get her.

I stopped what I was doing and walked down the sidewalk towards the parking lot. Danielle was standing not far from me, holding Kelly up, keeping her from falling to the cement. "Here, take your girlfriend. I'm finished with her!" I ran to where Kelly was before she could hit the sidewalk. I held onto her and helped her into the apartment.

She was muttering obscenities under her breath, cursing Danielle, Megan, Phil, Mission, and a slew of other names of people that I did not know. She looked at me with such venom in her eyes that I almost dropped her. I carefully lowered her onto the couch and tried to make her comfortable. I stood there for a moment looking at her.

She starting to pass out, then she would suddenly sit up and try to strike at me. This went on for about half an hour, then she finally passed out and went to sleep. I became suspicious, so I picked up her backpack, took it into the bedroom, and looked through it. As I dug deeply I found a small bag of meth and a glass pipe.

I took the pipe and meth to the bathroom, planning to flush the meth down the toilet and smash the pipe, but before I could do it Kelly was upon me, grabbing for both the pipe and the meth. I managed to flush the meth down the toilet, but Kelly grabbed the pipe from my hands and tried to run with it.

I was determined to destroy it, so I managed to get it back out of Kelly's hands and threw it to the bathroom floor. Kelly knocked me to the floor and put both of her hands around my throat, choking me. I could see that the pipe was behind the toilet, and I was almost able to reach it with my foot.

She continued to choke me, calling me a fucking bitch, whore and countless other names, telling me that was the last of her meth. I managed to scream out for help and someone heard me, yelling back that they were calling the police. Kelly let go of me and ran out of the bathroom and into the bedroom, locking the door behind herself.

I reached behind the toilet and got the pipe. I took it into the kitchen and wrapped it in paper towels, I stuffed it deep inside my purse. I then put on my apron and began straightening the kitchen, waiting for the police to arrive. Soon, I heard a knock on the door and answered it. There were two officers, concerned looks on their faces.

"Is everything okay ma'am?", one of them asked me. I replied that everything was fine. He asked if I was alone, and I told him that I was the only one at home. He said they had received a call about someone yelling for help and I told him that I had heard someone yelling, but I didn't know who it was.

"I'm just getting ready to attend the Pride Parade in Santa Cruz officer. If that is all I really need to be leaving." They apologized for any inconvenience and left my door. I was relieved. I certainly did not want to have another police invasion of my home. I watched out the window for them to leave, then I got my purse and ran out to my car.

I drove to a nearby gas station. I went inside the convenience store and bought myself a coffee. Then I went back out to my car to sit and think. I had to dispose of the pipe. I had seen a trash can close to the entrance of the convenience store, so I walked over as nonchalantly as possible, with the pipe in my hand and put it into the container.

I pushed it as far down into the trash as I could get it. Of course, throwing away the pipe didn't stop Kelly from using meth. In fact, I think that it provoked her into using even more, and she began spending more time away from the apartment with Danielle at her meth house.

When I returned home I heard Kelly crying. I walked into the bedroom and saw her on the bed. I knew that she was having withdrawals and asked her if I could get her anything that might help. Suddenly, she lifted her shirt up and exposed her breasts. They were covered with festering ulcers.

I was shocked. I asked her what the sores were from and she told me that Danielle had been injecting meth into her breasts. She couldn't stand a needle in her arm, or between her toes, or any other place on her body, so she had allowed Danielle to inject meth into her breasts over and over again.

I was stirred to anger. I knew that Kelly was by no means innocent, but I believed that Danielle had taken advantage of her in her weakened state. I took Kelly's phone from her and phoned Danielle. I told her that I knew what she had done to Kelly, and that if she ever saw me on the streets that she had better run like hell.

A few days later, June 8th, was the ninth anniversary of my brother Danny's murder. I was feeling rather low on that day, and Kelly noticed. She asked me what was wrong, and I told her that I was mourning the death of my brother. Not one for either sympathy or empathy, she crassly

told me to just "get the fuck over it".

I reminded her that not only had my brother been murdered, but my mother had as well, in July of 1972. She said "Susan, they're dead. It doesn't matter so just stop." I asked her how she would feel if one of her loved ones were to be murdered, and she said that she wouldn't care, they didn't love her anyway.

I was stunned by her cavalier attitude. I reminded her that she had told me that her family was everything to her, and that she loved each one of them with all of her heart. She replied, "Susan, my family hates me because I'm Gay. All that matters to me are my friends, and maybe a bitch here and there."

Of course, I didn't believe her. Kelly tended to be pernicious in many respects, especially when she was trying to get her way or push her opinions on others. Although I knew that she had been abused by both of her parents, from what I had observed they loved her, albeit not unconditionally, and her sisters both appeared to love her.

In early July, Kelly asked me if I would like to go to camping at the North Fork American River with Mary, her husband John, and their children. The river is located in the Tahoe National Forest, a truly beautiful place, so of course I wanted to go. Kelly told me that we would have a tent with sleeping bags, which was fine with me.

It was a four and a half hour drive, so I prepared sandwiches for us to take with us to eat on the way, as well as a large container of food to share with Mary and her family. I was very excited since I had not visited a river in many years. Kelly fueled up her truck and, as usual, told me to hit the toilet before we left.

We bought coffee and sodas for the drive. On the way I noticed that all of the hills in East San Jose were already dry and golden, but it wasn't a hot day. We were mostly silent, but that was fine with me. Halfway through our drive Kelly's cell phone rang, and being who she is, she answered it. Suddenly she had a big smile on her face.

She became quite animated. I tried to hear who was on the other line, but Kelly kept her phone held to her left ear, away from me. When we came to the turnoff towards the river I asked her who she was talking to and she said, "Danielle and Mission, not that it's any of your business." I felt defeated.

I had thought that she was finished with them, but apparently that was far from the truth. She talked to them the rest of the way to the campgrounds, and reluctantly hung up the phone when we arrived at the campsite. I became depressed, and Kelly noticed. She told me that I had better perk up before we saw Mary, or else.

I wasn't sure what 'or else' meant, but I put a smile on my face anyway. She parked the truck and got out, running to where Mary and John were sitting under a canopy by their RV. I lingered behind to carry some of our things to the campsite. I said hello to everyone, and since they had already set up a tent for us, I went inside and lay down.

I had just begun to relax when Kelly unzipped the tent and told me to get my ass outside. I sat up and crawled out of the opening. I could see that Mary was serving food underneath the canopy, so I walked over to visit with her. Kelly had disappeared, and I asked Mary where she had gone. "She's at the river with my daughter" was her reply.

I didn't know Mary very well, even though she had been at the Camp the same time that I was. She always had her dog by her side, an Australian Shepherd by the name of Pepper, and I saw the dog was lying beside Mary's chair wagging her tail. I gave her a pat on the head and sat down in one of the camp chairs.

I tried to enjoy myself. The campsite was a good one, overlooking the river and covered by the shade of trees. I ended up staying at the campsite mostly, going for walks by myself, and helping Mary to keep the campsite neat and tidy. I even helped her in preparing meals for all of us.

Kelly spent her time on the river, tubing with Mary's teenaged daughter. I tried not to be jealous, but Kelly didn't know the meaning of fidelity, and she was a notorious flirt with any girl or woman she considered to be 'hot'. And me being the age that I was, even though I was quite attractive, it did bother me.

When she wasn't on the river Kelly was talking on her cell phone to Danielle and her group of meth users. I was so happy when Mary told us that their stay was over and they were heading back to Capitola. I helped to break down the tent, thanked her and John for their hospitality, and was delighted to be leaving to go home.

A few weeks later, five months after moving into the apartment, I overheard Kelly on the phone with Danielle. Kelly was making plans to take her to Vacaville for a celebration of her Grandmother's 90th birthday. I asked her why she was taking her instead of me and she said that she didn't think that I would want to go.

I told her that of course I would love to go, that I really liked her grandmother, whom I had met several times, and she said, "Fine, I'll take you." I could tell that she resented me for wanting to go. We traveled the next day to Vacaville, in virtual silence. I knew that Kelly was not in the least bit happy having me with her.

I couldn't understand why she was so profoundly disappointed that Danielle was not with her, or why she was behaving the way she was towards me. It almost felt as if she hated me. I spent almost the entire drive to Vacaville looking out my window, while Kelly was played dark, twisted music on the stereo.

Kelly had made arrangements to stay at her younger sister Beth's apartment while she was there for the celebration. It was late afternoon when we arrived. Kelly got her things out of the car, leaving me to handle my own luggage. That was fine, I had certainly done it before and taken care of my own things for years.

I walked through the door of Beth's apartment, which was in sad disarray as usual. Her children Ricky and Abbey were bouncing up and down on one of the couches, excited to see both Kelly and me. It was close to five p.m., and I was a bit hungry as I had not eaten anything that day.

Beth told us that she had prepared dinner, which was frozen lasagna, frozen bread and a salad. I didn't fault her for taking shortcuts. I knew that she worked full-time and had little or no help from her husband. The children were too young to assign serious chores to. So, Beth left most things in her apartment undone.

There was no vacuuming, no cleaning the bathrooms, no making the beds, and rarely doing the dishes, and her home always had a soured smell. At least the children were clean and dressed. After dinner Kelly and went out in front of the apartment in a small commons area to sit and smoke cigarettes.

She still had not spoken more than a few words to me. I figured that it would be okay, whatever she was going through she would get over soon enough. An older woman from across the courtyard came out of her apartment and ran towards us. She swooped down on Kelly and started hugging and kissing her.

She pulled away from Kelly long enough to say hello to me, and then went back to hugging and kissing. "Susan", Kelly said, looking at me with a grin on her face, "This is Estelle. I have known her for years." Of course, Kelly introduced me as her 'friend from Aptos'. I told Estelle that it was a pleasure to meet her and shook her hand.

She told Kelly that she wanted to just swoop her up and take her to bed, right then and there. I laughed, somewhat nervously. Estelle was apparently either bisexual or lesbian, and she was a nice enough woman, so I welcomed her company and tried not to be suspect of their relationship.

We all visited for a while. Estelle went into her apartment and came back with a six-pack of beer. The alcohol relaxed Kelly a bit and she began laughing and talking to me, as if the drive up with no conversation between us had not happened. I thought that perhaps things would return to what normalcy we had.

Ricky and Abbey came out of their apartment and began chasing one another up and down the sidewalk having the time of their lives. They had to expend their energy somehow after being cooped up in their apartment for hours on end. Beth came out shortly after and told them, amidst their protests, that it was time for them to get ready for bed.

Kelly abruptly stood up and said that she was tired and was going to lie down. She stared at me and I knew that she wanted me to follow, but I didn't feel like going to sleep just yet. Estelle and I visited for about another hour, comparing notes on life, sharing our experiences down through the years, and really enjoying ourselves.

I told her that I had better get inside and lie down, as we had a big day ahead of us, and that it was very nice meeting her. I opened the door to Beth's apartment. It was completely dark inside. I felt my way in, when all of a sudden Kelly had me by my upper arms, digging her fingernails deep into my flesh.

She whispered, "What did you fucking think you were doing???" I told her that she was hurting me, and that is when I blacked out. I didn't regain consciousness until the next morning. The sun was already up, and Beth and her family were walking back and forth through the living room. The sounds stirred me from my sleep.

I sat up, finding myself on the couch and looked around. Kelly was still asleep in a sleeping bag on the floor. I needed to use the restroom so I stood up. Suddenly I felt dizzy, and almost fell. I had to grab the couch to keep from falling to the floor. My body hurt, my head hurt, and I couldn't figure out why.

I said good morning to Beth, but she averted her eyes. I went into the bathroom and looked in the mirror, and what I saw was horrifying. I had deep, bloody abrasions across the top of my nose, and dried blood below both of my nostrils. My eyes were both blackened and swollen almost shut, and my right cheek was swollen almost three times its normal size.

I rushed out of the bathroom to get help. Beth was in the kitchen and I ran in to show her my face. She looked at me and walked away. I went to where Kelly was sleeping and gently shook her. She opened her eyes and looked at me. I asked her what had happened, what had she done.

She laughed and said "Oh, you did that to yourself. I've already told everyone here as much." I was in utter shock. I remembered how she had dug her nails into my flesh the night before and felt my arms. There were large wounds on both of my upper arms, some slightly scabbed over, others still oozing blood.

I cried out, "You did this to me!" She laughed, stretched and got up off the floor. She pushed past me to go to the bathroom. I could hear Beth laughing in the kitchen. I went into the kitchen and told her that I needed help, that I should go to the hospital because I might have a concussion. She ignored me and walked out of the room.

I didn't know what else to do, so I picked up the phone and called 911. I told them that my girlfriend had severely abused me and that I was in extremely bad shape. The dispatcher told me to avoid her, even if it meant going outside or leaving, and that they would sent some officers immediately to assess the situation.

While I waited for the police to arrive I quickly got my belongings together. I was not going to stay there any longer than I had to. Kelly and Beth were watching me and laughing. I felt badly for the grandmother, because that day was her birthday, and we were all supposed to be going to her celebration.

As I was walking towards the door I noticed Kelly's truck keys on a counter and grabbed them. I didn't have any way to get home and I rationalized that I should be able to take her car after what she had done to me. I sat in one of the chairs in front of Beth's apartment and waited for the police to come.

Estelle came out of her apartment, took one look at me and sat down. She had a worried look on her face. She held one of my hands and sighed. She asked me what had happened and I told her that I really didn't know, but explained to her how Kelly had manhandled my arms when I went into the apartment the night before.

She looked down at the ground and shook her head. She sighed and said, "That sounds like Kelly." But that is all that she said. She got up from her chair and walked back into her apartment. I wondered why she had not offered to help me. But then again, the adults in Beth's apartment had walked past me like I was a ghost or didn't exist.

I was, needless to say, quite befuddled, and it didn't help that my head felt like it was exploding and my entire body ached like an abscessed tooth. I was becoming angry. Angry with Kelly, angry with her sister, and angry with the situation. And it took a lot to make me angry. By the time the police arrived I had managed to contain my emotions.

They all took a look at me, and one of them knelt down in front of me and examined my face and arms while the other two went inside Beth's apartment. He said that he could call an ambulance if I wanted, but I declined. All that I wanted to do was go home. The door to Beth's apartment opened and I saw Kelly in handcuffs.

She looked at me and screamed, "Give me my truck keys!" One of the police officers asked if I had her keys and I told him, yes, and handed them to him. Now I really had no way to get home. He told me that they had filed an emergency protective order on my behalf, and that Kelly was not to come closer than one hundred yards to me.

I could hear Beth yelling at me, cursing me, but I left, not looking behind myself. I didn't want to see any of their faces. I walked through an overgrown field, to a shopping center that I saw in the distance. I went into one of the stores and bought an iced tea, and going outside found a table in front of a pizza parlor to sit and think.

I called Stephanie and told her what had happened. She asked me how I planned to get home and I told her that I was working on it. One of the delivery drivers came out of the pizza parlor and I asked him if he wanted to make $80.00. He asked how and I told him that I needed a ride to Santa Cruz.

He scrutinized me for a minute, then said yes, and he went inside, told his boss that he was going to give me a ride, and helped me into his car with my luggage. I was so relieved. By the time we arrived in Aptos I was exhausted. The man helped me into my apartment, bringing my suitcase in, making sure that I was safe.

He left and I was alone. I took a shower and put on fresh clothing. There was a knock at my door, and when I opened it I saw Shana standing there. She took one look at me, and not taking no for an answer, put me in her car and drove me to the emergency room at Dominican Hospital in Santa Cruz.

When the doctor came to examine me he looked at my upper arms where Kelly had dug her nails into my flesh. They were puffy, black and purple, and oozing with pus and old blood. He cleaned those as gently as he could and told me that I would need a tetanus vaccination, just in case.

Next he examined my face. He told me that I had an orbital fracture on my right eye, and that my right cheekbone was also fractured. He suggested scans, but I told him that I just wanted to go home. He gave me a morphine injection, prescribed antibiotics and Percocet for the pain, and discharged me.

Shana drove me home and helped me to my apartment and into bed. She gave me her phone number and told me to call her if I needed anything.

She was glad that a temporary restraining order had been place on Kelly. She didn't like her at all, a feeling that I was to discover was shared by many other people, my family included.

What I did next was beyond bizarre. I left my apartment, got in my car and drove to Danielle's apartment. I was going to confront her and fight her if I had to. I blamed her for everything that had happened. For some reason I could never hold Kelly accountable for any of her actions. Perhaps I was weak, or maybe I actually was mentally ill.

I walked up to the door and knocked. Danielle answered the door and I told her to step out, that we were going to discuss her involvement with Kelly, even if it meant a physical confrontation. Now, I only weighed 115 pounds, and just 5'2" tall. Danielle was well over 250 pounds and much taller than me.

It was not as if I could actually do any damage, but I could definitely be damaged. Instead of stepping out she took me by the hand and walked me inside her apartment. She asked me what had happened and I told her everything, starting with the drive to Vacaville the day before.

She acted as if she were shocked, but I knew that she was aware that I had gone instead of her. She asked if I had been to the hospital and I said yes. I told her that I had an orbital fracture on my right eye, and that my right cheek bone was fractured as well. I showed her my u[[er arms and how infected the injuries had become.

She immediately made a phone call to Kelly and began shouting at her, telling her that I was there and that she was never welcome back in her home again. As if in a trance, I allowed her to lead me upstairs and put me in her bed. I had no power left in me. All that I wanted to do was sleep.

I pulled the blankets over myself, not caring if they were clean or not, and fell into a deep slumber. Hours later I found myself sitting on a bed in a different room looking out a window at trees. My head and body were buzzing, and I couldn't understand what was happening to me. I thought perhaps that it was the morphine the doctor had given me.

Danielle came into the room and sat down next to me. She asked me how I was feeling, and I told her that I felt peculiar. That is when she let me know that she had injected me with methamphetamine while I was sleeping thinking that it would help me, and that how I was feeling was normal.

My reaction was not of shock, anger or rage, which it should have been, especially since I had never been injected with an illegal substance. Instead, I thanked her and told her that I was feeling really, really good. I had smoked meth with Kelly those few times in the past, but it was nothing like this feeling of complete euphoria.

This was a different type of high. In fact, I felt the best that I had for an exceptionally long time. Danielle asked me if I wanted to move in with her clan for protection and I told her yes, absolutely. I was definitely not in my right mind. She ran downstairs and told everyone that the house had a car now and someone with money.

I didn't even care. All I wanted to do was maintain the thrill that I was feeling. I told Danielle that I had to go to my apartment and get a few things, so she and her boyfriend Phil left with me and I drove, like a bat out of hell. I hit a speed bump and damaged my engine, but I kept driving anyway.

The three of us went into my apartment and I packed a few personal items, along with all of the food that I had, and we returned to Danielle's. The following days are a dim memory for me. I know that Danielle drove me to the municipal court to file a permanent restraining order against Kelly, which would be in effect for three years.

A few days later, it was as if my eyes were opened for the first time. I had put myself in a very precarious situation with this meth clan. They were using my car, which was barely running, eating my food, and spending my money. Checks were missing from my checkbook, and I received several email alerts regarding my credit cards.

When I was sure that everyone was asleep, I got my belongings and went back to my apartment as fast as I could. I later called Danielle and told her that I no longer wanted anything to do with her or any of her clan, and never, ever wanted to see them again. I was finally by myself and dealing with the psychosis of the withdrawals from meth.

Only Stephanie knew what had happened to me in Vacaville, and I had been avoiding her phone calls since going to Danielle's, so I went out onto the deck and called her. When I was finished I called David. I didn't tell either of them that I had used meth, rather choosing to tell them that I was ill.

I hadn't lied. I was sick. I had infected ulcers all along the inside of my left elbow where Danielle had repeatedly injected me with meth. My lungs were filled with fluid and I could not breathe from my nose. I developed a hacking cough that would not go away. I could not go to the hospital because I was afraid that they would know I used meth.

I called Maggie, my youngest child, and confided in her. She counseled with me, encouraging me to stay away from Danielle and her clan, and to just get through the next days and weeks that it would take me to heal from the trauma of the drug. No matter what time I needed her she always answered my calls.

She phoned my upstairs neighbor, Joanne, and asked her if she would please check on me. Not only did she check on me, but she also carried meals to my apartment and watched as I ate them, insisting that I eat every single bite, and I could barely swallow. Joanne brought me medicine to help with my cough and congestion.

I was determined never to use any substance like meth again. I had my cellphone and landline phone numbers changed because I didn't want to hear from Kelly, her family or her friends. I just wanted to be left alone. I had gone through enough trauma. I was enjoying my newfound freedom from Kelly and beginning to find myself again.

One evening, I decided that I wanted pizza, so I phoned Dominoes. I ordered pizza, salad and a dessert. It wasn't long before the delivery driver knocked on the door. I opened it carefully, since I didn't have a peephole to see who was there. The driver handed me my pizza and I went to get the money to pay him.

He happened to look inside my apartment and complimented me on how nice it was and how he wished he had a place like mine. He looked like a nice enough fellow, so I invited him inside to talk, and maybe have a slice of pizza. His name was John, but I never did know his last name.

I asked him how long he had lived in the area and he replied that he had lived there all of his life. I inquired how long he had been working at Dominoe's as a delivery driver and he said it was for over ten years. I don't know what compelled me, but I asked him "Would you be interested in renting a room here for $400.00 per month?"

He practically jumped out of his seat. He exclaimed, "Yes, yes I would!" I took him into the guest bedroom, the bathroom and kitchen. He said that he had an older cat by the name of Blackie and asked if that would be a problem, and I told him none whatsoever, that I had a young male cat as well.

I told him to drop by the next day so that we could go over the details. I awoke the next morning feeling so alive and filled with vitality. I had finally recovered from both the meth and the lung infection, and now I was going to have a roommate! I was really looking forward to John coming by later that morning.

I got up, put on a pot of coffee, and went out on the deck to have a cigarette. Kudos came outside with me. Kelly never allowed him to go outside, but we were virtually in the country, and Kudos loved lying out on the porch and watching the birds in the beautiful gardens that I had planted, as well as sauntering down by the creek.

I knew that Kelly was not coming here any time soon, so I didn't really care how she felt. I got a cup of coffee and returned to the deck. I loved the view, even though there were a few houses across the ravine. The vegetable and herb gardens were maturing, and the Calla Lilies I had planted along the fence line were in full bloom.

I listened to the wide variety of birds singing in the Oak trees that surrounded the property. I could hear crows overhead cawing as they made their way to the coast. My heart was light and carefree, and I was enjoying my newfound freedom from the incessant abuse, neglect and trauma that Kelly brought with her.

It was not long before John showed up. He was ready to move in without any further ado. He had packed all of his belongings, along with his cat Blackie, and brought everything with him in his car. John handed me $400.00 in cash, which I promptly put away in one of the drawers of my nightstand.

I asked him to wait a moment while I put Kudos in my bedroom. I certainly didn't want him running out the front door. I watched as he huffed and puffed, carrying everything in, but he finally finished. John had brought Blackie in first, in a pet carrier, and put her on the bed in his new room.

He was so excited, and I could tell that we were going to become good friends. I asked if he wanted to join me for dinner that evening but he told me that he had to work, perhaps another time. He was a nice man, but somewhat peculiar. He walked with a pronounced limp but never told me how he had injured himself.

He kept the door to his room shut at all times with Blackie inside. Occasionally he would let her out to play with Kudos. Kudos and Blackie didn't get along very well at first, but he was still just a kitten, only two years old, and Blackie was an old gal and frequently put him in his place. They were fun to watch.

I happened to glance in John's room and saw some type of apparatus. I asked him what it was and he put his fingers to his mouth, shushing me. He invited me inside and I sat on the bed. He told me that he had a friend who had a marijuana grow down towards Freedom, and he was given the waste from the plants after it had been processed.

John would then take that waste, leaves and stems and turn it into hashish, a fairly lengthy process, but with excellent results. I smoked some with him and told him that my children would certainly enjoy it.

For the most part I was remaining sober from all substances, but indulging in a bit of hashish did me no harm at all.

On his days off we would go shopping together, drive to the beach, or just spend time talking on the deck. My car was dead after my soiree with Danielle, so he would drive us in his old beater BMW. One day we went to Pier One Imports, where I had shopped with Kelly for wall décor earlier that year when she was busy spending my money.

Even though I was slowly running out of funds and disability benefits, I bought a large, beautiful green glass mushroom, a lead crystal butter dish from Shannon, Ireland, and a large square porcelain plate decorated with elephants. I was pleased with my purchases, and I still have all three items to this day.

One day, I was able to start my car, so I took her to a mechanic to see if it was salvageable, but it was hopeless. He happened to have a car that he had just restored, a nice baby blue Buick sedan, and he was asking $3000.00 for it. I needed a car, but I didn't have enough in the bank to purchase it, and I really wanted this one. It was perfect for me.

I thought about it for a few minutes, the I asked the owner of the shop if it would be possible for me to split the amount he was asking between two of my credit cards and he said absolutely. I was ecstatic. The car was beautiful and drove like a dream. I took it home with me that very day.

The weeks flew by and I started to become my old self, the person that I was before my trip to Ireland, before the suicide attempt, and before I met my abuser Kelly. My love for life itself was returning. I was finally able to have my children come on their days off to visit, have barbeques and family fun.

Seeing my children and grandchildren filled my heart with the greatest of joy. I also took the time to drive down to the Bay Area to spend time with them. I continued to apply for jobs, but no one seemed to be hiring. With my years of working experience, it was difficult to understand, but I remained optimistic.

One afternoon in mid-September there was a knock at the door. Without thinking I opened it and there stood Kelly. I panicked, and tried to slam the door shut, but she forced her way in. She told me that nothing was going to keep her away from me. I shrank away from her, expecting to be hit. Instead, she smiled engagingly and kissed me.

She told me that she forgave me for having her arrested, and that the restraining orders meant nothing to her. I have explanation for my reaction, other than to say that I must have been under some type of strange spell or twisted hypnosis. I couldn't resist her. I told her to go ahead and bring her things inside the apartment.

I realized that even if I had said no she would have done so anyway. I felt so helpless and frightened. John came out of his room and I introduced them. They both had surprised looks on their faces. Kelly didn't know about John. How could she? But John knew the backstory to Kelly and me.

He knew that she was a methamphetamine addict, a narcissist, a freeloader and an abuser. He didn't shake her hand, only acknowledging her with a nod of his head. He told me that he had to get to work and to take care of myself. He let me know that if I needed anything, all I had to do was call his cell phone.

I thanked him and I went over and sat down on the couch. "Who the hell is he???" Kelly screamed the question at me. I told her that he was my roommate, and that he had lived with me since the beginning of August. I tried to rationalize with her, telling her that I needed the $400.00 per month that he was paying to help with rent and utilities.

She walked away in a huff, heading for the bedroom. She came back out after only a few minutes. "Where's Kudos?" I told her that he was out in the backyard enjoying himself. She flew out the patio door and ran down the steps calling his name. He finally came out of the ravine, and really didn't recognize her, so he was hesitant to come to her.

I called him and he immediately ran to me. She grabbed him up and took him inside. She demanded that I never let him out of the apartment again, but I knew that she would not always be there. I simply nodded my head in agreement, knowing that Kudos and I would continue to enjoy the deck and yard.

In her haste to get Kudos she had brushed up against Poison Oak, which she was highly allergic to. She immediately began to break out in hives, her eyes swelling shut, her lips swollen to twice their normal size. Even though she had just yelled at me I felt sorry for her, so I drove to the store and bought calamine lotion and oatmeal.

I drew a warm bath, dissolved the oatmeal in the water, and helped Kelly into the tub. I gently poured the solution over her body, and with a washcloth I cleansed as much of her face as possible. Afterwards, I applied the calamine lotion to her body. She did recover, but it took several days, and she was miserable the entire time.

I had reclaimed enough of my old self back to be able to stand up for the things that I believed in. For instance, I wore some of the jewelry which I had kept, pieces Kelly found demonic. I read my devotionals, which she thought were from the pits of hell. I vowed that I would never let go of those things again, regardless of what she said or did.

I admit, I did have some fear of her, knowing that, as a schizophrenic, she could snap and become violent in a moment's notice, but I was determined to stand up for myself again. There had been way too many times that she had aggressed me, abused me, and damaged my body.

One day I was preparing dinner and decided to take a break. I poured myself a tumbler of iced tea and walked towards the sliding glass doors. Kelly was in the living room, and I noticed her giving me a hard look. I told her that we needed to have a serious discussion and lay down some ground rules if we were going to remain together.

She was sitting on the loveseat, so I sat down on the couch. I began. "First of all, I don't know what happened at your sister's apartment after you grabbed my arms. Maybe Beth, or her husband, or perhaps even Estelle beat me, but I highly suspect that it was you." Kelly hung her head and said, "It was me."

She continued. "I was jealous of the time you were spending with Estelle." She looked at me and said "Susan, I love you, and I am so sorry that happened, and I promise it will never happen again!" Believing that I loved her, I told her that I hoped she had learned her lesson.

The second thing that I insisted on is that she immediately find employment, that I would no longer tolerate her sponging off of me. She agreed and said that she would find something right away. The third thing I spoke about was Danielle and the meth clan. I would not approve of her fraternizing with them any longer. Ever again. Period.

She promised me that she would not ever contact any of them again, saying that she didn't even like them, that all she had been interested in was the meth. Then I went on to discuss our new roommate. I told her that John was a good fellow, and that she was not to make life difficult for him.

Not only was he a wonderful roommate, but I needed the $400.00 a month from him in order to make ends meet. She nodded her head, and although I was a bit suspicious of her agreeable attitude, I felt that things just might work out for us. I told her that I had filed a three year protective order against her, and she asked what we could do.

I knew that if I did not have the protective order quashed it that she could go to jail for breaking the order, so I told her that I would be willing to go to the court the next day and have the protective order lifted. so that she would not go to jail for being with me. She gave me a warm hug and kiss and thanked me for giving her another chance.

Kelly did get a job as a merchandiser, working at local stores, stocking inventory and building displays. She didn't make a lot of money, but she ended up helping with buying groceries and some of the household bills. She had her truck with her so she drove herself to work and back five days a week.

She was often late coming home from work, but I thought that perhaps she was visiting with her coworkers after work and decompressing. Everything seemed to be going fine for us. John mostly kept to himself and stayed in his room when Kelly was at home. He didn't care much for her.

Unbeknownst to me, Kelly continued to visit Danielle and the meth clan. I discovered this in a most distressing way. She began insisting on dressing in private, which reminded me of when she had been injecting meth with Danielle. One day I went into the bedroom without thinking and saw her as she was getting dressed.

I took one look at her and was shocked by what I saw. Both of her breasts were covered with bruises and infected ulcers. I asked her if she was using meth. She began crying and told me that she had been hanging out with Danielle again and had started injecting methamphetamine into her breasts.

I reminded her of her promise to me, that she would not seek out those people any longer. I told her that this would not work if she continued to fraternize with them. She promised once again that she would not see them anymore. Weeks passed and our lives appeared to be normalizing.

Kelly worked, I kept the house up, shopped, prepared the meals and was always there for her when she got home from work. October 8th came, a day that was immensely difficult for me. It was my brother Danny's birthday, a day that I could barely get through. When Kelly came home she noticed that I was not doing well.

"What's the matter honey?" I told her that it was Danny's birthday and I was having a hard time. She asked, "What did I tell you before??? You just have to get over it!" I was dumbfounded by her callousness. She knew how deeply I was affected by his murder, as well as that of my mother's murder.

She had brought a large bottle of Long Island Tea home with her, and she poured me a tall glass. She said "Here, drink this. It will make you feel better." Instead of feeling better it got me drunk and I ended up passing out. The next morning, I awoke a bit hungover. Kelly was already gone to work, and I wanted more liquor.

So, stupidly, I got in my car and drove to a liquor store. I bought a couple of bottles of Long Island Tea and drove home. Pulling into the driveway my car jumped the curb and hit the water main. I was not drunk. I was hungover. I managed to park my car, which was crushed on one side, and went into my apartment to drink.

I fell asleep shortly after drinking one of the bottles and was awakened by loud pounding on the front door. I got up and went to the door. I asked who it was and a voice said, "It is the Highway Patrol ma'am. Open up." So, I innocently opened the door. Several officers came rushing into the apartment.

 One of them threw me to the floor and slapped handcuffs on me. I asked them what was happening and I was told that I was under arrest for DUI. They drug me out to an emergency vehicle where they attempted to do a blood draw. I could see the water from the main that I had crashed into rushing onto the property.

One of the officers said, "Yes, you did that." I was silent. I was not drunk when I was driving, but I was drunk when I answered the door, so they all assumed that I was DUI. They took me to a local hospital and forced me to have a blood draw done to test for the percentage of alcohol in my system.

I was mortified! I had never even had a single traffic ticket in my entire life. Since I had drank a bottle of liquor, my blood alcohol level was .25%, which was way above the accepted amount of alcohol to be driving. But I had not driven drunk! The officers took me to the police station and put me in a cell.

I sat there for hours wondering what was going to happen to me. Would I go to prison? This was all unimaginable, something that nightmares are made of. It was close to midnight when the cell door finally opened and an officer told me that I was free to go. They had not even fingerprinted me, nor did they take a mugshot.

So, there I was in my pajamas, no shoes, no money, and I had to find the way home. I asked if I could use a phone and a clerk placed one on the counter. I tried calling both Kelly and John, but there was no answer. I was at least five miles from my apartment, it was dark, and I was in a dangerous part of town.

I walked out the doors of the police station, trying to orient myself. I didn't even know which direction to go in, so I just started walking and hoped that I would see a landmark or familiar area. I walked and walked. My feet hurt from the cement and asphalt, and I was shivering from the cold. It took me what seemed like hours to get home.

Kelly's truck was nowhere to be seen. Someone or something was watching over me because I was not attacked or assaulted on that long walk. I didn't have my key to the apartment, so I knocked on John's window and woke him up. I saw his surprised face looking back at me, and I asked him to please open the door.

I went inside and sat down on the couch. He asked me what had happened and I told him. He was astonished. I told him that I needed to take a shower and that we would talk more when I was finished. After my shower I got dressed, put some makeup on and pulled my hair up into a bun.

I went out into the living room where John was waiting for me. I told him more of what had happened and took him outside to assess the damage to my car. He said "Susan, it is totaled. You will never be able to drive it again." I was beyond miserable. I went inside to look for my purse and when I did I noticed that my driver's license was missing.

I mentioned this to John. He told me that the officers must have taken it, considering that I had been charged with DUI. I phoned the local Highway Patrol office and questioned them. I was told that they would have to look into it and call me back. I called my children and told them what had happened.

They were all shocked, but not entirely surprised. They all felt that my disastrous relationship with Kelly was only going to continue to bring me to ruin. About an hour later the phone rang and it was a Highway Patrol officer on the line. He told me that they had confiscated my license, and that I would have be seen at the DMV to get it back.

I supposed that I would cross that bridge when it was time. For now, I had a bicycle that I had purchased shortly after moving into the apartment, and I knew that John would give me rides when he had the time. When Kelly came home that evening she asked me what had happened and I told her.

Her response was "Well, you got what you deserved." It was not "are you okay babe?", or "do you need to go to the hospital?" Once again she told me to just get the fuck over the murders of my brother and mother, that this would happen again and again if I let their losses get me down.

I had no choice but to accept what had happened. I didn't know if I was supposed to go to a court hearing for the DUI ticket. I had not been told anything at the jail, I never had to post bail, so I simply waited to hear from them. I didn't even think about calling the courthouse. They had my address and phone number.

A few weeks later, On October 29th, I was asleep in my bed when Kelly came home from work. I heard her coming through the door and sat up to greet her. She walked into the bedroom and put both of her hands on her hips. Her face was twisted, and purple with fury. I didn't know what was happening.

She asked me why I was having sex with Steve, the man whom we had met at the after graduation meetings at the Camp, and whom she had worked for briefly months before. I told her that I didn't know what she was talking about. And I honestly didn't. She told me that I had been seen around town with him.

She told me that I had been 'unfaithful' to her. I laughed and said that whoever told her that was wrong and intentionally lying. Kelly pushed me back on the bed and pinned my shoulders down. She slapped me in the face and started screaming at me. Then she did the unthinkable. She put both of her hands around my throat and started strangling me.

I tried to fight her but her strength overwhelmed me. I screamed, but all that came out of my throat were faint gurgling sounds. My hands were free, so I tried to fight her off and started pounding on the headboard with all of the power I could muster. I began to lose consciousness.

Suddenly the bedroom door opened and John popped his head in. He yelled at Kelly to stop. Kelly stood up and told him that we had just been wrestling and that everything was just fine. She loosened her grip and I got up off the bed, bolted out the door, and went out to the deck, hoping to get away from her.

She followed me out and apologized, telling me that she had done it because she was angry with me. I didn't say a word. All that I could do was look at her. I smoked a cigarette and looked out at the darkened yard. I wondered what was wrong with Kelly. She had actually tried to murder me in an unfounded fit of jealousy.

Finally, not coming up with an answer, I went back inside. Kelly was laying on the couch watching television, acting as if nothing at all had happened. I walked past her into the bedroom and lay down in the bed. I fell into a very troubled and restless sleep, with a twilight awareness the entire time.

The next morning, I woke up with Kelly beside me in the bed. I quietly got up and went into the bathroom. I looked at my reflection in the mirror and saw that my throat was swollen and livid with black and purple bruises. I was crushed. I started a pot of coffee, got the landline phone, and went out onto the deck to smoke a cigarette.

I reflected on the events of the night before, but none of it made any sense to me. The phone rang. It was Stephanie calling to check on me and to talk for a while. I tried to speak but all that came out was a hoarse whisper. She asked me if I was sick, and I whispered no. She knew that something was wrong, so she pressed me.

I finally broke down and told her what Kelly had done the night before. She was frantic and asked if I had called the police. I said no, no more police, please. She said that she was going to try and get Landon to drive her up to see me. I told her that would be so nice, since I had not seen any of my family since Kelly's return.

Stephanie said that she had to go take care of a few things around her house but would call to check up on me later. Kelly finally got up and went out on the deck to smoke a cigarette. I poured a cup of coffee for each of us and followed after her. She didn't mention the night before and acted as if nothing had happened.

She told me that she was going to make me a special breakfast, and I thought maybe that was her way of making up to me. We had just sat down to eat when there was a knock at the door. John was still asleep, and I knew he needed his rest so I went to answer it before whoever it was could knock again.

There stood two police officers. I wondered what they were doing there as I certainly had not called them, and I was certain that John had not either. One of them asked me to step outside to talk with her. The other one remained at the open door, watching Kelly.

I looked over my shoulder at Kelly and she put her hands into a praying position. She was silently pleading with me not to say anything to them. I could see tears streaming down her cheeks and I actually felt sorry for her. I walked down the corridor and onto the front sidewalk.

The officer asked if she could see my neck, so I put my head back. She asked me what had happened and I told her the truth. She took some photos of my neck and told me to wait where I was. She went back inside the apartment and moments later both officers emerged leading a handcuffed Kelly.

She didn't even look at me as she passed. They put her in the back seat of their cruiser and then came back to talk to me. The male officer told me that they had filed an emergency protective order against Kelly. He also let me know that this was going to the District Attorney's office, and that he would be filing charges against her.

I don't know why I was not relieved. Rather, I was baffled. It was as if I was living in a waking nightmare. None of this seemed real, as if it couldn't have possibly happened to me. The cruiser pulled off of the property and I went back inside. John came out of his room, wondering what was going on.

I told him that Kelly had been arrested for domestic violence and elder abuse, but that I had not called the police, nor had I pressed charges against her. All that he said was "Good!" I thanked him for intervening the night before but asked him why he had not phoned the police then. He told me that it was because of the hashish in his room.

I said that I understood when I actually didn't. In my mind, if a person were to see someone being attacked they would either stop the attack themselves or call someone who could. I would not hesitate to intercede if I were to see someone's life being threatened. Nevertheless, I was grateful that he had at least said something.

I was numb, still in shock. I phoned Stephanie and told her what had happened. She let me know that she had spoken with Maggie and they both agreed that enough was enough, and they had phoned the police. I thanked her but told her how sad I was that this had occurred. "Mama, you were almost killed last night! This had to be stopped!"

I agreed, I knew that she was right, and still I was sad. Stephanie told me that she and Maggie were going to come visit me as soon as they were able. David called me that evening. He was beside himself with rage. He was so incredibly angry with Kelly. He told me that he didn't know what he might do if he ever saw her again.

He told me that he was going to come and pick me up on the afternoon of the 31st to spend Samhain (known widely as Halloween) with the family. He told me to pack enough for a night's stay. And so I went to David's. All of the children and grandchildren were there. They all gathered around me and hugged me.

My heart was filled with so much love for them, and I was grateful to be there. We had a nice dinner and all of us went out Trick or Treating together in the neighborhood. The grandchildren had so much fun, but they soon tired and we returned to David's apartment. The next day David drove me back to my apartment.

He told me that he was relieved that Kelly had been arrested and made me promise him not to have anything to do with her any longer. I promised him that I would do my best. The days became pleasant again with Kelly gone. I no longer had to wait in lurid anticipation of what violence she might do next.

When Kelly first moved in with me she had brought into the apartment many items that belonged to her previous lover, Eleanor. I didn't believe that she deserved these things, so I sent a message to Eleanor asking if she would like me to forward everything to her. This was her reply:

"I am sorry for what you have been through...I dont know what to say....I supported Kelly for five years and she abused me and my son (who is now 16) physically, verbally, and mentally...I left Kelly a year ago and it was the best decision I ever made. I drove around for a year with an extension cord under my driver side seat...hoping to run into her....i have not seen her...if I had, I'd probably be in jail....

When I left Kelly, she took everything I owned, and I dont want anything back...please, anything you have that may or may not have been mine, burn it, beat it with a bat, do whatever you need to to get out your own pain and frustration....that girl has some bad bad Kudos and a couple ass kicking's coming her way...

I dont want anything in my life to remind me of what I went through...my kids and I are reminded daily by the struggles we still face in counselling and our current circumstances...You would be smart to stay away from Kelly, there is no love in her heart....Please take care of yourself and good luck on your journey to healing...."

I took this as yet another warning about Kelly, but instead of taking it to heart and actually considering what she had said, I put it to the back of my mind. Compartmentalization is only useful when you actually take the time to sort through everything stored. I failed, yet again, to do so.

John saw that I was not doing as well as I should be, so he stepped up and started taking me for drives along the coast just for the sheer pleasure of it. Sometimes we would stop for lunch, other times just drive. I was finally learning how to just relax again and thoroughly enjoy myself.

One day he decided to take me to his friends place in Freedom, the one who had a marijuana grow farm. We drove about fifteen miles South of Aptos and out into the countryside. I had no idea where we were going, and even if I tried I would never be able to find the place again on my own.

John parked his car alongside a dirt road and we got out. We had to make our way through low growing bushes and brambles, and I tried to be careful not to get scratched by the thorns. We finally came to a clearing and I saw before me a ramshackle, run down trailer where his friend lived.

We were greeted by his friend and led to a place outside where we could sit and visit. The friend brought out some soft drinks and we sat and talked. He asked me if I wanted to see his farm, and I said of course I did. He led me over a small hill and there before me was a vast forest of marijuana plants.

I was impressed. I had never actually seen a marijuana grow site. We returned to the trailer and sat visiting for a while longer. We didn't stay too long though. He gave John a large bag of waste products, which John would render into hashish. I didn't mind him doing this. It was harmless as far as I was concerned.

The days passed by and I had not heard anything from Kelly, for which I was grateful. No one from her life tried to contact me, not her parents, her sisters, or her friends. I hoped that she would be sentenced to prison for what she had done, or at least put on formal probation for a good long time.

I have heard it said that heartbreak is the catalyst for a new path, and I was more than ready to walk mine. I finally had my life back and Kelly was, hopefully, in the past, and would stay there, never to grace my sight again. I had a renewed sense of purpose and a potentially wonderful life ahead of me.

How To Lose Your Family In One Easy Step

One day in mid-November, I received a phone call from my daughter Maggie. She was in tears. She told me that she had just been terminated from her job for underperformance and given five days to vacate her townhome. I was not in the least bit surprised. In fact, I had been expecting this for some time.

You see, Maggie had never fully recovered from discovering the body of the suicide at the property she worked for in San Mateo. I asked her if she wanted to come and stay with me until she could sort through things and she said that she would talk to her husband Jesse and see what he thought. I felt that would be the right thing to do.

I told her that I would wait for her call, which didn't take long, because no sooner had I hung up than Maggie called me back and told me that they would appreciate the help. I asked her to come and pick me up and I would help her pack and clean. She told me that she would come the next day to get me.

I sat down with John and told what had happened, and that Maggie, Jesse and their toddler Caitie were going to be living with us for a while. He had met Maggie and was delighted that she was coming to live with us.

He said that we had both the couch and loveseat for them to sleep on.

The next day Maggie picked me up and we drove to Mountain View. We stopped first for boxes and then went to her townhome. Jesse was pretty much useless. All he could do was stand and watch us work. It took us three days and many, many trips in Maggie's van to my apartment to move everything. Most of their belongings had to go into my storage unit.

I lifted so many heavy items that I ruptured an already damaged ligament in my right knee. Nevertheless, I cleaned the townhome from top to bottom, and when Sherry, the head property manager (the same one who had terminated me) came to inspect the townhome, it passed her scrutiny. I would expect nothing less.

This was in mid-November, which came at a fortuitous time in my life as I had run out of money and disability payments were soon to follow. My credit cards were maxed out, so those were no longer an option. Maggie had some money saved, and she was approved for unemployment compensation right away.

We both applied and were approved for food stamps, so we would be fine paying the rent and utilities, as well as buying groceries. Instead of having them sleep on the couch, Maggie and Caitie shared my bed with me at night, and Jesse, who would stay up all night playing video games, would sleep in it during the day.

We had such good times for the next many months. Maggie and I would garden together and let Caitie play outside when the weather was good. We shopped and cooked together, and it was a blessing having family so close again. I was grateful that Maggie had her van as it made shopping and medical appointments so much easier for everyone.

She took me to the DMV to ask about my driver's license, where I found out that I would have to address the court about it. That is something I was confused about. I had called the courts several times and inquired when a hearing might be, but the clerks couldn't find me in the computer so they couldn't really help me.

I let go of worrying as I figured that I would get something in the mail eventually ordering me to go to court. I decided that I would try to plead my case by myself. The DA's office sent me the protective order against Kelly, as well as the charges they had filed, and advised me that she had to be served with the paperwork in order to validate it.

I had no idea how I was going to accomplish this. But the perfect time presented itself. Kelly phoned me a couple of days later and asked if I could meet her at a coffee shop to talk things over. Maggie and I decided that this would be when we would serve her with the order. I agreed to meet with her the next day.

Maggie wore full clown makeup on her face, and we drove together to a coffee shop. I saw Kelly's truck in the parking lot and told Maggie that she must already be inside. Maggie got out of the van and walked to the coffee shop. I can only imagine the look on Kelly's face when Maggie served her with the order.

Now she knew that I was serious. At least I hoped so. A couple of days later I received a call from the Sheriff's Department that they had a request for a civil standby for Kelly to pick up her belongings. I was delighted to have her things gone from my apartment. I agreed on the date, and Maggie and I began packing her things.

I was not going to allow her to take Kudos though. He didn't need any further trauma in his life, and I felt that all that Kelly could offer him was suffering and chaos. The day came for her to pick her belongings up and I watched for her out of the kitchen window. I saw her pull into the parking lot and park her car.

She had been followed by someone in another truck, which I assumed was to help haul her things away. I was stunned to see that she had Drew, my nemesis from Vacaville, and Danielle, the head of the meth clan house, with her. I was to learn later that she had moved in with Danielle and that they became lovers.

Maggie, Jesse and I had already placed all of her belongings onto the front sidewalk so that she would have no need to come to the apartment. Two deputies stood by to keep the peace. But there was no incident, for which I was grateful. I was relieved when they had the last of her boxes in the trucks and they pulled off of the property.

That was that, or so I thought. I still had to go to court in January 2010 to make the protective order official, and I knew that I would most likely see her there. In the meantime, I had received a letter from the courts stating that I needed to make an appearance before a judge on December 10th. Maggie was busy, so John drove me instead.

We arrived at the courthouse in downtown Santa Cruz and walked up the stairs. We went through security, then I asked one of the deputies where I could find the court I was supposed to appear in. He told me to look at the rosters on the wall in the hallway. John and I walked over and looked at the rosters and my name was nowhere to be found.

I was perplexed. I looked again, carefully scrutinizing each page that was posted on the wall and still couldn't see my name. I had the order in my hand, but I was not scheduled to appear according to the rosters. We went to the clerk's office to see if we could get more information. We had to wait in line for an hour to see a clerk.

When we got to her window I showed her the letter and she took it from me. She searched her computer and couldn't find my name anywhere. She told me that notice must have been a mistake, and to wait until I received another notice. I was still a bit confused. I wanted this to be over with, but I had no choice but to wait.

The holidays came and I had nary a thought about Kelly. We were all too busy celebrating and having an enjoyable time. Maggie, Jesse, Caitie, John and I had a lovely celebration in Aptos, and then I visited with the rest of the children and grandchildren in Campbell, where David lived and worked, and where Stephanie lived.

The New Year arrived and January was upon us. The day for me to go to court for the finalization of the protective order against Kelly had finally arrived. I had just gotten up and started a pot of coffee when there was a knock on the door. I wondered who could be there so early in the morning.

I opened the door and there were two police officers standing there. I asked if I could help them and they asked if I was Susan Sheehan. I said, yes, that is me. One of the officers told me to put my hands behind my back and informed me that they were taking me into the precinct.

I was in shock. I asked them why. The female officer said that a bench warrant had been issued because of failure to appear. I was baffled. I asked if I could have enough time to please get dressed, brush my hair and put some shoes on, and the female officer told me, fine, but that she had to accompany me.

She stood behind me in the bathroom while I brushed my hair, then followed me into the bedroom and watched as I dressed myself. When I told her I was ready she handcuffed me. Out to the cruiser we went. I was put in the back seat and the male officer drove us to the precinct. Once again they didn't fingerprint me or take a mugshot.

At the precinct I was told to take a seat in their lobby. So, I sat and waited. And waited and waited some more. A well-dressed man walked by and looked at me. He said, "You don't look like you belong here." I told him that I didn't think so either. He went over to the sergeants desk and spoke with one of the officers.

He came back and said, "I knew you didn't belong here. You have a new hearing set for two weeks from now. Make sure you're there." I practically hugged him! I asked to use a phone so I could call Maggie to pick me up. We only had an hour to drive to Watsonville to the courthouse to finalize the protective order.

Maggie told me she would be there to pick me up in a flash. I walked outside to wait for her. I still had to put appropriate clothing on for the court hearing and freshen my makeup as well. Before I knew it Maggie was pulling up to the sidewalk. I jumped in the van and she headed back to the apartment.

I got dressed in clothing appropriate for the court as quickly as possible and we headed out the door to the van. Maggie drove as fast as the speed limit would allow, and we made it to the courthouse with a half hour to spare. Maggie parked the van and we got out. We decided to have cigarettes before going in.

I looked down the sidewalk and there was Kelly, with Danielle holding her arm. She kissed Kelly intimately, making sure that I saw. I turned my head away and ignored them. Maggie and I finished our cigarettes and went inside to find out where the hearing was being held in.

Noting it, we located the room and went into the courtroom, taking our seats, and waiting for the judge to come from his chambers.   Kelly and Danielle sat across from us, but a few rows forward. Danielle turned and grinned at me, then ran her fingers through Kelly's hair and gave her a kiss. It turned my stomach to watch her.

The judge came into the courtroom and we all stood. The court was called into session. It was about a half hours wait before my case was called. All the while Danielle kept turning to look at me, as if she were goading me into a reaction. I didn't play into it. I could really care less if she was with Kelly now.

The judge asked me if I wanted to pursue the protective order, and I told him that if I could make it a lifetime order I would. He said that it would only last for three years, but at that time I could renew it. I felt relieved. He went over Kelly's charges and gave her a hard look. He ordered Kelly to have no contact with me whatsoever.

No phone calls, no emails, no text messages, and definitely no person to person. She nodded her head, indicating that she understood, but I could tell that she was bristling inside. Danielle rubbed her back, kissed her, hugged her, all the while looking at me with a smirk on her face. I smiled back and silently mouthed "Good luck."

Maggie and I left, went to the van, and drove back to the apartment. I was finally free of the sick, psychotic, schizophrenic, bitter, vindictive, and violent woman that Kelly was. I could reclaim myself fully and genuinely enjoy my life again, which is what I had actually been doing since the day that she was arrested.

A week later I went to Stephanie's home to watch over Zaccheus and Corryn while she gave birth to her third child, Maxxim. What a blessed time it was, but I was sad that I was not able to be at the hospital with her. While she was in the hospital I cleaned and arranged her home to make it spotless and comfortable.

I had to return to Aptos before she came home, but I made a nice dinner for her return, putting it in the refrigerator. I was able to travel down to Campbell a month later and stay with Stephanie, enjoying my newest grandbaby, along with the other grandchildren who lived on the same property. It was an amazing time for me.

The day for the hearing finally arrived and Maggie accompanied me to court. I dressed nicely, wanting to make a good impression on the judge. We found the right courtroom and walked inside. We sat near the back of the courtroom. I was almost in tears. I was sure that this was not going to go well.

The judge entered the courtroom and everyone stood. We waited almost an hour for my name to be called. Listening to the judge deal with all of those who had cases before me she seemed to be a fair woman. I could only hope for her leniency. Finally, my name was called and I was asked to come forward.

I waited for the judge to speak. She looked my file over and said, "I am sentencing you to five years of court probation, fining you $2800.00, and you must attend six months of DUI drivers class in order to regain your driver's license." I nearly fell to my knees. I was so grateful.

She was finished with me and told me to proceed to her clerks desk to get all of the information. Her clerk handed me paperwork and asked me when I would be able to pay the fine. I told him the truth, that I didn't have any money in the bank and was not employed. He said that he could extend the deadline to one year hence. I shook his hand and thanked him.

The following months were filled with so much wonder and love. Maggie adopted a little Chihuahua mixed puppy, whom she named Bella. She was adorable, and we all loved her, but she would never take to house training. As a result, and I was fortunate to have a steam cleaner, one of us ended up steam cleaning the living room every single day.

I had continued seeing Dr. Stein, but I didn't care for him. All that it seemed that he wanted to do was medicate me with the cocktail of medications that he had prescribed for me, most of which didn't even seem to work. I decided to find one who might be able to actually help me.

My visits with her were enjoyable, and Maggie attended every single session with me as a show of support. The new psychiatrist took me off all of the medication that Dr. Stein had prescribed, noting that they were not suitable for my issues, and placed me on some that truly seemed to work.

I began feeling a bit more stable and able to think more clearly for the first time in a long while. Maggie took the time to regroup herself and heal from the trauma she had experienced in discovering the suicide. I helped her with this by allowing her to express her feelings freely and giving her pointers on how to manage those feelings.

David, Stephanie and their families would all come for visits regularly. It was such a blessing seeing them. We barbequed in the back yard, and even invited Joanna , her husband Willy, and her little girl Sonique down to join us. Willy worked at a local BBQ joint, and he knew how to make a wicked sauce.

Jesse was present, but you would not know it. He was obsessed with playing video games, and that is all he did or talked about. He didn't bother looking for work. In fact, he had never looked for work in the six years that I had known him. The reason for this would become apparent in the not too distant future.

Since I had not been able to find employment I decided to enroll at

Cabrillo College, with my major in nursing and minor in medical terminology. I also registered for a class on psychology. I was due to begin my coursework in the Fall. I wanted to move my life forward, be productive with my life, and do something to help others.

It was a bonus that I would be receiving stipends regularly, which would help us financially. I had begun feeling a little bit under the weather, but I was confident that I would be able to attend classes every single day, get a degree under my belt and move on to a new career that would be fulfilling.

It was still early Spring, so we couldn't do much in the yard. It was chilly and rainy, and no one wanted to catch a cold. One day I mentioned to Maggie that my health felt as if it was declining. She asked if I wanted to see a doctor and I told her yes, but not right then. I thought that I could wait it out.

But as the weeks progressed I continued to feel worse. Even though I was reclaiming myself as a person, my body was sickening. In late April I told Maggie that I was going to make an appointment for a physical to find out what was happening in my body. I didn't have a primary physician, but making an appointment was not an issue.

Maggie drove me to the clinic and I signed in at the front desk. We waited until my name was called and both of us walked to the exam room. The doctor came in, and I was relieved to see that it was a woman, especially since I would be getting a vaginal exam and pap smear.

I had already been weighed and my blood pressure taken by the nurse and put on one of their attractive exam gowns. The doctor listened to my heart and lungs, then had me lie down on the table and she began feeling my abdomen and thumping around on it. She asked me to sit up so that she could test my reflexes, which were excellent.

She sat down and looked at me. She asked if I had ever been tested for Hepatitis C. I replied that I hadn't and asked her why. She told me that she thought that my liver felt enlarged when she had palpated it. She ordered a series of blood tests, including one for Hepatitis C, and a baseline mammogram was well.

The doctor then said that she thought that I had cerebral atrophy, which sent me into an immediate panic. I didn't know what cerebral atrophy was, but it didn't sound good. She ordered a CT scan of my brain to confirm this. When she was finished she asked me to make an appointment to return in a month for the results.

I went in for the CT scan and mammogram the next day. I was really quite anxious about the cerebral atrophy. I thought that it was a death sentence, instead of being a simple progression of aging. I called David and Stephanie and told them. I felt that I might die at any time. They both told me not to worry, to wait and see what the scan showed.

Thinking that I was terminal I decided to send emails to Joel and Tom, my first and second husbands, and one to Kelly. I wanted closure with them, resolution to what had happened between us. Joel never answered my email, but Tom did reply with his usual A-tom dialogue and sympathy.

Kelly did end up replying to my email. I had changed my cellphone and landline phone numbers after she was arrested, so she was not able to call me. Thus, I began having daily email conversations with Kelly. She had moved out of Danielle's and back with her parents after the restraining order hearing, and still didn't have a job.

As the conversations continued she told me that she hated living with her parents. They continued to derogate her sexual orientation and forced her to attend church with them. She told me that she longed to return to Aptos, even if we couldn't live together. She wondered if I had heard of the Salvation Army rehabilitation center for addicts.

I told her that I would look into it and let her know what I found out. I did some research and found a phone number in San Jose to call. I sent

Kelly an email, encouraging her to phone the facility, which she did. When she called them she told the coordinator that she was a Lesbian and she was turned down immediately.

At that time, 2010, the Salvation Army was decidedly homophobic, and outright refused to help anyone who were known to be or acknowledged that they were a member of the Gay community. I decided, against my better judgement, to phone Kelly. I knew that as soon as I heard her voice I would once again fall under her spell.

She was out of breath when she answered the phone. "I can't believe that you actually called me!" I could hear the excitement in her voice. I told her that I thought that phone calls would be faster than emails, and hopefully, together, we could come up with a plan to help her find a place that would be willing to give her a chance.

She said, "I was given three years formal probation and ordered to complete two years of weekly domestic violence classes." I asked if she had been attending the classes and how she was going to manage her probation and classes if she moved back to Aptos, and she told me yes she was, and that she could have everything transferred there.

Maggie and Jesse were planning a trip to Washington State to visit his mother, Bridgette, who had never met Maggie or her granddaughter

Caitie, in late May. I decided to have Kelly come down while they were gone to see if we could work things out, so I sat down to talk to both Maggie and Jesse about it and see what they thought.

Jesse became violently outraged, and Maggie protested. She reminded me of what Kelly had done to me, more times than once, and that she had stood by me, serving Kelly the restraining order and going to the court hearing for the order. My other children responded in a similar manner. They had absolutely not one shred of love for Kelly.

I decided that perhaps it would be a good idea for Kelly to write a letter of apology via email and send it to all three of my children. The following is her email verbatim:

"At first all I wanted was for Susan to forgive me. It took me some months, a couple of scary blackouts and the willingness to want to get sober and a trip home to even realize what the hell I honestly did. I understand about pressing full charges on me if otherwise. Fuck, you have no idea, really! That person was put away for 7 years, and it takes alot of will, work, patience and staying clean to keep that person. I, believe it or not only want the best for Susan also and as much as it hurt both of us I'm glad that she and Maggie had me arrested that day, I was out of fuckin control and hated myself for what I was doing. I really, barley remember some of the summer. I agree it is a waste of time to get back together if I'm not clean, and thats the only reason I commented back to her when she finally got a hold of me, because it still hadn't dawned on me what was goingng on. I still hadn't felt any feelings about any of it until 1/2 a month before I moved home. I stayed so high I was numb.All I knew was I missed her and couldn't believe my actions you know? Sorry I'm just talking I really haven't had anyone to talk to about it except your mom. And I am so glad she forgives me because until she did, I was in a commatose miserble fog. I am clean and would never of asked for forgiveness if I wasn't. I was the one who started the abuse between Susan and I, I was the one who finished it. But, that was not an all the time thing , which is how everyone has made it sound. I was hardly ever home to be abusing her all the time, But Susan sees neglect as abuse too which, I would have to agree with that. But, that night NO, I agree Susan didn't deserve what I did. I had to face her questions about that night and it broke my heart trying to explain to her where my head was at because truly all I new was love never entered my mind only drugs and alcohol were on my mind and it hurt to tell her that I didn't see her I saw someone who was trying to take my masking medicine away, I saw her as evil.If that was my mom you are right I would be over protective and probably actually beat the persons ass who hurt her. But if that person came to my family how I am coming to yours with a real and true compassion andas sorry as I am for what he did and was working on changing themselve, I wwould have to put my anger aside , as an adult and remember that I was raised with love and forgiveness. Also, as an addict who has had to endure staying clean for the sake of phisically hurting my blood, my family I would then have to understand the power ofd addiction. BI would have to accept people change, people get clean and the person they are on drugs is not really them. I'm sorry I'm babbling, I really did try and endure all of you as part of my family, and this time around I was tewlling Susan fuck them(at 1st) they know nothing about our relationship, but I do understand and can picture the shoe on the other foot. Plus, Susan said if I really and truly am sorry and in love with her, than I would apporpreatly deal with all of your feelings as far as letting you guys vent it out and then I would tell you guys my true heart since I never really would sit down and have heart to heart with you guys like she wanted it to be before. So with my heart and soul on the line spread fully exposed, I ask for everyones forgiveness and a chance to prove I'm really not a monster and have had time to deal with what led me back to the drugs.

Kelly"

Rachel, my daughter-in-law, replied with the following:

"Kelly, I really do not think it is fair that you are manipulating Susan again, and I will tell you something right now David and I are in no way afraid of you and if you ever hurt Susan again we will be pressing full charges, getting a lawyer and not giving up without a fight. I highly

doubt that you have changed you are nothing but a women beater drug addict. I think you are trying to get in good with Susan so she will drop the charges, but you aren't fooling us! What is it that you want from her? And please do not try to say Love because that is a complete load of crap! If you would like to discuss this further feel free to call me. Susan is a great person and doesn't deserve this abuse, obsession, bullying, and trauma! Leave her alone!!!!! Get a damn life of your own, and proper help before you decide to destroy people's lives. I want Susan to stay with me while Maggie is gone, because I think you will try to hurt her. I see you and I know you. So, what do you think about that?
Rachel"

Rachel put into words what all of my children thought and felt. They had absolutely no love for Kelly, and zero tolerance. They knew of only a few of the abuses that I had endured, and if they had known everything I doubt that Kelly would have been long for this earth. As much as I appreciated it, I still wanted to help Kelly if possible.

As the time neared for Maggie and Jesse to take their trip I reminded them about my plan for Kelly visiting. I certainly didn't want any problems, and I didn't want them to spend their time in Washington worrying about me. I told Maggie that I really wanted her to come down, that I had to see Kelly, that I believed that I still loved her.

Maggie pointed out all of the abuses I had suffered at Kelly's hands, and all of the help that she had given me and asked me how I could even consider this. I told her I was sorry, that Kelly had already purchased a round trip bus ticket to come see me, and I had made arrangements with Joanna to pick her up at the bus station.

I could see no harm in this. None at all. But nothing is as it seems. Jesse immediately began removing his video game equipment and taking it out to the van. Next, he unplugged his computer and took it out as well. He told Maggie to start packing their clothes and the rest of their belongings.

He looked at me with the cruelest contempt and demanded the rent money they had given me. I told him that he was overreacting, and that I needed the money to pay June's rent. He acted as if I were some foul creature. He knew where I kept the money and pushed past me to get into the bedroom and my nightstand drawer.

I tried to stop him, but he shoved past me so hard that he knocked me to the floor. When I got up he knocked me down again. I asked Maggie to help me, but she was too busy hurriedly packing and trying to take care of little Caitie, who was crying hysterically. I went outside with my cellphone and called the Sheriff's Department.

I hated being involved with the law, but I needed someone there to protect me from Jesse. I tried to look through the sliding glass doors to see what was happening, but the apartment was dimly lit. I was afraid to go back inside for fear of what might happen. So, I waited until I thought they were gone.

A Sheriff's deputy came around the side of the apartment to see if I was okay. I told him I was a bit shaken up, but that I was fine. I asked if they were gone, and he told me that he would let me know as soon as they were. I am sure that the neighbors, especially Shana, were watching everything. It was not the first drama filled event at my apartment.

The deputy asked if I wanted to press charges against Jesse, and I told him no, please do not. I simply wanted him out of my home. It was not long before the deputy came around the side of the building again to let me know that they had left the property. I went up the steps to the deck and opened the sliding glass door.

The apartment was in shambles. There was dirty laundry and trash strewn throughout all of the rooms except for John's, whose door was closed. In fact, I had wondered where he was during all of the commotion and chaos. I called both David and Stephanie and told them what had happened and why.

They were both shocked and disapproved of it. They asked me what in the world I was thinking to consider having Kelly come back. I told them it was only for a weekend visit, and that I was only trying to help her find a place to stay, but that I also felt as if I still loved her in some way.

Soon John returned home. He told me that he had been at his mother's, who was ill, and wondered what was happening. I told him everything, including the fact that Kelly was coming down for a weekend visit. He didn't say anything, he just walked into his room and closed the door behind him.

It was evident that he didn't approve either. I understood, since he had witnessed her abuses, and he was the one who intervened when Kelly was strangling me. I began picking up the debris on the floors. I bagged it, along with the clothing, and took everything out to the dumpster. I vacuumed the carpets and wiped down the tables.

My bedroom was in sad disarray, so I set to straightening everything. It seemed to me that while Jesse and Maggie were frantically packing that they didn't care what happened to my belongings. I decided to send an email to Maggie, just wanting an open line of communication with her, but I had no Internet.

I began looking at the connection and saw that the cable had been severed in two. There was a pair of scissors left behind, almost as a taunt.

I did not know who cut it, but I suspected it had been Jesse, just one final jab before he left. I didn't understand why things had gone the way they did. I was utterly confused by the entire event.

It took several hours, but I was finally able to get everything in the apartment in satisfactory order. I knocked on John's door and asked if he could give me a ride to the grocery store as well as the local Staples to purchase a new cable for the internet. He said yes, and I thanked him.

I was able to stock up on a few groceries and buy a new cable for my computer. John was mostly silent on the trip, and I understood why the next day. The next morning, Joanna drove me to the bus station in town to pick Kelly up. Joanna was such a good friend to me and supported even the worst of my decisions without making judgements.

She pulled into the bus station and parked her car. We waited for half an hour for the bus which Kelly was on to arrive. I watched the passengers disembark, and then I saw Kelly. I jumped out of Joanna's car and ran to her. She only gave me a brief hug and kiss on the cheek, said hello to Joanna, and put her duffle bag in the trunk.

I was so excited to see her, but I sensed that the feeling was not mutual. When we arrived at the apartment the first thing that she did was look for Kudos, who was hiding under my bed. She pulled him out and sat down on the couch, kissing and petting him. He acted as if he didn't know her and kept trying to pull out of her arms.

Kelly looked around the room and asked me why it was so 'dirty'. I had already told her about Maggie and Jesse, the confusion, violence and them leaving. I said that I had done the best that I could to clean and organize everything. The least she could have done was to be understanding and appreciative of what I had just gone through.

I had not seen John's car in the parking lot, but I knocked on his door anyway. I would usually hear Blackie meow when I knocked, but I didn't this time, so I opened the door just a crack. I peeked inside and saw that the room was emptied of his belongings. John had moved out!

I was dumbfounded. He had not said a word to me about leaving, and I certainly didn't anticipate this happening. I told Kelly that he was gone as well, and she said, "Good riddance!" But I was sad because he and I had become what I thought were close friends. I began to feel ill, thinking that perhaps I had made a terrible choice.

The weekend turned out to be fairly enjoyable. Kelly seemed to still be attracted to me physically, and I to her. We cuddled on the couch, watched movies together and went for a couple of walks to a nearby café. She apologized repeatedly for her abuse of me, and asked if there would ever be a chance that we could be together again.

I told her that I would deeply consider this, but that she would need to gain my trust. She promised me that she would never see Danielle or any of the other members of the meth clan again, and that she would stay clean of meth and alcohol. Although I was a bit hesitant to believe her it made me feel a bit better to hear her say it.

Joanna drove Kelly back to the bus station on Monday morning for her return trip to Vacaville. I was incredibly sad to see her go, even though I was not completely convinced of her sincerity. Now I was going to be absolutely alone. I had no car to travel to Campbell to visit David, Stephanie and their families.

I sat down that evening, even before Kelly had a chance to return home, and sent her an email. I asked her to come back, and that we would give it another chance. That chance was ill-fated, and it took another three and a half years for me to realize that welcoming her back into my life was one of the worst decisions I had ever made.

The Definition Of Insanity

I am sure that you, the reader, have heard what one definition of insanity is, but if not I will tell you. It is doing the same thing over and over again expecting an entirely different result. I was hopelessly stuck in a maddening cycle of insanity, believing that, because of my love for her, Kelly would change for the good.

It took Kelly less than a week to get her things together and move back in with me. Her parents were angry that she was back with me, but that didn't deter her from coming. During that week she was able to make arrangements to have her formal probation and domestic violence classes transferred to the area.

Joanna drove me once more to the bus station, and this time Kelly hugged and kissed me as if she genuinely loved me. We sat together in the back seat of Joanna's car on the drive to the apartment holding each other tightly. Kelly whispered words of love and comfort into my ear, promising to take care of me from that day forward.

Together we carried her belongings into the apartment. I was very tired afterwards, so I sat on the couch while she put her things away. I had told her that I thought that the cerebral atrophy was the cause of my fatigue, but I had yet to see the doctor again to learn the results of the scan, mammogram and labs.

Kelly told me that she was going to find work immediately to help out financially. I let her know that I had applied for nursing school and been accepted, and that I would have a stipend every few months that would help with money. I had also placed an ad in the classifieds looking for a roommate to replace John.

She didn't like the idea, but I told her that we needed the money, and it would do no harm to have a roommate. The following days were peaceful. Kelly actually got down on her knees one day to beg my forgiveness for all that she had done, and my heart broke just watching her. I kissed her and told her that I forgave everything.

A couple of days later I received a call from the manager of the storage facility where I had rented a unit. He told me that my payment for the unit was late, and if not paid by the end of the day he would put a lock on the door. I told him that he had to be mistaken, that Maggie had paid for it the month before.

He replied that he had never received a payment, and in fact had seen Maggie and Jesse at the facility moving their belongings out. I immediately went to the bus stop and caught a bus to Capitola. I walked the rest of the way, went into the office and spoke with the manager. We went to the unit together and I unlocked the door.

Walking inside, I saw that all of my belongings were in sad disarray, and that all of Maggie's belongings that had been stored were gone. She hadn't even bothered to tell me. I begged the manager to please give me a couple of days to sort this problem out. He assured me that he could offer me three days, but then he would have to lock the unit.

I called David and asked for his help. He told me that he couldn't afford to pay the rent on the unit, and he would not be able to help with another storage unit either. I asked if he could help me rent a truck to move everything to my apartment, and he agreed. I didn't know where I would put everything, but I would try my best.

With David, Rachel and myself, we had the storage unit emptied in about four hours. We drove to my apartment but could only fit a few items inside. We ended up placing everything else in front of my apartment, on the sidewalk and on the lawn of the commons. Everything was helter-skelter, disorganized and unsightly.

My metal and slate dining room table and upholstered chairs, which matched my coffee and end tables, my computerized Singer sewing machine, and boxes filled with personal belongings were outside. There were boxes of dinnerware, glassware, photos, my daughters footlockers filled with their memories from childhood.

There was truly little memorabilia Kelly had allowed me to keep when I first rented the storage unit in 2008. Over the next week I tried to find a way to store everything inside. Kelly refused to help me, telling me that it was not her problem. I was so tired, yet I still worked on re-boxing and organizing everything.

Stephanie and Landon drove up and picked up the footlockers, along with a few other items. Kelly 'allowed' me to keep a few dinner plates, salad plates, soup bowls and mugs to take inside the apartment, and those were chosen from a service for sixteen people. I was beside myself with worry about someone stealing what was left outdoors.

Shana had been at odds with me since Maggie moved out and it seemed that she wanted me to get into trouble. She phoned the property manager to complain about my belongings, not giving me the chance to try and manage them. Not long after that I received a phone call from Lewis, the property manager.

He told me that he had received complaints about the items outside. He said that if I didn't have everything gone by the end of the week that he was going to evict me. I thought about storing some items in the guest bedroom, but I needed that room to rent out. I desperately needed the money that the rental would generate.

Kelly was heartless and called a local thrift shop, arranging to have everything picked up as donations. She gave me no other alternative. In my mind, I imagined that my house had burned to the ground, along with everything that was inside. This was the only way that I was able to accept losing almost everything that I owned.

Life took an upturn as one morning shortly after this I received a call from a young man answering the classified ad I had placed looking for a roommate. He was interested in renting the guest bedroom. I made an appointment with him for later that day. I excitedly told Kelly that he would be coming by in a few hours to see the room and meet us.

She was not in the least bit happy though since she didn't want a roommate. I reassured her that it would be fine and reminded her that she still didn't have a job and that we needed the money to get by. I was still receiving food stamps and insisted that Kelly apply for them as well. Thankfully, she was approved.

Peter, the young man who had phoned me earlier, called and told me that he couldn't find the property. I asked where he was and he told me that he was in front of the strip mall by the road. I told him we were just down the sloping driveway, to walk down the drive and that I would meet him outside.

He was a nice looking young fellow, with longish hair and dressed in Hippie fashion. He followed me down the narrow corridor and into the apartment. I showed him the kitchen, deck, living room and bathroom, and then I led him into the guest room. He asked if he would be the only occupant, and I told him of course he would be.

Peter already knew that I was charging $600.00 per month, along with a $400.00 refundable security and cleaning deposit. I had also created a legally binding lease agreement for him to sign. I was not about to allow what John did to me to happen again. Peter would have to give me a thirty day notice to vacate or he would forfeit his deposit.

He told me that he would take the room that very day. I gave him the lease agreement to look over and we both signed it. He paid the $1000.00 in cash and said that he needed to get to the college to sign up for his courses. It would be nice to have a fellow student as a roommate.

With Peter moved in I had a bit of stress lifted from me. Not only did the money he would be paying monthly help, but he also pitched in to buy groceries as well. I was so appreciative of this. Soon I would also be receiving my first stipend from school, which would boost our ability to live day to day.

A few days later I had my follow-up appointment with the doctor. I had asked Joanna if she could give me a ride to the clinic, but she was busy and not able to drive me, so I took the bus. The bus stop where I got off was about two miles from the clinic, and it was all I could do to walk there.

I arrived and checked in with the receptionist. She asked me to take a seat and told me that I would be called in shortly. Soon a nurse came through the doors that led to the exam rooms and called my name. I followed her back but she led me directly to the doctor's office instead of an exam room.

The doctor was seated at her desk and invited me to sit in the chair opposite her. My heart was racing. She opened my file and looked it over. She said "Your brain scan and mammogram both came back clear. No cerebral atrophy or suspicious masses in your breasts." I sighed with relief.

"But Susan," she continued, "you do have Hepatitis C." I almost fell off out of my chair. My heart raced and I could feel my blood pressure soar. She asked if I had ever used intravenous drugs. I could feel my face turning red with embarrassment and humiliation. I had told very few others about my time with Danielle.

I knew that she had injected me with meth, but what I was to learn after the fact is that she used her own filthy syringe to do so. I confided this in the doctor who looked at me with empathy. She said, "I am making you an appointment with a gastroenterologist who will oversee your treatment."

"You are going to have to do a course of chemotherapy in order to manage the Hepatitis C." She shuffled some papers on her desk and picked up her telephone. She made a call, and when she was finished I had an appointment with yet another doctor. This was not something that I had ever anticipated happening to me.

I walked the two miles back to the bus stop, despising myself more with every single step I took. When I got to the bus stop I decided to phone my younger brother who had become infected with Hepatitis C when he was tattooed. I thought that he might be able to give me support and advice.

I was relieved when he answered his phone. I told him what I had just learned, and he assured me that I was going to be fine, just follow the doctor's orders and take whatever medication that I was prescribed. He had undergone a year of chemo and survived it. The most difficult part was ahead of me, as I had to tell Kelly.

I got back to the apartment and saw that she was out on the deck. I made myself a cup of tea and went outside to join her. I took her hand in mine and looked her in the eyes. "I do not know how to tell you this, and I'm so sorry, but I have Hepatitis C." She pulled away from me and stood up.

"How could you do this to me???" She fairly screamed the words. I told her that I had not done anything to her, it was my body that was sick, and that she was welcome to leave at any time. I certainly didn't need this type of reaction, I needed support, but I also knew that I could manage alone.

She said that she was not going anywhere, that she was willing to support me, and that she was just shocked. She asked how it happened and I told her that I believed that Danielle had injected me with her dirty syringe. I told her about my upcoming appointment and that I was going to have to undergo chemotherapy.

Kelly said that she had taken Danielle to the same clinic many times for something to do with her liver, and that she was on some type of medication but she had not considered it to be Hepatitis C. That made her think about herself, because Danielle had used her syringe when she was injecting meth into Kelly's breasts.

I phoned my children to tell them of my new diagnosis, but also that I didn't have cerebral atrophy. They were relieved to hear that, but shocked to hear that I had Hepatitis C and worried about chemotherapy. I assured them that I should be fine, that millions of other people had undergone the same treatment successfully.

In good conscience I had to change my college courses. I didn't want to be responsible for infecting someone else with Hepatitis C, and as a nurse I would have been responsible for drawing patients' blood at times. My counselor thanked me for my honesty and helped me in making my decision to change my major to psychology.

I was already signed up for medical transcription, which I knew that I would be able to pass with ease. School would not begin for two more months, and I would be seeing the gastro doctor before then. I was hoping, with all of my heart, that the chemotherapy would not affect my performance at school.

I received my first stipend in mid-June, which covered two months' worth of rent, as well as paid for the utilities. With the food stamps that Kelly and I received I was also able to stock up on groceries for the household. My only issue was that I had to ride my bike to the store, shop, and ride back to the apartment alone.

When Kelly was sentenced for strangling me she was, in addition to probation and domestic violence classes, given eighty hours of community service, but for whatever reason she was not able to find a place to serve those hours while she was in Vacaville. I began calling local businesses and churches hoping to find one.

I finally found Santa Cruz Bible Church that was willing to give her five hours a day of community service for working on their landscaping. I set up a meeting for Kelly with the pastor of the church for the following day. She was able to impress him enough that he told her that she could begin the next week.

Kelly and I would take a bus to the church each weekday, and I would sit on one of the cement curbs, watching as she pulled weeds and mowed the lawns. Kelly was raised in a fundamental Christian home, and this church happened to be fundamental, so she decided that she wanted to start attending services there.

In order to keep the peace, I agreed to attend Sunday services with her. But this church was not Gay affirming. In fact, they were anti-Gay, and made no secret of how they believed. As a result of this we had to keep our relationship a secret, and Kelly told everyone that I was her mother, which was rather embarrassing for me.

As time went on we started to attend the Sunday and Wednesday evening services and became involved in their Friday night dinners for the homeless. We spent many hours every Friday afternoon helping to prepare and set up for the dinners, and I would often end up at one of the tables serving others.

I have to say that I enjoyed doing this, even though I didn't share their spiritual philosophy. I loved helping others, preparing the meals, caring for their wellbeing, and ensuring that they had at least one proper meal a week was one way of expressing this love. After serving Kelly and I were allowed to enjoy a meal ourselves.

Sundays, Wednesdays and Fridays were taken up by church activities, and I was happy to do this both for Kelly and the needy. There were even times that I went by myself on Fridays as Kelly often didn't want to go to help. Five days a week I accompanied her to the church so that she could fulfill her community service.

Summer was in full bloom, and I saw the gastroenterologist in July. He informed me that I would not begin the chemotherapy until the end of September and went on to assure me that I would be fine until then. He had his nurse make an appointment for me in August so that he could instruct me on how to self-inject the poisonous chemo.

That Summer I found that I needed to go to food pantries to supplement our resources. Going to food pantries was a first for me, and I would end up walking or taking the bus and carrying the heavy loads for miles back to the apartment. Kelly was too embarrassed to go, so I volunteered to do it myself.

But the Summer months were mostly lovely. I found that I was unable to garden as much as previously as I found myself tiring easily. But even so, I puttered around the yard, making sure there were no weeds, and I did what I could to maintain the beauty of the yard and spent as many hours in the gardens as possible.

Kelly didn't care for gardening, but we would go for longs, sometimes stopping for a cup of coffee or tea. A few times we biked down to Potbelly Beach, taking blankets, lunch and drinks with us. We would spend hours just gazing out upon the waters, little or no conversation between, simply enjoying our shared experience.

I had my second appointment with the gastroenterologist in mid-August. He took me into an exam room to show me how to self-inject the Interferon, which was one of the chemo drugs I would be taking. He told me that he would be sending me home with a packet of syringes, and starter packs of Interferon and Ribavirin.

The Interferon I was to inject subcutaneously once a week, and I was prescribed six Ribavirin every single day. The doctor had an empty syringe and an orange on a stainless steel cart. He said, "Now watch me." I watched as he picked up the syringe and orange, deftly slipping the needle just under the rind of the orange.

"Now you try it." I picked up the syringe with shaking hands and tried to slip the needle under the rind, just as the doctor had, but I broke the needle off the syringe. He laughed. "Look, it's easy. You are going to have to learn how to do this yourself. Take a deep breath and try again."

I picked up the orange and syringe, but this time I was successful. He patted me on the shoulder. "You'll be just fine. Now, your first injection is scheduled for September 29th. Lift your blouse and let me show you where the injection site should be." I lifted my blouse and he pinched the skin on my waistline on one side.

"This is where you'll inject. Each week you should change sides so that you don't become too bruised. You can take this box of Interferon, along with the Ribavirin, home with you now." He continued "I need to find someone to introduce you to." He left the room for a brief moment and returned with a social worker.

"This is Mary" he said. "She's going to help you apply for a program that will supply you with your Interferon and Ribavirin at no cost to you. Go with her, and I'll see you after your first treatment." I followed Mary out of the room. In her office, I filled out a few forms, but they already knew my financial situation.

She asked me to be patient while she made a phone call. She was on the phone for almost half an hour, but when she was finished she told me that I was all set, and that the Interferon and Ribavirin would be sent to me in the mail once a month for a year. Boy, I was not looking forward to it!

The end of August arrived and school began for me. I would either ride my bike or walk the mile to the college. I often took my lunch with me, but sometimes I could afford to eat in the cafeteria. I thoroughly enjoyed all of my classes and instructors, all but one of the classes was held during the day.

The night class was for my course in medical transcription. Sometimes I would feel strange walking the campus alone at night and finding my way home along Soquel Drive in the dark, with the hair standing up on my neck, but I never missed a class, nor was I ever late, and fortunately nothing ever actually happened to me.

The classrooms, as on any college campus, were located quite a distance away from each other, so I would find myself running from class to class along with the other students, all of whom were young enough to be my children, or even my grandchildren. But I had the tenacity to not give up on furthering my education.

I still accompanied Kelly when she went to her weekly domestic violence classes in Capitola, and monthly when she had to report to her probation officer in Watsonville. We would usually take the bus to Capitola, but sometimes we would ride our bikes. We always took the bus to Watsonville.

While Kelly was in her domestic violence classes I would wait for her at a Burger King that was adjacent to the building that her class was in. I always took a book with me to pass the time, and when she was finished, would sometimes have a snack, then we would ride our bikes or catch the bus home.

One night at Burger King, I met a young Hispanic man by the name of Francisco. He ran a small mercantile out of the back of his van. He would often join me at my table and regale me with stories of his life in Mexico, how he came to be in California, and what his plans for his life were.

He was a pleasant young fellow, and we shared many conversations. Often he would eat dinner while I read my book. He brought his wife and little son in to meet me one evening, and I treated them to dinner and sundaes for dessert and enjoyed their company as well. Surprisingly, Kelly was jealous of him, for no good reason.

During one of her domestic violence classes one evening, there was a guest speaker by the name of Jeannie. Kelly became friends with her and insisted that I meet her. Jeannie was bisexual, which piqued my interest, especially since Kelly seemed to be head over heels with her. Jeannie was a paralegal giving advice to the clients of the class.

One day shortly after Kelly mentioned Jeannie, she had me ride with her to Jeannie's house. She had invited the both of us to dinner. I liked her immediately. She was a charming and lovely woman and treated us to an absolutely delicious dinner of roast beef and root vegetables. We went outside after dinner to chat for a while.

Jeannie told us that she was moving to another place soon and asked if we could help her. Kelly immediately said yes, not bothering to ask if I was willing to help. That was often the case with Kelly, disregarding how others, especially myself, might have felt. Looking at Kelly I said "Jeannie, I would love to help in any way that I am able."

And so it was that the following weekend we helped Jeannie to pack her belongings and clean the house that she was moving from. Kelly drove the moving truck to her new apartment, and we all carried boxes up the stairs to the new apartment. Jeannie ordered pizza as a way of thanking us for our help.

It was a lovely apartment, which had a beautiful view of the Pacific Ocean and the Santa Cruz boardwalk. I told her that she was lucky to have found such a wonderful place to live, and she replied that her married lover, who was an attorney at the firm where she worked, had found it for her.

We had pizza along with some soft drinks, and some enjoyable conversation. Before we left Jeannie invited us to join her for drinks in Santa Cruz the following Saturday. I was the first to speak up and told her that it sounded wonderful, even though it meant riding our bikes over five miles to the downtown area.

We had to return the moving truck still, and ride our bikes back to our apartment, so we told Jeannie goodbye for then. Kelly drove the truck to the lot in Capitola, and she pulled our bikes out of the back of it. It was dark by the time we were finished returning it, and the bike ride to our apartment was challenging, but we made it safely.

I had already completed my third week of school. I was excelling in all of my courses. Often it was a challenge as I didn't have a printer, so I had to email many of my papers to myself, go to the college library, log onto a computer, download the papers and print them there. But I always pulled through.

Saturday came, so Kelly and I got ready to meet with Jeannie in town. It was a lovely, warm late Summer day, so I dressed in parachute cargo pants, a tank top and tennis shoes. I didn't own a helmet, although in retrospect I know that I probably should have. The bike ride into town was easy since it was mostly downhill.

The bike lane was situated along Soquel Drive for most of the way into Santa Cruz, with cars zooming by us so close that we could feel the wind from them, which added to the sense of exhilaration. We neared downtown and had to ride through San Lorenzo park to get to our destination.

Kelly was ahead of me and yelled for me to change gears on my bike. I yelled back that I was doing fine. She circled back and got beside me, reaching out and grabbing my handlebars, trying to change the gear, and I lost control of my bike. I fell to the asphalt, landing under the bike.

The speed at which I had been traveling had enough momentum to drag me with it for several yards. I landed on my side and back and skidded along the asphalt. I could feel the burn of the skid on my flesh. When the bike finally stopped I tried to get up but I was trapped underneath it. Instead of trying to help me Kelly rode ahead.

There happened to be a worker in the park who saw the accident. He ran to where I was, picked the bike up off of me, and helped me to his truck. My pants were torn, and I was bleeding from my knee and back.   I warned him not to touch me, that I had Hepatitis C, and he said, "I do not give a damn what you have, I'm going to help you."

So, he got his first aid kit out from behind the seat of his truck and began doctoring me. Kelly stood in the distance watching. Not once did she come to see if I was okay. The man finished his ministrations, and I thanked him for helping me. I went to my bike, checked it for damages, then rode to where Kelly was.

I was hurting, and I am certain that I looked like hell, but I followed after her anyway. There was a footbridge ahead of us with people on it, so we walked our bikes across it and found our way into the downtown area, locating the bar where we were to meet with Jeannie. She was waiting for us on the sidewalk outside of the bar.

She took one look at me and lead me inside, not even saying hello to Kelly. She asked me if I wanted a drink, and I told her no alcohol, but that I would love to have a glass of water. We stood at a counter by the wall, as there were no tables available to seat at. Kelly joined us and ordered an alcoholic drink.

The server brought our beverages and I downed mine in literally one gulp. I reached into my fanny pack for my cigarettes, but they were not there. I figured that they must have fallen out when my bike crashed. I told them both that I was going to walk to the nearest store to buy a pack.

Jeannie was worried that I might have a concussion, but I assured her that I had not hit my head, it was just my knee, back and shoulders that were injured. I walked to the corner where I found a convenience store. I went inside, walked up to the counter and asked for a pack of menthols.

A girl who was standing behind me saw my back and asked if I was okay, and I replied "Yes, just watch out for a woman named Kelly. She is nothing but trouble." I winked at her and laughed, but I was mostly serious. I mean, what was wrong with Kelly doing that in the park? I had been riding along fine without her help.

I paid for my purchase, went outside and lit a cigarette. I could see that Jeannie was standing outside watching my return. I walked slowly towards her, not really wishing to go back into the bar. I was irritated with Kelly for what she had done. We both went back inside where Kelly was having another drink.

Jeannie mentioned that she felt unattractive, and wondered if anyone would ever want to be with her. Kelly spoke up and said, "I think you are attractive and I would fuck you if I had the chance." I was mortified and Jeannie appeared to be shocked.

Jeannie quickly changed the subject, saying that she needed to return to her place and get ready for a dinner engagement with the man that she was having an affair with from her law firm. She asked me if I wanted to rest at her apartment for a while, and when she got back from her dinner she would drive me home.

I did need to rest, so I said that would be fine. Hepatitis C had weakened me and falling off of my bike only added to that weakness. Kelly put my bike in the trunk of Jeannie's car, but hers would not fit, so she said that she would follow behind us. Jeannie helped me into her car she drove to her place.

Kelly did not keep up with us and was far behind us at that point. Jeannie parked and helped me up the stairs to her apartment. She suggested that I lie down on the couch. She brought me a glass of water and a pain pill. I was not sure if I should take it, especially with Hepatitis C, but I swallowed the pill anyway.

I vaguely heard Kelly come through the front door. I heard Jeannie tell her that she be leaving soon and asked that we wait for her. I could tell by the tone in her voice that Kelly was really was irritated with me, but I paid no mind as I suddenly became very sleepy from the pain pill, so I allowed myself to doze off.

I could vaguely hear the television that Kelly was watching while I slumbered. But the pain pill soon wore off and I sat up on the couch, sore and stiff. I asked Kelly how long I had been asleep. "Probably around two hours" she said. I asked her why she had said that about Jeannie, and she replied that she would have sex with her if she could.

I suddenly became angry, and said that I just wanted to go home, that I didn't want to be there anymore. Kelly said that we had to wait for Jeannie to return. I got up off the couch, got my backpack and looked for my cellphone. Kelly told me to go sit back down, but I wanted to call a taxi to come pick me up.

I put my backpack on and began to dial the number on my phone when Kelly grabbed me, ripping my backpack off of my back and slamming me against a wall. She told me that I was not going anywhere and to just sit back down. And here I had thought that her violence was in the past.

I sat down, waiting for an opportunity to run out the door. I didn't know where, but I needed to get away. I went into the bathroom and looked in the mirror. My left eye was blackened, my jaw felt like it was dislocated and I had bruises up and down my arms. I returned to the living room, sat down on the couch, and waited for a chance to leave.

Kelly continued to watch television, all the while keeping an eye on me. I waited, watching her the entire time, in fear of further violence. Finally, Kelly got up to use the toilet. She told me to stay where I was if I knew what was good for me. She left the room, I got up, grabbed my backpack and ran out the front door.

I didn't have a lot of strength, but I managed to get down the stairs and away from Jeannie's. I walked as quickly as I could down the sidewalk, all the while listening for Kelly. I got to the end of the street, called a taxi and waited. I could see Kelly in front of Jeannie's apartment looking for me, but it was too dark for her to see me.

The taxi arrived and took me to my apartment. I went inside, locking the door behind me. Peter was on the couch watching television. He saw my torn slacks and blackeye and asked me what had happened. I told him about the bike accident and then I let him know that I had run away from Kelly, who I was sure was not far behind.

He followed me into the bathroom and looked at my back. He said it looked bad, scratched deeply and still oozing blood. He dabbed at it with a warm washcloth, but that hurt, so I asked him to stop. I got my towels and pajamas and went into the bathroom to take a shower. The water from the shower hit my back and I let out a scream.

Peter asked if I were okay and I told him that I was fine, and that I would be out in a few minutes. I finished, got dressed and went into the living room. Kelly was there, both of her hands on her waist, as was her custom. She had an angry look on her face. I told her to just let me be, that I needed to rest.

She gave up and sat down next to Peter to watch television. I awoke the next morning stiff and sore. I needed to feel better since the following day was Monday and I would be returning to school. Kelly was still asleep, so I quietly got out of bed and went into the bathroom.

After washing up I started a pot of coffee and went out onto the deck to wait for it to brew. My body hurt, and I was not looking forward to the coming Friday, November 29th, as that would be the day of my first Interferon injection along with six doses of Ribavirin. I already knew that both of them were going to make me extremely sick.

I wondered how I was going to manage going to school and continue to be successful in my classes. I went back inside and poured a cup of steaming hot coffee and returned to the deck. There was nothing that I could do about it anyway. Life was going to happen regardless of what I thought or my how many fears that I might have.

The following week passed quickly and Friday was upon me before I knew it. I took the box of Interferon out of the refrigerator and went into the bathroom with it and a syringe. The doctor had shown me how to pull the sterile water out of one vial with the syringe and fill the other one that contained powdered Interferon.

I asked Kelly to stand by me for support, but she refused, saying that it was a trigger. I sucked the mixture into the syringe and pulled my pajama top up. Pinching what little fat I had with two fingers I inserted the syringe just under the flesh. It burned going in, and I could feel the poison as it coursed through my body.

I managed to get through my day of school but could feel my body flagging. I only had that day of classes left, and then I could rest and recover over the weekend. I had walked to school, as riding my bike was the last thing that I wanted to do. The weekend came and with it much needed rest.

But before I could do that I had to get the laundry washed, dried and folded. From day one, I had been responsible for all of the cleaning, shopping, cooking, laundry and any other chores that had to be done.

I spent most of the day afterwards lying down in bed. Peter had offered to prepare dinner, for which I was grateful.

The Interferon was still affecting my body, and I took six doses of Ribavirin every day, which was also having an adverse effect. We had rice and pinto beans for dinner, with shredded cheese and sour cream. Quite a simple meal, but I ate every single bite. Kelly complained about the food, saying that she didn't care for beans at all.

On Sunday, October 2nd, Kelly and I set out for her weekly domestic violence class. We took the bus as far as we could, then walked the mile and a half to the building where the building in Capitola where her class was held. I walked over to Burger King to sit and wait. I ordered a coffee and sat down in my regular booth.

I had brought schoolwork with me, "Kitchen Confidential", by Anthony Bourdain, which my instructor in literature class had assigned the class to read and draft a report on, and a notebook to begin drafting the report in. I was enjoying a cup of coffee when I saw Francisco walk in.

He sat down at my booth across from me and we talked for a while. He asked what I was reading and I showed him, but since his English was not particularly good he couldn't he read the words, and I didn't think that he knew who the author was. He stood up and told me that he would be right back.

I sipped on my coffee and read. When he returned he had a chocolate sundae in his hand. He said, "This is for you." I thanked him and took it from him. He told me that he had customers outside by his van waiting for him and we said goodbye. I ate the sundae and read more of my book.

I would not be able to draft my book report just yet, as I was not finished reading the book. I watched out of the window for Kelly as it was getting near the time that her class was finished. I saw her walking down the stairs with a woman by the name of Leela, whom Kelly had said was a meth addict.

I finished my sundae and coffee, put the containers in the trash, and walked outside to meet Kelly. Leela said hello to me and I simply nodded my head. I told Kelly that it was getting late, and that we had best be heading to the bus stop so that we would not be late for our bus.

We had walked about half a mile when suddenly I felt as if my abdomen had been cut in half. I was bent over in agony and told Kelly that I was not able to walk any further. She just stood there looking at me, tapping her foot. "Come on woman, we'll miss our bus!" She didn't even wait for me, she simply started walking.

I couldn't understand what was happening to my body. The pain was excruciating, but somehow I managed to walk the rest of the way to the bus stop. I sat down on a bench to try and catch my breath. The pain was growing in intensity. Kelly didn't try to comfort me. Instead, she became impatient.

The bus finally came. We got on and rode the four miles to a bus stop close to the apartment. Due to the pain, it took me a moment to get down the steps of the bus. Kelly was already walking to the apartment and was inside by the time I got there. I went into the bedroom and lay down on the bed, groaning in agony.

Kelly came in to look at me, and I asked her to get the thermometer because I was beginning to feel very warm. She took my temperature, which was 102 degrees. I asked her for water and aspirin, then pled with her to call the hospital and speak with a triage nurse. She hesitated, but finally phoned the emergency room.

The nurse asked her to bring me in, but Kelly told her that we didn't have a car. She then instructed Kelly to either call an ambulance or to put me in a tepid shower to bring my temperature down. Kelly unceremoniously dragged me into the bathroom and put me in the shower with my clothes on.

The water was freezing cold, not tepid, and I began to shiver uncontrollably. She left me there alone. I had not even one ounce of strength. Whatever was wrong with me, and I blamed Interferon, was debilitating my body. Somehow I managed to get out of the shower, go to the bedroom, dry off and put on my pajamas.

I had taken three aspirins, so I felt that would help with the fever. I do not even know where Kelly was, but I spent the night in delirious dreams, nightmares, running from shadows that I couldn't even see. The next morning, I woke up with a vague aura surrounding me. I was burning up and my body was in severe pain.

Somehow I managed to make it through the day. Kelly would pop in and out of the room just to look at me. I do not remember her bringing more aspirin or fresh water, or even taking my temperature again. I realized that I had missed school, and that upset me more than being sick.

I made my way from the bedroom to the couch and lay there trying to watch television, which in my state of feverish disorientation made absolutely no sense whatsoever. I heard Peter come through the front door. He saw me and asked Kelly what was wrong. She told him that she didn't know, but that I would be fine.

He walked over and felt my forehead, which must have been scorching, because the next thing I knew I was being carried to his brothers truck and taken to Dominican hospital. I don't even remember the ride to the hospital. I do remember having my temperature taken, which was 104 degrees.

When my blood pressure taken, which was 53/38, three nurses, each with a blood pressure cuff, checked and rechecked my blood pressure. The next thing I knew I was on a cold, stainless steel table. Two nurses were working on me. One was trying to insert an IV, and the other one was attempting to place a catheter in my bladder.

Neither one was successful. I know that I lost consciousness again, only to come to awareness long enough to realize that I was in a surgical suite having an IV port inserted into the artery just above my heart. I vaguely remember the doctor making the incision to insert the line.

I lost consciousness again, and when I woke up I was in an ICU room surrounded by machinery. A Black male nurse was attending me, and I remember him telling me to just lie still, that I would be fine. He assured me that he was giving me the absolute best of care. But I couldn't have moved if I tried.

I very dimly remember David and daughter-in-law Rachel coming to visit me. I heard my nurse tell them that I was not permitted to have flowers in the ICU, and to take them out of the room, that I couldn't have them. He suggested leaving them at the nurse's station.

I had two heart attacks while in the ICU. I was diagnosed with E coli Sepsis, which I discovered after the fact has a mortality rate of 30% if caught in time, and almost certain death if it is left to incubate for more than three days. Thanks to Peter's quick actions my life was saved.

But even so, I was given a 20-70% chance of dying within two years of recovery. I spent five days in the ICU, then moved to the Cardiology floor, where I spent another four days. I didn't see Kelly the entire time that I was in the ICU, but she came to visit me the first afternoon that I was on the Cardiology floor.

I woke up to her sitting in a chair beside the bed that I was in. She was just staring at me. I tried to sit up in bed but I didn't have the strength. She asked how I was feeling and I told her that I was very weak. I had not had food since I had eaten that sundae, which is what I was beginning to suspect had made me so sick.

She looked at me and said, "When you get out of here we are breaking up." Just like that. I didn't say a word. All that I could do was look at her. She stayed a few more minutes then left without saying goodbye. The head Cardiologist came into the room a few minutes after she left. He was there to get family history.

I told him that my father had two heart attacks and a stroke. His heart issues had been managed with Procardia and Nitroglycerin tablets. The doctor said that the heart attacks I had experienced were as a result of the E coli Sepsis, and that I should be able to manage myself by taking baby aspirin every day.

He told me that there was a possibility that I could develop kidney failure in the future and have a need for dialysis. This worried me, but I didn't dwell on it, as with so many of the other that life had brought to me. He left some literature on caring for the heart and told me to make a follow-up appointment with his office.

I spent the rest of the afternoon and evening thinking about Kelly and what she had said. I didn't understand why she would break up with me. Being in the hospital was not my fault. But I would come to learn there were other reasons. Of course, her words broke my heart, but it was not the first time.

The next morning, I asked a nurse to help me find the number for the fast food restaurant, as well as the Santa Cruz County Health Department. I knew that it must have been the sundae that had made me so ill, and I wanted to ask for an investigation to find out if others had become ill as well.

The fast food restaurant manager refused to talk to me, but the agent at the health department took all of my information and told me that they would follow up by inspecting the kitchen of the restaurant, and that they would contact me soon. I hoped that no one else had been affected by the tainted sundae mixture.

Considering the fact that I never received a bill for the nine days that I was in the hospital led me to believe that the health department did indeed discover something, and that the fast food restaurant paid my entire bill. I am sure that this was to avoid a hefty lawsuit. I never did hear from the health department.

I didn't worry about it though, as I had other things on my mind that were more important. On October 13th, nine days after being hospitalized, I was discharged to go home. I had phoned Joanne a couple of days before and she agreed to pick me up. A nurse helped me into a wheelchair and took me to the front doors.

I walked out of the hospital slowly, still weakened by the illness I had been almost overcome by. I sat on a stone ledge by one of the gardens and waited. Soon I saw Joanne's car pulling into the circular drive. I was incredibly surprised to see Kelly was with her. I had intense uncertain feelings seeing her.

Joanne got out of her car and helped me walk. It was going to take some time for me to regain what strength that I had before this happened. I had Joanna stop at a convenience store for cigarettes. I knew that I probably didn't have any at home and I definitely wanted to make sure that I had a least a pack.

It had been almost two weeks since I had last smoked, and I had thought while I was in the hospital that I might quit, but that was not the case. We arrived home and Kelly helped me into the apartment. Surprisingly, it was clean, every single room. I went directly into the bedroom and lay down.

Just that little bit of movement, walking to and from the car and into the apartment, had taken every ounce of energy from me. Kelly brought me a glass of iced tea along with an ashtray and my cigarettes. I sat up in the bed with my pillows behind me and took a sip of tea.

She sat on the edge of the bed and told me that she needed to talk to me about a few things. I braced myself for the worst, but it really was not what I thought. "I didn't mean anything that I said in the hospital. I have been smoking meth with Leela, and I am so sorry." She had tears in her eyes.

I had already suspected that she was using meth again. In fact, a couple of weeks before I became ill I confronted Leela in the parking lot of the domestic violence class building. I told her that I knew that she was a meth addict and extracted a promise from her to stay away from Kelly, a promise that she obviously didn't honor.

But so much for promises, though I certainly didn't blame the entirety on Leela. Kelly was responsible for her own actions. I couldn't force Kelly to not smoke or inject meth, but I could let her know how adamantly against it I was. I was finished extracting promises from her that I knew would be broken.

Peter had disappeared while I was in the hospital. He had not paid his rent and he left all of his belongings behind. I contacted his brother, who had no idea where he was, and then his parents, who came the next day to talk to me and collect his things. I told them that since he had not given a thirty day notice that he had forfeited his deposit.

I went on to tell them that he still owed for the month of October. I showed them the signed lease agreement, and they paid the $600.00 for the month, but they were not happy that they had to pay it. I couldn't understand why he had left in such a hurry, and I never heard from Peter again.

I had missed too much college to try to go back, so I was forced to officially withdraw. I was then held responsible for paying back the stipends I had received, in full, with no income whatsoever. I didn't know what I was going to do. Over the course of the next week and a half I began to recover from the E coli sepsis.

I had lost a significant amount of weight during the sickness, leaving me at close to 105 pounds. I was still a bit weak, but my strength was returning, slowly but surely, and I was able to accompany Kelly to the grocery store, her classes and her monthly probation meeting. I knew that eventually I would regain my health again.

On October 25th, my daughter Stephanie's twenty-eighth birthday, I received a phone call from my daughter-in-law Rachel, informing me that a property close to her in Campbell was searching for an onsite resident manager. I told her that there was truly little chance that I would be hired but asked her for the contact information anyway.

I took a deep breath and dialed the phone number. A woman by the name of Laurie answered. I asked if she was looking for a resident manager and she excitedly said yes. She explained to me that her last resident manager had died a few months before from breast cancer, and they needed a replacement as soon as possible.

Her father, John, owned the property, and she had been filling in as manager. I let her know that I had years of property management experience, and that I would gladly be able to provide a letter of recommendation. She asked when I could come for an interview and I asked when she would like to meet with me.

She replied that she would like to meet with me the next day if at all possible, and that it would be greatly appreciated. I replied that I would phone her back within the hour to let her know if I would be able to make it to the interview. When I hung up the phone I nearly jumped with joy.

This was the first real interview that I had been offered in almost two years. I phoned David and asked if he could pick me up that evening and take me to the interview. He said absolutely! I phoned Lauren back and told her that I would be more than happy to meet with her, and we agreed on ten a.m. the next morning for the interview.

After hanging up I told Kelly the good news, but she was hesitant about moving to Campbell. She immediately began arguing with me, telling me that this was not a suitable choice, and that I shouldn't go to the interview. I didn't listen to her. I was determined to forge my own path, and being given this opportunity would help me do that.

In my heart of hearts, I really didn't want to take Kelly with me, but I would end up doing so, against my better judgement. Again, remember one of the definitions of insanity. Hoping for a different outcome as you do the same thing over and over again. And that was what I was doing with Kelly.

It seemed that the Universe was taking me through lessons that I thought I would never have to learn, but that it must have felt that I truly needed them in order to grow. The following year in Campbell would bring that home to me in the most chaotic and heartbreaking of ways.

Chapter Four: Campbell, California

I gave Kelly a hug and assured her that this was the opportunity of a lifetime for us. I went into the bedroom and packed my suitcase. I was so glad that I had purchased a very professional black two piece pant suit right after graduating rehab that would fit me absolutely fine. I had to think who I could approach for a letter of recommendation.

My former employer would not be a good choice, but one of my friends, Michael, still worked there, and even though I had not seen him for several years I decided to send him an email. He replied soon after I sent the email, and attached to the email was a generous letter endorsing my qualifications as an onsite resident property manager.

I wished that he had been near me so that I could give him a big hug. David arrived shortly after six that evening. He carried my suitcase to his car and we drove to his apartment in Campbell. He was still an onsite manager for the company that I had been terminated from a few weeks after my botched suicide attempt.

We all had a wonderful time visiting, and I was able to rest on the couch for the night. The next morning, I awoke with renewed hope in life. I got up, had some coffee and a cigarette, and then got myself ready for the interview. David drove me to the property and told me to call him when I needed to be picked up.

It was a good sized property, one hundred and fifty-five units. It had beautiful and well maintained landscaping and was located in a wonderful neighborhood. I located the office and walked inside. There were two desks, one at which a woman was seated. I introduced myself and she told me that she was Laurie.

She led me to an area by a fireplace with a couch and two chairs. I had printed both my resume and the letter of recommendation from Michael. I handed them to her and waited while she looked them over. She said "This looks great. I want to show you the property. So, we left the office and she gave me a tour.

As we walked she began asking me questions. I was able to answer every one of them quite effectively. I really did know about property management, and caring for the residents was my primary concern. It took about half an hour to walk to the property, after which time we returned to the office.

Laurie told me that if it were up to her that she would hire me on the spot, but she said that her father would like to meet me first, and asked if I could return at the same time the next day. I said that I would be more than happy to come back. I shook her hand and left the office.

It was all I could do to keep from kicking my heels together and shouting aloud. I phoned David and told him that I was ready to be picked up, and asked if I could stay another night, letting him know that I had an interview with the owner the following day. He was excited and told me that he could pick me up within the hour.

This was the first job opportunity that I had received since being terminated shortly after my botched suicide attempt. If I were offered this position I promised myself that I would not allow it to be compromised. I phoned Kelly, letting her know that I would be staying another night, and that the interview had gone really well.

I told her that I was scheduled to meet with the owner the following morning. She sighed and said that she didn't want to move from Santa Cruz, that she liked it there, and moving only meant that she would have to request transfers for her probation and domestic violence classes and it was all too much of a hassle.

I listened to her, then said "Kelly, if you want to stay, stay. It is fine with me. Should I be offered this job I will take it and move here by myself. Maybe you could ask Lila if you could be her roommate." I knew that it was a snide remark, but I was not going to allow Kelly to deter me this time.

The next morning, I met with the owner. He was an elderly gentleman by the name of John, probably the same age my own father would have been, and a seemingly nice fellow. We talked for about an hour, and when we were finished he offered me the job. My heart was racing, but I managed to keep myself under control.

He said "I am willing to offer you $3500.00 per month, a two bedroom, two bath apartment, all utilities, cable and internet paid, as well as complete coverage health insurance. Does that sound fair to you?" He smiled and waited. I thought to myself "Fair?" Oh, my goodness, this was a dream come true.

I remained calm and told him that was more than fair, and I asked him when he would like me to start the position. "We want you to start on November 1st. Now, you need to choose an apartment. Laurie will show them to you." He stood up, shook my hand, and left the office to walk the property.

There were two apartments available. An upstairs unit and a downstairs unit. I immediately chose the downstairs unit. Not only had the previous manager lived there, but I also did not want to be a disturbance to those who lived below me. I could, however, live with people walking above me.

When Laurie and I returned to the office her dad was sitting in front of the fireplace. He stood up and handed me an envelope. "Here is a little something to help you with moving, plus a sign on bonus", he said with a smile. I opened the envelope to see a check for $2000.00. I was speechless but managed to remain calm.

I shook his hand, thanked him, and asked when I could start moving in and he replied that the upcoming weekend would be fine, if that worked for me. I told him absolutely. Laurie gave me the key to the apartment. I thanked them both and went outside to phone David. I was both elated and relieved.

I was going to be able to pay back the stipends, pay the fine for the DUI which had been ordered by the judge, and enroll in DUI classes. I would also be able to start paying down my credit cards. Life was beginning to become bright once again. I was hired two years and a day after I was terminated from my last job.

I took this as an omen filled with blessings. I phoned David and told him the good news. He picked me up shortly thereafter, and then drove me back to Aptos when he got off of work. While I waited for David I phoned Kelly to let her know that I had been hired. She sighed, and once again insisted that she didn't want to move.

I told her about the sign on bonus, my new monthly income, the two bedroom apartment, and all of the benefits. I was overjoyed. But she only tried to bring me down. Her reaction to my fantastic news was less than enthusiastic. When I mentioned that we could move in over the upcoming weekend she told me that would be impossible.

I informed her that we would talk more when I got home that evening. I took the time to phone Lewis, the manager of the property for my apartment in Aptos and told him that I would be moving that weekend, and I would be paying him any money that I might owe for the rental. He thanked me and told me that would be fine.

On my way home I asked David to stop at my bank so that I could deposit the two thousand dollar check, and a Home Depot so that I could purchase moving boxes and tape for packing. My mind was racing, and I was determined to get packed and moved into the new apartment before November 1st.

But plans do not always play out the way we want them to. I arrived at the apartment to an unhappy and depressed Kelly. She was obstinate over the move and I knew that I would not be able to set up the new apartment that weekend. I ended up packing all that I could before Monday by myself.

Sunday came, and David drove to Aptos to pick me up. I had decided to stay with him for the first week, then return to Aptos to pack the rest of my belongings the following weekend. Kelly had disappeared, and I had no idea where she had gone, so I left without saying goodbye to her.

My first week of work went by quickly. I had to learn a new rental payment program, which was easy enough. There were a couple of move-ins, one move-out, and loads of potential new residents to tour and discuss renting on my new property. Current residents came in to meet me, and I was incredibly pleased to meet them.

Laurie was only there on Monday to ease me into the job. I didn't see her again until Friday, which would prove to be the only day of the week that she set foot on the property. She knew that she could trust me, and that the property would be more than well cared for with while I managed it.

I spoke to Kelly during the week and she told me that she was working on packing the apartment, and that she had Lila with her. This upset me. I had an extraordinarily strong suspicion that they had been using meth. On Saturday I rode with David and Landon to Aptos to pick up my belongings, and hopefully Kelly's as well.

I rented a moving truck and David drove it to the apartment. I was shocked when I opened the door. Everything was disorganized and in disarray. Kelly was sitting on the couch and Lila was on the loveseat. I took one look at Lila and asked her to leave. I looked at Kelly and asked what had happened and she said they had tried their best.

What I was sure of is that they tried their best to stay high. I began putting boxes together and packing the kitchen. When I was finished with that I began in the bathroom, then the guest room and my bedroom. As I packed, David and Landon loaded the truck. It was pouring rain, so that made it particularly difficult.

Together they moved all of the heavy furniture into the moving truck, and while they were doing that I went into the back yard to get as many of my garden statues as possible. I had a wishing well and a bench set with planters that Kelly's parents had given me and I wanted those for the garden patio at the new apartment.

All the while Kelly stood and watched. She kept telling me that she didn't want to move. Finally, I said "Kelly, please just stay here. I know that you can move in with your friend Lila. I am certain that the two of you would make perfect roommates." She looked at me with her mouth agape.

She insisted that I was not understanding her, that it was about her probation and domestic violence classes. But I knew otherwise. I had an extremely unsettling feeling about her coming with me, almost a sense of dread and doom. In the end, she relented. Finally, everything was packed in the moving truck and we headed for Campbell.

I rode with David in his car while Kelly rode with Landon. It was pouring rain as we drove to Campbell, and I hoped that we would be able to get everything moved in with minimal damage. The drive down the hill was over almost as soon as it started, and we were at the new apartment before I knew it.

During the drive David expressed his worry over Kelly coming with me. I agreed with him, telling him that I had a sense of foreboding. We arrived, and in less than two hours everything was in the apartment. Kudos was in a pet carrier, and we put him in one of the bathrooms while we got everything inside.

David and Landon were so organized that they placed all of the right furniture and boxes in the corresponding rooms, leaving only the kitchen and living room items in the dining area to unpack. I didn't have a dining room table any longer, so I planned to purchase one with my first paycheck.

They set up the beds in the appropriate bedrooms, along with my beautiful nightstands in the master bedroom and my computer desk in the guest bedroom. Yes, when I say 'my' I mean that everything was either mine when I met Kelly or I had purchased it with my own money.

I asked David if he could drive me to the grocery store so that I could stock the kitchen. I had thrown all of the food away at the old apartment as it didn't make sense to bring it with me. We followed Landon, who drove the moving truck, and returned it, then dropped him off at his home afterwards.

After I paid for the moving truck I still had plenty of money left to buy groceries and to get us through until my first paycheck. I filled a grocery cart with meat, fresh fruit and vegetables, and an assortment of dried goods, breads and snacks. I made sure to stock up on laundry supplies, as well as toiletries and bathroom items.

I even made sure to buy Kelly's special toiletries that she had always insisted on having for herself. I purchased a supply of kitty litter for Kudos, who I was sure was getting acquainted with his new home. David helped me into the apartment with the groceries, then left to go home for the rest of the day.

I gave him a hug and kiss and thanked him for all of his help over the past few weeks. Having no transportation of my own, and without anyone that I could truly rely upon, I knew that I could never have possibly accomplished all of it without him. He was my hero in so very many ways.

I was entirely thrilled to be here, even though Kelly remained recalcitrant. In fact, she planted herself on the couch, holding Kudos, and refused to help me unpack. I busied myself in the kitchen first. There was so much more space in this kitchen than the old apartment had, and plenty of cupboards and cabinets to store items.

I unpacked the coffee maker and put a pot of coffee on to brew while I put away the groceries and organized all of the other kitchen items. I was pleased with the results. When I was finished with the kitchen I went into the master bedroom and made the bed and put away our clothing.

I then went into the master bathroom and began organizing it. There was only a toilet and shower stall in this bathroom, so I planned to use the hall bath, which was larger, for my showers. I put Kudo's kitty litter box in the master bathroom. There was a large vanity that was separate from the bathroom, and it was large and accommodating.

I took a break and poured myself a cup of coffee, offering some to Kelly, but she declined. I went out onto the garden patio which was already set up with the benches and the wishing well, allowing myself a few minutes to relax. I had taken my fourth dose of Interferon the day before and it was sapping much of my strength away from me.

Both the Interferon and Ribavirin were powerful chemo drugs, and they tended to take my breath away, so to speak. Nevertheless, I wanted to get as much done as possible, as the next day was Sunday and all I really wanted to do was rest up before the start of my second week on the new property.

I really wished that Kelly would help, but instead she spent her time pouting. Next came the guest bedroom, which was pretty much sorted out. All that I needed to do in there was make the bed and lay a rug beside it. The hall bath was easy to set up. There were sliding glass doors, and I planned to purchase a nice swag curtain for it.

Kelly finally got up off of the couch and began setting up the entertainment center. Apparently she needed to have the television and stereo up and running so that she could spend her time watching TV and listening to music. Other than that, she had done absolutely nothing.

David had placed my bookshelves next to the patio door in the dining room, so I pulled the boxes of books that Kelly had allowed me to keep over to it and unpacked them. When that was finished I went into the kitchen to start some dinner. I made a nice pasta dinner complete with salad and garlic bread.

Kelly and I sat in the living room together on the couch and watched television while we ate. I wished that she were more grateful, and that she understood what a great blessing this was, but she was the way she was, and I couldn't change her, nor would I try. After dinner I cleaned the kitchen, took a shower and got ready for bed.

There were only a few boxes left to be unpacked, so the next day I would finish those and complete all of the organizing, then try to rest. I wanted to be bright eyed and bushy tailed for my second week of work. I planned to give my all to this job, to the property, and prove myself to John and his daughter Laurie.

I promised myself that I would attend to the residents needs as if they were my own need. I drifted off to sleep alone, with Kelly in the living room still watching television. I wondered what the future was going to hold for us, but I had a feeling that things might not go the way I wanted them to.

A Place To Call Home

My days at work were good, and certainly not strenuous, which I was grateful for. Not much changed day to day, just the usual property manager responsibilities, which was attending to my residents, creating work orders, taking phone calls and making appointments for tours.

I was truly fortunate in being provided with an excellent insurance plan provided by the company, so I felt free to make an appointment with a Gastro doctor at the closest Kaiser Permanente location, which was in Sunnyvale. I knew that I needed to have my Hepatitis C monitored. My appointment was for Friday, November 12th.

A few days before the appointment I went in for a blood draw to assess where my levels were. Laurie came in to cover for me the day of my appointment, and David drove me to Kaiser. He waited in the lobby for me while I was being seen. The doctor gave me a thumbs up when she came in and told me that my liver levels were excellent.

She was concerned with my weight, as well as my iron levels. She told me to eat a couple of rare hamburgers or steaks at least once a week. I talked to her about not having a vehicle and told her that it would be rather difficult for me to get to my appointments. She told me that it was not protocol, but that she could do phone appointments.

She extracted the promise from me that I would continue to have weekly blood draws at the clinic, up my intake of rare beef, and continue my regimen of Interferon weekly and Ribavirin daily. She told me that she would have her nurse book the phone appointments for me but asked that I try to come in at least once every few months.

During my first week on the job, I had asked John for a new printer for the office. The one that they had been using was antiquated and barely worked, and I wanted to be able to make monthly fliers for the community. During my third week in the office, he came in with a big smile on his face. He had purchased the new printer.

I sat at my desk while he installed it on a cart behind me. I busied myself with a new move-in file and some repair requests while he worked. Everything about the office was rather archaic. The only things that were put into the computer were the rental checks. Repair requests were written on four inch by six inch pieces of paper.

There was no way to track how many times a particular unit had the same repair problems, or even which unit had had repairs done. I kept all of the repair requests that I issued from the day that I started clipped together and hanging on a wall by the filing cabinets. It was a MacGyver move,

365

but it would have to do.

I turned around and saw that John was finished installing the new printer, so I sat down at the computer behind me to install the printer driver on it. It only took me a few minutes, and he watched me the entire time. When I sat back down at my desk he walked towards me.

He looked down at me with a creepy smile on his lips, then he put his decrepit old hand on one of my knees and began squeezing and rubbing it provocatively. He was so close to me that I could smell his fetid breath. I shrunk away from him, appalled. I asked him to please stop immediately.

I informed him that I was a lesbian, and I didn't appreciate his advances. The look on his face was one of complete revulsion. He took the empty printer box and left the office, slamming the door behind himself. I knew at once, only three weeks into my new job, that my employer loathed me and that I had made a dreadful enemy.

My heart sank, and I wondered if this had been his regular behavior with the previous manager. For the remainder of the days that I worked there, as I walked to the office in the mornings, I felt as if I were going to my own execution, and I feared his phone calls and visits to the office.

I never told Kelly or Laurie, nor did I report the sexual harassment to the authorities, and I have always regretted not having done so. Regardless of this I did my absolute best every single day. I was never late to the office, and I always stayed several minutes after closing time just in case a resident needed help or a phone call came in.

I only took the allotted hour for lunch each day. I was an exemplary employee. Whenever John phoned or came into the office I would put on my brightest smile and pretended that nothing had happened, even though it tore at my very soul to do so. I needed this job and enduring his one sexual advancement was a price I felt that I had to pay.

I began putting a little money towards each of my credit cards every payday. I even managed to open a savings account without Kelly's knowledge with the plan to purchase a car as soon as I had enough money. I was so pleased with how this job was providing for the things I really needed to do.

Things at home were not going very well. Kelly had fallen into a deep depression from which I was not able to rouse her. She complained that I was turning her into a girl, but I really didn't understand what she meant. She didn't have insurance, but I was able to help her connect with a county clinic to get help with her mental issues.

She really didn't want to go, but I convinced her that it was for her benefit, as well as our relationship. She went to her first appointment and was prescribed medication to manage her schizoid-personality disorder, but she refused to take the medication and never saw the psychiatrist again.

Instead, she waxed worse and worse, staying up all night and sleeping most of the days. I already knew that she had several severe mental disorders, some from her years of meth use, and some from the years of abuse that she had endured at the hands of both of her parents. I couldn't help but feel sadness for her and only wanted to help.

I tried hard to understand what she was going through, even though I was dealing with so much on my own. She refused to find employment, depending on me for everything. I gave her leeway because I did love her, even when she went through her darkest moments, and I always tried to be there for her.

It wasn't always bleak for us though. Often, in the evenings after work and we had eaten dinner, Kelly and I would walk to the jacuzzi and relax for an hour or so before going to bed. This was something that she genuinely enjoyed, and I didn't mind it at all. It seemed to relieve some of the stress of my workdays.

Saturdays were taken up with laundry and household chores since Kelly couldn't find it in herself to help with any of it. Those responsibilities fell upon my shoulders. Often times when I was finished with these chores she would pressure me into going for long walks with her. Sometimes, even though tired, I actually enjoyed it.

We discovered a unique restaurant just down the block from the property, and we would have dinner there at least once a week. That was when I would have the rare hamburgers or steaks that my gastro doctor had ordered me to eat. I loved the atmosphere, and actually allowed myself a small cocktail every now and then.

I loved Kelly and wanted to see her at peace. We didn't talk seriously as often as I would have wished, but the times we did I always felt that we were getting somewhere in our relationship. At least, that is what I wanted. Not having a car, I was delighted when I found a grocery store that made home deliveries.

I would place an online order for groceries every Saturday. When I did Kelly she always insisted that I purchase alcohol for her, which I did, even though, because of Hepatitis, I was not supposed to have any alcohol as it could increase my chances of having a damaged liver. I had mostly given it up for the time being.

Every Sunday afternoon, without fail, I would accompany Kelly to her domestic violence class in Capitola. We would walk the half mile to the tram stop in Campbell and take the train to the downtown bus station. From there we caught a bus that took us up the mountain to Santa Cruz, and a bus to Capitola

I refused to go into the Burger King because I knew I had caught the E coli sepsis. Instead, I spent the hour that Kelly was in her class in the atrium of the building where the class was held. It was only an hours wait, there were lovely plants all around, and I always took a book to read to pass the time.

We would get home around 11 p.m., so I was never well rested to begin my work week on Monday morning. On the other nights of the week, I would go to bed at a reasonable hour to try and get the rest that I needed in order to be present both mentally and physically in the office.

Kelly didn't like me going to bed early. She would complain that she was lonely while I was working, and that it was not fair that I wanted to rest when I got home. She insisted on waking me from sleep late at night to 'hang out' with her, watch television, listen to music, or sit on the patio.

What she didn't understand was that not only was I twenty-five years older her senior, but I was also undergoing aggressive chemotherapy, and even though my job was not strenuous it did wear me down. Every so often I would try to stay up with her, but most of the time I would fall asleep watching television.

Not long after we moved Kelly asked me if I could help her find a church to attend. I didn't want to go to one like the church in Santa Cruz, so I began researching online, trying to find one that was gay affirming. I finally found one that was within reasonable walking distance from the apartment.

And so it was that church services were added to our weekly Sunday schedule. But church didn't help Kelly. She continued to be depressed, even though I had found her the psychiatrist, even though I had found the church, and even though almost everything I did was for her, barely taking the time to consider myself.

I signed both of us up for a weekly group meeting for Gays and Lesbians at the church and approached the pastor of the church, asking her to help us get through this issue through counselling. She would come to the apartment once a week during my lunch break and have a half hour sit down with Kelly and myself.

I absorbed everything that she said, taking to heart the advice that she gave. She had given us a book on what relationships mean, which I read, but Kelly didn't. It was frustrating, because try as I might ,nothing that I did or tried seemed to be helping Kelly to overcome her depression.

Kelly would blast music all night in the living room. She would sit on the patio in the middle of the night and cry or talk loudly on her phone with friends, disturbing the neighbors and myself. I was to discover much later that John's son lived directly across from us and reported everything he heard or saw to either John or Laurie.

Kelly didn't realize how her actions were affecting me as well as my job. She knew I was undergoing chemo with two immensely powerful drugs. She saw me struggle physically on a daily basis. But still, it didn't deter her from her activities. It became habitual and a terrible cross to bear.

Often, after I had dozed off, she would turn the light on in the bedroom, pull the covers off of me and demand that I get up and 'hang out' with her. She would literally drag me out to the living room to watch her 'dance' to her music, but sometimes I would fall asleep while I tried to 'hang out' with her.

Of course, this didn't sit well with her, so she would pull my hair or slap my face to wake me up. I would be so worn down the next morning that I could hardly get out of bed. When I woke up I would start the coffee and lay on the couch, just wishing that this would all be over.

I felt like I was trapped, but in feeling that I knew that I had brought all of this upon myself. I wished that she had stayed in Aptos and moved in with Lila. I wished that she would change. But as my grandfather would say, wish in one hand and shit in the other and see which one fills up the fastest.

There were actually joyful times during our first few months at the new apartment. At Christmas, Laurie presented me with a $500.00 bonus check, and we had two of my children and five of my grandchildren over for dinner and to celebrate. We bought gifts for everyone, and I did have a wonderful time.

Occasionally, after I got off of work, we would take the train downtown to window shop, and once in a while, when I could afford to, I would purchase something for Kelly or the apartment, and maybe once or twice for myself. I was desperately trying to make this a home for us, but I was almost always met with resistance.

One day I was speaking with my daughter Stephanie and she mentioned that she and Landon were looking to move from where they lived. I told her that she was more than welcome to come apply for an apartment at my property, which is exactly what they did. They had to go through the same process as any other prospective resident.

I was incredibly happy to be able to approve them for an apartment. They moved in during the middle of January, and I couldn't have been more pleased to have my family living on the same property as I was. Almost every evening after work, instead of going to my apartment, I would go and visit with Stephanie and the three little grandchildren.

Kelly had always seemed to like Stephanie, but now she was exhibiting signs of jealousy over my visits with her. Interestingly enough, Kelly began going to Stephanie's apartment late at night after I had gone to sleep to 'hang out' with her. Stephanie didn't appreciate the visits.

Her family kept what is considered by many to be normal hours, getting up early in the morning and going to sleep at a reasonable hour. Kelly would always show up at Stephanie's apartment extremely late, always drunk and crying, and would wake up the children and disturb the neighbors.

Stephanie talked to me about it, but there was little that I could do since Kelly always waited until I was asleep. I did have a conversation with her, but she told me that I didn't have the right to tell her what to do, where to go and who to see. Eventually the visits to Stephanie's became more infrequent but didn't stop altogether.

Kelly was now becoming a burden on my family and I was not in the least bit happy about it. And without me knowing it she was beginning to have an effect on my job. My residents knew who she was, and often they would wait until Laurie was in the office to complain about her.

The months passed and I continued to do an excellent job on the property. The residents loved me. I never referred to them as 'tenants', as that term was always abrasive to me for some reason. Perhaps because I am Irish. I always went to bat for them, making sure that they were comfortable living there.

In the Spring I filed my income tax return and received a hefty refund. I was able to pay off the fine for my DUI in its entirety, as well as register for the DUI class that the judge had ordered. I would walk the three miles to the class, and sometimes, if I were fortunate enough, one of my children would give me a ride there and back.

One day I was getting ready for my class. Kelly insisted that I ride my bike. She rode along with me, but I was unable to ride more than a few blocks before collapsing. I just didn't have the strength. That had been sapped from me thanks to the chemo drugs. She stood on the sidewalk looking at me and laughing, deriding me for being so weak.

I ended up leaving my bike and walking the rest of the way without Kelly. I am not sure why, but I never once thought about calling for a taxi. Upon reflection I think that I was in money saving mode after being without a job for so long. I would rather wear myself down walking than spend the money on something that I deemed frivolous.

In late February I received a phone call from my son David. He told me that Maggie was in an unbelievably bad situation and asked if I could help. Now, I had not heard from or seen Maggie since she and her husband moved out of the apartment in Aptos in May 2010, but this was my daughter and I asked David how I could help.

He gave me Maggie's phone number and suggested that I call her. He didn't tell me what had happened. I replied that I would call her when I got off work later that afternoon. I finished my day at the office worrying about Maggie, not knowing what had happened, but knowing that I would help.

When I got home I told Kelly about David's phone call and told her that I was going to contact Maggie. She began yelling, telling me that all my children wanted to do was use me, which had never been the case. I took my telephone and went out on the patio to make the call. Maggie answered the phone with the name of a motel.

When she heard my voice she broke down crying hysterically. I calmed her down and asked her what had happened. She told me that Jesse had taken Caitie to the boardwalk that morning, and when he tried to bring her home she threw a tantrum. When Jesse tried to quiet her down Caitie began screaming that she wanted her daddy.

Not realizing that Jesse was her daddy a bystander heard this and phoned the police. The police arrived to assess the situation, and when they ran Jesse's identification they found that he had an outstanding warrant in the state of Colorado. He was immediately arrested.

Years before, when Maggie had first met Jesse, my oldest daughter Stephanie warned her about him. Jesse had told Stephanie that he had absconded from Colorado when he was nineteen years old after being arrested for sexually assaulting a thirteen year old girl. Maggie refused to listen.

Now it had all caught up with Jesse and he was in police custody. Five year old Caitie was taken to the police station with him, and Maggie had to drive there to pick her up. Maggie told me that she was losing her job as a motel manager because it was a type of team position, and now Jesse was gone.

It all became perfectly clear to me why in all of those years, from 2002 to the moment he was arrested, that Jesse never tried to find a job, why he forced Maggie to work, even at two weeks post-delivery of Caitie. Of course, I didn't want to see my granddaughter's father go to prison, but he had to pay for his hideous crime.

I told Maggie not to worry, that I would have David drive me to Santa Cruz and help her pack her belongings, and that she and Caitie could come and stay with me until she sorted out her life. I didn't know it, but Kelly was listening to the conversation from just inside the patio door. I hung up and went inside. Kelly was waiting for me.

She told me, plainly, that Maggie was not welcome in our home after what she and Jesse had done in Aptos. OUR home! The home that I paid for with my employment. I told her in plain words that it was not up to her, and that Maggie and Caitie were coming to live with us whether she liked it or not.

Kelly argued defiantly with me and I told her that she could move out if that was the way she felt. She had become such a burden on me anyway, with her depression and drunkenness, and keeping me up all hours of the night. I could hardly stand it anymore. In the end she relented. She realized that I was going to stand my ground on this.

Maggie and little Caitie moved into the guest bedroom. Anything that we were unable to fit in the apartment and guest bedroom went into storage. I was thrilled to have my daughter and little granddaughter staying with me, and another daughter living only three buildings away.

Stephanie would visit me at times, bringing the three grandchildren with her. They, along with Caitie, would run on the lawn in front of my apartment, picking up leaves and throwing them at each other. I cherished watching them frolic, something that I had missed over the past few years.

It was my greatest hope that now this would become a place to call home, a sanctuary and refuge, somewhere to find peace after working the long week at the office, and a place where my family could gather as we did in years past. But Kelly had other plans in the works, and she was not intending to make it easy for anyone concerned.

Working For The Enemy

Time was passing quickly and April was upon us. I was a little more than halfway through the chemotherapy treatment for Hepatitis C. I faithfully injected the poison into my body every Friday morning. I was so happy to have Maggie with me, as she stood beside me and supported me with every injection while she was there.

When I had first begun the injections in September of 2010 I asked Kelly to please sit in the bathroom with me as a show of support. She refused, citing that it would only serve to 'trigger' her into wanting to run out and find meth. Although I didn't understand this, I respected her and so I went it alone.

I was doing well at the office. I had managed to have all of the washers and driers in the laundry centers set up to take payment cards that were provided by the company that we leased the units from. Since my employment began, the laundry centers had been robbed several times, and I knew that this was the answer to the problem.

I also took it upon myself to conduct monthly property audits to check for trip hazards, illegal satellite dishes, items hanging from the patio fences or off of the balconies, or anything else that could cause injury or detract from the beauty of the property. I took my position as resident manager seriously, and both Laurie and her father knew it.

But that didn't prevent John from bullying me as often as possible. On one of his visits to the office he asked how my daughter was enjoying living in an upstairs apartment with "all of those children". Of course, he was referring to Stephanie. He asked why she didn't keep her children under control, but he was not speaking the truth.

I replied that she loved it there, and really appreciated the neighborhood and school district, since her oldest child attended the local elementary school. He then went on to command me, and I mean command, not to ever allow my grandchildren to run and play on the lawns again if I knew what was good for me.

His voice was actually shrill as he said the words, and his face twisted, making him look like a shriveled old apple. I was literally in shock. I couldn't believe that he would say something like that. I asked him what harm it had done. My grandchildren were seven, five, four years old, with the youngest child only one year old.

He became infuriated. I sat back in my chair fully expecting him to strike me. He spat the words at me again. I thought that he was going to have a heart attack. I didn't know what else to do, so I assured him that I would see to it that it didn't happen again. I asked Stephanie to have the children play on the lawn in front of her apartment, away from prying eyes.

At this point I already knew that his son lived across from me, watching me like a stalker, but he most certainly couldn't see three buildings away where Stephanie lived. What I found particularly interesting about this is that other children played on the lawn with no repercussions whatsoever.

Early on in my employment I had confided my Hepatitis C diagnosis in Laurie. I wanted her to be aware that I was undergoing chemotherapy, and that there might be times when I would appear fatigued. John was visiting the office on another day when he sidled up to me and asked, "How is your Hepatitis C?"

I replied that I was still in treatment and would be until sometime in November. He nodded, looked at Laurie and left. I could practically see the wheels turning in his head. Remember, in the third week of my employment I had thwarted his attempt to touch me in a sexual way, and I knew at that time that I had made an enemy out of my employer.

Home life was going as well as could be expected. Kelly continued to be depressed and began consuming more alcohol as time went on. She still tried to get me out of bed late at night, but while Maggie was there she would intercede and take Kelly out on the patio to talk and allow me to rest.

Stephanie would come sometimes in the evenings to visit and talk out on the patio. One such evening she, Maggie, Kelly and I were sitting out enjoying the lovely summer air, talking and joking about all sorts of things. We all had a cocktail in our hands, and it was a very relaxing mood.

Stephanie had a stick in her hand, playing with it, and Kelly tried to take it away. Stephanie was able to overpower her and take the stick, and Kelly became so angry that she punched Stephanie in the mouth. Maggie, Stephanie and I were all in shock, especially me, since I had always taken the brunt of Kelly's aggressions in the past.

Stephanie held her mouth, which was bleeding. I got a wet paper towel for her to press against the cut on her lip. I wanted to knock Kelly in her mouth, but I restrained myself. I asked her why she had done it, and she couldn't come up with a satisfactory answer. Stephanie only visited my apartment a few times after that.

May came, and with it an influx of thirty day notices. In my experience as a property manager, residents with children made their moves at the end of the school year. This left me with loads of paperwork and pre-move inspections, but I managed to get through all of it with ease.

Renting the units was just as easy. I loved touring the property with prospects, and I almost always had a full capacity property, which I had hoped would please John somewhat. After all, the property, according to Giovanni, the head maintenance tech, was John's 'cash cow', what he had built his life's work on.

One day in May, John paid a visit to the office. He always came unannounced, and when I least expected him. As soon as he came through the door he ordered me to turn the 'God damn" radio off. I replied that was the station that his daughter Laurie listened to all of the time.

He said "I don't care. When you are in this office you aren't to listen to the radio." So, I stood up and walked over to the radio and turned it off. He asked me about Maggie and Caitie, wondering why they were living with me. I replied that they had moved in a few months before, and they would have been homeless had I not opened my home to them.

"They have two weeks to get out." Just like that. No ifs, ands or buts. He never said that he would fire me, but the insinuation was there. I panicked and didn't know what to do. I couldn't turn my daughter out on the street. I hung my head, with tears rolling down my cheeks. He scoffed at me and walked out the door.

That evening I sat down with Maggie and told her what John had said. She said that it would be fine, that she would find somewhere else to live. She let me know that she had met a man a few weeks before who wanted her to move in with him, and that she was already kind of planning to move anyway.

She asked me to give her a couple of days. My heart ached and I worried. But Kelly was overjoyed. She had been against Maggie moving in to begin with, and I knew that she could hardly wait for her to leave. I would miss both Maggie and Caitie dearly, but Maggie said that she would only be a few miles away, and still in the same town.

The next day was a Friday, and Laurie was scheduled to come into the office. I let her get settled, then I told her to let her father know that Maggie would be moving out in a few days from then. I asked her if her father had always been so cruel and heartless, and she pursed her lips. She never did answer my question.

Maggie moved out that weekend, and she did it alone. I helped her pack, but I wasn't able to carry the heavy boxes, and Kelly just stood by watching. But Maggie managed fine and was gone from the apartment within four hours. Still, it made me sad. I had never even met this person that she was moving in with.

Maggie had already filed for divorce from Jesse, who had been transported to Colorado and sentenced to a year in the state penitentiary. I could only hope that I would see her and little Caitie often, and that soon I could meet the man that she had moved in with. I wanted to be assured that both she and Caitie were safe.

I spent Sunday organizing the guest bedroom, washing the linens, dusting and vacuuming. Mind you, it was not in bad condition after Maggie moved out, but I wanted it to be fresh and welcoming in the event that we ever had a guest in our home who wanted to stay a night or two.

June came, and with it warmer weather. Kelly and I spent many of our evenings relaxing in the community pool and the jacuzzi. Home life was good, even without Maggie there, and although Kelly was still not employed and continued to neglect the household chores I was able to manage.

Maggie and her new boyfriend came over for dinner one evening. I was overjoyed to see her and Caitie. We had a lovely get together, or so I thought. The adults were sitting at the dining room table after dinner enjoying coffee, and Caitie was in the living room playing with some toys.

Maggie's boyfriend was complaining about having issues. Kelly chimed in and said that everyone has issues. The man slammed his chair back, got up, and ran out of the apartment. I looked at Maggie, and she shrugged her shoulders. He reminded me of a man-baby, and my first impression of him was not a particularly good one.

Maggie ran after him, apologizing for her boyfriend's behavior. A week later Kelly invited both of them to accompany us to a family reunion BBQ-picnic that her family was holding at a park about twenty miles from where we lived. I knew that Kelly had invited them for the sole purpose of getting a ride there.

I honestly didn't want to go as I felt like I would not fit in well, but when the day came I got up and ready for the day. Maggie came by and picked us up, and she drove us to the park. There were literally hundreds of Kelly's relatives there, including her parents and sisters. Kelly introduced me to many of the relatives that I didn't know.

I tried to include Maggie and her boyfriend. Caitie made friends with some of the children and went to the playground to have fun. About an hour into the festivities when Maggie's new boyfriend disappeared. I asked her where he had gone, and she told me that he was sitting in her van.

She told me that he was not enjoying himself because someone had said something that offended him, and that he just wanted to go home. I told her that she was our ride, but she insisted that she needed to take him home right away. I told her that I understood, and that Kelly and I would make other arrangements to get home.

Home life continued on pretty much the same. I was not getting much support from Kelly, and she began sinking into another depression. I asked her to please make an appointment with the psychiatrist I had found for her, but she refused, saying that she didn't believe that she had any mental health issues.

I had managed to save enough money to purchase an older Ford Taurus sedan, which ended up being an extremely poor investment, but at least we had transportation to the stores and appointments. Kelly was not thrilled with it, but it had not been her money that had paid for it.

Even though she had fought against Maggie and Caitie living with us she behaved as if she missed them. My company was just not enough for her. She begged me to allow her to have one of her friends from Vacaville come and visit, assuring me that everything would be fine, and after days of her begging I finally relented.

A few days later Kelly told me that her friend, who she still had not named, would be there later in the evening. I must have fallen asleep before the person came, because the next morning, when I went to start a pot of coffee, who should I see at the dining room table but Kale, Kelly's old meth dealer!

I tried not to be upset, but now my suspicions were aroused. I told him good morning and left the room to take my shower and get ready for the day. Kelly was still sound asleep, so I would be leaving for work hoping that Kale did not rummage through the apartment while I was at the office. I did not trust drug addicts.

When I went out the front door I saw his motorcycle parked underneath the stairwell which I knew belonged to Kale. As I walked to the office I noticed that one of the beautiful lawns had deeply furrowed ruts in it, the area almost completely ruined. I continued to the office and put my key in the lock, but the door was already open.

I walked inside and saw John waiting there for me. I could see that he was visibly upset. He told me that a man on a motorcycle had been seen doing 'donuts' on one of the lawns, and that the same man was seen entering my apartment shortly thereafter. I was stunned. I knew that his son Richard must have been watching.

I told him that I had had no knowledge of damage to the lawn until that morning when I was walking to the office, and that I was thoroughly shocked. He asked me if I knew the man, and I told him that he was Kelly's visitor who had come to stay with her for a few days and assured him that I would be speaking with both of them.

I was thoroughly embarrassed, as you might imagine. I was the manager of this property and I was being made a proper ass by Kelly and Kale. John told me that I was treading on thin ice and I had better watch out if I knew what was good for me, yet again. I apologized, but it didn't abate his anger.

He stormed out of the office, leaving me to deal with the aftermath of what Kelly's dear, dear meth dealer friend had done. I phoned home, but there was no answer. I still had several hours before my lunch break, so confronting Kelly and Kale, which I was determined to do, would have to wait until then.

I knew that I was being watched by John's son Richard, who lived across from me. In the past this would not have bothered me in the least bit. My life had always been an open book, but now it was a book of embarrassments brought about by Kelly, her lifestyle and her friends.

I tried to busy myself in the office but was unable to concentrate fully. Giovanni, the head maintenance tech, came into the office, smiling at me knowingly. He was deep in the pockets of John, and although he didn't live on the property, his eyes were always watching. He feigned checking to see if there were any work orders, but I knew better.

He was another set of eyes and ears for John, as was his stepson Jeremiah, who also worked on the property as a maintenance tech. I had thought that Jeremiah and I were friends, but I had learned otherwise. I told him that there were no work orders, and he left, glancing at me over his shoulders.

Lunchtime came and I went to my apartment. Kelly was just getting out of bed. I asked both she and Kale to come into the living room, letting that know that we all needed to talk. Her friend was close to my age but had not an ounce of sense about him. He had apparently been a meth addict for years.

I asked about the lawn and he admitted that he had dug the ruts into it with his motorcycle, explaining that somehow it had gotten stuck in it. They laughed. I told both he and Kelly that he would have to leave that very day, offering no apologies. I was not going to put up with this any further.

Kelly tried to argue with me, but I told her this was my decision, I paid for the apartment, and I would say who was allowed to be there. Kale went into the guest bedroom, packed his belongings and went out the door. Kelly started crying, begging him not to leave. She followed after him and I sat at the dining room table trying to think.

There would be no lunch for me that day. When she returned her eyes were ablaze with anger. She began slinging profanities at me, telling me that I was worthless, and that she almost hated me. It was my turn to laugh. I almost felt as if Kelly was doing all of this on purpose, perhaps to pay me back for all of the arrests for her assaults on me.

Or, perhaps she was truly ignorant and had never grown mentally, having begun using meth at such an early age. My laughter only served to fuel her anger. She ran into our bedroom and slammed the door, rattling it on its hinges. I made myself a cup of tea and went out on the patio to smoke a cigarette.

I had always been the first to admit any mistakes that I had made, but now I was being made to pay for other's mistakes by association. I regretted ever having allowed her to come with me to the new property. I was being scrutinized for her actions, and ultimately I would pay a dear price for them.

Kelly followed me onto the patio and told me that I was useless. I didn't respond to that, instead telling her that I had to go back to the office. A couple of days later Kelly told me that she had invited a former lover to come visit over the next weekend. I was stunned. I couldn't believe that she lacked understanding of what I had told her.

I told her no, absolutely not. She went into the living room and sulked for the rest of the evening. From that day forward Kelly began sinking into a deeper, darker depression. Nothing that I said or did was effective. We knew friends from a local church that I had agreed to attend with her and told her that they could come and visit her.

That is not what she wanted. She yearned for those she had used meth or had alcoholic binges with. I suggested that we go visit my children, or even take the Greyhound to Vacaville to visit her family, but that didn't sit well with her. She wanted what she wanted and nothing I said made a bit of difference. She waxed worse as the days passed.

One evening in late September I returned home from work to a darkened apartment. When my eyes adjusted to the room I saw Kelly sitting on the couch holding Kudos in one hand and a butcher knife in the other. I was alarmed, but maintained my composure, not wanting to provoke Kelly.

I asked her what she was doing and she told me that she was going to kill Kudos and then kill herself. I told her to put the knife down, but she held it up, pointed towards me instead. I stayed close to the front door, watching her, talking to her and trying to calm her down. I wanted to phone for help, but the phone was too far away from me.

Nothing I said was working, so in my desperation I ran to Stephanie's apartment to get help. I told her that Kelly was threatening to kill Kudos and herself. Stephanie immediately phoned the police to have them do a welfare check on Kelly. I waited about ten minutes then returned to my apartment to wait until the police arrived.

They arrived quite quickly, along with paramedics. They asked me to please wait outside while they went in to speak with her. Less than five minutes later she was being led out of the door in handcuffs. They were placing her in a 5150, which is a mandatory seventy-two hour psychiatric hold in a hospital.

This was the icing on the cake for me. I didn't want her to come back. I phoned her parents and told them what had happened, and how hard I had tried to get Kelly the help that she needed. I asked them to please contact her, and to please, please allow her to come stay with them in Vacaville.

They agreed and told me that they would be by to collect her belongings, and I was so very relieved. Of course, I wanted Kelly to get the help she needed, and to heal from whatever trauma was causing her mental psychosis, but I also needed for her to be somewhere else when she was discharged from the psychiatric ward.

I spent that evening going over and over again in my mind why Kelly might have done this. Her actions were not only against herself and poor little Kudos, but they were also against me as well. Having been with her for the better part of almost three years I had developed a deep attachment that would be unbearable to break.

I tried to eat dinner but couldn't manage to get a single bite down. Kelly's parents phoned me and let me know that they had spoken with her, and that they would be by as soon as she was discharged from the psychiatric ward, and asked if I could get her things together. I assured them that I would.

As you can imagine, I didn't sleep well that night. I still had to work the next morning, and being unrested was not going to make it that easy. I woke up and got ready anyway, dreading the day ahead of me. As I sipped my coffee on the patio, I realized that John's son had seen everything that had happened.

Shortly after I opened the office for the day John came in. I smiled my brightest smile and asked how he was doing. He didn't answer. Instead, he demanded to know why the police had been at my door the evening before. I took a deep breath, in fear of what his reaction might be.

Nevertheless, I was completely honest with him, telling him that Kelly had had a psychotic break, and had been hospitalized in a local hospitals psychiatric ward. He replied that she was giving the property a bad name, and then went on to ask if she was coming back. I told him that she would be staying with her parents for a while.

"Make sure that this never happens again!" He screamed the words at me, causing me to jump in my chair. I didn't know how to respond, except to say that I would do my best. He told me that I had better if I knew what was good for me. The look on his face changed to that of perverse pleasure.

He informed me that instead of the maintenance crew checking in with me for the day, that I was to go to them and check in with them, and that I would have to walk the property to look for them to give them any work orders. I was shocked, as this was highly unusual and completely unprofessional.

Never in my experience as a resident manager was I considered to be managed by the maintenance crew, but I nodded my head that I understood him. With that being said he stormed out the door and slammed it behind himself. I put my coat on and went in search of Giovanni and his crew.

I walked from one end of the property to the other, and finally found them in a vacant unit. I asked how they were doing, but no one responded. I told Giovannie that there were no work orders so far for the day. I assured them that if any came in that I would search the property for them again.

I was, as you might think, dismayed by this sudden change, but I managed to get through the day, handling all of the issues that were presented by residents, taking phone calls and creating work orders for the Giovanni and his crew. I smiled through everything, making sure that I put others at ease.

I went directly to Stephanie's apartment after work to talk to her about everything that had happened, and to get her opinion on what I should actually do. I was conflicted, or perhaps I had lost my mind as well, but I was considering to allowing Kelly to come back. I thought that if she received the psychiatric treatment that maybe it would be fine.

Stephanie strongly objected. She knew the chaotic history that Kelly and I shared. I tried to reason it out with her, but she poked holes in my reasoning. Nothing I said made a good argument, and I knew that. I was just so sad that Kelly had done this. I had thought that we could be happy together.

Kelly was discharged from the hospital the following Saturday. Her parents, David and Sharon, picked her up. They arrived at my apartment with Kelly, who stood just outside the front door. I had already packed her belongings as neatly as possible. I thanked them for coming by and wished them the best of luck with their daughter.

Neither Kelly nor I spoke. After all, what could we really say? I already knew that she blamed me for her depression, but I knew that she had dealt with this very same issue since she was young, having been institutionalized for a year when she was fourteen years of age. I admit, I was relieved that she was gone.

I thought that perhaps I would still have a chance to salvage my job and prove to John that it was not my actions that had caused all of the turmoil and chaos that accompanied Kelly. At the age of fifty-seven, another job such as this was not likely to be offered to me again in my life. I put everything I had into my work.

Kelly was gone for a month, and during that time my life returned to what I considered to be normal. Going to bed at a reasonable hour, getting up early and greeting the day, eating well, getting the right kind of exercise, performing well at work, all things that I was not able to do while Kelly was with me.

My children and grandchildren began visiting me again, joining me for lunches and dinners. They had always been reluctant to come by with Kelly there. None of them really cared much for her. They didn't like the fact that she had abused me so many times and then acted as if everything was fine.

One evening, after I had eaten my dinner and cleaned the kitchen, I was sitting on the couch cuddling with Kudos. The phone rang and I answered it. I heard Kelly's voice. It was almost a whisper, so I had to ask her to speak up. She was apologizing for what she had done and told me that she was now on the right medications.

I told her that I was incredibly happy for her, which I actually was. I still had deep feelings for her that I was not able to shake, nor could I really understand them. She told me that she missed me, and asked if she could come down and visit me sometime. I told her that I would have to think about it.

I wanted her to realize that she had caused such drama that I almost lost my job. She needed time to reflect on her actions. I should never have considered allowing her back into my life. But Kelly was my weakness, and for whatever reason I was not able to resist her. It was almost as if she were a deadly disease for which there was no cure.

In the end, Kelly returned. Her parents drove her down, and I prepared a lovely meal for all of us. We visited, and I thanked them for having cared for Kelly while she was with them, even though I knew that they did it under duress. I could tell by the looks on their faces that they were relieved that she would not be returning with them.

When they were gone Kelly reached into one of her bags and pulled out a book, handing it to me. It was titled "If Only I Knew". I opened the book. On the inside of the cover, she had written following words:

"This is a gift of truths that we both should have looked at before. A gift of I am sorry's from the bottom of my heart. A gift of promises I plan to live by with you from now on. A gift for when you get sick and forget us, also for us to reference when we disagree or argue. A gift given for both of our hearts to help the healing process. I love you and want to thank you for forgiving me." It was signed "A gift for my love, Susan Sheehan, with love from the bottom of my heart, Kelly". I have kept the book to this very day.

My heart melted. Kelly was different, seemingly transformed. She was demure in her approach, somewhat feminized, whereas before she was proud of what she considered to be her masculinity. She began helping around the apartment, even going as far as preparing lunches and dinners, rather than depending on me for these.

Kelly was home just in time to celebrate Stephanie and David's birthdays. Everyone came: Maggie, Rachel, Landon and all of the grandchildren. We had a wonderful celebration, with dinner first and then cake. The adult children noticed the change in Kelly, but they were not convinced that she was actually different.

They believed that she was putting on a show. I believed that it was the medication that she was on, Wellbutrin, which was making the difference, that she was finally able to be her true self, rather than the one she had convinced herself that she was. She also had weekly appointments with a therapist which seemed to be also helping.

One Sunday shortly after the birthdays we paid our weekly visit to UCC Campbell, the church that we had been attending for almost a year. Even though my energy was slowly returning I was delighted that we finally were able to drive to the church. I didn't mind going, since it satisfied a certain need in Kelly.

We spent some time after the services visiting with a few of the friends that we had made, then returned to the apartment to relax for the rest of the day. I was sitting at the dining room table when the phone rang. It was Jeremiah, one of the maintenance techs who happened to be on call that weekend.

He informed me that a resident had phoned him, asking him to come to their apartment and remove dead flies. I told him that was not our job and suggested that he let the resident know. Shortly after hanging up the phone rang again. The tech had given the resident my phone number for me to deal with.

I listened to man complain about the flies, then asked if he had a broom and dustpan. He replied yes that he did. I then told him to use those to sweep up the flies. It was not my job to clean apartments, and I felt free to let the resident know this. I hung up the phone, not thinking another thing about it.

Monday morning came and I went to the office as usual. I went inside, took the phone off of the service, checked for messages, then went in search of Giovanni and his crew to let them know that there were no work orders for them. When I returned to the office John was waiting for me.

With him was a younger man who I didn't recognize. He turned out to be the one who had phoned complaining about the flies. Angry with me, he had researched the property, found John's home address and phone number, and contacted him. He told John that I was not doing my job. John's face was purple with anger.

He told me, plainly, that if a resident called me with a complaint, no matter what it was, that I was to take care of it immediately. I looked at the young man and asked if he was a resident. He replied no that he had been visiting his girlfriend, who was a resident. I was rendered speechless.

John had sided with someone who was not even a resident and had demanded that I perform work that was outside the scope of my employment. I didn't even consider such a thing to be within the realms of the maintenance staffs responsibilities. Nevertheless, I told John that I would make sure that this didn't happen again.

When they left, the younger man turned around and laughed scornfully at me, relishing in the fact that he had caused me discomfort and embarrassment. What I planned to do was have him sign a change of occupancy or remove himself from the property immediately. But I never had the opportunity.

The apartment that he stayed in happened to be almost directly across from my apartment, and right next to Richard, John's son. Somehow he was able to curry the favor of John, who, in my honest opinion, erroneously sided with this man, who was not only not a resident, but who was quite obviously devious.

I managed to get through my day without any other issues and took care of everything that my job expectations actually covered. But I was definitely getting tired of the incessant harassment at the hands of John, tired of reporting to Giovanni and his crew, and tired of living in fear of losing my job.

I was fast approaching the end of my chemotherapy treatments. My blood work continued to come back clear, so my gastroenterologist let me know that November 11th would be my last injection of Interferon, and at that time I could also cease taking the Ribavirin. I was beyond thrilled.

My sides were perma-bruised from all of the injections I had taken, and hopefully those bruises would fade quickly. I was looking forward to being permanently clear of Hepatitis C, as well as regaining my strength and stamina. It had been a long, difficult year, but I had managed to get through it.

At the office that day I mentioned to Laurie that my treatment was almost complete and apparently successful. She smiled and replied that she was happy for me. Later that day, John visited the office. He was unusually pleasant, greeting me as if I were a family member, which should have aroused my suspicions.

He asked me how I was feeling and I replied that I was feeling wonderful. He mentioned that he knew that I had almost complete with my chemo and said that he was glad. He knew that I had only one vacant apartment, and he asked me to hold it off the market for his niece who was planning to move to the area soon.

I marked the apartment as rented, even though I was the only one leasing the apartments. Laurie never even gave a tour to any prospects the entire time that I worked with her. I didn't give it much thought, though, as I was simply doing as my employer requested. Even so, I was left with an uneasy feeling.

We were invited to Stephanie's to share a beautiful Thanksgiving dinner with her, Landon and the grandchildren. I prepared my famous homemade Cranberry Sauce. It was a lovely celebration, even though I have not agreed with the observance of that day for many years. It did, however, allow time off to spend with my loved ones.

The next day Kelly and I took my granddaughter Caitie to the San Francisco Zoo, and had a really wonderful day. We had lunch in Half Moon Bay, then drove back to the apartment through the mountains to San Mateo, where we caught the freeway home. The forest was breathtaking, and we all enjoyed the drive.

The rest of the weekend was spent relaxing and recovering from the past few days. I was looking forward to work on Monday, as I had a sense of renewed purpose, as well as returning strength. Without the chemo in my system and the change in Kelly, life appeared to be brighter and more hopeful.

Monday morning came, and with it energy that I had thought was gone forever. I had my coffee and cigarette, took my morning shower, and got dressed for the day. Kelly was still asleep, as was her custom, so I gave her a quick kiss on the cheek and left for my day at the office.

I unlocked the door and went to my desk. I didn't bother taking my coat off since I had to go and report to Giovanni, as if he were my boss. I took the phone off of forwarding and checked for any messages that might have been important. I then went in search of Giovanni, who was obviously savoring this new requirement.

I found him in one of the parking lots laughing with the other two maintenance techs. I said good morning to all of them, told Giovanni that there were no work orders, then returned to the office. I had no sooner sat down at my desk than Laurie walked through the door. I was surprised, as she never came in Monday through Thursday.

She didn't look at me or speak when I greeted her, instead she went directly to her desk. She opened her briefcase and pulled out an envelope. I was busy filing paperwork, so I was not paying close attention to her. I sat down at my desk, straightening it, as I always prided myself on being tidy.

Suddenly, Laurie stood up and walked over to me. She had the envelope that I had seen in her hand. She placed it on the desk and said "Susan, you are terminated effective immediately. Hand over the property keys and company credit card and gather your personal items. You have three days to vacate the premises."

My heart dropped and my eyes filled with tears. I couldn't believe what I had heard. My head began reeling and I felt as if I were going to faint. I didn't understand why this was happening. I handed her the keys and took the credit card out of my wallet, handing that to her as well.

I took a deep breath, and without saying a single word I picked up the envelope, my books and my mug of water and walked slowly out of the office. It was almost as if I could barely drag myself to the apartment. I couldn't believe that this was happening. I had done not one single thing wrong, except for allowing Kelly on the property.

Fortunately, Laurie had allowed me to keep the apartment key, so I let myself in. Kelly was just getting up. I said good morning to her and let her get a cup of coffee and have a cigarette before speaking with her. I poured myself a cup of coffee and followed her outside onto the patio.

I took her hands in mine and said quietly, "I don't know how to tell you this except just to do it. I have been terminated, and we have three days to move." Kelly's mouth dropped open. She asked me why, and I told her that I really didn't know. She asked what we were going to do, and I replied that I had no idea.

I opened the envelope that Laurie had handed me, and saw two checks, each of them in the amount of $2500.00. There was a note inside the envelope that Laurie had written. The note indicated that one check was my final pay and the other check was severance pay.
This was not going to allow us to get by for long.

My anxiety level began to rise. I phoned John, one of the deacons from UCC Campbell. I told him what had happened and he said to give him a couple of hours, that he thought that he might be able to help us. Those two hours felt like an eternity. He finally called back and told me that he had contacted the church attorney.

He had given her my phone number, and to expect a call from her before the end of the day, and told me not to worry at all, that she had a great plan. While I waited I tried to console Kelly, who was falling apart. She blamed this tragedy on me, on Maggie, on everything and everyone but herself.

It was not long before the attorney phoned me. The first thing that she asked is whether or not I had a contract with the employer. I told her no, everything was verbal. She laughed, and told me not to worry about it, that they had no right to expect us to move out in three days, and that she was going to take care of it for us.

Only an hour passed before she called again. She told me that we had sixty days to vacate, and that she would be calling my former employer the next day. I felt relieved. That should give us plenty of time to plan for a move, and also give me a chance to find other employment.

In the meantime, I considered filing for unemployment, but since Laurie's plans were not going to pan out I doubted that she would approve my application. We spent the rest of the evening talking about what we could do. I began searching online for job opportunities, but they were slim to none.

Kelly mostly sat on the patio, smoking cigarette after cigarette and drinking alcohol. It was too much for me to hope that she might look for employment as well. The next morning, I decided to swallow my pride and go to the office and speak with Laurie. I went into the office and there was already another woman at the desk that once was mine.

Laurie looked at me like I was scum, trash, someone who was lower than her. I told her that I needed to file for unemployment, but I had to know if she was going to reject it. She didn't reply. All that she did was stare at me. I all but got down on my knees to beg her. I told her that it was going to prove difficult for me to find another job.

I said "If I am not able to be approved for unemployment benefits Kelly and I will become homeless. Please, consider approving my application." She told me that she would see what she could do, and then told me that I was not permitted to be in the office and asked me to leave. She turned away, not saying another word.

I went back to the apartment and immediately filed for unemployment. I also applied for food stamps and state health insurance, something that I encouraged Kelly to do as well. I still had not told my children, so I picked up the phone to make the calls and tell them the dreadful news.

They all had encouraging words, telling me that I should have no problem finding another job. My reply was that I couldn't possibly ask Laurie or John for a recommendation considering all of the drama that Kelly had caused. They all asked me why I endured her, especially after all the turmoil she had caused and what it had cost me.

A few days later I received my approval for unemployment in the mail, which was close to three thousand dollars per month, along with my approval for food stamps. I silently thanked Laurie. Kelly still had not heard anything about her food stamps, and of course she couldn't file for unemployment since had really never worked.

I felt stuck. Kelly had told me that she might go live with her parents, which gave me immense relief. I felt that would work out so much better than me having to drag her along and pay her way. I might even be able to go and stay with one of my children until another opportunity came along.

I waited for Kelly to make a decision. But that decision never came, and here we were, needing to pack what we could, rent a storage unit to store items that we didn't need, and look for a place to live in the meantime. All that I could afford was a room for the two of us and Kudos, but nothing we found suited Kelly.

Because we had to move I found that I had to drop out of my DUI class. I was disheartened, as I was only a couple of months away from completing the classes. I went into the office to see if I could get a refund, but I was told that they didn't issue refunds, ever. I had lost two months' worth of payments, equaling almost two hundred dollars.

Kelly and I both spent hours looking for possible places to move to. All that we needed was a safe and comfortable room, with amenable roommates, somewhere that we could start over and perhaps give both of us a chance to find jobs. I really wanted to find a position that would offer an apartment and utilities as part of the pay.

Some of the places we found were homophobic but allowed pets. Other places were gay friendly but didn't accept pets. We just couldn't find a place to live, and I had all but given up hope. Kelly said that maybe we should just live in the car, but that was not something that I considered an option.

I kept looking, even though I was deeply discouraged. The days turned into weeks, swiftly moving into the holidays, but we had nothing to celebrate. I didn't go to my children's homes. I was embarrassed, and rightly so. Each one of them phoned me though, wishing me the absolute best.

I was so beside myself with worry. The deadline for our move was fast approaching, and we had absolutely nowhere to live. My heart was breaking increasingly each day. I had given so much of myself to the job, only to have every ounce of my efforts thwarted by Kelly's selfishness and lack of self-control.

She was my lover and my enemy, my friend and abuser, and she had ruined my hopes and dreams of a better life. I continued to search for a place to live, but seemingly to no avail. Little did I know that a place was ready for us, a place that would turn into an unimaginable nightmare. A place that I would come to call Hell House.

Hell House

One day, shortly after the New Year, Kelly told me that she had found the perfect place for us. It was located in the foothills of East San Jose, about fifteen miles outside of town. They were gay friendly and they allowed pets. I told her that I really didn't want to live that far away from the children.

She replied that we could visit them anytime that I wished, and they come to see us as well. I told her to go ahead and make an appointment, and that at the very least we could take a look at it. We got ready and drove out to the foothills. It was easy to find the house, which in that neighborhood was referred to as a mini-mansion.

The street that it was on was lined with cars, but we were finally able to find a place to park. We walked up to the door and rang the bell. A dark haired petite woman holding a baby answered the door. We introduced ourselves. She told us that her name was Emma and she invited us inside.

We followed closely behind her through the foyer. As we walked I noticed an area to the left that was blocked by drywall. I asked her what it was and she told me that she was having her living room remodeled. She led us past the staircase and into the kitchen. There were a couple of younger girls preparing meals.

The girls were scantily clad, in only shirts and underwear, which I found highly inappropriate. They giggled and left the room. It was a sizable kitchen, with two ovens and an extra-large refrigerator. I asked Emma if we needed to supply our own cookware and she replied that we were welcome to use whatever was in the kitchen.

We followed Emma up the staircase. At the top she pointed to a room with two doors and told us that we were to never knock on the doors or try to go into the room. She led us on down a hallway, and as we walked past other doors I noticed two young girls from the kitchen, watching us from behind their door.

Emma showed us the shared bathroom. It was good sized, but very dirty and disorderly. There were towels and toiletries scattered everywhere. The shower/tub was filthy, and the toilet looked as if it had not been cleaned for months. I asked Emma who was responsible for cleaning and she said, "You are".

Back down the stairs she led us down a short hallway just past the kitchen and unlocked a door. "This will be your room. It is eight hundred per month, including all utilities and internet." The room was good sized, but it would certainly not accommodate very much of our furniture.

There was a half bath just outside the entry door, and the room had a window and a door that led outside to a small garden area. Emma opened the door and took us into the backyard. "You can barbeque or have bonfires out here." It was a fairly nice yard, although the landscaping had seen better days.

I looked at Kelly and asked to speak with her privately. I told her that we really needed to think about this, that something felt off to me. Emma overheard me and said, "You had better make a decision soon as I have more people coming to look at the room." I asked her to give us the afternoon to think about it and that we would get back to her.

She told us that was fine, and with that being said she left us and went back into the house. On the drive back to the apartment Kelly told me that this was our only chance, and I had to agree with her. But the place had made me a bit nervous. There was something about it that just didn't seem right.

In the end, I finally conceded to Kelly, and we called Emma, telling her that we would like to take the place, and asked when we could move in. She told us that January 14th would be fine. That gave us a week to decide what to take and what to store. Everything felt confusing, and it seemed like my life was spiraling out of control.

Most of all of our belongings were already packed neatly in boxes, so we rented a storage unit and a moving truck and began taking boxes to the unit. We figured that we could fit our bed, the loveseat, entertainment center and the coffee table in the room. Everything else went into storage.

I had received my second unemployment payment, so I was able to withdraw eight hundred dollars to pay for the room. The morning of the 14th came. We rented a small moving van to move the furniture that we were taking with us to Emma's. We ended up leaving my beautiful couch behind. Emma was waiting for us at the door.

She had her hand out, waiting for the money. I paid her, asking for a receipt, and she told me that she would get one for me later that day. We worked most of the afternoon setting up the room to our satisfaction. Kudos had been in his carrier all day, so I let him out to roam the room and try to get used to yet another strange home.

I went out the side door to smoke a cigarette when a woman accompanied by large dog popped her head over the gate. She introduced herself as L.J. and told me that she was one of the roommates, and that her room was upstairs. I called Kelly outside to introduce them.

She seemed like a pleasant enough person, and as it turned out she was also a lesbian. I returned to the room to sit and relax, leaving Kelly outside to visit with L.J. Kudos was roaming the room, and seemed to be at ease. I had set up his food and water station, along with his kitty litter, as well as a few of his toys.

It was getting close to dinner time, and neither Kelly nor myself had eaten that day, so I opened the door and told her that we should be going out to get a bite to eat. We had not purchased any food yet, and I really didn't want to try to navigate the kitchen yet even if we had. She gave L.J. a hug, which was fine with me.

While we were out we did a bit of shopping. We stopped by a Dollar Tree and bought totes to put our toiletries in so that we didn't have to leave them in the shared bathroom. We found a local grocery store and stocked up on what groceries we thought we would need, and we made sure that Kudos had enough food and kitty litter to last.

When we got back to the room I labeled all of the perishable food and placed it on an empty shelf in the refrigerator. The non-perishable items were kept in our room. We bought our own toilet paper, which we would take with us when using the toilet, and paper towels just in case of any spills.

I could hear people moving about behind closed doors, but I didn't see anyone. It seemed as if sounds were emanating from behind every door that I passed by. I wondered if they were Emma's family. I got an eerie feeling, and chills ran up and down my spine. I almost ran to get back into the room.

Back in the room, I suggested that Kelly invite L.J. down to the room to chat and watch a bit of television or listen to music. Kelly was only gone for a few minutes, returning with L.J. and a younger girl who L.J. introduced as her girlfriend. We had an enjoyable time, laughing and joking.

We exchanged emails and phone numbers, as well as adding each other on social media. After the first day though, we realized that things were not what we thought. We were under the impression that Emma lived in the home with her husband and baby, perhaps with extended family members as well.

That was not the case. People started coming out of the rooms, introducing themselves as our roommates. Apparently, Emma had renovated the five thousand square foot house, creating ten separate rooms. She had in turn rented these rooms out to seventeen different people, plus ten dogs and two cats.

She had even removed the washer and dryer from the laundry room and rented the tiny room to a younger woman who owned four of the dogs. I was astonished when I discovered this. I knew that I had not been imaging the noises coming from behind the doors. I continued to have the peculiar feeling.

There was Heinrich and Phyliss, who lived in the master suite upstairs, Julio and his fiancée Jaimie, who lived in a room just down the hall, Alma and her little girl, who lived in what had been the living room, Mike, who lived upstairs and had a girlfriend, and Cami, who also lived upstairs with her miniature Chihuahua Mimi.

There were various others whose names I never really knew. It was a real hodge podge of people, a true circus of characters, some of whom I would learn to love and others to dislike immensely. All that we had wanted was a fresh start. About a week after we moved in Kelly received an email from L.J.

Attached to the email was a PDF document. The document was certification from the courts that the FORECLOSED house had been sold at auction to Bank of America on November 14th, 2011, and we had moved in on January 14th, 2012, two months later. Emma had rented the room to us illegally.

In fact, she had rented ALL of the rooms illegally, and was absconding with the money! She had defrauded everyone in the house! I found out about all of this on Sunday, January 22nd. I immediately went online and searched for an attorney to represent Kelly and me.

I sent them an email inquiry telling them everything that I knew. The next morning, I had an email reply from the attorney's office. I called and made an appointment for that very morning. We drove to downtown San Jose, were both interviewed by one of the paralegals for the firm.

She informed us that we definitely had a case, and that Emma no longer had any right to access the home or the property. She advised us to have the locks changed on all of the entry doors, place padlocks on the garage, and we were given appointments for the next day to meet with an attorney.

I was in shock, but I was also infuriated. On our way back to the house, we stopped at a hardware store and purchased a new lock for the front door and padlocks for the garage. We had keys made for all of the roommates. We were going to protect ourselves, our pet, our few possessions and the other roommates from this woman, who allegedly had ties to a local Vietnamese gang.

We told several of the roommates that we had been to an attorney, and Cami asked if she could go with us to our appointment the next day. We told her of course it would be fine. The next day at our appointment, in

the middle of our interview with the attorney, I received a phone call from yet another roommate.

Emma had arrived at the house with a moving truck, a group of immigrants, and a locksmith. She had the lock we had installed removed from the front door, the padlocks cut from the garage, ransacked the house, removed the refrigerator, and poured bleach over all of the food.

She also poured bleach over all of the floors, and poured quick drying cement down all of the drains, including the tubs, showers, toilets, disposals, and sinks. I instructed the roommate to phone the police, and we left our appointment unfinished. We raced back to the house to find Emma inside attempting to remove the ovens and ranges.

The refrigerator was already in the back of the moving truck. Kelly shoved her out of the house and refused to allow her back inside. Emma then proceeded to destroy as many of the outside plants as she could before the police arrived. We told the immigrants that the 'policia' were on their way, and they hit the pavement running.

One of the roommates pulled their car in front of the moving truck to prevent Emma from driving away. She sat in the back of the moving truck, refusing to allow us to get to anything in it. The police finally arrived, listened to our story, and even spoke with the attorney for the bank, who told them NOT to allow her to drive away with anything.

Guess what they did? You are right! They let her drive away, with a smirk on her face, gloating over what she had just done. This woman, who had been fraudulently renting rooms in the house for months, to the tune of $8000.00 to $10,000.00 each month, was allowed to get away with further causing harm to us. We had no protection.

The energy of the house, which was already very tense, began to change into one so bizarre that it was unbelievable. It appeared that all but a few of the roommates were living actively in alcoholism or drug addiction, and those people tried to persuade us to join them. I refused, but Kelly was weak.

She began drinking with other roommates. Not only drinking but snorting cocaine with L.J. She had Kale, her old meth dealer, come down from Fairfield as often as possible and together they used meth. She would stay away from our room for nights on end, only coming back to the room to detox from the alcohol and drugs.

I did my best to have the roommates all come together to hold meetings regarding the potential eviction and upcoming court hearings. I encouraged them to be involved for their own sakes. But getting everyone in the same room only served to make things worse. I couldn't get my voice heard over the din of intense arguments.

Most of the heated arguments were with Heinrich, almost coming to a physical fight on occasion. One day there was a knock on our bedroom door, and I heard Heinrich say that he had left a gift in the half-bath for us. I cautiously opened the bedroom door, not knowing exactly what to expect.

I went into the bathroom and was hit with the most foul of odors. I looked in the sink and it was empty. Then I lifted the toilet seat to discover it filled with feces and empty toilet paper cores. The stench was malodorous, absolutely disgusting. I gathered a few of the other roommates to ask them to help me clean it, but they all refused.

The responsibility lay on my shoulders to clear the toilet out, so, very carefully, and with much repulsion, I scooped out all of the feces and toilet paper cores, retching, and placed them in a plastic trash bag, and took the bag out to the waste bin at the curb. I washed my hands, over and over, and still felt that I had to wash them again and again.

If I had ever had even an ounce of respect for Heinrich it was completely gone, along with any that I may have had for his wife Phyllis. I had thought that they were both professionals. Phyllis worked for the IRS, and Heinrich was supposedly topnotch in the field of computer technology. I never wanted to see either of them again.

Our story made the front page of The Mercury News, we were on the local television news, (CBS), and there were several more stories about us in the local newspapers. Even though our stories were told the bank continued their attempts to take possession of the house and evict everyone.

Kelly and I began arguing more, and she argued with the other roommates as well, was verbally abusive, and often remarkably close to being physically abusive. The police were called on her over sixteen times, and eventually Heinrich filed a restraining order against her as a result of the threats she had made.

One night she tried to enter our room with her drunken friends, and I pushed her away. She overpowered me, and drove me into the wall, hands around my neck, subduing me. The next day I packed a few bags and left everything else behind, including Kudos. Maggie picked me up and drove me to her apartment in Campbell.

I thought that it was all behind me. All that I wished for was peace. One day I received a phone call from Barbara, one of my roommates from the Camp. She asked how I was doing, and I told her that I was fine. She said that she had heard from Kelly and told me that Kelly loved me with all of her heart and needed me to come back to her.

Barbara told me that if I loved Kelly at all that I needed to call her. My heart felt like it was going to stop. I honestly didn't know what to do. I had only been gone for a week, regaining my freedom, but I foolishly called her and allowed myself to be convinced to return to Hell House.

Kelly told me that she loved me, and promised that she would do the right thing, that she would stay away from all of the other roommates and would avoid the drugs and alcohol. That was an outright lie, and that very night she resumed the same path she had started just days after we had moved into Hell House.

She drank, she used drugs and she fought with everyone, including another one of the men, threatening him physically, and yet another restraining order was filed against her. With two restraining orders she was forced to stay away from the house during the day, but she would sneak into our room late at night.

Our car was parked down the street so Heinrich, who had filed the restraining orders, would not see it. Kelly would bring food with her so that at least I had one meal per day. Tension continued to mount, and there was at least one verbally abusive fight between roommates every single day.

I couldn't tolerate it any longer. It only took a few days for me to have to leave again. I had endured all that I could. I had become a hardhearted person. I was becoming verbally abusive. And I was depressed. Kelly happened to be in the room, so I waited for her to go to the bathroom.

I had moved my car into the driveway earlier when Kelly was not paying attention, and I had already put a few bags in the car, and even though I didn't have my driver's license, I took the car keys and ran. Kelly heard me and ran after me to the car, trying to get the keys out of my hand.

The keyring broke and keys flew everywhere, but I still had the car key. I put it in the ignition, started the car, put it in reverse and fled for my life. I left, with the intention of not ever going back for the few possessions I still had. Not even the cat. But that was not to be the case.

I drove to Campbell, to Stephanie's apartment, even though I was not supposed to be on the same property, having been terminated three months prior. A few days later I discovered that Kelly had come into town and taken my car. I tried calling her, but instead she texted me that she would return it when she was finished with it.

I was furious. She told me that her cousin was giving her a car, and she needed to transfer the title and get it insured. It took all day. It was evening when she called Stephanie and told her that she was downstairs with the keys to my car. Stephanie told me to stay in her apartment and went down the stairs to get the key.

Kelly pled with her, begging to speak with me. Stephanie returned without the key, and told me that Kelly had purchased a gun, and that she planned to commit suicide. Against my better judgement I decided to go and talk to her. I asked Stephanie to come down with me. Kelly was crying hysterically, asking why I had left her in such a mess.

I told her that it was not my choice for her to turn into a drug addled demon. I asked Kelly if she actually had a firearm, and if she were planning to commit suicide, and she said yes, lifting her shirt so that I could see the handle. I looked at Stephanie and signaled her to call 911.

The police came, and once again, Kelly was placed in handcuffs and put into a mandatory 5150 for suicide observation. She had the hospital call me, asking me to come down to visit with her. I decided to talk with her on the phone instead, but she was able to convince me, through crying and pleading, to come and see her in person.

I went the next day. On medication, Kelly was calm and logical, able to rationalize. I hugged her and told her that I loved her, that I always would, but that I would probably not return. She clung to me, begging me, telling me that she had no one else to turn to or talk to, and she cried until I promised her that I would come back in a few days.

Her birthday, April 7th, was coming up, so I went to the store and found two cards that spoke to my heart, and most certainly would speak to hers. They communicated what I truly felt for Kelly. Love. At one time unconditional. Now not so much. So, I went to visit her on her birthday.

As I was signing in for the visit, I noticed that the last signature, L.J., was that of the lesbian Kelly had spent so many nights with at Hell House. I was infuriated. I went in and waited for Kelly. When she came out, I stood up and handed her the cards, telling her that I was finished with her.

She grabbed me, holding me very tightly. I couldn't move and had to motion for help from one of the nurses. She asked Kelly to release me. Kelly told me that she was being discharged that day and had no place to go. I considered helping her, but then I remembered who her last visitor was.

I said "That's too bad. Why don't you phone L.J.? I'm sure that she would be more than happy to come and pick you up". I was angry, disappointed and so very deeply hurt. I got in my car and drove away. I didn't get far before turning around. I couldn't just leave Kelly stranded, or hand her over to people who didn't really care for her.

I picked her up and drove her to where she had left her cousins car. What a mistake. But didn't I already state that I have made many mistakes? I drove on to my daughter's house and parked my car on the street. As I was walking down the sidewalk to the property gate, Kelly came racing up behind me crying.

Her cousin had taken the car. She had no place to go. She begged me for help. Then, she got down on her knees and pleaded with me to marry her, swearing her eternal love. Damn my heart! I looked at her for a long time, then made one of the worst decisions I have ever made, I said yes.

So, here we were, stuck in a dreadful situation. She couldn't go back to the foreclosed house because of the restraining orders, and I certainly couldn't go back to that snake pit, so we ended up renting a cheap fleabag motel room, at the rate of eight hundred dollars for two weeks. We were fast running out of money and options.

Kelly was convinced that she needed to attend AA/NA meetings in order to maintain her sobriety. I agreed to go with her. The first place that she chose was in a rundown church in an unsavory part of San Jose. I sat through the worship services with her, helped in the kitchen, and attended the meetings after lunch was served.

We didn't go there for long though as I didn't feel comfortable with either the people or the neighborhood. Kelly found another meeting place closer to the motel where we were staying. This one was a little bit better, but I really didn't want to even be there. I went outside for frequent smoke breaks during the meetings.

I had had enough of AA/NA to last me a lifetime. On April 14th, which happened to be my mother's birthday, while I was standing outside, my phone rang. A man on the other line introduced himself as a police sergeant. He asked me if I was Susan Sheehan, to which I replied yes.

He then went on to ask if I had recently rented a room from Emma Nguyen. I told him that I had. He asked me if I knew where her relatives lived. I told him that I didn't, but Kelly did, having gone there in the past with L.J. I took his information and told him that I would have Kelly give him a call.

When the meeting was over I told Kelly that she needed to phone the police sergeant and why. She spoke to him for a few minutes, then told me that we needed to meet the Sargent and have him follow us out to Emma's relatives home in the East Foothills, close by Hell House.

It took about a half hour to drive there, the police sergeant following close behind us. Kelly pulled to the side of the road and pointed to the house where Emma's family lived. The sergeant requested that we drive on and told us that he would take it from there. I was, of course, very curious about why he needed to see Emma's relatives.

I suggested that Kelly phone L.J., who certainly would know what was going on. We learned that Emma had been murdered, in front of her eighteen month old baby girl, by her ex-boyfriend, who then committed suicide. Even if I tried to forget her, I couldn't, since she lost her life on my mother's eighty-fifth birthday, on April 14th, 2012.

Some of the roommates called me, saying that Emma got what she deserved. That made me sick to my stomach. I couldn't believe that they would be so heartless as to have those kind of thoughts. I was sad for Emma, for her boyfriend, and for the little baby girl that was left behind as an orphan.

Try as we might, we couldn't find a place to live, I couldn't find employment, and my children refused to help me because I was with Kelly. One evening, while we were watching television, an ad for the state of Arizona came on. I didn't pay much attention to it, but Kelly was intrigued.

She said, "That is where we need to go. You have family there; I have family there. We can make a fresh start". I argued that I wanted to stay in the Bay Area, but she didn't give up. So, foolishly I allowed her to convince me to move. To Arizona. At Kelly's insistence. The land of my birth, and the last place on earth that I wanted to live.

Reluctantly, I spent most of the rest of what money I had in the bank on the move, only to discover that we were moving into yet another situation that Kelly once again turned into a nightmare. I phoned my younger brothers, Peter and Michael, and let them know that Kelly and I would be moving to the Valley of the Sun in just a few days.

They were excited, but they were also suspicious of Kelly, knowing all of the horrible abuse that I had suffered. I searched online for a room to rent, knowing full well that was all that I could afford. I still had my unemployment for at least another year, so in renting a room I knew that I could pay for that and everything else that we might need.

I finally found a room on the Phoenix/Glendale border. I exchanged several emails with Mike, the man who was renting the room out. I looked his social media profile over and could see nothing out of the ordinary. He appeared to be a respectable person, and someone that Kelly and I both would be able get along with.

After much consideration I told Kelly that we could take the room, and I let the man, Mike, know. I rented a large moving truck, along with a car dolly to tow our car behind us with. I contacted all of my children and told them that Kelly and I would be moving to Arizona within a few days.

Chapter Five: The Valley of the Sun

The morning of Thursday April 19th came, and with it an extremely elevated level of anxiety and sense of dread. I knew, deep within my soul, that I was making one of the most terrible mistakes of my life in agreeing to this move. Nevertheless, we picked moved forward in picking up the moving truck and car dolly.

Kelly drove to the storage unit and together we cleared it out, loading the truck, box by box, and all of the heavy furniture. It took almost all day, and we still had to travel to Hell House to retrieve our belongings from the room and the few items we had stored in the garage. I didn't know about Kelly, but my body was exhausted.

It was a rather precarious situation going to Hell House, as Kelly still had restraining orders on her and was not allowed to be within one hundred yards of the house. Kelly backed the truck into the driveway and we snuck through the side gate and into the room. I was hoping that Heinrich and Phyliss were not watching from their window.

Heinrich had always made it a practice to spy out the windows from upstairs, standing on the landing and peering out. We had to rush to pack all of the loose items, putting them helter-skelter into boxes and large plastic bags. It was all that we could do to carry the mattress and box springs, which proved to be unwieldy.

We emptied the room in under two hours, then went to open the garage door. Much to our surprise, although it shouldn't have been that much of a surprise, someone had cut our padlock off of the door and replaced it with a different one. We had no way to get into the garage, and we needed the items that were inside.

Kelly began searching for something to break the lock off when suddenly Phyllis appeared. She had her cell phone in her hand. She told us that she was going to call the police and have Kelly arrested for breaking the restraining orders and threatened to have me arrested as an accomplice.

I took one look at Kelly and told her that we had to leave immediately. I had never in my life had so much police activity in and around me until I met Kelly. And still, here I was, ready to travel over seven hundred years miles to a place that I didn't want to be, all for the sake of what I considered to be love.

I got in the truck and waited for Kelly, who was hell bent on arguing with Phyliss. Heinrich came out the front door and started throwing his arms around and yelling. I got back out of the truck and physically pulled Kelly away from them, and using all of my strength forced her into the driver's seat of the truck.

More roommates ran out of the house, yelling at us, yelling at Heinrich, and yelling at each other. I told her to move it fast, that we needed to get away before the police arrived. She reluctantly started the truck and pulled away slowly, all the while watching Phyliss and Heinrich in the side mirror of the truck.

It seemed as if all she wanted was a fight. I had lost so much already that what little that I left behind at Hell House seemed insignificant in comparison. We drove back to the motel, with plans to leave the next morning. Kelly loaded my car onto the car dolly and did a visual on the moving truck, making sure that it was ready for the drive.

I went inside to prepare some food for the both of us. Kudos was in his carrier yowling, and I could tell that he was agitated. I am certain that he could sense the overwhelming confusion and dreaded anticipation that I was experiencing. I let him out to try and calm him down.

We weren't even supposed to have him in the room and had taken him to Stephanie's apartment when we first rented the room, but he attacked her and the children and she was not able to keep him, so he remained hidden at the motel and we didn't allow anyone else in our room for the duration of our stay, not even maid service.

I fed Kudos, then made dinner for Kelly and myself. After we had eaten we both took showers. I went over everything in the room, making sure that all of our belongings were packed and secure. The food I would leave. Perhaps the maids or someone else would be able to use it.

Kelly was already lying down watching television, so I joined her. Soon she was snoring, but sleep didn't come easily for me. The seven hundred mile trip that lay ahead of us was more than I was looking forward to, and I worried that Kelly would not be able to drive it.
I lay there worrying for over an hour.

I decided to go outside to smoke and think about the future and what it may hold for us. I was leaning against the building, smoking in the dark, when all of a sudden eight police cars, no lights or sirens, pulled silently into the parking lot. Officers piled out of the cars, weapons in their hands.

One of them was shouting at a man who was walking through the parking lot. I went back inside as quickly as I could, but not before watching as the man was thrown to the ground and handcuffed. I sat inside at the little table by the window listening to what was happening outside.

Morning couldn't come soon enough! Even though the motel was in a fairly decent part of town there seemed to be regular criminal and police activity. I could hardly wait to get out of there. Kelly had slept through the entire thing, and since she was driving the moving truck I decided not to wake her up.

I pulled back the covers and carefully eased myself into the bed, being careful not to awaken Kelly. I knew that I needed to sleep as well. But sleep was hard to come by. I was worried about leaving my children and grandchildren behind, not knowing when I would be able to see them again.

I must have finally dozed off because I was awakened to the sound of the toilet flushing. I looked at the clock and saw that it was just past 5 a.m. Kelly, already dressed, told me to get my ass out of bed and get ready to head out. I sat up on the edge of the bed and rubbed my eyes. After washing up I made each of us a cup of coffee.

Kelly didn't sit to drink her coffee. Instead, she began hauling our luggage and boxes out to the moving truck. I watched as she worked, and I didn't mind letting her do it. I was too sore and so very tired from having to load the moving truck with our belongings from the storage unit.

I gave Kudos some food, and when he was finished eating I carefully placed him in his carrier. This trip was not going to be easy on him. Poor thing, he had been through so much, and most of it was put on him by

Kelly. Even though he and I didn't always get along I did love him.

Kelly was finished loading the last of our belongings. She told me that it was time to hit the road. My heart sank. I didn't want to do this, didn't want to move to Arizona. I felt like a rabbit caught in a trap, helplessly watching the inevitableness of my fate closing in on me. I got my purse and coat and reluctantly followed Kelly out of the door.

We had one last stop to make before getting on the freeway. David had a television that he was giving me, and this was an opportunity to see him and his family before leaving. But it was not a pleasant visit, as David was so incredibly angry that I was moving. He had sent me a message the night before, which I choose not to share with Kelly.

This following is what he wrote:

""Hey Mom. I really don't know why you're letting this evil person tell you where you should be heading in life. All we can say is we warned you. I can't tell you what to do, but I do know this.....SHE WON'T ONLY CONTINUE TO RUIN YOUR LIFE BUT WILL ULTIMATELY BE YOUR DEMISE!!!!!!!! She must be so proud of herself that she is finally going to have you where she wants you. Alone, vulnerable, and so far away from the ones who would protect you. If you are reading this Kelly, FUCK YOU!!! You ruined my Moms life!!! You are what's wrong with the world. I wish you had never gone to that f**king camp Mom, you would have eventually been much better off!!! She has made you lose and lose and lose. And do you know what?? You could just lose the one thing you really have left that is truly yours....YOUR LIFE!!!! Be warned, she is a fucking leech, an emotional vampire/wreck/killer/psychopath. Nothing good could ever come of this poorly planned and thought out decision. Love you, miss you, and truly don't understand. Your Son, David. p.s. Remember your promise???"

He was right. I had made a promise to my children and grandchildren to never be far from them, but I found myself trapped in an unstoppable whirlpool that was slowly dragging me down. But I did it anyway, at Kelly's urging, and it was a choice that I would come to regret as one of the most dreadful ones in my entire life.

David stood in the driveway waiting for us. He begrudgingly loaded the television into the back of the moving truck, and barely gave me a kiss before we drove away. I could see him in the sideview mirror watching us as we drove away. My heart broke into a millions pieces.

Kelly didn't care. I am certain that she was relieved to be moving me away from my family as she had always felt threatened by my love for them. She made her down Interstate 101 South to Highway 152 East which would connect us to Interstate 5 Southbound, headed towards Los

Angeles.

We drove mostly in silence. I gazed out my window at the passing cars and landscape. Kudos was in his carrier on the seat between Kelly and me. Fortunately, he was sleeping, and I hoped that he would continue to sleep most of the way. We stopped in Gilroy for a quick breakfast but didn't linger since Kelly wanted to get back on the road.

She was confident that she could make it to Phoenix before nightfall. The radio was blasting as we drove, Kelly yelling the lyrics at the top of her lungs. This made for a fairly miserable ride. It was rap music, definitely not one of my favorites, but I kept silent, not wishing to stir the pot with her.

I continued watching the landscape. We were in what was once known as the Salad Bowl of California, now a bleak landscape. The miles disappeared behind us and before I knew it we were climbing up and over the Grapevine. It only has an elevation of about 1500 feet, but the moving truck was having a hard time getting up and over it.

Kelly shifted into low gear, but the truck was barely hitting fifteen miles per hour. It took us more than an hour to get over the hill. By the time we were on the other side it was already early evening. So much for us making it to Phoenix by nightfall. Kelly told me that she was not going to be able to drive much longer, that she needed to rest.

I began looking for a motel. We had driven close to three hundred miles, and perhaps it was best to just stop for the night. We found a motel in the small town of Lebec, just on the other side of the Grapevine. They didn't allow animals in the rooms, so we had to leave Kudos in the cab of the truck.

We got a few personal items from the back of the truck and walked to the room. The room was, shall we say, not quite up to my level of expectations, but better than the fleabag we had been staying in. Of course, it was not super expensive, and I certainly didn't expect a penthouse suite, but it was pretty run down.

The carpets were worn, the drapes were worn, and the bedding had seen better days. There was only one set of towels in the bathroom. It was more like a flop house. Kelly lay down on the bed and told me not to wake her up. I nodded at her, picked up my cigarettes, and went outside to smoke.

The moving truck was parked about one hundred yards away from the room, not far, so I decided to walk down and peer through the window to check on Kudos. He saw me and started yowling loudly. I put my hand on the window, trying to comfort him from a distance, but that only seemed to upset him.

I wished that I had the keys. I could have at least sat beside him for a while to calm him down. I went back to the room and went inside. Kelly was on the bed, still fully clothed, and snoring. I couldn't turn on the television for fear of wakening her, so I sat at the old, wobbly table, watching her and thinking about the future.

I must have dozed off because the next thing that I knew Kelly was moving around the room gathering our belongings. She told me that she had gotten enough rest and that she wanted to get back on the road. It was a little past ten p.m. I wondered if she was going to be able to drive in the dark, but she assured me that she would be fine.

There was a small truck stop café at the end of the motel driveway and we decided that we should get a bite to eat before heading out. We walked there, leaving the moving truck parked where it was. We each had breakfast food, and before we left we ordered coffee to go for the road.

Walking back to the truck Kelly took my hand and told me that everything was going to be fine. Of course, I highly doubted that, especially considering the last several years of chaos and turmoil. But here I was, on the road, and determined to make the best of what I knew was going to be a miserable situation.

We got into the cab and Kelly drove the truck around the motel and back onto the road that led to the freeway. We were back on Interstate 5 in no time. Traffic was virtually non-existent, which I thought to be unusual as we were coming close to the Los Angeles area where we would connect to Interstate 10, which would take us to Phoenix.

I leaned against my door and closed my eyes. The movement of the truck on the road eventually lulled me to sleep. I awoke soon afterwards though. We were approaching L.A., and the traffic was beginning to build up. We had to drive almost into the heart of Los Angeles in order to connect to Interstate 10.

Even at this hour of the night traffic was bumper to bumper. Of course, it was Friday night, and I knew that this was normal for the area. It took Kelly a little over an hour to get through the traffic, but once we were on Interstate 10 it was smooth sailing. It was already close to midnight and we still had almost four hundred miles to travel.

By the time we reached Blythe it was just a bit past 4a.m. We pulled into a truck stop to get a bite to eat and refresh ourselves. Kudos was traveling well, sleeping most of the time. I was relieved. I comforted him and gave him some food and water before going into the restaurant. I wanted to make sure that he was taken care of.

We were back on the road by 5a.m., and Kelly made good time. There were no hills or mountains to climb, just a straight and flat road almost all of the way to Phoenix. Even though I had a lot of apprehension over this journey, I was actually beginning to get excited at the thought of seeing my younger brothers once again.

Finding Peace

We arrived at my brother's house sometime around 10 a.m. They both came of out the house, running down the driveway, and scooped me into their arms. Kelly stood behind me watching. They shook her hand and invited us inside for coffee. I made sure that Kudos was comfortable in his carrier, then followed them all inside.

My brothers had agreed that they would help us to get moved into the room at Mike's house in Glendale. Whatever we couldn't fit into the room was going into storage, and they would help us with that as well. I had already rented a storage unit not far from Mike's house so that it would be easy for us to store those items.

My brothers led the way to the house which was located just on the border of Phoenix and Glendale. As we approached the house I noticed how run down the neighborhood was. In fact, it was so run down that it felt as if we had entered another very strange world. I was utterly disappointed, but I tried to look on the bright side.

We didn't have to stay here long, and we could pretty much keep to ourselves, in our room, or visiting with my brothers. I got out of the moving truck and went to the front door. A youngish man opened the door. This would be Mike, who we were renting the room from. He was tall, podgy, disheveled and very pasty looking.

Being born and raised in this part of Arizona I knew that not everyone is tanned and vigorous looking, but he had the appearance of someone who spent every waking hour inside the house, in a darkened room. I introduced myself. Kelly was behind me and my brothers were behind her.

He invited us into the house and gave us a brief tour. It was very dark, shabbily furnished, smelled sour and stale, and was in sad disarray. We went inside and we followed him through the living room and down a hallway. There were bedrooms on each side of the hallway, but he kept going, opening a door at the end.

What I saw was a remodelers nightmare, with old sheet rock and rusty cans of paint lying about, drapes hanging here and there, a vain attempt at privacy I suppose. Even though it was almost Summer, it was damp and musty. Mike told us that this was where his children slept when they were visiting.

Unkempt and dirty, there were several old and stained mattresses on the floor for the children to sleep on, with ragged blankets to cover themselves with. I asked him why they were not sleeping in the bedrooms we had passed by as we walked down the hallway, but he didn't answer me.

We walked back through the house and finally came to the room we were renting, which definitely left a lot to be desired. The room itself was fairly good sized, approximately ten foot by twenty foot. There was an entrance door from the kitchen area, a door to the bathroom, and another door which led to the hallway.

Mike had the lease agreement for us to sign. The rent for the room was $400.00 per month, including utilities and cable, and I had already sent him a check from California in the amount of $135.00 a week prior for the prorated amount. I read the simple lease agreement once again and Kelly and I signed it.

My brothers, Kelly and I got to work unloading the moving truck. I wanted all of my kitchen items of course, plus the bedroom and personal items that we would need. Mike had told us that we could use any cabinets that we wanted, and that we were free to store our food in them, as well as anywhere in the refrigerator.

Having just recently lived through the nightmare experience at Hell House I was a bit reluctant to spread my belongings throughout this house. I didn't know this person, and he could very well be just like

Emma, but I did want to unpack my kitchen items, so I decided to go ahead and do so.

It was not long before we had everything in the house, all of the extras in storage, and the moving truck and dolly returned to the truck company. Peter and Michael went home, and Kelly and I returned to the room after picking up cleaning supplies at the store. I wanted to start cleaning and arranging everything for the night.

Due to the odd configuration of the room my beautiful California Kind sized bed didn't fit, so we decided to list it for free on Craigslist. It was quite an expensive bed, and in exceptionally good condition. Within an hour we had over a dozen inquiries, and the bed was gone before the day was over.

That first night we slept on the floor. It was almost unbearable. I woke up stiff and feeling bruised all over, so I went to the local Walmart and bought an air mattress as a temporary solution. I would purchase another bed as soon as I received my next unemployment payment, which would be soon.

We worked together on the room and bathroom. I put a few of my dishes and assorted pots and pans in the kitchen, along with my collection of beautiful wooden serving bowls. I avoided the living room and the other areas of the house as they felt very odd to me, almost like something from a nightmare.

We didn't smoke inside, so I sat in the carport to smoke, and was able to meet the next door neighbor, Anita, who was a nice younger woman. She and I spent hours talking and watching her young children play in her driveway. For some reason she didn't like Mike but refrained from telling me why exactly.

Kelly would come out from the room occasionally, and only then to smoke. She avoided having conversations with Anita, and I really didn't understand why. Kelly was developing a relationship with Mike though. I personally didn't care for him. There was someone not quite right about him.

I would often awaken at night to Kelly not being in bed, but I didn't bother looking for her. I knew that she was spending time with Mike. I didn't worry too much about it. She needed a friend outside of our relationship and I didn't think that any harm could come of the friendship.

Mike had a part time job as a night clerk at a motel located along Interstate 17 not far from the house. That was great for him since he had no vehicle and had to walk everywhere that he went. I enjoyed the evenings with him gone as he was quite an awkward fellow. Once or twice a week his three little children would visit.

I had the opportunity to meet all three of them a few days after we had moved in. I heard the voices of children coming from the kitchen, so I went to investigate. There, in the kitchen, I saw three small children, all under the age of five, two boys and a girl, the youngest boy still in diapers.

Mike told me that this was his scheduled visit and introduced me to them. I smiled as they ran around the kitchen and dining area, laughing and playing. I told them that I was happy to make their acquaintances and went back into my room. I could still hear the children from beyond my closed door.

Mike asked if I would be willing to watch the children while he worked. I asked him what that entailed, considering that he worked from 10 p.m. to 6 a.m. He said that all that I would need to do was check on them a couple of times during the night, and that he would take twenty dollars off of the rent for each night that I watched them.

That sounded fair to me. Watching them twice a week or so would shave off close to $200.00 from the monthly rent, and I could certainly use that extra money to make purchases for Kelly, who had zero income, and myself. I told him that I would be happy to do so. He looked relieved.

I began that very night. I set my cell phone alarm for two hour intervals beginning at midnight. I felt that would be adequate for checking on the sleeping children. They were sleeping peacefully each time that I checked on them. Getting back to sleep was a bit of an issue, but I figured that I could always take a nap during the day.

A couple of weeks after we moved in my niece Samantha came down from Nebraska to visit. I had not seen her since she was five years old, so this was a real treat for both of us. I was extremely glad that Mike was not working on the days she visited as I didn't have to get up at night to check on the children.

She spent time with my brother Michael, of course. After all he is her dad. She also stayed with Kelly and I for a few days, which I was so happy for. Samantha slept on the loveseat, which was amazingly comfortable but not really suited for more than a nap, but she managed.

We treated Samantha to lunch at the Three Hippies hamburger shop in Phoenix. She was not feeling well but was able to eat a Magic Mushroom burger. Afterwards she took a bottle of water and went out to the car to lie down and wait for us to finish. By the time we went to the car she was, fortunately, feeling better.

I asked Samantha if she had ever visited her grandmother's (my mother's) grave, and she told me no. I told Kelly that I wanted to drive to Saint Francis cemetery where my mother's grave is located. Out of her eleven grandchildren, only my three children had ever visited her grave.

I hadn't been there for eighteen years, and it must have been a strange but wonderful experience for Samantha. She shares the same middle name as my mother, Belle, but my mother had passed fourteen years before Samantha was born, therefore she never knew her grandmother.

We had brought flowers, (White Spider Chrysanthemums, my mother's favorite) and a pack of Salem menthol cigarettes, which was my mother's favorite brand. We lingered by her grave for a short while, then decided to go, dropping Samantha off at her dad's house on our way home.

Samantha returned to Nebraska not too long afterwards, and even though I really enjoyed seeing my niece, I was relieved since Kelly was making sexual advances towards her every time she was around. That was an ongoing thing with Kelly, as anyone reading this well knows.

Soon after Samantha's visit I received a message from Kelly's cousin Tara inviting us to join her at an IHOP for a Mother's Day brunch. She also invited us to spend the night at her home in Queen Creek. I had never met this cousin, so I thought that it would be a nice diversion, and a chance to meet more of Kelly's relatives.

That night I awakened around midnight and noticed that Kelly was not in the room. I got up and went into the kitchen. I heard Kelly's voice coming from the living room, so I walked around the corner. She and Mike were sitting on the couch talking and watching television. They looked up and saw me.

I didn't say anything. I nodded my head and went back to the room. I knew that she was going out of the room at night, I just didn't know that she was 'hanging out' with Mike so often. I began to worry, especially after Anita told me that Mike was a meth user and knowing that Kelly was a 'recovering' meth addict.

I went back to bed, and I was up early the next morning, eager to meet Tara. I let Kelly sleep in. I didn't even know what time she came back to bed. I washed up and went out to the kitchen to get a cup of coffee. It was still dark out, but I sat in the carport to smoke, drink my coffee, and wake up.

Kelly came stumbling out of the house with a cup of coffee in her hands about an hour later. I suggested to her that we both needed to get ready if we were going to be on time to meet Tara. She, of course, needed to wake up a bit, while I, on the other hand, was wide awake. I went ahead and took a shower, got dressed and put on some makeup.

By the time I was finished Kelly was getting her things together to take a shower. It was close to 9 a.m., and I knew that we needed to leave fairly soon. I told her as much and she promised to be as quick as possible. Soon she was ready and we hurried out the door and drove to the restaurant.

Tara was already inside waiting for us. She had reserved a table, which was smart since the place was packed. Soon we were seated and the server brought water and coffee to the table. We perused the menus and made our selections. The server took our orders and told us that the food would be out soon.

Afterwards we followed Tara down Interstate 17 to Queen Creek. She lived in a newer subdivision. I was amazed at how much the town had grown since I had last been there, but I had left Arizona in 1996, sixteen years earlier, so I shouldn't have been so surprised. Progress, or so they say.

I enjoyed myself at Tara's, had an opportunity to meet her mother, father, husband and children, and take a nice breather from the house on Lawrence Road. Tara's father, Richard Ortiz, who is Kelly's blood uncle, prepared the barbecue while the rest of us put the side dishes together.

The next day, before traveling back to Phoenix, I stopped by the mechanics shop where Tara's husband worked for an estimate for a tune-up for my car. It was more than I could afford, so I asked Jeremy if he would be willing to come to Phoenix to do the tune-up. He agreed, much to my relief.

Kelly and I shopped before returning to the house. No one was home when we got there, which I was actually happy about. I really wished that we could afford a house of our own, but such is life. We put away the groceries and retired to our room to watch some television before going to bed.

Jeremy traveled up from Queen Creek the very next day. He replaced the frieze plug, changed the oil, and replaced the spark plugs. He told me that it shouldn't need to be serviced for a while, which was a relief. I thanked him for taking the time and paid him generously.

Kelly and I decided to go to a restaurant, get a bite to eat, and do some more shopping since I noticed that we were low on a few of our toiletries. As we were on our way out the door Mike stopped me and asked if I might be available to watch the children while he was at work that night and I told him of course I would.

Before we got to the restaurant Kelly decided that she wanted to visit a secondhand store. I told her that would be fine, but instead of pulling into the right lane to turn right, she made the turn from the outside lane and hit a car in the right lane. The impact threw me into the dashboard, but I was not injured.

Kelly pulled into the parking lot and parked the car. The other car followed and parked. I got out of the car to access the damage and saw that the right front fender was completely crushed in and almost hitting the tire. I noticed two women emerge from the other car, which had sustained little or no damage.

One of the women was pregnant, looking to be close to full term. I had already phoned 911, so I walked over to make sure that they were both okay. Of course, they were shook up, but neither one was injured. I felt relieved. Kelly was fine, and still sitting behind the wheel of the car.

The police came, but no ambulance. The officers investigated the scene on the road and came to the conclusion that Kelly was at fault. They cited her for failure to yield, a citation that she never paid or appeared in court for as far as I know. I was really quite upset with Kelly. Now my car was no more than a piece of junk.

Needless to say we didn't go out to eat or do any shopping that day. I was miserable. I had worked hard and sacrificed so much to buy my little old car, plus I had just, the day before, put more money into it to keep it in good running condition. Kelly was careless and could actually care less.

I had already reported the accident to my insurance company, making sure that they knew that I was not the driver. After all, I was planning to get my driver's license back, and an accident might make it more difficult. It would feel good to be able to drive myself on errands, and maybe visits with my brothers without Kelly.

I made some dinner for both of us, and afterwards went out to the carport and had a cigarette. Anita was sitting outside and came over to join me. As we were talking, she began whispering. She reminded me to be wary of Mike, that he was a known methamphetamine addict. I replied that I was keeping my eyes wide open, at least during the day.

Mike came outside to join us. I looked at Anita and wondered if he had heard us. He asked if I would be watching the children that night and I told him of course I was. Mike's shift started at 10 p.m. and he left the house to walk to work at 9:30 p.m., so there was time for me to get myself prepared.

I set the alarm on my cell phone and fell asleep watching television. Kelly had been particularly silent all evening. I wondered what was wrong, but I supposed she may have been thinking about the car accident she had caused, but it was doubtful. Perhaps she was going to miss hanging out with Mike that night.

I awakened at midnight for my first check of the children. I made my way down the hallway to the strange addition where they slept. Their eyes were closed and they looked peaceful. I listened carefully to make sure that they were asleep, and I made sure that they were covered with the raggedy blankets before I left.

I fell back to sleep, but it took more time than usual. It seemed like only moments had passed when my alarm went off at 2 a.m. I was groggy, but managed to get to where the children were. They were all three still blissfully asleep. Only two more checks to go before Mike returned from his job.

I continued watching the children for the next month, but one morning I woke up nearly exhausted to tears. I checked one more time on the children, then started a pot of coffee. I decided that I would not be able to continue watching them. Mike would either have to take the children to their mother's house or find someone else to help.

When Mike came home I told him. He was, needless to say, extremely disappointed. In fact, his normally pasty looking face turned bright red. I was not too worried about that though; plus, the $20.00 a night was simply not worth losing sleep over. I finished my cigarette and went to wait for Kelly to wake up.

While she slept I went online to check for messages from my children. I didn't hear from them very often. I realized that they were really quite disappointed that I had moved to Arizona, but there was little that I could do about it at that point. I missed them so much, they and my grandchildren.

There was nothing for me to do in the room so I went out to the kitchen. I heard a low, painful moaning coming from the living room. I walked through the doorway and peered into the darkened room. There, laying on the couch, was Mike, his little girl straddled across his lap.

His eyes were closed and his hips were undulating in a way that was sexually suggestive. The girl continued to moan, and I could see that she was trying to push away from him. I walked further into the room and Mike's eyes opened. Seeing me he lurched up from the couch, knocking his small daughter to the floor.

He hurriedly explained that they were playing one of their favorite games, but that his daughter was too tired to play. He told her to get up off of the floor and go to her room and wait for her mother. I simply looked at him. I didn't believe him. It didn't look like a game. It looked like molestation.

I walked back into the kitchen, my mind racing. I could have phoned 911, but I had no proof of what I had seen, and my words would only be considered hearsay. Perhaps I should talk to their mother when she came to pick them up. I would be listening, though, for any more sounds like the moaning that I had heard.

I went outside to clear my mind. Anita was standing by her back door and walked over to join me. I didn't tell her what I saw. I was still digesting the scene, which thoroughly disturbed and disgusted me. I knew that the children's mother was coming soon to pick them up, and I decided to speak with her when she arrived.

Kelly finally woke up and came outside to join us. She had a cup of coffee in her hand which was sloshing over the sides. I asked her if she had slept well. She looked at me strangely, and she asked me what I meant by that. I sighed and didn't reply. Kelly just didn't know how to answer a simple question.

She was mostly sullen in the mornings but had been particularly so since the car accident. There was nothing that I could do to change that. I could only hope that she would not get too depressed, get over it and get on with life, maybe find a job and get my car repaired. Or perhaps she needed to find a new psychiatrist.

I told her that I needed to go out and do some shopping, but that I wanted to wait until the children were picked up before we left. Kelly asked why, and I told her that I had a few things to speak to their mother about. I didn't want to share with her about what I had seen. Not yet. I went back inside to wait for the mother to arrive.

I made the bed and straightened the room. I checked the computer again for any messages. I got my purse together for the store, then I sat on the loveseat and waited. Finally, I heard a car pull up into the driveway. I went outside and saw not only the mother, but the grandmother as well.

The children ran out the door and past me to the SUV. They scrambled into the back seat of the car, laughing and pulling on each other. I walked to the driver's side and the grandmother rolled the window down. I had met the mother once, but not the grandmother. I introduced myself.

I was not sure how to begin the conversation, so I just started telling them what I had heard and seen. The grandmother pursed her lips, and the mother shook her head. She told me that they both had suspected something strange going on with the little girl but couldn't put their finger on anything with certainty.

The mother asked if I would be willing to keep watch when the children were with Mike and report anything else that was suspicious. They invited me to come to grandmother's house to talk more and wondered if I would be interested in speaking with the children's caseworker.

I told them that I was no longer able to watch the children at night, but that I wanted to make sure that these children, in particular the little girl, were not harmed in any way, any shape, or any form. I gave them both my cell phone number and told them to call me and let me know when a good time was for me to pay them a visit.

I turned back to the house as they drove away and saw Mike standing in the carport just outside the kitchen door. He asked me what we had been talking about and I lied, telling him that we were just exchanging pleasantries. I certainly didn't want to give him any indication regarding the conversation I had with his ex-wife.

I walked past him and into the house. Kelly was in the kitchen, and I told her that I was ready to go. I grabbed my purse from the room and walked out to the car. I saw Kelly and Mike talking at the back door and wondered what it was that conversation was about. I was becoming suspicious of their friendship.

On our way to the store I told Kelly what I had seen that morning in the living room, and also told her that I had spoken to the children's mother and grandmother. Kelly cast a sideways glance in my direction, but really didn't have much to say about it. I wondered if she really cared at all.

I let her know that I would be meeting with the mother soon, as well as potentially speaking with the children's caseworker. I refused to allow even the suggestion of abuse. Kelly knew full well how I felt about it. She told me that she would drive me to the mother's house when the time came.

I was not sure how she would react, but I had to ask Kelly if Mike had ever offered her meth when she visited with him at night. She laughed and told me that he had, but that she had refused. I wanted to believe her but given my past experience with her I had a difficult time doing so.

I didn't tell Kelly, but I decided to have a talk with Mike about this. There was no way that I was going to live through yet another round of Kelly's meth use, which always led to her abuse of myself and others. I just had to time the conversation with Mike when she was not around.

That afternoon I receive a phone call from the children's grandmother asking if I could drop by her house the next day. While she was still on the phone I asked Kelly if she could drive me there and she told me that would be fine, as long as she could come inside. I let the grandmother know that Kelly and I both would be there.

We arrived at the grandmother's house shortly after noon the next day. She had prepared light refreshments and offered both of us either coffee or tea. We sat in the living room waiting for the children's mother to join us. We exchanged pleasantries, just chit-chat while we waited.

It was not long before the mother arrived, with all three of the children in tow. She sent them to their rooms and sat down on the couch next to the grandmother. She was obviously nervous, which was understandable. She asked if I was ready to speak with the caseworker and I said yes, of course I was.

She dialed the number and put the phone on speaker. I introduced myself to the caseworker and she asked me to recount what I had witnessed. I told her that I was certain of what I had seen, and she said that Mike was being investigated for this very issue. I was not surprised.

When I was finished with the conversation I asked about the mother and grandmother about Mike's meth addiction. The mother rolled her eyes. She told us that this was the very reason she had divorced Mike, and that she had fought to gain full custody of the children as she considered him to be extremely unstable.

Kelly didn't seem to be interested in the conversation. Perhaps she thought that Mike was a good guy, or maybe he really was her meth buddy. I wouldn't be surprised. I decided to talk to him about the meth when we got back to the house, but I didn't tell Kelly. I knew that she would have stopped me.

We did some shopping before returning to the house. I was putting the groceries away when Mike walked into the kitchen. He asked if I needed any help and I told him that I was fine. He went into the living room and turned on the television. I saw this as an opportunity to have a conversation with him.

I finished putting the groceries away and asked Mike if I could speak to him for a minute. He got up off of the couch and walked into the dining room. I went in and stood about five inches from him. Keep in mind that he was well over six feet tall and I am only five foot two inches.

I told him that I was aware of his meth use, and that I knew that he had offered it to Kelly. I took a deep breath, and looking directly into his eyes, I told him that if I ever caught wind of him offering meth to Kelly again that I would hunt him down. He didn't say a word. He abruptly pushed past me and went outside.

I got a glass of iced tea and went into the room. I sat down on the loveseat taking deep breaths. I could feel the adrenaline flowing through my body and had to somehow calm myself down. Kelly asked if I was okay, and I told her that I was fine. I didn't want her to know about the conversation with Mike.

I decided to prepare a home cooked meal for our dinner. It was a bit early, but I knew that would calm me down. Kelly and I ate in our room, and afterwards we went out into the carport and smoked cigarettes. Mike was nowhere to be seen, and I wondered where he had gone to.

I went back inside the room and put my pajamas on. I was tired from the days happenings, the conversations about the children, and confronting Mike about the meth. All that I wanted to do was watch a bit of television and relax. Kelly joined me soon after. I asked if she had seen Mike and she said no.

We were both fast asleep when there was a very loud banging on the door of our room. We both jumped out of bed and Kelly opened the door. There, in the kitchen, stood two police officers with Mike right behind them. One of the officers ordered us to leave the house. I was in shock.

I asked what was going on, and the officer showed me restraining orders against both Kelly and me. He said that we needed to leave the house immediately, and that we could make arrangements with Mike and the police department to return to pick up our belongings. It was almost midnight and I had no clue what to do.

I went into the room and put Kudos in his carrier, grabbed my purse, and out the door we went, restraining orders in hand. Kelly pulled the car out of the driveway and parked down the street from Mike's house. I hesitated to call my brothers, but I knew that I really didn't have much of a choice.

I dialed Michael's number and he answered in a drowsy voice. I told him what had just happened and he told me to just come on over, that we could stay with them until we could get everything sorted out. I was somewhat relieved. He and Peter were waiting for us when we pulled into the carport.

They had made a pot of coffee, so we sat in the carport and talked while we sipped the fresh brew. Michael told me that we could sleep in their spare room, but that there was no bed. He did have pillows and blankets for us. I wished that I had thought about bringing the air mattress. I thanked him and told him that would work fine.

I awoke early the next morning in somewhat of a panic. I had never had a restraining order placed on me, and I couldn't for the life of me understand why Mike had done this, except that he was guilty of what I had accused him of. I got a cup of coffee and took the paperwork the officer had given me outside to look it over.

My brothers were having coffee and cigarettes. They had already been up for a while. I read the order and was shocked to see that I had to appear in court. Mike was pressing charges against me for threatening him when I told him that I would hunt him down. The hearing was scheduled for two days away.

I certainly didn't know what to expect, but I did know that I wanted to be 'courtroom' presentable, so later that day I went shopping for an outfit that was befitting a woman of my age. Afterwards I asked my brothers if they could help us retrieve our belongings from Mike's house.

I would rent and pay for a moving truck, but I needed someone with muscles to move certain items. They said that would be fine, and that they had talked and decided that we could stay with them until we found another room. I thanked them. I would not have to worry right away about finding another place.

I told them that I could pay them a fair amount of money and help out with groceries, and asked if three hundred dollars to start would be acceptable. They said that would be perfect. I was so excited. When Kelly woke up I told her the good news, but she refused to stay with my brothers.

She insisted on finding a place of our own. I told her that we could try, but first we needed to move our things out of Mike's house, and almost everything would go into storage. I sent Mike a message online and asked when we could come by to pick up our belongings. It took him a while but he finally replied.

He told me that we could come by that afternoon at 3 p.m., and that he would have the police there for a civil standby. I let my brothers and Kelly know that the move would be in just a few hours. Kelly rode with Michael to a local moving truck company and rented a truck for the day.

Peter's girlfriend Janet came by and offered to help us move. I thanked her and told her the more people we had the quicker we could be out of that house. Michael had the presence of mind to buy moving boxes when he and Kelly picked up the truck. He and Kelly drove the truck to Mike's house, and Peter, Janet and I followed in her truck.

As we drove up to the house I saw two police cars and four uniformed officers standing in front of the house. We were told by one of the officers that we had fifteen minutes to remove our possessions. I started to protest but seeing the look in his eye I decided against it. I certainly didn't want any more trouble.

The five of us went inside the house and began packing all of the loose items first. I started in the kitchen, the others in the bedroom and bath. I began opening the cabinets and cupboards, but much to my dismay discovered that eighty percent of my personal belongings were missing, including tableware, flatware, and all of my wooden bowls.

Even the food that I had bought was gone. I tried to tell one of the officers, but he turned his back on me and walked out of the room. It was not long before we had everything out of the house and in the back of the moving truck. Janet, Peter and I followed behind Michael and Kelly to the storage unit, which was not far away.

The only items that we took to my brother's house was the queen sized bed I had just purchased, my nightstands, television and the table it went on. These just fit in the spare room, but it was very cozy. Kelly, though, continued to be obstinate, refusing to find the good in anything.

The next morning was my court appearance. We arrived in downtown Phoenix, a few blocks from the courthouse, and several hours early. I bought both of us lunch from a cart, along with some coffee, and we sat on a bench across from the courthouse to eat. I wondered if Mike was even going to show up.

When it was close to the hearing time we walked to the courthouse, went through security and into the main lobby. I looked at the dockets on the wall and found the correct courtroom, which was on the second floor. We took the elevator up, and as soon as we got off the elevator I saw Mike.

He saw us and smirked in a rather sickening manner. I turned and looked the other way and found a bench to sit on which was close to the courtroom door. I knew that he was watching us, but I chose to ignore him. Soon the bailiff called us into the courtroom for the hearing.

There were a few hearings before mine, but finally the judge called out our both of our names. I stood when she said my name, but Mike remained seated. She read the charges that Mike was attempting to bring against me. Mind you, I had not been arrested, I had not been charged, and I didn't really know why I was there.

Mike finally stood up and began speaking over the judge. She said, quite loudly, "Young man, sit down immediately or I will have you removed from the courtroom." I looked at him, seeing that his face was beet red. She looked at me, looked at Mike, and said "This case is quashed". He couldn't pursue his accusations any further.

I turned around and smiled at him as he stormed out of the courtroom. I never saw or heard from him again, but I did hear from his ex-wife a few weeks later. She told me that charges were being brought against him for molestation and that he no longer had visitation with any of the children.

The next several weeks were spent with Kelly looking for another place to live. She would search online every evening, write down addresses, and we would drive to the houses. Not even one of them was in a decent neighborhood, and all were in even worse shape than Mike's was.

She argued with me non-stop, often to the point of shouting. She insisted that my brothers were just using me for my money, even though they had not moved me to Arizona. She told me that I couldn't give them money or buy groceries, even though the money belonged to me.

During this period of time I started pursuing obtaining my driver's license. I went to the Arizona MVD and asked what I needed to do to get an Arizona driver's license. They asked for my social security number and told me that all I had to do was pass the written and driving tests.

Now remember, I had been cited for a DUI in November of 2009, had my license revoked, was sentenced to five years court probation and had to complete a DUI class before becoming eligible to apply for a new license. Apparently none of that mattered in Arizona, and I was very excited with this.

I had brought with me certified copies of my divorces, including the one which legally returned my birth name of Sheehan to me, my California identification card, my Social Security card, letters addressed to me at my brother's house, and numerous other identifications to prove who I was.

I filled out the application, had my photo taken, and waited four hours before being told that I needed to also provide my birth certificate and passport. I was a bit frustrated but decided to return the next day with those documents. The next day I had another photo taken, and waited to be seen, with all of my documentation in order.

I was prepared to take both the written and driving tests in order to get my license. At the window I gave all of my documents to the customer service representative, who took everything and went into a room along with three other people. I sat at the window for about twenty minutes.

When the representative returned, she told me that I would now have to provide marriage certificates for both of my marriages. "You have to connect all of the names you have had." I was livid when I left their office, crumpled my paperwork up, threw it in the trash bin, and was completely discouraged.

Regardless, I was not one to give up easily, so when I got back home I went online and was able to order both marriage certificates. It took about a week for them to arrive. I returned to the MVD, passed both the written and driving tests, and finally had my temporary license, with the hard copy to arrive by mail within two weeks.

I was so incredibly happy. I was finally going to be able to drive my own car. I drove home that day, the first time that I had driven in almost four years. Kelly was silent on the way home, and I could tell that she was getting angry. I tried not to let that bother me, so I ignored her, choosing not to argue.

When we got to my brother's house I went in and told them my good news. They hugged me and told me that they were proud of me and my determination. Kelly remained silent and sullen. She went into the bedroom and closed the door behind her. I followed her. I wanted to find out what she was thinking and why.

She was sitting on the edge of the bed with her head down. I put my hand on her shoulder and asked her what was wrong. She told me that she knew that I had gotten my license so that I would no longer have to depend on her driving me. I reminded her that I had a license for years before we met, as well as my own cars.

She told me that she was going to move out on her own since nothing she had found was good enough for me to live in, and I certainly didn't need her anymore. I was a bit hurt. I didn't understand. However, I told her that if that is what she wanted to do that I would not stand in her way.

From the moment we had arrived in Arizona to that present time she had been falling deeper and deeper into some type of depression, something that I was not equipped to help her through. I silently wondered if it was her recent use of meth causing this. I damned Mike for his interference in her life.

Week after week, she stayed in a slump, depressed over anything and everything. She barely left the bedroom. She claimed that I was ignoring her when I repeatedly attempted to engage with her in meaningful conversation. I held her at night, rubbed her back, talked to her, loved her. Nothing was working.

My brothers had a gym membership and added both Kelly and me to their account. Even though it was like pulling teeth from a chicken I somehow managed to talk her into going with us every morning. I thought that some vigorous exercise would do her good, and it would be healthy for both of us.

I asked her if she wanted to make an appointment with behavioral health, that perhaps she needed to be back on medication, but she refused. She began avoiding everyone in the house, including me, and stayed in the room with the door closed. She barely ate, and hardly came out of the room except to smoke a cigarette.

When I would go to the bedroom to get anything, or to go to bed, she would be curled up on the bed, a hoodie pulled tight over her face, and with her head turned away. Kelly refused to speak to me or anyone else, even though I tried time and time again. I didn't know what to do for her.

She rarely allowed Kudos out of the room, even though he got along well with my brothers pup Sugar. I knew that Kelly was desperate to move out of their house, even though it was not practical, and she fought me paying anything to live there. This ended up becoming her undoing.

One day I woke up and was simply finished with her. I had added her to both of my bank accounts, so I drove to the local branch, closed both accounts, and reopened them in my name only. I withdrew $500.00 to give to Kelly as I was not going to have her penniless. Deep in my heart I still loved and cared for her.

I returned home and went into the bedroom to look for her. Kelly was just getting out of bed. I told her that I needed to talk to her, but she brushed by me without responding. I followed her into the kitchen and told her that she may as well destroy her bank card since it would not work any longer.

That caught her attention. She asked me what I meant and I told her what I had done at the bank. I handed her the $500.00 and I suggested that she start looking for a roommate situation that she could afford. She ran to the bedroom and I followed her. She was hurriedly getting dressed.

I had given her half of a gold Mizpah that I had had for years to wear around her neck and asked that she give it back. It was a gesture of love on my part, and since I no longer felt that there was love in this relationship I didn't want her to have it. Kind of like returning an engagement ring.

She refused, and when I reached for it she yelled "Don't make me get physical with you." My brother Peter must have been close by because he came to the door and told Kelly that she had an hour to leave the house. She was in shock, but what did she expect? She was threatening me yet again.

My entire family knew the abuse that I had endured at her hands over the past almost four years. Peter was being protective of me. She said that she had nowhere to go and began to plead with both of us. I told her that it was not up to me, it was not my house, and that I would be staying.

Kelly began panicking. I messaged her cousin Tara and told her what had happened and asked if Kelly could stay with her for a while. She said that she would talk to Jeremy and let me know. I told her that my brother had given Kelly only an hour to leave the house. That built a fire under Tara.

She said that she could be at the house in less than an hour to pick Kelly up. I let Kelly know and told her that she needed to start packing her belongings. Kelly was crying, hysterical, and my heart was breaking. I had no choice in the matter, and I let it happen. I let her leave.

Since she didn't have any luggage she haphazardly threw her clothing and toiletries into plastic trash bags. She told me that she needed to go to storage to get a few things out and I replied that it was not going to happen that day, that she would need to come back. My brothers helped Kelly carry her belongings out to the curb and left her there.

It was not long before Tara pulled up. Together they loaded the trash bags into Tara's car and I watched as they drove away. I felt so bad, but I was relieved. Saddened, but I was glad to have finally found peace. I was still in very much in love with Kelly, but I would learn to live without her once again.

Losing Your Family Part Deux

Living with my brothers was not so bad. There had been some unbelievably bad blood between my brother Peter and myself, but I was willing to forgive, although never forget. We actually shared time together, cooked meals, went shopping and continued going to the gym.

I helped around the house and put my hand to planting a small vegetable and flower garden in the back yard. About two weeks after Kelly left the owner of the house stopped by to talk to my brothers. He was an older gentleman, and I thought quite pleasant. I spoke with him while he waited for my brothers.

Suddenly he looked at me and said, "You are nothing more than a grifter and leech." I was taken aback. I told him that I was nothing of the kind, that I had always paid my own way. I went inside the house and told Peter what he had said. Peter immediately went out to the carport and gave his thirty day notice to vacate, no ifs, ands or buts.

The old man looked confused and stumbled to his car. I thought that he was going to have a heart attack. I don't think that he imagined having said what he said to me would have such a consequence. Giving the notice put us in the position of having to find a new place to live, and we immediately began searching.

Peter's girlfriend Janet offered to help find a house for us. She drove through neighborhoods looking for rental signs and found several that would be right for us. One of the houses she found, located in Glendale, was the perfect house. Three bedrooms, two baths, a back yard the size of a satellite park, and a swimming pool.

She gave us the phone number and Michael called the owner, and he set up an appointment for us to tour the home. We were all extremely excited. This would be a fresh start for the three of us together as a family, something that was a long time coming, and we all looked forward to viewing the property.

In the meantime we began packing in earnest. One way or another we were going to have to move out. I didn't have a lot of my own possessions to pack since most everything was still in storage, however I did pitch in and packed the kitchen, bathrooms and part of the carport.

The rent on the new property was $1200.00 per month, so the three of us agreed to divide that amount equally amongst us. Michael said that he would take care of all the utilities, including cable and internet, and that we could all chip in to pay for those each month, along with sharing the cost of groceries.

The day finally arrived for us to view the property. Janet joined us, and we all rode there in her truck. The owners daughter Cami was there to greet us. Janet pulled into the driveway and parked her truck. We all got out and walked over to her. She was a nice woman, taking care of her father's business.

She walked us through the front door, which is where the living room was located. The dining room/kitchen area was large and inviting, featuring an island with cabinets and drawers. There was a beautiful fireplace along one of the walls which would be wonderful to use in the Winter months.

There were two large bedrooms at one end of the house with a shared bathroom in the hallway. On the other end was the master bedroom, with its own master bath and walk-in closet, and quite spacious. There were large, beautiful French Doors leading that out to the covered patio.

Cami stayed inside while we walked out to the back yard. There was so much potential. I was already planning a meditation garden on the patio and a vegetable garden along one of the fences. The yard was surrounded by slump block fences that were tall enough to keep Kudos contained.

There was a smaller sized built-in swimming pool, yet it was big enough to swim laps in, and would be a plus for us in the hot Arizona summer months. Cami came outside to show us her father's workshop, which was located on the East side of the property, as well as the pool pump.

She wanted us to know that the workshop was off limits to anyone, including us, and that her father frequently did work inside the shop. That felt a bit strange to me. I was under the impression that we would be renting the entire property, including all of the buildings on site, but I chose not to say anything.

I looked at my brothers and nodded my head. This was the house for us. We all went back inside. Cami asked us what we thought and we told her that we were ready to sign the lease and move in. She smiled and told us that they could have everything ready for us by October 1st.

She asked if we were willing to put the deposit down and we told her yes. I wrote a check for $1200.00, for which my brothers reimbursed me $400.00 each. She said that she would meet us there on the morning of October 1st, which was only a week away, for the lease signing and move-in.

I was already in love with the house and the yard. The kitchen was magnificent, filled with beautiful cabinetry, and the island was large enough to prepare anything that we needed for our dinners or baking, plus plenty of space to store anything that didn't fit in the other cabinets.

We returned to the house in Phoenix to make our plans.

That evening my brothers approached me and said that they had decided I would get the master bedroom. I had not really thought about it. I was just grateful to be able to move into the house. This was a huge plus for me, especially with the master bathroom, doors opening to the patio and the large walk-in closet.

We reserved a moving truck and spent the next week finishing up the packing. The night before we moved we all slept on our floors, with blankets and pillows of course. Even though my body ached the next morning I was still extremely excited to be moving to the new house, with yet another fresh start in life.

It had only been six weeks since Kelly had been asked to leave, and she was almost always on my mind. After she left I began receiving harassing emails and social media comments from her, her family and her friends. Even though I didn't want to I had to block her and the rest from contacting me.

It did break my heart to have to do so, but I didn't want to deal with the emotional trauma that the harassments brought with them. Kelly rang my cell phone repeatedly and never left voicemails. She sent text messages begging me to take her back. I couldn't relent. I blocked her phone number as well.

I knew, down deep in my heart, that we were better off separated. Our relationship had been and continued to be toxic. Even going through couples counseling didn't help. The twenty-five years age difference was one factor that made our being together difficult, but it was so much more than just that.

Putting Kelly to the back of my mind, I busied myself in helping to set up our new home. We had picked all of my belongings up from the storage unit, and what didn't fit in the house was stored in a small shed in the back yard, including all of Kelly's belongings that she had left behind.

My brothers did all of the heavy lifting and helped me to set up my bed and arrange the furniture. I had kept Kudos in his carrier in my bathroom while we were getting things inside the house, but once we were finished I let him out to explore. I placed his litter box in one corner of the bedroom, and his feeding station in the kitchen.

I set his cat tree up next to the bedroom door and not far from my bed. He loved taking naps either on the top or in one of the hidey holes. Once we were settled I opened the French Doors of my bedroom and allowed him outside to mark his territory. He immediately claimed the fence and yard as his own.

Kelly had always refused to allow him outside, but each time that we were separated in the past, and he was left with me, and I allowed him outside whenever he wanted, except for during the night of course. He was king of his kingdom, and the yard was his savannah. He was happy, and that mattered to me.

Shortly after moving in, and once we were comfortably established, my brothers and I started working on a large vegetable garden along one of the fences. They did the heavy work; shoveling, chopping and digging, while I prepared the seeds for planting. It was early Autumn, so we planted accordingly.

Michael assumed the responsibility of spiffing the house every day (with the exception of my quarters), while Peter took the job of managing Sugar, their Jack Russell Terrier. I helped in the kitchen and kept my own space clean and tidy. We took turns preparing food, and occasionally we sat down together to eat.

Much of the time I sat in my bedroom to eat. I wasn't a recluse, but I enjoyed my own space and privacy. I would watch television once in a while, but really didn't spend too much time doing so. I spent most of my time either outside in the back yard and on the patio or creating art or writings on my computer. I always tried to stay busy.

I had joined a group for my elementary school on a social media site, and one day I read that my seventh and eighth grade math teacher, Mr. Battina, had passed away. There was going to be a memorial service at St. Simon and Jude Cathedral in Phoenix, which happened to be the parish that I was raised in.

Around the same time, I had reconnected with my best childhood friend, Connie, whom I had known since the second grade. I contacted her and asked if she would like to go to the memorial service with me. She did want to go, and we made arrangements to meet in the parking lot of the Cathedral.

I had not seen Connie for over forty years. We had been in touch on and off down through the years and promised each other that we would always do so. I was sad to go to the memorial service, but extremely excited to be able to see Connie again, and I wondered what it would be like.

I parked in the lot and waited. Soon I saw Connie pull in, driving her Jeep. I got out of my car and ran over, gathering her in my arms and hugging her. It was as if the years had never passed, except for the fact that we were both fast approaching sixty years of age. I was overcome with joy.

We sat together throughout the memorial. I didn't see anyone else there from grade school that I remembered. Afterwards we drove to a Garcias, lovely Mexican restaurant, where we enjoyed a wonderful lunch and hours upon hours of lively conversation. It was all we could do to tear ourselves away.

We had fun together during the weeks that followed. Connie's roommate had given her tickets to a college football playoff game, between the Arizona State University Sun Devils and the UCLA Bruins. She invited me to go with her, and believe it or not, this was my very first football game, ever.

We took the Metro Rail to Sun Devil Stadium in Tempe. It was a beautiful Autumn day and I really enjoyed the ride. The Metro conveniently let us off in front of the stadium. The crowd was immense, and there were Homeland Security agents mingling in the crowd. I was curious as to why they were there.

Being who I am I walked up to one of the agents and asked what they were doing at a football game. He replied, "We are here for people like you", and winked. We all laughed, but it actually made me feel a bit strange for him to say that. Regardless, we went on into the stadium to find our seats.

It felt as if we had walked a half mile when we finally found where the seats were. Much to my dismay, they were at the very top of the 'nosebleed' section. Now, I have acrophobia, and have had it since I fell from the high dive onto the cement at our neighborhood swimming pool when I was four years old.

I tried to get up the steps, but only got about five feet before I began experiencing extreme vertigo. I held onto Connie's arm and told her that I just couldn't go any further. She sighed, but said it was okay, that she understood, and that perhaps we should just go back to her house.

Even though Connie had said it was okay I knew that she was disappointed. As we walked through the crowds by the concession stands I spotted a man who I thought might be in authority. I walked up to him and asked, and he told me that he was a supervisor. I related to him my dilemma.

I told him that this was a special day for my friend and myself. I asked if there might be seats available in a lower section, seats that I would actually be able to get to. He told us both to follow him, so we did. Lo and behold, he had led us to the VIP section, with only three steps down to the seats.

Now, there were not any refreshments, but that didn't matter to us. We were in a glass enclosed temperature controlled room with a fantastic birds eye view of the playing field. Unfortunately, the Sun Devils lost to the Bruins 45-43, in what I came to find out was a remarkably close game.

Connie and I also went to the Arizona State Fair, enjoyed visiting Sahuaro Park, and spent time visiting at both her house and mine. I genuinely enjoyed spending time with her. We met for lunch several times, but our reunion was to be short lived as Connie, being a career truck driver, was called back on the road.

Peter and Michael's fifty-third birthday was right around the corner. They are twins, born on October 31st. I prepared a beautiful dinner and ordered a cake complete with Halloween decorations. Janet joined us and we had a lovely celebration for them, the first that I had participated in for over seventeen years.

I was a bit sad though. I had missed so many of my children's and grandchildren's birthdays since living in Arizona. Of course, I phoned them, but having been with them for most of their lives it was an exceedingly difficult thing for me to cope with, and this caused a bit of emotional distress.

The holidays were fast approaching and I wanted to prepare the dinners.

My brothers and I went shopping for our Thanksgiving dinner, purchasing a nice, fat turkey, along with all of the side dishes. Everything that I made was from scratch, including the Cranberry relish and dinner rolls.

Yule dinner was a standing ribeye roast, and I cooked it to perfection. I made a fresh pecan pie for dessert, which was absolutely delicious. Janet joined us for both meals, even after she had eaten with her daughters. New Years dinner was just my brothers and myself, with a traditional Southern good luck meal to enjoy.

In early January I phoned my son David and told him that I wanted to come and visit before the end of the month. He was so excited and said that it would be wonderful to see me. I was able to purchase round trip airfare to San Jose Mineta Airport for only $200.00 and planned to stay there for a week.

I departed Sky Harbor International on the morning of January 15th and arrived in San Jose less than two hours later. David was waiting for me outside the terminal in the arrivals area. He ran to me, giving me a tight hug, and he took my luggage from me, stowing it in the trunk of his car.

My plan was to spend a couple of days with David and Rachel in Campbell, then be driven out to Morgan Hill to visit with Stephanie and

Landon. Instead of visiting Maggie at her home, she drove to David's to spend time with me because her boyfriend did not care for me.

On the second day Maggie and I joined two of our oldest friends, Luanne and Jennifer, for lunch at a local restaurant. It had been several years since I had seen them, and we all had an absolutely wonderful time. They followed us back to David's to continue the visit.

Two days after my arrival I became ill. Fever, headache, sore throat, everything that accompanies the flu. Determined not to be thwarted, I stayed out of bed and visited with my family. Landon came by and picked me up for my visit in Morgan Hill, but there I became so ill that I had to take to a bed.

I was miserable. I certainly didn't want my entire visit to be taken up with the flu. I phoned the airline and talked to them about my situation. I asked if I might be able to extend my stay and reschedule my flight for another week out, and they, amazingly, were able to do so, without charging me any more money.

The visit ended up being a wonderful one. I recovered and was able to spend time with all of the children and grandchildren and build memories that would sustain me for the months ahead. Before I reluctantly returned to Arizona I told them all that I would be back very soon.

Almost as soon as I was home I went online and made reservations to return to the Bay Area in May. This gave me something to really look forward to in the months ahead. Things were going fine with my brothers, but I had never been separated from my children and grandchildren this long before.

The first time was we were separated was when they all decided, at the drop of a hat, to move to Nevada to be near their father. He drove from Reno, picked Stephanie and Landon up in Washington State, drove back to the Portland area and picked up David, Rachel, Maggie, Jesse and the grandchildren.

My heart broke, but they were adults, quite capable of making their own decisions. I knew deep down in my heart that it would not last long, and that someday they would be close to me again. Now, though, the shoe was on the other foot, and it was I who had moved far away.

Not long after returning from the Bay Area I received a message from a mutual friend of Kelly's and mine. She told me that Kelly was frantically trying to get in touch with me and asked if I would please call her. Of course, I had Kelly's phone number, but this was something that I really had to consider.

So, I considered it. I thought about it, and thought about it, until calling

Kelly was the only thing that I could think about. You see, I still felt that I was in love with her. Yes, our relationship had been highly dysfunctional and toxic, but the least I could do was call and find out why she needed to talk.

So I called her. I took my phone and sat under the giant Olive tree in the back yard. I didn't want my brothers to know that I was calling her. That would only lead to an argument. I sat down and dialed her number, making sure that I blocked my number so that she would not have it.

She answered the phone and my heart began beating wildly. It took me a moment before I could reply to her. I finally gathered myself together and said hello. She started to cry, telling me that she knew that she was the reason we were no longer together, and that she would be willing to do anything in order to be a part of my life again.

I quietly listened while she spoke, begging me to please consider reconciliation. Finally, I broke in and told her that was not going to happen, that I was just beginning to get my life back together, and that I was really quite happy with the way things were. I asked her about how things were going for her.

She told me that she had broken both of her feet when a dumpster filled with granite fell on them. I told her that I was deeply sorry and that I hoped she was getting medical care. I asked if she was living with her parents and she said no. She told me that she was living with Drew's sister Nicole and her girlfriend Isis.

This was the same Nicole that Drew had tried to convince Kelly to have a relationship with while we were still together. I certainly didn't like the sound of that, but I had nothing to say about it. I asked if she had found a job and she told me that she didn't, but that she was attending domestic violence counseling.

She went on to tell me that it was helping her to better understand herself and her anger. I said that was nice, and I hoped that she could find peace in her life. I was finished with the conversation and said my goodbyes. As I hung up the phone I heard her pleading with me to please give her another chance.

I sat outside underneath the Olive tree for a while, thinking about the conversation, knowing full well that I needed to just file it away in my mental 'do not touch' folder. I knew that I was way better off without her, that all that could possibly come of us being together would be more chaos, and possibly tragedy.

That night, as I was trying to sleep, all that I could think about was Kelly. I wished that things had not gone so awry, I wished that she and I were still together, but I could see no way for that to happen. Plus, I suspected that she was involved sexually with the girls she was living with.

I finally managed to drift off to sleep, but it was not a restful night. My mind was racing, trying to think of ways to bring Kelly back, and as much as I tried to get the thoughts to stop, knowing that I was making impossible plans, the thoughts continued of their own volition.

I spoke with Kelly often in the following weeks. I would always sit under the Olive tree, away from the house, hoping that my brothers were not listening. Kelly and I argued a lot during those conversations, which should have been an indicator that what I was conjuring up was not a good idea.

We began exchanging emails, and again, those were filled with arguments and misunderstandings. I should have known better, the arguments should have given me pause to reconsider, but I was like a confused, ill-fated teenager in love for the very first time, almost in a hypnotic state.

My fifty-ninth birthday was fast approaching, and my brothers planned a surprise party for me. They made a wonderful Mexican food dinner, ordered a lovely ice cream cake for dessert, and presented me with several gifts that I fell in love with. It was a wonderful day.

I received birthday phone calls and messages from my children, and all of those I cherished just as much, if not more, as what my brothers had done for me. I was a bit disappointed that they had not sent cards, but that was fine. At least I had the chance to speak with them. It was a great birthday, one to remember.

The next morning I woke up with two things on my mind; I was going to enroll in an online school to earn my degree in psychology and I was going to create a non-profit for combat veterans and their family members, not for myself, but on behalf of my oldest brother, who was a Vietnam War veteran.

I told my brothers and children what I was planning on doing and they all applauded me. They knew that I had the fortitude to see these things through, and that when I put my mind to something that I was usually quite successful. This gave me even more confidence to move forward with my plans.

I applied at the school and was accepted. I did the research to find out what I needed in order to start a non-profit. I loved staying busy and applying myself to those things that I felt were important in helping others. I worked in our little garden and helped around the house, but those things truly took little of my time.

I emailed Kelly and let her know what I was doing, and she replied by saying that she thought that I was stupid, that a person my age couldn't possibly be successful in school or business. We argued back and forth for a while via email, but then I decided to just ignore her. I didn't need the opposition.

Time was passing quickly now. I took all of my college entrance exams and passed them with high scores. I sent off all the paperwork necessary to the State of Arizona for the non-profit, which I decided to name A Circle of Warriors. Everything was moving along smoothly, and I was really quite happy.

My brothers and I still went to the gym regularly. Even if I was not able to lose the extra weight that I had gained at Hell House, I at least wanted to be healthy and stay fit. I continued to receive emails from Kelly but held back from phoning her. Even when we argued her voice moved me somehow.

One day I received an email from Kelly that was compelling enough for me to phone her. Call it what you will; foolhardy, brainless, reckless, or even downright irrational, I was not able to resist calling her. I went out and sat under the Olive tree and dialed her number. She answered, already knowing that it was me calling.

She was somewhat breathless and I asked if she was okay. She told me that she had been kicked out of Nicole's house and that she was in desperate need of a place to live. I asked about her parents, sisters or friends. She told me that none of them were offering her a place to stay, and that she was living behind the store where she was working.

I asked what she thought that I could do to help her and she replied that she believed that she might be able to come live with myself and my brothers. I knew, deep in my heart of hearts that this would be a grave mistake, but I told her that I would consider it and talk to my brothers.

Just then Michael walked out the back door and asked who I was talking to. I lied and told him that it was one of my daughters.
I ended the phone call with a heart that was filled with both hope and dread. I went into the house to talk to my brothers, knowing full well that I was opening the proverbial can of worms.

If they agreed to have Kelly return then perhaps she could fly back to Phoenix with me in May after I had visited with the children and grandchildren. I found them in the garage playing their music. They had been aspiring musicians since their late teens, and had a measure of success, as well as a fairly good fan following.

They stopped what they were doing when they saw me and I asked them if we could talk. They asked me what was up and I, hesitating, began to tell them about Kelly's situation, and that I wanted her to come live with us. I insisted that I still loved her and thought that there was a good possibility that this would work out.

I knew that they were shocked, and I am sure that they were in disbelief. They both knew the abuses that I had endured during the years that I was with Kelly. They had seen firsthand that she was prone to depression and addiction. They told me that they would think about it and let me know.

I immediately phoned Kelly and let her know that I had talked to my brothers. She was conflicted on whether or not she really wanted to come, and I didn't press her. I knew that she didn't really care for my brothers, and that she was afraid of them. It would need to be her decision to make, and she had to be ready to make changes in herself.

I refused to go back to how things were before. The four years of experience that I had with Kelly were tumultuous to say the least, and all that I wanted was peace in my life. Now I was waiting for both my brothers and Kelly to make decisions. Instead of dwelling on it I submerged myself in schoolwork and plans for my non-profit.

I figured that what was intended to would be, and put everything in the hands of the Universe, which of course meant that I needed to be able to accept the outcome. Soon my brothers approached me with a plan. They said that Kelly would be welcome, but that she would have to adhere to certain rules.

She would have to be employed, agree to mental health counseling, and not raise a hand to me. I assured them that I would talk to her and let them know that she was still deciding. Of course, I didn't know why she would have difficulty deciding on moving here. According to her she was homeless with absolutely nowhere to live.

No one wanted her around, even her family members, and we were willing to give her a chance. A few days later I received an email from Kelly. She told me that she was ready to come down, and wanted to know how to make a reservation on the same flight I was taking back from my visit to the Bay Area.

I went outside and sat under the Olive tree. I dialed her number and she answered excitedly. She told me that she loved me, and that she wanted to spend the rest of our lives together. She said that she would prove it to me and was grateful for the chance to do so. I laid out my brothers rules, all of which she agreed to.

Even though I still had a bit of apprehension I began to become just as excited as she was. Kelly told me that as soon as she got to work that day she was going to put in for a transfer to the Glendale store. I asked if she were going to be able to afford to pay for her flight, and she said it would be no problem.

After we hung up I sent her an email with my itinerary, including the flight number I was taking for my return to Arizona. I made sure that she understood that time was of the essence, and that if she were going to be on the same flight as mine that she needed to make her reservation soon.

My trip to the Bay Area was less than a week away and I was extremely excited to be able to see my children and grandchildren and hoped to be able to visit with a few of my friends as well. As the days passed I made sure that everything at home was in order. I really appreciated being organized.

I arranged with my brothers to care for Pumpkin and all of the outdoor plants while I was away. That was an extremely easy task for them. I had purchased a new food dispenser for Pumpkin, as well as an electric fountain water dish. I had a litter box for him even though he mostly went outdoors.

I awakened quite early the morning of May 6th. My flight was scheduled to leave at six a.m. that morning, and I wanted to have plenty of time to get through the TSA checkpoint. Michael drove me to Sky Harbor

International and told me that he would be there to pick Kelly and I up on the fourteenth.

The flight was brief, and Landon picked me up at the airport, driving me to his and Stephanie's home in Morgan Hill. I stayed with them and three of my grandchildren for three enjoyable days then left for Campbell to visit with David, Rachel, Maggie and the other grandchildren.

We had a lovely Mother's Day celebration at David's. He gave me a beautiful blown glass swan, which I still have, filled with a small, but lovely bouquet of a single rose and baby's breath. The visit was shorter than I would have wanted, and before I knew it the day had come for me to return to Arizona.

I had spoken with Kelly several times during my visit. She was concerned because she was not able to find a ride from Vacaville to the airport in San Jose. No one from her family was willing to help her, and none of her friends had the time to do so. I told her to just keep trying.

She told me that she had asked everyone, and finally her parents next door neighbor agreed to drive her, but for a price. Since Kelly had already purchased her airfare I was not too worried about her having to pay for the ride. After all, she was going to be working within the first week of arriving at the house.

I was confident that she would be able to recoup quickly financially. Our arguments had ceased for the most part, which I was grateful for. We didn't need to get started on the wrong foot again. One thing that did bother me was that her sister Brenna told her that I was the devil whispering in her ear, which was a vile thing to say of me.

Landon drove me to San Jose Mineta airport, unloaded my luggage, gave me a hug and drove away. I didn't see Kelly at first. I walked to the end of the building to smoke a cigarette before checking in for my flight and found her there, leaning against the wall and smoking a cigarette.

I gave her a hug, but her body was very rigid, and she didn't hug me back. I dismissed this as her being nervous. I told her that we had a few minutes before we needed to get checked in and go through the TSA security checkpoint, but that was all that we had. She stomped her cigarette out and walked to the front door.

I took a couple of more drags and followed after her. I used the kiosk to check in. Kelly watched me and asked me to help her, which I did. I checked my bags in with the airline and then proceeded to the TSA line, which was not too long fortunately. In fact, we were through in less than fifteen minutes.

All the while Kelly was silent. We walked together to the departure gate to wait for our flight. We only had a half hour until boarding time. Soon, we were called to board and we were in our seats on the jet and ready for takeoff. I was rather excited, ready to begin a new chapter of my life with Kelly.

Kelly remained silent during our flight for the most part. I tried to hold her hand but she pulled away from me. I really didn't know what to think, but then, if she didn't want to be with me she should have said something instead of agreeing to move back to Arizona. I was confused.

Our flight was short, less than two hours, and Michael was waiting for us outside the terminal. Even though it was mid-May, and still morning, the weather was already beginning to get hot. On our drive home my car overheated, something Michael said had been happening since I left for my trip.

Peter was waiting in the driveway for us. He gave me a hug, shook Kelly's hand, and helped me in the house with my luggage. Kelly followed behind, lugging her belongings, still silent, and really quite sullen. I had not seen a single smile on her lips. I wondered what was going on in her mind.

The first thing that Kelly did, after stowing her luggage in the bedroom, was look for Pumpkin, whom I had renamed after she had left the last year, and whom she immediately renamed Kudos. She held him like he was a long lost loved one, which I suppose he was. She had not seen him for nine months.

Before I left to visit the children I had purchased a locking handle for my bedroom door so that Kelly and I would be assured privacy. I knew that was important for her. That evening, we had a small dinner and visited with my brothers before going to the bedroom. I closed and locked the door behind us.

I got my pajamas and went into the bathroom to change. As I was washing my face Kelly came up behind me and gave me a big hug. I looked at her reflection in the mirror and saw a smile on her face. I turned around and hugged her back. She was genuinely showing affection.

She told me that she loved me, the new house, our bedroom, and that she thought she would like it here. I asked her if she would be able to get along with my brothers and she said that wouldn't be a problem. All that she wanted to do was spend the rest of her life with me, and I felt the same towards her.

We were intimate that night for the first time in almost a year, and the passions ran high. Kelly gave me a love bite on the left side of my neck that was quite noticeable, but I really didn't think anything of it. It had happened so many times in the past that it didn't bother me. I failed to consider what others might think.

I awoke fairly early the next morning. I went out into the kitchen, poured a cup of coffee, and walked out to the Meditation Garden. It was still dark out, and I could hear the birds just beginning to chirrup in the trees around the property. I lit a cigarette and sipped slowly on the hot brew in my cup.

Michael came out to the garden, said good morning, and asked if I was doing okay, to which I replied I was doing simply fine. He asked if I was sure, and I told him that I was. He went back into the house and closed the door behind him. I decided to take a look at my precious plants around the yard.

Janet came out and sat on the edge of the pool, dangling her feet in the water. I said good morning to her and she asked how I was doing. I told her the same thing that I told Michael, that I was fine. The sun was coming up and I was finally able to see my plants, and I was astonished.

Several of my very delicate and beautiful plants were shriveled, and the soil in the pots was bone dry. There was no reviving them. I became quite angry and muttered some profanity, not directed towards anyone specifically, but Janet heard me. She suddenly jumped up and ran into the house.

I made my way through the yard, checked the vegetable garden, which I was happy to see healthy. My coffee cup was empty, so I headed back into the house to get some more. As I was pouring coffee Peter came running towards me shouting at the top of his lungs. I was so shocked that I dropped my cup.

He grabbed my neck, scrutinizing it, and said that he knew that Kelly had hurt me again and that he was going to take care of her. I laughed, telling him that it was just a love bite. Before I could stop him he ran to the bedroom door, threw it open, and began screaming for Kelly to get out of bed.

I was in shock, but I went inside my bedroom and pulled him out. Kelly was sitting on the side of the bed, her eyes as big as saucers. I walked Peter into the kitchen and tried to reason with him, telling him that he was in the wrong, but he anger escalated and he started to become violent with me.

I demanded that he stand down and walk away, or I might have to call the authorities, but he continued to behave irrationally. All the while Michael and Janet were watching but not doing or saying anything to help. I asked Michael to please contain Peter, at least take him out of the house, which he finally did.

He walked Peter into the garage to try and calm him down, but it was to no avail. Peter was behaving like a madman for no reason whatsoever. Michael came back into the house and told me that either I was moving out of the house, or he and Peter would. I didn't know what to say. Here I was, once again losing family over Kelly.

I asked him to give me a few minutes to think. I sat in the meditation garden. My unemployment was running out the next month, and I could hardly afford the utilities, let alone the $1200.00 a month rent. I felt dizzy and numb, but I decided that I would keep the house myself. I would find a way to work it all out.

I went back into the house and Michael was already packing. He asked if I wanted to buy his computer, printer, desk and dining room table, and I told him I would. I wanted to help him and Peter as well. Peter and Janet had gone to rent a moving truck. Michael told me that they would be gone within the next few hours.

Kelly had stayed in the bedroom the entire time. I went in and told her that my brothers were moving out, and that I needed to drive to the bank to get money out to buy the items that Michael was selling me. She started to protest, but I shut her down immediately. I told her plainly that this was what I was going to do.

I had saved a bit of money back and I had enough to buy the items from Michael. We had paid May's rent two weeks before, so I had a few weeks to figure out what I was going to do about money. I pulled into the driveway and saw the moving truck. Michael and Janet were loading it with belongings.

I went into the house to look for Kelly. She was not in the bedroom or kitchen, so I walked out the back door to find her. She was sitting on one of the benches smoking a cigarette. She asked me what we were going to do I and told her that I was developing a plan to save us, and that I was certain it would work.

By the time I went back inside the house all of my brothers belongings were gone. In fact, they were gone. I was heartbroken. I didn't understand, just couldn't fathom the reason for this happening. But it did happen, and I would not hear from my brothers again for many years.

Insanity Revisited

I immediately began to work on my plan. I took photos of the house and gardens and put them on Craigslist with an ad looking for roommates. I phoned the utility companies to put everything in my name. When I phoned the water company they told me that they couldn't do this.

They let me know that the bill had not been paid in several months, that to continue service I would need to pay over four hundred dollars to bring the account current, and that the account would have to stay in Michael's name. I assured them that I would get them paid within the week.

Since I was not able to contact my brothers I sent Janet a message asking her to have Michael disconnect the phone and internet services, as well as the electricity, so that I could put those utilities in my name. She messaged me back when he had done so. It cost a bit of money to have the services turned back on, but I managed to get it done.

Of course I was miserable that my brothers were gone, but I had to move forward. I had school to attend five days a week, and I was continuing to work on my non-profit, A Circle of Warriors, so I couldn't just sit and wait. I knew that everything would work out for Kelly and me. I just knew it.

The same day that I placed the roommate ad I received several inquiries. I made appointments for those interested. One genuinely nice gentleman came and put a holding deposit down, but later that day called to say that his situation had changed and that he would not be moving in. Still, I was not going to be discouraged.

Kelly suddenly became stubborn again, and somewhat sullen. She didn't like the idea of having roommates. I, on the other hand, welcomed having them. I still was not completely comfortable living alone with Kelly, and I was delighted to have the chance for others to live with us.

Before the end of the week I had both bedrooms rented, one to a gentleman by the name of Terry, the other to a young lady by the name of Hailey. They both paid two hundred dollars each in security deposits as well as their first month's rent of six hundred dollars each. Things were definitely going to work out.

I let Kelly know that she was going to have to contribute to the rent and utilities, so she needed to get her job going, but that took a few weeks. The manager at the secondhand store in Glendale had heard from the manager in Vacaville, but there were no openings for Kelly yet.

Soon, Terry and Hailey moved in. I gave them freedom of the house and gardens, told them that they could use anything in the kitchen and store their food in the refrigerator without worrying that Kelly or I would eat it. They shared the hall bath but had no problem with doing so.

It took Kelly several weeks after my brothers moved out to start work. She agreed to pay four hundred dollars a month towards rent, including utilities, and to help with groceries whenever she felt she could afford to. I had my college stipend coming at the end of June, all of which I would put toward the household.

My brothers had taken the living room furniture, which was fine. It belonged to them, but it left us with an empty room that I was not in the position to refurnish. Kelly began taking me to furniture stores to look at sofas, loveseats, end and coffee tables, but I simply couldn't afford to purchase them.

We were getting along fairly well. Since she worked outside of the home Kelly didn't feel obligated to help with household chores. I was left to do them myself, and it began to become increasingly difficult for me. Rheumatoid Arthritis was starting to spread throughout my body.

Occasionally, Terry and Hailey would pitch in and help, but not very often. But when they did I was appreciative of the help. I kept the house and gardens in order, made lunch for Kelly every morning before she left for work, and always had a nice dinner ready when she returned in the afternoons.

Kelly didn't like me doing schoolwork when she was home, so in order to accommodate her I woke up early in the mornings, completed as many units as possible before she got up, then finished the rest of my units while she was at work. In between everything I continued working on my non-profit. I was anxious to get it up and running.

I created the articles of incorporation, by-laws, and all legal documents in order to file with the State of Arizona as a corporation, and the Internal Revenue Service when I filed the non-profit paperwork. It took me several days, but when I was finished it was as polished as if an attorney had created them.

I worked on the one hundred and thirty two pages of the 501 C-3 exemption paperwork for the Internal Revenue Service, which was going to cost eight hundred and fifty dollars to file. I had my son-in-law Landon help me build a website and included a donation button on it for anyone willing to help me out.

I created two social media pages and posted daily updates, and I was not in the least bit shy about asking for donations. Even though it exhausted me I worked on everything that I needed to in order to get my non-profit going. Kelly was not really interested and told me so one day.

She called me a con artist and a charlatan, accusing me of defrauding people out of their donations. Reasoning with her was hopeless. As I have mentioned before, Kelly was really quite ignorant of many things, and this was just one example. Her accusations didn't stop me, even though they were a cause for contention.

For the Fourth of July Kelly decided that we were going to attend the Arizona Public Service Electric Light Parade. I thought it would be fine and agreed. At dusk we drove to Central Avenue and Camelback Road and found a place to park. There was already a huge crowd, but we were able to make our way through it.

I did have a bit of a challenge walking. The Rheumatoid Arthritis had moved into my hips, making it difficult to walk more than ten yards without a high degree of pain. Kelly was unsympathetic. She took my hand and dragged me behind her, ignoring my pleas to stop and let me rest.

Even though I was in pain I still enjoyed the parade. By the time it was finished I was fatigued and could barely walk to the car. Once again, Kelly grabbed me by the hand and pulled me along. I refrained from saying anything. In her limited capacity to understand it would have done no good.

In mid-July I finally had enough funds in the donation account to send all of the paperwork to the Internal Revenue Service. I was so proud of myself for remaining undaunted and for following through on my dreams. I wanted to achieve something that would bring hope to combat veterans and their families.

I continued to do well in school. One day I received a call from one of my instructors. We spoke for a while, and then she said "I have been teaching for ten years. During those ten years, I have conducted approximately forty-five classes with an average of fourteen students per class, making that around seven hundred students I have taught."

She went on to say, "That doesn't count the number of students I have taught part time at my local community college. I was told when I first began teaching that once in a blue moon a student would come along who would be a shining star 100% of the time. Susan, you are that student, and I am so proud of all of your achievements."

My head began spinning. I was honored, and more than a little flattered as well. Her compliments only served to make me want to work harder and longer on my courses. So far I had received nothing below an A-, and that was in finance. For some reason I couldn't stomach the voice of the narrator, who happened to be Suze Orman.

The summer was in full force, the days long and so extremely hot. I was grateful to have air conditioning inside the house. Even so, I would spend several hours a day in the gardens, especially the vegetable garden which was beginning to produce tomatoes, chilis and beautiful zucchini squashes.

Kelly helped in the garden a handful of times, leaving most of the responsibility to me, which I had no problem with. I had always loved gardening, and when it came time to harvest the bounty I busied myself making fresh Pico de Gallo from the tomatoes and chilis. All that I had to buy were onions to complete it.

The Zucchini was sauteed, baked and made into the most delicious bread pudding that I had ever tasted. Kelly was not impressed. In fact, life between us was beginning to take a turn for the worse. Even so I pressed onward. I continued to care for her, cook for her, and did her laundry. But my heart was heavy with foreboding.

Her feet began to bother her to the point that it was painful to stand or walk. She had begun her job in receiving but could no longer work in that position. Her manager, as much as she didn't want to, moved Kelly to one of the cash registers. She even provided a stool for Kelly to sit on so that her feet didn't hurt so much.

Her job provided insurance, so I found and orthopedist and made an appointment for her. I wanted to see what was going on in her feet. There were a series of x-rays taken. There were no fractures, even old ones. The x-rays did reveal some damage to the ligaments, which would heal in time.

The orthopedist referred Kelly to physical therapy three times a week which did only a small amount of good. Shortly after she began physical therapy she developed extremely painful headaches, so I researched and found a neurologist to see if she could be helped at all. I made an appointment and let Kelly know.

Her manager was understanding enough to give Kelly the time off for both the physical therapist and the neurologist. Of course, Kelly was losing hours, but I convinced her that we would be okay financially, and that this way she would be able to manage both her feet and the terrible headaches.

At one of the podiatrists appointments I asked if there might be specially fitted shoes that could help her. There happened to be a good pair and the podiatrist placed an order for them. Kelly hated them, telling me that they looked like 'old peoples' shoes. She did end up wearing them, and they seemed to help.

The neurologist ordered a series of x-rays for Kelly's head. What came back was startling. There were what appeared to be empty spaces, what are called vugs, or cell damage. I suspected that these were from her many years of methamphetamine use and possibly why she was experiencing severe headaches.

The doctor asked Kelly to make several future appointments for lidocaine injections at the base of her skull. She was reluctant, but I insisted that these might very well help her. Now Kelly had her feet and headaches being taken care of by professionals, and I was hoping that her attitude towards me would change.

One day I caught her going through some of my prescriptions. I asked her what she was doing. She told me that someone at work wanted to buy some and she thought I would be okay with it. I told her, plainly, that I was not okay with it and to keep her hands out of my personal belongings.

She became furious, ranting about how I never wanted to help others. I told her that was not the truth, and that she was only trying to profit financially from illegally selling my prescriptions. I hid my prescriptions the best that I was able to, hoping that Kelly couldn't find them.

I actually didn't take the prescriptions, and didn't need them, so the next day I took the container that my laundry soap was in, poured all of the pills into it, added hot water, and threw the container in the trash. I cancelled any further refills. I didn't wish to go through anything like this again.

Our already fragile relationship began to crumble, piece by piece. Kelly would wait for me to go outside in the mornings and leave for work without saying goodbye. She would come home when she knew that I would already be in bed asleep. I still loved her, but the unraveling was occurring even with my love.

Kelly spent the weekends away from the house, taking my car whenever she wanted and without asking me. I had no problem with her using it when she needed it for work, or if she was running errands, but I began to develop a sort of resentment that I fought hard against. I so wanted our relationship to work.

I still made her lunches each day that she worked, although I had a suspicion that she threw it away as soon as she went to work. I still accompanied Kelly to her medical appointments, but those times together were mostly silent. I was helpless, and I could feel her pulling away from me by slow degrees.

Autumn arrived, and with it cooler days. The vegetable garden was still producing, and all of my flowers in the meditation garden were thriving and beautiful. Halloween, or in my Irish tradition, Samhain, was approaching, but I already knew that I would not be celebrating it openly. Kelly despised my celebrations.

The days went on. Kelly was doing reasonably well with her physical therapy, and her new orthopedic shoes seemed to be helping considerably. The same couldn't be said about her headaches and neurology appointments. At every visit she was given painful Lidocaine injections which didn't help.

I did my best to make her comfortable when she was home. In fact, when she was there she was my only concern. I rubbed her feet, massaged her neck, and made sure that she had a delicious dinner every evening. Even so, she continued to slip away to work without any goodbyes and stayed away late into the night.

When she was not at home I turned all of my attention to school and to the non-profit. My grades and performance were excellent, and I received accolades from my instructors and fellow students. I worked on the pages I created on social media for the non-profit, and with the help of my son-in-law I was able to keep the website up and running.

Terry and Hailey were rarely home, and when they were they mostly stayed in their rooms. Occasionally Hailey would sit out in the meditation garden with me and visit. She was such a fun young woman, and I thoroughly enjoyed chatting with her. It helped to ease the pain of Kelly not being home.

One evening, Hailey and I were visiting in the garden. I happened to say something funny and she laughed with her usual loud, boisterous laugh. I laughed along with her. We talked about life and love. She asked me where Kelly was, and why Kelly yelled at me when she was at home.

I told her, excusing Kelly as I often did, that Kelly was having issues with her feet, issues with headaches, and issues with her job, so she was often irritated, and taking it out on me was her way of managing that irritation. Hailey found that to be intolerable, but I told her it was okay, I was really quite used to it.

Unbeknownst to me, Kelly was home and in the bedroom. Hailey had gone back into the house and I sat outside finishing my cigarette. Kelly came outside and sat on one of the benches. I said hello, but she didn't acknowledge me. She lit a cigarette and looked at me. "Why do you allow Hailey to be so loud and not me?"

I thought for a minute. I didn't want to upset her, but she needed to know the truth of the matter. I told her that when she raised her voice it was in anger, that she belittled everything that I did, and that it was abusive. I let her know that raising her voice had nothing to do with amusement or pleasure.

She stood up, angrily stomped her cigarette on the patio and went into the house. I chose not to follow, at least not immediately. I was not frightened since both Terry and Hailey were home, but I didn't want to get involved in a yelling match with Kelly, which had become more frequent of late.

I sat outside for a while, reflecting on my choices. Welcoming Kelly back into my world was fast beginning to feel like another grave mistake. The repercussions were many. I lost my relationship with my younger brothers, my children contacted me less frequently, and friends I had reconnected with kept their distance.

But what was I to do? I was convinced that I still loved her. I was trying hard to make the relationship work, but it felt as if I was beating a dead horse. I went inside and into the bedroom. Kelly was lying on the bed, her back turned to me, and I was certain she was feigning sleep to avoid me.

The following days brought more trouble between us, but I tried to ignore those troubles, staying busy with school, promoting the non-profit, running errands and keeping up with the housework and gardening. When we did come together the atmosphere was strained and filled with tension.

Thanksgiving was approaching, and Kelly wanted to celebrate it. I was worried about being able to afford food to prepare for the dinner. Kelly didn't contribute much to groceries, and I was mostly left alone with the task of making ends meet as far as purchasing food and dry goods.

I had not celebrated the 'holiday' for many years. It went against my code of ethics knowing that it represented the 'pilgrims', and that these 'pilgrims' almost decimated the Native peoples who had lived on the North American continent for centuries before the English claimed the land as their own.

Terry was flying back to Tennessee to be with his family and would not be returning until after New Year's, and Hailey planned to spend the holidays with her family, so Kelly and I would be on our own. I looked forward to this since Kelly seemed to have a problem with both of them.

Wanting to please Kelly, I reached out to my children to see if they could help me financially. This took a bit of humbling on my part. I was the mom, the provider in times past, and asking them felt like I was admitting some type of failing. But my eldest daughter responded and sent enough funds for me to make a wonderful dinner.

Kelly requested that I make the stuffing from artisan olive bread, and I agreed to do so. I went to the store and bought everything that we would need for our repast. I purchased Cornish Game Hens, the artisan bread, fresh cranberries, and all of the assorted vegetables for sides and a lovely appetizer tray.

I also bought the ingredients for a walnut-chocolate chip pie, which Kelly wanted to make for dessert. Not being adept in and around the kitchen, she had a difficult time managing the preparation of the pie. I was glad to have a large enough kitchen with plenty of room for both of us to work on what we were individually making.

I prepared the roasted Cornish Game Hens with a pomegranate/sun dried tomato reduction, the stuffing Kelly had requested, made of olive artisan bread, goat cheese and sun dried tomatoes, double baked yams, homemade cranberry relish with walnuts and mandarin oranges, and green bean casserole.

I set the table with the last of my beautiful stoneware dishes and flatware. I placed an old vase in the middle of the table and filled it with fresh cut flowers from the meditation garden. I put the food on the table and went to find Kelly, who was in the bedroom playing games on her laptop.

She acted as if I were bothering her but she followed me into the dining room. We sat at the table together and I served her, and then myself. There were no compliments. In fact, there were very few words during the dinner. When Kelly was finished she took her plate to the sink and returned to the bedroom.

I was worried and more than a little perplexed. Our relationship was not what I thought it was going to be. We were more like roommates who slept in the same bed. I cleared the table, put away the leftovers and washed the dishes. I made a cup of tea and went out to the meditation garden to regroup and think.

It was a cool evening, and the sun was just beginning to go down. I should have been relaxed, but I was not. I wanted to have a serious conversation with Kelly but I didn't know how to go about it. She was often defensive whenever I tried, plus she spent most of her hours away from home.

I decided to talk to her the next day. Neither one of us needed our rest to be disturbed, especially since I suspected any conversation would end up in a shouting match. I finished my tea and went back inside. I walked into the bedroom and noticed that Kelly was not there. I walked into the garage and saw that my car was gone.

Once again, Kelly had left without saying goodbye. I locked all of the doors and went into the bedroom to wash up and put my pajamas on. I was not going to let her actions keep me from getting my sleep. Sometime after midnight I awoke and saw that Kelly was not in bed. I got up and walked through the house.

She was nowhere to be found, again. I went into the garage and my car was still gone. I opened the garage door and walked out to the driveway. Everything was silent, no one was around, and there certainly was no sign of Kelly. I shook my head and went back inside. I went back to bed but didn't rest.

The next morning I saw that Kelly was still not at home. I tried her cell phone and got voice mail. I made a pot of coffee and went outside to smoke a cigarette in the dark. I wondered where she was and what had actually gotten into her to be acting out this way. Going back inside I heard a sound coming from the garage.

I opened the door and saw that my car was parked inside. I peered through the windows and saw Kelly sleeping on the backseat, a quart of liquor cradled in her arms. I panicked and opened the driver's side back door. She lurched up from the seat, her eyes bloodshot and her hair disheveled.

She stumbled out the car and I tried to catch her, but she pushed me away. Into the house she went, straight into the bedroom. I cautiously followed after her, thinking that I could try and confront her. She collapsed on the bed, clothes and boots still on, and fell into an inebriated slumber.

I was relieved that she had the day off from work. She needed to be able to recover from the alcohol, and whatever else she had used, but she needed to really recover to be able to work on Saturday. I had the entire weekend off from school, and I was taking a break from the non-profit as well.

Kelly was making this a habit, staying out, stumbling in, going to work drunk. It bothered me that she was driving my car in that condition, so as many times as I was able I drove her to work in the mornings and picked her up in the afternoons. I just told her that I needed my car on those days.

Yule was coming in just a few weeks, but my stipend from school would not arrive beforehand. I was a member of an online forum for recovering Hepatitis C patients, and the members were paid for their contributions with gift cards from a popular online store. I had enough saved to buy a few nice gifts for Kelly.

I continued in my class work and was doing really well. The non-profit was not doing well though, and I wondered what I could do to promote it. I was not experienced at all in non-profits, fundraising, or even running promotions. I just wanted to help Veterans and I really needed help to get it going.

I had placed an ad on Craigslist looking for volunteers to help me with A Circle of Warriors, and within a couple of days I received a reply from a Veteran by the name of Kathleen. She was an Iraqi/Afghan Veteran and was interested in helping me get the non-profit going. Needless to say, I was thrilled.

The first week of December I received a call from the unit commander of the Arizona Honor Guard. He told me that he had been given my phone number by one of the members of the Guard, and that he was extending an invitation to me to join them at the Pearl Harbor Remembrance Day at Wesley Bolin Plaza.

Receiving this invitation and having my first volunteer was heartening. So far, I had received no help, with the exception of Kelly helping me hand out flyers on that extremely hot day in July. This gave me hope to keep pressing forward and to not give up. Cathleen agreed to accompany me to the commemoration.

That same week I received more good news. I was finally approved for health insurance, effective January 1st, 2014. It would cover one hundred percent of everything medical. I was so grateful for this. I had not had medical coverage since losing my employment at the apartment property in Campbell.

I immediately researched primary care physicians in my area and found one that I felt would be suitable for myself. I phoned his office to make sure that they accepted my insurance, which they did, then told them I would be calling back on December 31st, 2014, to make an appointment.

There was so much good news to begin my December that I was thrown off by the next thing that happened. The fifth of the month was mine and Kelly's fifth anniversary. I prepared a lovely dinner, made a special dessert, and had everything ready for when she came through the door from work.

I was so excited, wanting to spend a romantic evening with Kelly, but when she walked into the house my excitement was immediately quashed. She went into the bedroom without saying hello. I had already set the table so I sat down in my chair and waited for her to come back into the kitchen.

'What's that for?'. She pointed to the candles on the table, the flowers in a vase, and the spread of food that I had prepared. I replied that it was our fifth anniversary. 'Oh', she said, 'I forgot. Sorry.' But I already knew that she was not sorry. I served our dinners in silence, my heart silently breaking.

There was minimal conversation while we ate. Kelly avoided looking directly at me, but I could see her, out of the corner of my eye, glancing in my direction every so often. I finished my dinner first and carried my dishes to the sink. I went outside to have a cigarette, hoping that Kelly would follow.

Three out of four things being positive was a plus, but I was genuinely concerned with how our relationship was devolving. I was still very much in love with Kelly, and I so wanted everything to work out for us. I just couldn't figure out how to make this happen, especially with communication being so limited.

I finished my cigarette and went back inside the house. The table was still cluttered with dishes, so I cleared everything. I put the leftovers away in the refrigerator, scraped the plates and serving dishes, and put them in the sink to soak in hot, soapy water. I planned to finish those after I had a chance to talk to Kelly.

But she was nowhere to be found. I went out to the garage. The garage door was open and my car was gone. She had left again, without saying a word. My heart sank. I tried her cell phone, but there was no answer. I left a voicemail hoping that she would call me back and let me know that she was okay.

The evening progressed without a call from her. By the time ten p.m. came I was ready to retire for the night. I washed up, put on my pajamas and went to bed. It took a while to fall into slumber though. My mind was racing, worried thoughts about Kelly filling my mind. Eventually I fell into another night of troubled sleep.

I awoke the next morning with Kelly in bed beside me. She had her back turned to me with the comforter pulled tightly over her head. I silently got out of bed, not wishing to wake her. I used the toilet, washed up and started a pot of coffee. I made sure that Kudos dishes were filled and went out into the meditation garden.

It was still dark and rather cold. I pulled my robe tightly around my body. I lit a cigarette and gazed into the distance. Try as I might, I couldn't think of how I was going to repair whatever was going on between Kelly and myself, especially since I really didn't know what was wrong.

I went back inside and poured a cup of coffee. The next day was the Pearl Harbor Commemoration celebration. I was relieved that Cathleen was going with me since Kelly had to work and was not interested anyway. I needed to phone both Cathleen and the commander of the Honor Guard to coordinate the next morning.

By the time I went back into the house Kelly was already up and getting ready for work. I asked her if she wanted me to make lunch for her and she said that she would grab a bite at one of the fast food restaurants by her work. I went to give her a hug goodbye but she pushed past me and left.

I had too much to do to let that bother me, so I put it to the back of my mind and started on the house. I got dressed, started the laundry, tidied the bedroom, our bathroom, the kitchen and the rest of the house. I phoned Cathleen to confirm that she was coming with me and was pleased when she said yes.

Next, I phoned the unit commander of the Arizona Honor Guard. He told me that Cathleen and I would be joining their procession, along with hundreds of combat veterans. They were from all of the branches of the U.S. military and spanned from the Korean War all the way to the present. I was both humbled and honored.

He told me where to park and where to meet the procession the next morning. He asked that Cathleen and I be there by eight thirty a.m. I told him that would not be a problem. I just needed to make sure that Kelly had a ride to work since her shift didn't start until much later in the morning.

It was just past noon, so I made myself a small lunch and finished my coursework for the day. I was glad that the commemoration was on a Friday as I would be able to focus on that exclusively. I put some chicken breasts in the oven for dinner and pulled out the sides that I would be serving with them.

I was sitting outside in the meditation garden when I heard one of the doors in the house shut. I knew that Terry would not be back from Tennessee until after the first of the year, and Hailey was not home, so I went inside to investigate. I was surprised to see Kelly walking in from the garage.

She walked up to me and gave me a hug, not a warm hug, just a very brief one. She apologized for not remembering our anniversary. I told her that it was fine, and that I would get over it. She asked if she could help me with anything around the house and I told her that the vegetable garden needed some watering.

She immediately went outside to the back yard and began irrigating the garden. I was somewhat surprised since Kelly was never really interested in doing these things. I supposed that this was her way of making up with me regarding our anniversary. While she was watering I prepared the sides for our dinner.

By the time she was finished the food was ready to serve. I had already set the table, so all that I had to do was place the food on it. Kelly washed her hands and sat in the chair next to mine. She told me that she loved me and appreciated everything that I did. I thanked her, but I was skeptical.

I asked if she would be able to find a ride to work the next day and she told me that it would be no problem. She still didn't understand why I wanted to attend the Pearl Harbor Commemoration, and so I reminded her that my Uncle Thurmond was stationed at Pearl Harbor when it was attacked.

We had finished eating, so I started to clear the table. Kelly told me to go outside and relax, that she was going to put everything away and do the dishes. This was a rarity for her. It was so rare, in fact, that I could count on one hand the things she had done around the house since she had moved in.

I made myself a cup of hot tea and went outside. I wondered if Kelly was being sincere, or if she was trying to disarm me somehow. I supposed that it really didn't matter. I was glad to be able to relax for a while after dinner. Soon Kelly joined me in the meditation garden. She had a slight smile on her face.

She sat next to me and took my hand. Kelly told me that she had been preoccupied with work for months, and that she had let our relationship fade. She apologized and told me that she was going to work on herself and expected me to work on myself as well. I was comforted hearing this. After all, I had given her my heart and soul.

That night we made mad, passionate love, the first time in many months. I didn't question Kelly, or the change that she appeared to have made. I was taking this at face value, not wanting to do anything that would get in the way of our growth as a loving couple. The coming days would prove otherwise though.

I awoke early Friday morning, excited to be going to the commemoration. I started the coffee and went outside for a cigarette. I had a little over two hours before I needed to leave to pick Cathleen up. We would have plenty of time to drive to the state Capitol and find a parking space.

Kelly was still asleep when I left, and I hoped that she would not be late for work. I drove to Cathleen's, who was waiting for me just outside her front door. She got into the car and we drove twelve miles to the Capitol. I briefly looked at the neighborhood as we approached. My Grandmother had lived there for many years.

We arrived a half hour early and had no problem finding a good parking space. I could see a crowd gathered at the opening of the plaza. There were veterans in full dress, bikers in their leathers, and others in street clothes. We walked over and I asked where they would like us to assemble.

A younger veteran told us that we could walk in front, in back, or right in the middle. I was not sure about Cathleen, but this was an exciting day for me. Three of the nine living survivors of the attack on Pearl Harbor, all of whom were in their late nineties, were to be honored during the ceremony.

I could see the Honor Guard taking their place at the head of the group. I told Cathleen that we should get in formation with the rest of the people, and so we moved into the center of the group. I could hear the distant sound of marching music, and suddenly we were all moving forward.

We made our way through the plaza and onto the lawn in front of the stage. The lawn was filled with excited spectators, families and friends of veterans, and there were plenty of news reporters. I was led up to the stage by the commander of the Honor Guard, where he introduced me to Ken Bennett.

Mr. Bennett was the Arizona Secretary of State and was the driving force behind the retrieval and installation of the guns from the USS Arizona, which was sunk during the attack on Pearl Harbor, and from the USS Missouri, which is on display in a museum at Pearl Harbor. His achievement was impressive.

The entire ceremony only lasted about an hour. Afterwords I spoke again with Ken Bennett. I wanted to get his thoughts on my non-profit. He told me that I had a really great idea and that he couldn't see why I would not be successful in getting it noticed in the veteran communities throughout Arizona.

I was encouraged by his words. The crowds were milling about and I walked into them searching for Cathleen. It was time for us to leave. I wanted to get home before Kelly got off of work so that I would have time to prepare a nice dinner for both of us. I found her talking to an Army buddy with whom she had served.

I found the commander of the Honor Guard and thanked him again for the opportunity to attend the ceremony and be a part of the procession.

He invited me to a baby shower the following Saturday for one of the members of the Honor Guard and I accepted it. I felt that immersing myself in that community would be a good thing.

The ride home was pleasant. I dropped Cathleen off at her house and she told me that she was ready to help with the non-profit anytime. I replied that I wanted to wait until after the upcoming holidays to start rigorously promoting it, and that I would be contacting her soon to let her know what the plans were.

I arrived home well before Kelly did which gave me plenty of time to prepare a nice dinner. Kudos greeted me as I walked into the house from the garage. I checked his dishes to make sure that they were full, which they were. I was going into the bedroom to put my purse away, but the phone rang before I could.

I answered the phone. It was David, my son. Because I didn't receive phone calls from my family very often I thought that it was some type of emergency, but he assured me it was not. He wanted to know if I would like to fly to the Bay Area for the holidays to visit with the children and grandchildren.

I told him that I would love to, but that my finances were not healthy at that time. He told me that I need not worry about the cost, that he was going to pay for my airfare. I was thrilled but told David that I would have to talk to Kelly first and I would let him know. I was sure that she would be fine with it though.

I hung up the phone, excited with the thought of seeing my family. I had thawed out some pork chops for dinner, so I seasoned them and put them in the oven to roast. I was so glad that it was Friday, and that I didn't have any class course work to complete. I felt like I was actually going to be able to relax for a while.

While I worked in the kitchen I thought about Kelly and myself, our relationship and any future that we might have together. We had been through some trying times, had two long term separations, argued and made up, and even so were still clinging to the relationship. I hoped that we could last.

I had just sat down in the meditation garden with a cup of tea when I heard the front door open and shut. I went inside and saw Kelly in the kitchen. She was home early. She told me that she wanted to be able to spend more time with me, which was very heartwarming to hear. I asked if she wanted a cup of tea, to which she replied "sure".

She told me that she needed to wash up. I let her know that I would be outside in the garden with her tea. When her tea was made I went back outside, sipped my own tea and smoked a cigarette. I planned to talk to her about flying to the Bay Area to visit with the children and grandchildren over the upcoming holiday.

It was not long before Kelly came outside. She gave me a brief hug and sat on the bench adjacent to mine sipping her tea. I asked how her day had been and she began a long description of how work had been. She didn't get along well with her manager, but I attributed that to Kelly and her inability to follow direction.

When she was finished I asked if she would like to accompany me to the grocery store after dinner and she said that would be fine. I began to tell her about my day, about the commemoration ceremony, but I already knew that she was not interested. Remember, she thought that the non-profit was a scam.

I told her about David's phone call and let her know how much I wanted to go and visit my children and grandchildren. I told her that it would be a good time to visit with her parents and sisters, but she shook her head and emphatically said no. She was not in the least bit interested.

She abruptly stood up, knocking over her tea, the cup falling to the cement and shattering. Without looking at me she went into the house, muttering that she needed a shower, and slammed the door behind herself. I knew better than to follow her. Doing so would only lead to yet another shouting match, of which I had grown quite tired.

I lit another cigarette and waited before going inside. I hoped that by the time I did she would be calmed down. I bent over and carefully picked up the shards of the teacup, placing the jagged pieces in the small trash can on the patio. What a dilemma! I couldn't imagine why Kelly was so upset, but I planned to find out.

By the time I went back into the house Kelly had showered and was standing in the kitchen. She smiled and asked me what was for dinner. She said that she was starving. She acted as if nothing had happened. I told her that I had roasted some pork and that I was just getting ready to make the side dishes.

We made small talk while I prepared the rest of the food. She had her laptop on the table and was playing games while she waited. I glanced at her every so often trying to determine if she was still upset, but Kelly was always difficult to read. I set the table while the food finished cooking, trying not to disturb her.

When we were finished eating I cleared the table and tidied the kitchen. I asked Kelly if she was still going to accompany me to the grocery store and she said of course. I got my purse from the bedroom and walked into the garage to wait for her. We only needed a few items so the trip would be a short one.

As Kelly was backing the car out of the driveway she suddenly and violently hit the brakes. It was hard enough to throw me forward and into the dash. I was not injured, but I was shaken up a bit. She looked at me and said, "If you decide to visit your children and grandchildren I won't be here when you get back".

I was stunned. I had innocently thought that she would understand the need that I had to see my family, and that she might want to see hers as well. I was so wrong. Reluctantly, I told her that I would phone David and tell him that I would have to pass on the visit this time. My heart was broken though.

The remainder of the evening was spent in mostly silence. Not one word was spoken between us, with the exception of asking if Kelly needed anything from the grocery store. When we got home I put the few groceries away and then got ready for bed. I already knew that it was going to be a sleepless night.

There were only a few weeks left before the Yule holidays and I wanted to decorate the house, but without a lot of funds it might prove to be difficult. I had an artificial tree in the small storage shed in the backyard, so I decided to search for it amidst all of the boxes, hoping that it was still in good condition.

I hauled the box with the tree in it to the patio. I had decided to put it together outside then carry it into the living room. It was a white flocked tree complete with multi-colored miniature lights. The task was easy, and within fifteen minutes it was ready to go inside. I was really quite pleased with myself.

I carried it into the living and set it in a corner. Now all that I needed to do was buy some garlands and tinsel, and maybe a topper to complete it. I had taken Kelly to work so I had my car. I drove to the Dollar Tree and found most of what I needed there to decorate, with everything costing truly little.

I stopped by Ross to see what else I might be able to afford. I found a lovely serving tray with cardinals on it, and a statue of three cardinals. Those would look lovely on the dining room table. The year before I had purchased two Yule lanterns that were discounted at a local grocery store, which I would use as decorations as well.

I wanted to get the decorating finished before picking Kelly up from work so I drove home and got to work. First, I decorated the tree. Even though the living room was bereft of furniture it still looked quite charming, even elegant. I was happy with how well it had turned out.

Next, I went into the dining room. I strung colorful lights and garlands on the small bakers rack that Kelly had brought home from her work. I decorated the fireplace with poinsettia garlands, put a nice tablecloth on the dining room table, and placed the cardinal decorations on it. I completed the table by placing both of the lanterns in the center.

I noticed that it was time to pick Kelly up from work. The drive was a short one, less than two miles from our home. She was waiting by the front door of the thrift store. I was so excited to show her what I had done at home. Even though we didn't have a lot, we could still be grateful and celebrate the season together.

I parked the car and we went into the house together. I waited for Kelly to notice the beautiful tree and decorations, but she didn't even look. Instead, she went into the bathroom to wash up. I was patient though. I truly hoped that she was going to be delighted that I had been able to decorate for the holidays.

I made myself a cup of tea and sat at the dining room table waiting for her. I planned to make hot pot for dinner, and already had a nice piece of pork that I had roasted a few days before, as well as boiled eggs and fresh vegetables, to put in it. It was a simple and inexpensive dish that was also nutritious.

I sat at the dining room table, sipping my tea and waiting for Kelly. I hoped that she would look beyond me at the decorations and be happy. It took a while for her to come out of the bathroom, and when she did she had her pajamas on. She must have taken a shower while she was in the bathroom.

I asked if she would like a cup of tea and she said no. She walked past me without looking at the decorations and went outside to the meditation garden. I followed her, sitting beside her on one of the benches. She quickly got up and moved to the other bench. I wondered what was wrong now.

I lit a cigarette and waited for her to speak, but she remained silent. I told her that I had decorated a few areas of the house and asked if she would like to see. She just stared at me. Finished with my cigarette, I went back inside to sip on my tea. Eventually she came back inside. She looked around the room and smirked.

"Is this the best that you could do?" She shook her head disapprovingly. I told her that I truly had little money and that these decorations were all that I could afford. I asked if she wanted to see the tree, so she walked into the living room and looked. She turned around, laughing mockingly.

"This isn't decorating. It doesn't even feel like home or the holidays." She walked past me and into the bedroom, closing the door behind herself. I let out a heavy sigh. I was trying to make her comfortable, to make her get into the holiday spirit, but it was useless. Kelly was definitely not pleased at all.

Of course I was discouraged by her reaction, but I brushed that off and set about making our dinner. When the hot pot was ready I went to the bedroom to ask Kelly if she was hungry. She told me that she had eaten before I picked her up at work and asked me not to bother her. I told her that was I going to go ahead and have my dinner then.

The following days were rather miserable. I had nowhere to go, so I let Kelly drive my car to work. I focused myself on my class work, as well as the non-profit. When I was finished with those two things I made sure that the house was tidy and the gardens watered and groomed.

I had ordered a few gifts for Kelly with the gift cards that I received from my Hepatitis C online group, and I was happy when they were delivered prior to the holidays. I made sure that we had a nice meal for Yule, which of course we would celebrate on the twenty-fifth out of consideration for Kelly.

On Christmas Eve, Kelly came home from work frantic. She told me that she had not bought me anything, and that she had to go that very minute to try to find something. I told her that it was not necessary, but she had a meltdown. She asked if I would go with her and I replied that I would be happy to.

Kelly pulled the car into the street and drove down the block. I asked her where she planned on going and she said that there was something at one of the larger stores that she had been looking at. I told her that since it was Christmas Eve, and after seven o'clock, that she might find it was closed.

She began cursing, screaming profanities at me, at cars that she passed, even at pedestrians walking on the sidewalk. I told her that if it was going to upset her so much that we may as well turn around and go home. I really didn't need any holiday gifts, especially if buying one was going to make her so angry.

Kelly drove to the first store, which was locked up, then to another, and to another, finding every one of them closed for the holidays. She beat on the steering wheel with both of her hands, then began hitting herself on the head. I was ready to open my door and jump out of the car, but suddenly she calmed down.

She told me that we were going home, that she was sorry there would be no gifts for me. I reassured her that I was not upset, told her that birthdays were more important anyway, and that we could have wonderful celebrations for both of our birthdays which were only three months away.

Kelly isolated the rest of the evening, refusing to speak to me, acting as if I had caused the stores to be closed. I took a shower and got ready for bed. I watched some television, then dozed off into a restless sleep. Kelly never did come to bed that night, and I didn't bother going to look for her.

When I awoke the next morning I noticed that Kelly was not in the house. I went out to the garage and found her sleeping in my car. I left her there. I didn't feel like having any drama. I went back inside the house, poured myself a cup of coffee, and went outside to the meditation garden to wake up the rest of the way.

The sun was just cresting the horizon, and even though it was quite chilly it added a bit of warmth to the morning. I planned the day ahead. I had purchased a nice beef roast for our dinner, with fresh asparagus and potatoes au gratin. Even though Kelly was being obstinate I planned on having a lovely day.

I finished my coffee and went inside to put the roast in the oven. The sides would be quick and easy to prepare. I also made hard salami and green olive pinwheels for appetizers, and for dessert bakery style banana muffins and homemade French apple pie. The heat from the oven warmed the kitchen.

About two hours after I awoke Kelly walked through the door. She was disheveled and bleary eyed. I asked her if she wanted a cup of coffee but she walked past me and got a cup herself. I shrugged my shoulders. I had more than her to think about right now with all the cooking that I was doing.

I told her that I had once again invited my deceased loved ones to join us for dinner. She didn't say a word. I thought that she was going to argue, tell me that it gave her the heebie-jeebies, but she didn't protest. She went outside while I continued preparing the food. I put the pie in the oven and joined her outside.

I wanted to talk to her, but Kelly was in her own world. I lit a cigarette and wondered why she had slept in the car, again. I had done nothing, had been supportive, made sure that she had everything that she needed. Still, it appeared that nothing I said or did was enough for her. It broke my heart to realize this.

The hours passed and soon it was time to have dinner. We sat together at the dining room table. She told me that the food was delicious, but her eyes never met my gaze. I asked if she wanted to call her family and wish them happy holidays. She said that she would after we had finished with our dinner.

A few days later I received my second school stipend, which I was so grateful for. I put aside money for the rent and utilities, then went to the store to purchase food for New Year's Day dinner. I always prepared a traditional Southern style dinner which I had learned from my mother.

I was also excited for December 31st to arrive since I would be making my first appointment with Doctor Bitza, the primary physician I had chosen with my new health insurance plan. It had been over two years since I had last seen a doctor, and I wanted to make sure that everything in my body was healthy.

So a New Year, a new doctor, and so many new possibilities waiting for me. I wanted Kelly to be a part of everything in my world, so I would be working on our relationship from my end as much as I possibly could. With school and the non-profit, it looked like the New Year was going to be a busy and productive one for me.

Chapter Six:
Whatever Doesn't Kill You
Will Only Make You Stronger

December 31st, 2013, came, and I was excited to make an appointment with my new doctor for January 2nd. My new health insurance would take effect on January 1st, and I was looking forward to being able to at last get help for the Rheumatoid Arthritis and have my liver enzymes checked to make sure that I was still Hep C clear.

About an hour after making the appointment I was getting ready for a shower. I looked at my reflection in the mirror and noticed that my right nipple was puckered and pulled in. I put my hand on my breast and felt around the nipple. Much to my horror I discovered a lump in my breast the size of an apricot.

I took my shower, during which I felt my breast again to see if there really was a lump, and yes, it was still there. It was real. I quickly dressed and phoned the doctor's office, but they were already closed for New Years Eve. I phoned my daughter Stephanie. She asked if I was okay, but I was not. I was panicking.

I told her about the lump that I had discovered, and that I felt that it was most likely cancer. She said that I was jumping the gun, that it could be any number of things, but I detected deep concern in her voice. I assured her that I would be seeing the doctor on Thursday the 2nd.

She encouraged me to remain calm, saying that it might not be what I thought it was, cancer. I promised her that I would try, but it was difficult at best. My heart was racing, and even though I usually handled these types of things very well, my mind told me that it really was cancer.

I didn't know how I was going to tell Kelly. I was afraid of her reaction to a very real and life threatening problem. I decided to wait to talk to her, perhaps have a discussion the next day. I certainly didn't wish to alarm her if there were no reason, but she had to be told. I would talk to her on New Year's Day.

As much as I tried to put this discovery to the back of my mind it kept creeping out. I touched the lump gingerly, not wanting to disturb anything, perhaps aggravate it. I tidied the house and put a chicken in the oven for dinner. I went out to the garden and picked some fresh chard and zucchini to cook as a side.

Going into the backyard was a nice distraction. I irrigated the garden after picking the vegetables and watered the potted plants on the patio as well. Kelly would be home soon and I planned to be as calm as possible.

I didn't want to put a strain on the evening, especially since it was New Year's Eve.

Kelly came home fairly early and we had dinner together. I stayed awake with Kelly that night to ring in the New Year. She turned on the television so that we could watch the fireworks displays and the countdown to the end of 2013. We didn't have any wine or champagne to toast each other, but I was fine with that.

We watched the clocked tick down on the television as we held one another in what I thought was a loving embrace, and when the ball fell on Times Square our lips met and we kissed. I didn't know that it would be our last, or that any loving embraces were soon to become a thing of the past.

I awoke later than usual on Thursday morning. Kelly was already up and showered. I went into the kitchen after washing up and poured myself a cup of coffee. I saw Kelly sitting on one of the benches in the meditation garden so I went out to join her. I said good morning and took a sip of the hot brew.

Without looking at me she said good morning. I asked her how she was feeling and she replied that it really didn't matter. I lit a cigarette, took a long drag on it, and sipped my coffee. I supposed that Kelly hadn't gotten enough sleep and was grumpy, so I didn't press a conversation on her.

I went inside and began getting the food for our New Year's Day dinner together. I had purchased two nice slabs of salt pork, prepared black eyed peas, rice, and the fixings for cornbread. There was plenty of kale in the garden for the greens. This was going to be a traditional Southern style dinner intended for good luck.

Good luck. I was going to need all of the luck that I could get. As I prepared the food I thought about the next day when I would be seeing Dr. Bitza. Perhaps the lump was nothing, just a lump. There was no pain, so how could it be cancer? I tried not to think about it too much though and put my hand to preparing dinner.

While the cornbread was baking I made myself a cup of tea. Kelly was still outside so I went to join her. It was time to talk to her about the lump in my breast. I sat next to her on one of the benches and took her hand in mine. I lifted it to my breast and placed it over the lump. "Do you feel that?" I asked.

She jerked her hand away and stared at me wide eyed. "What is that?" I explained to her that I had discovered it the day before, and that I would be seeing my new doctor the next morning with the hope of founding out what it was. "Is it cancer?" I told her that I didn't know, and echoed

Stephanie, saying that we must not jump the gun.

Kelly avoided me for the rest of the day. She only joined me briefly for dinner, barely touching anything that I prepared, and left the table as soon as she was able to. I sighed heavily. Was she going to support me should this be cancer? I cleared the table, put away the leftovers and washed the dishes.

I went outside to relax, hoping that Kelly would join me, but she never did. I smoked a cigarette, sat a bit longer, then went back inside. I figured that I might as well get ready for bed. The day had not been what I had planned, and there was nothing I could do about it. I wondered where Kelly was.

I couldn't find her in the house so I went to the garage and saw that my car was gone. She had left, once again, in the midst of something that could be life altering. I had thought that she might have been more sympathetic, more loving, but such was not to be the case. I gave up wondering and went to bed alone.

The next morning I awoke in a state of anxiety. I had not slept well at all. Kelly had come in around three a.m., stumbling through the house and smelling heavily of liquor. I didn't bother speaking to her, let alone help her. I had too much going on that I knew I would most likely have to deal with on my own.

I poured a cup of coffee and went outside to the meditation garden to wake up. It was only six a.m., so I had two hours before my appointment with Dr. Bitza. I decided to phone Stephanie and let her know that I would be seeing the doctor shortly. My anxiety was too high to talk for long though.

I did mention Kelly's reaction to feeling the lump, and Stephanie told me that I should have expected it, that Kelly had never actually 'been' there for me in the past, and I shouldn't assume that she would be there now. I agreed. For as much as I loved her, Kelly just was not a compassionate partner.

Kelly was up and getting ready for work when I went back inside the house. I took a deep breath and dialed the doctor's office. The receptionist answered and I told her who I was. I let her know that I had discovered a lump in my right breast and she asked me to come in immediately.

First I had to drive Kelly to work, so I told the receptionist that I could be there by ten a.m.. She said that would be fine. I got dressed and waited for Kelly to finish in the bathroom. I let her know that I would only be a few minutes, that we could leave when I was finished with my makeup and hair.

I arrived at Dr. Bitza's office just before ten a.m. I checked in with the receptionist who asked for my insurance card and identification. She gave me a clipboard with forms on it to fill out. I waited while she copied my cards, then went to sit down to fill out all of the forms. I was still filling them out when I was called back to the exam room.

A nurse met me at the door. She led me to the back of the offices to an exam room where she took my weight and blood pressure. She asked me to take off my clothes from the waist up and handed me a paper shirt. She left, and within a few minutes the doctor walked through the door.

He introduced himself and sat down at a desk. He was an older, pudgy man who seemed to be thoroughly versed in the world of doctoring. We talked for a while as he went over my medical history. I told him 'I think that like you', which was a lot coming from me. I was always very particular where doctors are concerned.

He listened to my lungs, to my heart, and then said he wanted to examine my right breast. He asked me to lift my right arm straight up. He gently probed my breast, around the nipple and onto the lump. He looked at me and told me he was finished and that I could close the shirt.

He sat back down at the desk and began writing. He said that he was filling out forms for an emergency mammogram and ultrasound. He instructed me to go to Insight Imaging to have these done, and not to hesitate. I thanked him and left the office. I felt very surreal, as if none of this was really happening.

I drove the five miles to Insight Imaging and checked in with the receptionist, giving her the paperwork that Dr. Bitza had filled out. She told me that they didn't have an opening right away, and asked if I could return at two thirty p.m. for an appointment. I told her that I was extremely anxious, but that would be fine.

I left and drove home to wait, my nerves rattled. I barely remember the drive. My mind was racing. I didn't want to consider the horror of having cancer eating at my body. No one wants to think about something consuming their bodies. I tried to put it out of my mind by working on the non-profit website.

Needless to say I was not able to stop thinking about the lump. When I sat down at my computer it was one o'clock, and the entire time that I worked on the website I watched the clock. I was not able to get a lot completed and was actually relieved when two o'clock came. I got my purse, went to my car and drove back to the imaging center.

The same young lady was at the reception desk from earlier that day. She handed me a clipboard with several forms for me to fill out. She told me that it would only be a few minutes and someone would be out to get me. I sat and filled out the forms, my heart racing the entire time. I was exceptionally nervous.

It was not long before a technician came through the doors and called me by name. She led me back to the dressing room, handed me a cloth gown, and asked me to take my upper clothing off and put on the gown with the opening in front. When I was finished she took me into the mammogram room, which was the first imaging I received.

She opened the front of the gown and gently placed my left breast on the cold metal plate. I was prepared for a high degree of discomfort, but such was not the case. She then placed my right breast on the metal plate. This time there was a bit of discomfort, but not what I had experienced in the past.

The entire time the technician made light, small talk, told a couple of jokes, and generally tried to put me at ease. She was a kind and empathetic young lady. She asked to me go out into the waiting area in the hallway so that she could prepare the ultrasound room, which was the next imaging she was doing.

I was so nervous, actually scared. Soon the technician came back and asked me to follow her. We walked down the hallway and went into a small, dimly lit room. She asked me to lay down on the table and try to relax. I chuckled, telling her that would be a feat for me at this point in time.

She opened my gown and applied a warm sterile gel to my left breast. With the transducer in hand, she gently moved it over my breast until she was satisfied with the images. She then applied the gel to my right breast. As she performed this sonogram I could hear her making sounds that were rather discouraging.

Using a warm, damp towel, she gently wiped the gel from my breasts. She told me that she had to talk to the radiologist to see if he needed any further images. I waited alone in the room, trying to think about anything but what was happening, and attempting to listen to any conversations from beyond the door.

The technician was gone about fifteen minutes, and when she returned the radiologist was with her. He was not smiling. He took my hand in his own and squeezed it. "Susan, it is not good". Tears began silently coursing down my cheeks. I was numb, dumbstruck, and now, I was really frightened.

I asked what he had found, but he dodged my question. He told me that he had already phoned Dr. Bitza, and that they were transferring all of the images to a DVD that I was to give to him that afternoon. He let me know that I would be seeing a surgeon and having a biopsy, but that was all that he could tell me.

He continued holding my hand, helped me sit up from the bed, told me that he would be thinking of me, gave me a warm hug and then left the room. The technician came into the room with my clothing, glasses and purse. She told me to go ahead and get dressed in the ultrasound room while she finished her paperwork.

While I was dressing I asked the technician about the biopsy. She explained that it would most likely be a punch biopsy and that I would need to see a surgeon in order to have that scheduled and performed. She took me by the arm and led me through the lobby and to the door, where she gave me a warm hug, telling me that I would be fine.

I drove to Dr. Bitza's office to drop off the DVD with the ominous images. I handed it to the receptionist who told me that the doctor would be in touch with me soon. By the time I got home the doctor's office had left a voicemail to call them immediately, which I did, but they were already closed.

I would have to wait, anxiously of course, until eight a.m. Friday morning to speak with the doctor. I started a dinner for Kelly and myself, Pork Riblets in BBQ sauce with Hoppin' John and green beans. But my mind was not on food, it was on the uncertain future that lay ahead for me.

I picked Kelly up from work. She seemed to be in a good mood. She asked how my appointment had gone and I told her about Dr. Bitza, and that I had both mammograms and ultrasounds done that afternoon. She didn't say a thing, didn't respond. She just sat in her seat, looking out of the window.

We ate our dinner and then tried to distract ourselves by watching a movie. We both fell asleep before it was over, our backs to one another. The sleep that I had was troubling and broken. I couldn't stay in bed, so at three-thirty a.m. I got up, started the coffee, and went outside to sit in the dark.

When the coffee was done I poured a cup and returned to the meditation garden. I sipped on the coffee and thought about the past few days. It seemed as if so much had happened in such a short amount of time. Discovering the lump in my breast was more than I had ever bargained for.

I went back inside and made sure that the kitchen and dining rooms were tidied. I worked on the non-profit website for a while, checked in with my online school, and sent messages to my children. I didn't hear from them frequently, but I tried to be faithful in contacting them on a daily basis.

Kelly was up by seven a.m. I poured her a cup of coffee and went outside with her. I asked if she had slept well and she replied, "What's it to you?" I hung my head, feeling rather useless and defeated. I shrugged my shoulders, gave her a brief hug, and went back inside to get dressed and wait for eight a.m. to come.

Kelly came in shortly after and took her shower. I made the bed and straightened the bedroom, then gathered the laundry together to wash a couple of loads. By the time I was finished it was almost eight a.m., so I poured a cup of coffee, got the phone, and went outside to call Dr. Bitza's office.

The receptionist answered and transferred me to the nurse. She asked if I could be there at ten forty-five a.m., and I told her of course I could. Kelly was ready, so I drove her to work and came home to wait. I nervously puttered around the house straightening out things that didn't need it.

The time passed and soon it was time to drive to the doctor's office. I parked my car, went inside and checked in with the receptionist. It was not long before the nurse called my name. She led me through the door and into an exam room. She told me the doctor would be with me very soon.

She had no sooner shut the door than it opened again and she came back into the room. She asked me if the radiologist had mentioned any malignancy. I told her not really, just that he had told me that what he saw was not good. She nodded her head and left. This made me extremely uncomfortable and shaken.

She came back again within a few seconds. She told me that she had gone through stomach cancer, and that she was in remission. She told me to fight this, that I would be fine. She came over and gave me a big hug and patted my shoulder. She smiled, and again told me that I would be fine.

I thanked her, but I thought that it was extremely peculiar that she had told me about her stomach cancer, implying that I also had cancer. I had not been diagnosed so it felt rather inappropriate to me, even though I knew that she meant well. I tried to relax, but that was now beyond my reach.

Not long after the nurse left there was a knock on the door and the doctor walked in. He said that he had viewed the images and had spoken with the radiologist. He asked if I was in pain, and I told him only from Rheumatoid Arthritis. Then he said that he was scheduling me to see a breast surgeon right away.

The door opened and the nurse came in with the report from the radiologist and my doctor read it. He then read some of it to me. He was not smiling at all. I watched as he wrote the referral for the breast surgeon. While I was waited I asked him how this could have happened so quickly.

He didn't have an answer. I asked him if this was cancer and what stage I was in and he told me that we weren't going to talk about that right now, that we would discuss it after I had seen the breast surgeon. He gave the referral to the nurse so that she could get me a copy to take with me.

Dr. Bitza said "I am giving you two prescriptions. One for anxiety and one for pain. Take them when you need them. It is okay to take more than one." He then told me to go home and try to relax. He handed me the DVD with the images on it and told me to make sure to give it to the breast surgeon.

Even though Dr. Bitza had avoided the subject of cancer he told me that he was going to recommend excision and removal of the tumor and all surrounding tissue, or a lumpectomy. He said that I should be prepared for a biopsy, and that if the tumor was positive for cancer that the lymph glands on my right side would also be removed.

I stopped at the front desk to pick up the referral to the breast surgeon. The nurse told me that she had already made an appointment with the surgeon for ten a.m. the following Monday. I would have to wait an entire weekend without knowing what was actually happening to and in my body.

As I drove home I entered the world of surreal, as if I were dreaming everything. I shouted out loud "I AM NOT READY FOR THIS! I HAVE PLANS, I HAVE YEARS AHEAD OF ME! THIS CANNOT HAPPEN TO ME!!!!! TAKE THESE BREASTS, BOTH OF THEM, I DON'T NEED THEM, I DON'T EVEN CARE!!!"

Tears were streaming down my cheeks, tears of frustration and anger. I knew that I needed to get my emotions under control, that Kelly couldn't see me like this. I had been crying for days, not uncontrollably, and only when I was alone, but I needed to be strong for whatever the days ahead would bring.

My health insurance covered medication, so I composed myself and stopped by the pharmacy to get the prescriptions that Dr. Bitza had ordered for me. One was for Percodan, which was intended for pain, and the other was for Xanax, which was for anxiety. I didn't plan to use them unless absolutely necessary.

At home I hid the medications behind the coffee cannister in one of the kitchen cupboards. I didn't want Kelly to know that I had them. Knowing that she was an addict I didn't trust her to not to use them, and I knew that I might need them in the weeks to come. It consoled me a bit knowing that they were there if I needed them.

When Kelly came home that evening I spoke to her about my visit with Dr. Bitza, his concern. I told her that I was referred to a breast surgeon, and that I had an appointment that coming Monday. She asked if it was cancer, and I told her that I would not know until after a biopsy.

I asked if she could accompany me to the breast surgeons office, but she said that there was no way the company would give her the time off. I said that it was okay, I could take her to work and drive myself. But I really didn't want to go to the appointment alone. I wondered if it was work or if she actually didn't want to go with me.

The weekend came and went. Kelly worked both days, so I was left to myself. I tried to relax, to let go of the worry. I puttered around the house, prepared food for dinner, tried to take a nap, tried to stay busy, but the discovery of the lump and the reactions of the doctors kept plaguing me.

Terry had already returned from his extended visit with his family in Tennessee, and Haylie was home more often after the holidays. While Kelly was at work on Sunday I asked them both to join me in the meditation garden, telling them that I had some news that I wanted to share with them.

I brought them both a glass of iced tea. Haylie sat on one of the benches and Terry on a chair. I sat on the other bench. I told them both how much I appreciated them, that they were the best roommates anyone could possibly hope for. Then I told them of my discovery the Monday before.

Haylie gasped and immediately got up from where she was sitting and hugged me. Terry looked at me, shook his head and said he was sorry. I told them that there was no diagnosis yet, but that I was seeing the breast surgeon the next day. They asked if there was anything that I needed, or if they could do anything for me.

I told them that Kelly couldn't come with me and that I didn't want to go to the appointment alone, so I took the opportunity to ask Haylie if she would be willing to come with me, and she said yes, of course she would.

I was so relieved. It is not that I needed someone to hold my hand, I just needed some moral support.

Neither one of them cared much for Kelly. They had both either witnessed or heard her frequently yelling and belittling me. Terry had at one point tried to talk to her about it, but she made it out to be a joke and ignored his suggestions. She was who she was, and no one was going to change her.

When Kelly came home that evening she told me that she was taking me out for dinner and shopping so that she could buy me something to wear in case I had surgery, something comfortable but stylish. We ate dinner at McDonald's, then went shopping. I found a teal sweatpants outfit with one of the pant legs embroidered with 'HOPE'.

Hope is what I needed right now and wearing 'hope' would help me to continue feeling that my life was worth fighting for. By the time we returned home I was worn out. It had been an exhausting week, and the worst of it all was not over. I put on my pajamas and got ready for bed. I fell asleep almost immediately and slept all night.

The morning came and I awakened early as usual. I started the coffee and went outside to the meditation garden. My mind raced towards my appointment with the breast surgeon. In my heart of hearts, I already knew that I had breast cancer, but I tried not to think about it. I got a cup of coffee and went back outside.

Kelly woke up and joined me in the meditation garden. She didn't smile or say good morning. I thought that she might be worried or frightened about my appointment with the surgeon, but she didn't show it. I said good morning to her anyway and went into the house to get ready.

Haylie was awake and ready to go. I told her that I needed to get dressed, do my hair and put on some makeup and that I would only take a few minutes. I was certainly anxious to get this appointment over with, and hoped to find out that morning when I would be going into surgery. But that was not to be the case.

I told Kelly goodbye and wished her a good day at work. There were no hugs or kisses. The drive to the surgeons office was a short one. Haylie parked her car and we walked to the building, went through the door, and I checked in with the receptionist, handing her the referral from Dr. Bitza and DVD of images.

The receptionist handed me a clipboard with forms to fill out, four pages total. She said, "Take a seat, you'll be called shortly". A nurse came through the door about fifteen minutes later and we were led through several hallways to the very back of the rooms. She opened a door and invited us to walk in.

The doctor's office was warm and inviting. Dr. Kassenbrock stood and introduced himself to Haylie and me and invited us to be seated. He had already loaded the images on the DVD onto his computer. He turned the monitor around and began to explain to us what he saw. He pointed out the suspicious mass.

It was not too large, 2cm, about the size of a peanut, and located directly behind my right nipple. He said that my left breast looked fine, and that I need not worry about it. He explained the surgeries, chemotherapy and radiation that I would most likely be going through if it turned out to be malignant.

The doctor asked us to go to an exam room where I was told to take my upper clothing off and put on a paper shirt. Haylie sat on a chair while I changed behind a curtain. She told me that she was glad that she had come with me and would do her best to support me during this traumatic time.

Dr. Kassenbrock knocked on the door and walked into the room. I was already on the exam table. He listened to my lungs and heart, then he began examining my breasts. First the left, then the right. He asked me to lie down and put my left arm straight above my head. He performed another exam of the left breast.

Then he asked me to extend my right arm above my head and he examined my right breast. He felt the lump and moved along the lymph glands from the breast to the armpit. He helped me up, told me to get go ahead and get dressed, and for Haylie and me to meet him back in his office to discuss what he had found.

Haylie and I walked back to his office and took our seats. Dr. Kassenbrock said the mass was large but that he didn't feel anything unusual in the lymph nodes. He told me that his nurse was scheduling a biopsy for as soon as possible, and that if anything changed, or I had any questions whatsoever, to call him immediately.

He filled out a form and told me to take it to the front where the biopsy would be scheduled. I handed the paper to the receptionist who asked us to have a seat and wait. Soon I was called back up and given a paper to take to the outpatient surgery at Banner Hospital. The biopsy was scheduled for Thursday, January 9th, 2014.

We left the doctor's office and Haylie dropped me off at home but couldn't stay as she was scheduled to work that evening. I went into the house. I was numb and couldn't think. I wanted to cry, but there were no tears. I was scared, worried, and beside myself. I needed to rest, to try and escape through sleep.

First though, I needed to make some food for our dinner, so I put a small pork roast in the oven and pulled out some side dishes. I made sure that the house was tidy, that Kudos had plenty of food and water, and then I laid down on the bed. I turned on the television, the sound of which usually lulled me to sleep.

I had turned the phones off in the house so that I would not be disturbed. I slept through phone calls from Kelly and my children. I simply slept, a deep but troubled sleep. In fact, I slept so deeply that I didn't awaken until I heard Kelly come through the garage door into the house.

Slowly, I sat up on the edge of the bed. I was a bit disoriented. I had not taken any of the prescriptions that Dr. Bitza had ordered for me, so it was not drugs making me feel this way. I supposed it was because I rarely took naps. I got up and went into the bathroom to splash some water on my face.

I was anxious to talk to Kelly about what I had learned at the surgeon's office earlier in the day. She walked into the bedroom just as I was coming out of the bathroom. She gave me a brief hug, then pushed past me. She went into the bathroom to wash up, something that she always did after work.

I went out into the kitchen, poured myself a glass of iced tea and went outside to the mediation garden. Kelly came out soon after. I asked if she would like to hear about my visit with the surgeon, and she said "Sure", but I was not convinced that she was actually interested in listening.

I went over everything that the surgeon had told me and let her know that I was scheduled for a punch biopsy on Thursday, three days hence. I asked if she could possibly get the time off to go with me, but she hesitated, telling me that her manager was refusing to allow her to take the time off from work.

Needless to say I was disappointed, but it really was not unexpected. I remembered how Kelly had pulled her hand away from the lump in my breast, the look of shock on her face, actually close to revulsion. I supposed that I could drive myself to the appointment, but it sure would be nice to have her support.

I made it through the next few days. My schoolwork was always easy for me, so I was able to complete my entire week's work before Wednesday. I also worked on the non-profit on both the website and social media. In reality, I was not very well versed in non-profits, but I was doing my absolute best to promote it.

When Kelly got home she had a smile on her face, the first I had seen for a while. She told me that her manager had approved of her taking the following morning off in order to go with me to the biopsy. I was more than thrilled. I gave her a hug and kiss and thanked her for pursuing the request.

I knew that it had only been a little over a week since my discovery, but this would be the fifth appointment since then, three of which I had attended alone. I was a bit apprehensive about the one coming up, but after having researched and read about it I was more at ease. I wanted to be as prepared for the biopsy as possible.

We had a light dinner then retired to the bedroom for the night. Kelly actually let me rest my head on her shoulder for the first time in months. But rest is not what I had. After tossing, turning and having distorted dreams for hours I finally got up around five a.m. I started the coffee and went outside.

The biopsy appointment was scheduled for ten a.m., so I had plenty of time to wake up, get ready and compose myself. I certainly didn't want to arrive in an agitated state. I sipped my coffee, smoked a cigarette, and gazed into the darkness of morning. I was so glad that Kelly was going to be with me.

She was up by seven a.m., early for her, and she was well rested. She came outside with a cup of coffee and gave me a hug and kiss. Perhaps I had misunderstood her actions over the past week and a half. I know that she was under stress of some type. Who would not be when finding out that their partner might have cancer?

I straightened the house, put a load of clothes in the washer, washed the few dishes that were in the sink, and then finally I got in the shower. I decided to wear the new outfit that Kelly had bought for me, the one that had 'HOPE' embroidered on the left leg. I might not even need surgery, so I figured I didn't need to wait to wear it.

Kelly showered while I got dressed, styled my hair and put on some makeup. By the time she was finished I was anxious and ready to go. She took her time getting ready and I began to worry that we were going to be late, but it was only nine a.m. by the time she walked out of the bedroom.

The drive to the breast cancer center was brief. Kelly parked the car and we walked together to the outpatient clinic located next to Banner Hospital. I gave my name to the receptionist, who took my insurance information and asked me a few questions. He told us to have a seat and said that we would be called in shortly.

A door opened and the receptionist came through, calling my name. He led Kelly and me down a hallway, through two sets of doors, and told us to take a seat, that a nurse would be with me in a few minutes. I was extremely nervous. I know what the ultrasound technician had told me about the biopsy, but it was yet an unknown.

It was not long before a nurse came into the waiting area, took me by the arm and literally swept me away through the swinging doors. I didn't even have a chance to say anything to Kelly. She showed me to a dressing room and told me to undress from the waist up and put on one of the gowns provided.

She handed me a bag to place my clothing in. I changed into the gown and folded my clothes, placing them in the bag. I began coughing and asked the nurse for some water. She asked if I was sick and told me that she was worried that I might start coughing during the procedure, that I needed to be perfectly still.

I said, "I am just a bit nervous." She brought me a small cup of water which I drank and then she led me to another room. Dr. Kassenbrock walked by and waved at me. Everyone seemed so cheery, smiling and making jokes. I couldn't smile, even though I usually would have been the first one to do so.

The nurse explained some of the procedure to me, including that I would hear a pop, kind of like a champagne cork being dislodged. That would

579

be the biopsy needle going into my flesh. She left for a few minutes then returned to take me to the mammogram room, images the doctor needed for reference.

For some reason this mammogram was painful. Perhaps it was only my mind playing tricks on me, or maybe the tumor really was that sensitive. The technician was finished in less than five minutes, then I was told to go out and sit in the hallway to wait for the nurse to call me for the procedure.

I sat down and waited. There were doctors, nurses and technicians heading in different directions along the hallway, some going into procedure rooms, others into the main building. Soon the nurse returned and told me that it was time for my biopsy. I stood up, a bundle of nervousness, and followed her.

We walked across the hall and into a room with a narrow steel table. There was a hole in the table where I was told that my breast would hang through. The nurse helped me take the gown off then told me to get on the table and lay on my belly. She positioned me so that my right breast hung through the hole at a right angle.

Another nurse came in, along with Dr. Kassenbrock. They were both laughing and talking. The nurse that was already in the room joined in the joviality. I tried, but just couldn't get into the mood. The doctor said, "Now you'll feel something cold and wet." He rubbed my breast with a topical anesthetic.

The topical anesthetic was meant to numb my skin, getting it ready for an injection of Lidocaine. I could see the needle coming towards my breast and I jumped away from the doctor's hand. He told me to be still, and the second time he was successful. The medicine was hot, burning my flesh. I moaned aloud in discomfort.

Dr. Kassenbrock spoke in a soothing tone, telling me everything was going to be fine, that I just needed to let the anesthetic start working. Suddenly, both of my calves began cramping, painfully, and I couldn't move or do anything to stop them from doing this. The doctor told one of the nurses to massage my legs.

Suddenly I heard the 'POP'! Dear lord, if anyone EVER tries to tell you that a breast biopsy is relatively painless DON'T BELIEVE THEM!!! The pain was severe, and it lasted for what seemed a lifetime. The Dr. Kassenbrock said, "Hold on, I'm injecting Lidocaine through the biopsy needle."

I felt the burning and pain, but no numbing effect. I kept saying "Oh my god!", to which Dr. Kassenbrock replied, "No, I am not, but thank you anyway". He took two biopsies, but before he removed the needle he inserted a titanium clip to show where the biopsy tissue had been removed.

I went limp, there were no tears, but I had no energy. He walked around the bed and began massaging my legs trying to get the cramps out, which they eventually did. Even though it was a painful procedure, everyone involved was kind and funny and lighthearted, and really cared about me as a human.

Dr. Kassenbrock and one of the nurses left. The younger nurse stayed behind to make sure I was stable enough to sit up. She helped me sit, but I had to remain seated for a few minutes as I was dizzy. When I was able to she helped me get the gown back on and walk across the hall to have another mammogram done.

This one was to make sure the titanium marker was in the right position, marking where the biopsy had been taken. The technician finished and told me that I could get my clothes on and leave. I asked when I would hear the results of the biopsy and she told me that it would be several days.

I got dressed and went out to the lobby to find Kelly. She was nowhere to be seen. I asked the receptionist if he had noticed where she had gone, and he told me that she left shortly after I had been taken back for the biopsy. I thanked him and went outside in search of her.

I was still reeling from the biopsy, and not in a particularly good mood. I saw her sitting in the car. As I approached I could hear the stereo blasting the hip-hop music that Kelly loved to listen to. I opened the passenger door and got inside the car. Kelly asked if I was okay.

I told her that I was as good as could be expected and asked her why she had left the building. She said, "You didn't even hug me or say goodbye before going back, so I didn't think that I needed to be inside." I asked if she had seen the nurse whisk me away and she said that didn't matter, that I had ignored her.

I shrugged my shoulders. This was so typically Kelly. On the way home we stopped at an IHOP pancake house to have a late breakfast. Kelly had to go to work for the rest of the day afterwards, so I rode with her to the store and drove myself home. She said that she would be able to get a ride home and not to worry about her.

I was on my own for the rest of the day. I phoned my children to update them on everything so far. They all asked that I notify them as soon as I had the biopsy results. Stephanie told me that if I were to need surgery that she would be willing to fly down and stay with me while I recovered. I was relieved to hear this.

So far, since January 2nd, I had gone to five appointments. It was only Thursday, and I would have another weekend ahead of me to get through before hearing the results of the biopsy. It was all I could do to distract myself. I didn't have any school assignments as I had completed the entire week the day before.

There was nothing more to do on the non-profit website for the time being, so I decided to do some grocery shopping. I still had some funds leftover from my last stipend, as well as a months' worth of food stamps, so I would easily be able to afford some nice meals for the weeks ahead.

After shopping and putting away all of the groceries I decided to take a Xanax, my first, and lie down. I counted the pills in the bottle, along with the Percodan. They were all accounted for. I wanted to make sure that Kelly was not getting into them. I really didn't like being so suspicious of her, but such was the life she had created.

On Friday I called Dr. Kassenbrock's office to find out if the results of the biopsy were in yet but was told that I needed to be patient and to wait until the following week to hear back from the doctor. I was frustrated, but I knew that these types of things take time so I had to force myself to wait for his phone call.

The weekend passed incredibly slowly. In fact, it was if time itself had stood still. Kelly worked both days, so I was left to myself again. Even when she was home it was almost like she was not there anyway. I gardened, kept the house tidied, did the laundry, but still it seemed that time was dragging its toes.

Monday morning finally arrived. I awoke fairly early, started the coffee and went out on the patio while it brewed. I had no energy, and really wanted to go back to bed. I got a cup of coffee and went back outside. I sat thinking about all that was happening and what it was going to mean for the future.

Kelly awoke an hour or so after me. I got her a cup of coffee and asked how she was feeling. She didn't say much, so I went back inside the house. I poured myself another cup of coffee and tried to drink it. I became nauseated and decided to lie for a while to let it pass.

I must have dozed off because the next thing I knew Kelly had given me a quick kiss on the cheek and walked out the door to go to work.
I decided to get up and try to feel 'normal'. I poured myself a mug of iced tea and sat in the meditation garden for a few minutes. I kept the

phone close to me in case someone called.

'Normal' for me is making this house a home, a welcoming place to be, warm and inviting, so I decided to bake. I made apple muffins, bakery style. I left the flour on the counter in order to bake some cookies after I rested a bit. While the muffins baked I sat outside. The phone rang and I looked at the caller ID.

"General Surgeon", which meant it was a call from Dr. Kassenbrock's office, the surgeon who had performed the biopsy. I answered the phone and he asked how I was feeling. I told him that I felt drained, listless, had zero appetite, which was not normal for me. He said that I should get as much rest as I needed.

He then told me that the pathology report from the biopsy had come back. It was positive. I had cancer! I held back my emotions and spoke with him for a while. I asked so many questions, which he patiently answered. He told me that his staff would be working on scheduling the surgery.

Dr. Kassenbrock said that the tumor had doubled since the first images were taken, now the size of a walnut, and this indicated it was an aggressive tumor. This also meant that at this time the cancer was in stage two. The sooner that I had surgery the better my chances were at survival. I agreed that it should be soon.

He then asked if I wanted a lumpectomy or a mastectomy. I replied by asking him what he felt was the best course. He said a mastectomy, so trusting him I agreed with that. Then he wanted to know if I wanted just the right breast removed or both. I thought only briefly then replied that he may as well take both.

He asked me to make an appointment with Dr. Bitza for a pre-surgery physical. He said that his nurse was lining up restoration surgeons that he had worked with in the past, in the event that I wanted breast implants. I told him that I would phone Dr. Bitza and looked forward to hearing from his nurse regarding the surgery schedule.

I didn't allow myself tears until right before I hung up the phone. I was frightened and angry, and I didn't know what to do with myself. I phoned my children. I needed strong shoulders at that moment, those that I could lean on for support. All three were shocked, distressed and concerned.

I assured them, even though I was quite uneasy, that everything was going to be fine. Stephanie reminded me that she was going to try to come to be with me before the surgery and a week afterwards. I was so grateful for this. Kelly was not a nurse in any sense of the word and would not know the first thing about caring for me.

The first hurtle of informing my family was completed. Now to jump over the second one, and that was telling Kelly. I anxiously awaited her coming home. Since showing her the lump, she had been decidedly distant, even though she appeared from time to time to be understanding and compassionate.

My heart was racing, but I managed to get my emotions under control. I prepared a nice dinner for Kelly and me for that evening. I wanted everything to go smoothly and for her to be in a good mood when I spoke with her. Life was such a mixed bag with her, and I found that I often had to tread lightly.

I jumped when I heard the door from the garage open. Kelly had come home early. I turned to greet her but she walked past me into the bedroom, I figured to wash up. I poured each of us a glass of iced tea and went outside to sit in the meditation garden to wait for her. I could feel my blood pressure rising.

She finally came outside and sat on the bench opposite me. I asked her how her day had gone and she curtly replied that it was the same as always. She didn't have her tea, so I went into the kitchen and brought it to her. I sat down and gazed into the distance, wondering how this conversation was going to go.

I told her about the phone call from Dr. Kassenbrock, and that the biopsy was positive for cancer. She didn't say a word. I went on to let her know that I would be hearing from the nurse about the date of the surgery, and that they were giving me a list of restoration surgeons for possible implants.

"Well, I figured that you had cancer. Susan, I'm not going to be able to deal with this." She shook her head, avoiding my eyes. She said that she had already spoken to her mother, Sharon, who had suggested that Kelly encourage me to join a breast cancer support group. I told her that I felt it was too early for me to do so.

I asked if she were hungry and told her that I had prepared a nice dinner. She said that she had picked up a burger on the way home and was not interested. I felt so defeated. It seemed as if nothing I did or said was ever good enough for her. I went inside the house and put all of the dinner away. I had lost my appetite.

I thought about the restoration surgery, but that did little to comfort me. I thought about what it would be like to lose a limb, for instance an arm or a leg, putting myself in the place of someone who is paralyzed, someone who has experienced more trauma than I. My mind raced trying to make sense of it.

I barely slept at all that night. I awoke every ten minutes or so, tossed, turned, got out of bed as quietly as possible, paced the house, paced the patio, looked at the computer. All that I could think about was this 'thing' eating away at my flesh, and what had to be done to stop it, meaning that soon I would have no breasts.

I decided not to awaken Kelly. That would only cause problems. I couldn't call my children because it was the middle of the night. Around six a.m. Kelly came outside to where I was sitting and was able to convince me to come back to bed and rest a bit. I was able to doze for an hour or so.

By the time I woke up Kelly was gone for the day. I poured a cup of coffee, got the phone, and went outside. I had just lit a cigarette when the phone rang. It was Dr. Kassenbrock's nurse. She told me that my surgery had been scheduled for January 23rd. She reminded me to make an appointment for a pre-surgery physical.

She then gave me the names and phone numbers of three restoration surgeons that Dr. Kassenbrock recommended. I wrote them down and thanked her for her time. I decided that I would call them after I had spoken with Kelly. I was going to do my best to convince her to accompany me to the appointments.

The entire day was spent going through the motions of being alive. Somehow I managed to get everything done that I needed to. With surgery looking me in the eye, and as much as I didn't want to, I decided to contact my school and take an extended leave of absence starting the week before the surgery.

Through gentle persuasion I was able to convince Kelly to accompany me to at least one appointment with a restoration surgeon, which didn't go as well as I would have hoped. Not only was he inept and inexperienced, but his entire attitude was one of disdain, and I attributed that to homophobia.

I made an appointment with the second restoration surgeon on the list, but this one I went to on my own. His office was located in Scottsdale, which was a bit of a drive for me, but I had to find a surgeon. If he agreed to do the surgery then he would need to get special permission from the hospital. The appointment was set for Friday at two p.m.

Somehow I managed to get through the rest of the week. My nerves were constantly on edge, but I kept myself under control, even when dealing with Kelly's negative attitude. I continued my schoolwork as I wanted to have as much of it completed before my leave of absence began the following week.

I knew that we needed to renew the lease soon on the house, and Kelly had agreed to be added to it, so I phoned my landlord and told him that we planned to stay another year and to please draw up the lease contract. He told me that he would have it ready for us to sign sometime in mid-February.

Friday morning came, but I was not ready to get up. I was so comfortable in my little bed fortress that I had created. I finally worked my way out from under the comforter and blankets and got a cup of coffee. Kelly was already up and about. I sat in the meditation garden drinking my coffee and waking up.

I didn't have a lot of time to wake up though as I needed to make Kelly lunch and then drive her to work. I finished the cigarette that I was smoking and went back into the house. Kelly was already dressed, so I went into the bedroom, made the bed, showered, got dressed, styled my hair and put on some makeup.

I had plenty of time after dropping Kelly off and before going to my appointment, so I was able to return home and tidy the entire house, with the exception of Terry and Hailey's rooms, water the gardens, and put a small roast in the oven for dinner. I also spent some time working on the non-profit website.

There was only so much that I could do on the website, so when I was finished with that I took the time to write a last will and testament, as well as an advance directive. I didn't want to think about dying, but with any surgical procedure there are risks, and I wanted to be prepared just in case.

By the time I was finished writing those documents it was one p.m. and time for me to drive to Scottsdale. I had not been to that town for many years, and I didn't have the first inkling of where I was going, but I had drawn a detailed map that hopefully would get me there safely and on time.

After the visit to the first reconstruction surgeon earlier in the week I was actually dreading this appointment. I wanted my breast surgery to be as flawless as possible, so I was hoping that this doctor would be the one. If he were, then he would need to be pre-approved to perform the surgery at Banner Hospital.

I arrived at the medical complex a little more than a half hour later, so I was early for my appointment, which was a good thing since I had to find where to park for the surgeon's suite. I drove around the complex twice, then finally found the parking area. I took the elevator upstairs and walked the few steps to the office door.

As I walked through the door I was struck by the elegance of the entire waiting room. The walls were gilded and lined with bookshelves which were filled with books on art, travel and photography. There was a seventy inch television which was tuned to the Travel Channel, which was featuring a travel guide on Tibet.

I checked in with Rani, Dr. Jacobsen's receptionist/assistant. She handed me a clipboard which held several pages of medical history for me to fill out. It took me several minutes to do so, and when I was finished I gave all of the pages back to her. I asked where the restroom was and she pointed through a pair of swinging doors.

Even the restroom, which was quite accommodating, was also gilded. There were seasonal flowers in assorted vases, and actual cloth towels to dry hands with. When I was finished I went back out to the waiting room. The only other person who had been in the waiting room had been called back for his appointment, so I was next.

I had no sooner sat down than Rani called my name. She led me to an exam room, which of course was beautifully appointed. She said that I could choose either a short or long gown to wear, it was my choice. The gowns were Oriental in style, black silk, with gold buttons located on the side at the top.

I chose a long gown, put it on, and sat down to wait for the doctor. I glanced over a book about haute couture, from ancient times to present day. I gazed out the windows, hoping that this was going to work out. Then there was a knock at the door. It was Dr. William Jacobsen.

He was tall, with greyish hair, and had an arresting aura. He invited me to be seated on the exam table while he sat on a chair. He told me that he was there to help me get through this. He was not a breast surgeon, per se, in other words, his forte was reconstruction of devastating cancer trauma.

"However," he said, "I have a heart for breast cancer patients, and you are one of them. I am here to help you." I started to cry. I was, of course, frightened, bewildered, and so unsure. I let him know that I had been told the surgery would be outpatient, that I would be admitted briefly to the hospital afterwards, and then sent home.

This really bothered me. He said "I am part of the surgical team. You will be in the hospital for several days, in the care of skilled nurses. Don't worry, don't cry, it will be all right." He took my hand and said, "We will get you through this." He explained the mastectomy, along with the placement of the tissue expanders.

The expanders would be filled with saline solution after my chest had healed from the mastectomies. Optimally they would eventually be my normal size, which was D-DD. He then opened a drawer and pulled out an 'implant', one which he had helped in developing. It felt like a real breast, not hard, but flexible and soft.

He continued to hold my hand and reassure me. He said he would be with me every step of the way, that I could call him 24/7 to talk. His staff was already on the phone with Tisch, Dr. Kassenbrock's nurse, to let her know that he was agreeing to be a part of the surgical team and to move forward gaining Banner hospitals permission.

He then said that his part of the five hour surgery would be only a half hour, and that he would make sure I would be VERY WELL taken care of during the surgery and while I was in the hospital recovering. I left the office feeling confident, believing that everything was going to turn out simply fine.

I drove home feeling much better than I did earlier. Even though I was still somewhat apprehensive I was glad that everything was coming together so well for the surgeries. I had just enough time to pick Kelly up, so I drove to her work first before going home. She was waiting for me by the curb.

While we were driving home she asked me how the appointment went, and I told her that it couldn't have been more perfect, and that Dr. Jacobsen would be placing the tissue expanders after the mastectomies were completed. She said, "That's good". Nothing more than that, but what could I expect?

It was already the 17th of January, meaning that I only had six days before my surgeries. Six days of frazzled nerves, and of trying to make plans when I had no idea if those plans would ever come to fruition. I slept truly little that night. In fact, for the next several days and nights rest was difficult for me to find.

I received a phone call from my daughter Stephanie the next day. She was not going to be able to fly down after all, but she told me that she had contacted our former nanny/housekeeper, Annie, and that Annie was more than happy to come and watch over me. I was disappointed, of course, but delighted that other arrangements had been made.

Stephanie gave me Annie's phone number and I called her as soon I had hung up with Stephanie. It had been quite a few years since I had last spoken to Annie, but she recognized my voice right away. She told me that she would need to be picked up at her sister's house in Eloy, and I assured her that would not be a problem.

We spoke on the phone for over an hour, catching up on life. She told me that one of her daughters, Julie, had recently passed away, and that she had taken on the responsibility of raising her granddaughter Sofie. I told her that I was deeply sorry for her loss. I was sad for her, but really looking forward to seeing Annie again.

That evening I asked Kelly if she would be willing to pick Annie up the day of my surgeries and she agreed. I tried to talk to her about the surgeries but all she could say in return was that I needed to join a breast cancer support group. That was something I just was not ready to do. Not yet.

I managed, in an extreme state of high anxiety, to go grocery shopping, stock the kitchen with food, and prepare enough dinner meals for the first two weeks after surgery. I felt that it would be a nice gesture to have those ready for Annie so that she didn't have to spend a lot of her time in the kitchen cooking.

Somehow I able to get through the final days before having my breasts amputated. I had a high degree of apprehension, but I refrained from taking any of the Xanax that Dr. Bitza had prescribed for me. I did check the prescription bottles though and was pleased that they had not been pilfered.

The night before the surgeries I was not able to rest at all. I spent most of the night on the patio, not wishing to awaken Kelly. I didn't need to check in at the hospital's outpatient clinic until seven a.m., so I let Kelly sleep until five-thirty. She was groggy and not in a particularly good mood. I poured her a cup of coffee and let her be.

I had packed a small bag of personal items to take with me, making sure that I had my advance directive to give to the nurses. My last will and testament was tucked safely in a manila envelope and filed away. I had not shown it to Kelly since she was not named in the will at all. My children were the focus of that.

We arrived at the hospital fifteen minutes early. I checked in, had a wrist band placed on my left wrist, and was wheelchaired through a set of swinging doors. The aide who was wheeling me took me to a small cubicle where I was given a gown to change into. He told me that a nurse would be with me shortly.

Kelly was there, but not really. She had barely spoken five words to me all morning. I realized that she was somehow traumatized by all that had happened since the beginning of the year, but it was my body, my psyche, my being that had been attacked by cancer, not hers, and I sorely needed the support that she was unwilling to give me.

A nurse came into the cubicle to start my IV. I handed her the advance directive, making sure that she noted on my chart that I did want to be resuscitated in the event that something untoward happened during the surgeries. She slipped the document into my file and told me that someone would be by shortly to take me to nuclear medicine.

Kelly stood looking out of the window, not paying attention to what was happening in the room. I wanted her to hold me and tell me that everything was going to be fine, but instead she avoided me. I was, of course, incredibly sad about this, but there was simply nothing that I could do to change the way she was behaving.

Soon an aide came to wheel me to nuclear medicine. I was to be injected with a nuclear material in order to pinpoint the largest lymph node. This would be biopsied during the mastectomies in order to stage the cancer, one to four. When the procedure was finished I was wheeled back to the cubicle to await surgery.

I was just getting back into the bed when a nurse opened the curtains and told me it was time for my surgeries. Kelly gave me a brief hug and wished me luck. She told me that she was going to Eloy to pick Annie up so that she would be at home when I was discharged from the hospital, and that she would see me later.

From that moment on everything became somewhat dreamlike. I must have already had a sedative in my IV. I remember being helped onto the steel surgical bed and being positioned. I remember watching Dr. Kassenbrock draw on my chest with a marker. Then darkness descended upon me and I became blissfully unaware.

Revelations: Old Friends And New Enemies

I didn't regain consciousness until after I was taken to my room. I was vaguely aware of post-surgical pain, so I knew that the anesthetic was still working. Dr. Kassenbrock was sitting on a chair next to the bed waiting for me to wake up. I tried to speak but all that came out of my mouth was a hoarse, dry whisper.

"Don't try to talk Susan," Dr. Kassenbrock said. "You were intubated during surgery so it will be difficult for you to speak for now." He went on to tell me that the surgery had been a success, that not only had he removed all of my mammary tissue, but also most of the lymph nodes on my right upper side.

He told me that the tumor he had removed was seven centimeters, or the size of a peach. That meant it had grown four times the size it was when I first discovered it. "You will stay here overnight for observation, but tomorrow morning you should be fine to go home." I was relieved. I never did care for being in a hospital.

"I'll be seeing you in a week for a follow-up. I have given written instructions to the nurse for you to take home. Make sure that you do exactly what the instructions say and you should heal fine." He smiled as he talked, a reassuring smile, which gave me just a bit of comfort in such an uncomfortable situation.

He patted my hand and left the room. I tried to sit up, and that is when I felt the pain. The anesthetic was wearing off. It was a searing, excruciating pain. I placed both of my hands over my chest and felt a rather thick wrapping over the area where my breasts had been. Then I felt a tug on my flesh just under my right armpit.

When I put my hand under the hospital gown I discovered a tube coming out from my side. I immediately rang for a nurse. I needed to know what it was that was sticking out of my flesh. I felt around on my left side and found that there was a tube coming out of my body on that side as well.

A nurse came into the room and asked what I needed. I told her, in a raspy voice, that I had found tubes coming out of my sides and wondered what they were. She helped me sit up and opened my gown. She told me that they were surgical drains with bulbs attached on the ends to catch any fluid that drained from the surgical sites.

I asked if she knew how long I would have to have them and she told me that it was normal to have the drains in for up to two weeks after surgery, and that I needed to be careful not to pull on them too hard as I might dislodge them. I was a bit upset since I had no prior knowledge that I was going to have them.

I asked her if she knew where Kelly was and she replied that she had no idea. I reached for the phone but that increased the pain. The nurse saw me wince and pushed a button on my IV, which immediately dispensed pain medication. She asked if I needed to make a phone call and I said yes, please. She placed the phone on my tray.

I waited for the nurse to leave the room and then I dialed Kelly's cell phone. It went directly to voice mail. The only thing that I could think of is that she was still driving with Annie and had not made it home yet. I hung up the receiver and slowly lay back on the pillows. Even the small effort of using the phone was almost too much for me.

I somehow managed to doze off, although I was aware of the pain the entire time. When I opened my eyes I saw Kelly sitting in the dark in one of the chairs in the room. She was watching some kind of travel program on the television. She noticed that I was awake and asked how I was feeling.

I told her that other than the high degree of pain that I was in that I was fine. She said that she had picked Annie up and that Annie was getting the house ready for my return. I was so relieved. I actually did wish that Stephanie had been there, but Annie was a good friend and a wonderful woman, so I was grateful.

I let Kelly know that I would be discharged the next morning and asked if she was going to be there to pick me up. She acted shocked that I would ask such a question. She said that she would be there, that all I had to do was give her a call. She told me that she had taken the day off so that she could be with me.

That night I spent alone, miserable, in pain and sad. I regretted losing my breasts, one of the things that I identified with as being female. I was distressed that Kelly had chosen not to stay with me. I mean, it was only one night and she was taking the next day off from work. What would that have hurt?

I awoke the next morning after a night of broken sleep. Even the slightest move caused extreme pain. I needed to use the toilet so I slowly, carefully turned to my side and pushed myself up off of the bed. It was all that I could do to keep from screaming aloud. I also had to pay attention to the surgical drains that were dangling.

Shortly afterwards an aide brought in a breakfast tray. I really had no appetite, even though I had not eaten for a day or so. I drank the juice and coffee and tried a bite of the unbuttered toast. It was useless though. I pushed the tray aside and waited for Dr. Kassenbrock to come in to discharge me.

About half an hour later both Dr. Kassenbrock and Dr. Jacobsen came in to see me. Dr. Jacobsen told me that he had stopped by the room the evening before, but that I was resting and he didn't wish to disturb me. Dr. Kassenbrock told me that he was discharging me and that the nurse would give me the post-surgical instructions.

Dr. Kassenbrock let me know that someone would be bringing me several prescriptions to take. One was for pain, another was for pumping up my iron, and another was for anxiety. I told him that I had pain and anxiety medications at home already, and that the bottles were still full.

He said, "Susan, you're going to need more that what you have at home. Make sure that you get plenty of rest, absolutely no lifting whatsoever, no cooking, no cleaning, just stay in bed unless you have to use the toilet." I replied that I would do my best and told him that I had Annie coming from Eloy to care for me.

Dr. Jacobsen said that one of his staff would be phoning me with my first appointment and that he would see me then. I thanked both of them, yes thanked, because the cancerous tumor was gone. But I was devastated that my breasts were gone as well. I feared that I would never be the same.

Dr. Kassenbrock gave the discharge paperwork to a nurse who stayed behind when he and Dr. Jacobsen left. I asked for the phone and called Kelly. After several rings she answered. I told her that I was getting ready to go and asked if she could pick me up and she said that she would head to the hospital soon.

The nurse helped me out of bed. She took me into the bathroom to show me how to empty the collection bulbs at the end of the surgical drains. It was actually quite easy but also extremely uncomfortable. The bulbs swung like pendulums at the end of the drain tubes and felt as if they were going to pull the tubes right out from my flesh.

She told me that a visiting nurse had been arranged for, and that the nurse would be stopping by my house at least twice a week for the first month of recovery. That was a relief since I didn't have another appointment with any of my doctors for at least a week or more. I needed someone that I could trust medically.

I had brought a comfortable pair of pajamas to wear home and the nurse helped me to dress in them. Together we made sure that I had all of my belongings. I sat on the edge of the bed waiting for Kelly to come and pick me up, but it was taking her quite a while to arrive. I tried phoning her again but it went to voicemail.

The minutes ticked by slowly as I waited for Kelly. It turned into half an hour, then an hour. I rang for the nurse. I figured that rather than sit and wait in the room that I may as well wait outside in the patient pick-up area. The nurse came and I told her what I wanted to do. She frowned but got a wheelchair anyway.

I called Kelly once more, but there was still no answer. The nurse wheeled me out of the front doors of the hospital. She handed me a bag which contained the medications Dr. Kassenbrock had prescribed for me to take at home. She said that she had to take the wheelchair back inside and pointed to a bench saying that I could sit there to wait.

I thanked her and crept slowly towards the bench. The pain was overwhelming. The muscles in my chest wall seemed like they were screaming every time that I moved. I had just sat down when I saw my car coming down the entry road to the hospital. I carefully stood up and gathered my belongings.

Kelly didn't bother getting out of the car. I hobbled over and opened the passenger door. Bracing myself, I slowly lowered myself into the seat. She asked if I were all right and I replied that I would be fine. Annie was in the driveway of the house waiting for us. She opened my car door and helped me out.

She carefully put her arms around me and gave me a gentle hug. Taking my by the elbow, Annie helped me into the house and straight to the bed. The covers on my bed were already turned back, so all that I had to do was sit and gingerly lie down. She asked me if I wanted to watch television while she made me some lunch.

I told her that television would be fine. I asked for a glass of water and a pain pill. The medication from the hospital had already worn off and I was hurting. Annie brought me a glass of ice water and the pain medicine from the hospital. I took a pill, drank the entire glass of water and then snuggled into my pillow.

I tried to relax, but it was impossible until the pain medication started soothing away the discomfort. I found myself dozing somewhat peacefully. Soon Annie came into the bedroom with a tray of food. She helped me to sit up and placed the tray on my lap. It was almost like old times, as if the years had melted away.

After I finished eating Annie took the tray away. I told her that I was going to try and get some sleep. She patted my shoulder and pulled the bedroom door shut as she left the room. Kelly had not checked on me since bringing me home. I wondered where she was, but I was too tired to worry excessively.

I was awakened by Kelly roughly shaking my shoulder, causing intense pain to shoot through my chest. She told me that I had to get up and show Annie how to backwash the pool filter. When my brothers had lived in the house they were responsible for doing this, but when they moved out the task fell upon my shoulders.

I sat up slowly, trying my best not to strain my chest muscles, but that did no good. I was struck by the pain anyway. I got out of bed and made my way to the kitchen where Annie was waiting. I led her outside to where the pool pump was located. It was all I could do to turn the handle to start the backwash.

She watched what I was doing and told me that she understood. I apologized for not being able to take care of it, but she would not hear it. She helped me back into the house and tucked me into bed. Kelly came in and asked if the pool was okay, and I told her everything was taken care of.

That day I received a phone call from Dr. Jacobsen's assistant Rani. She informed me that they had made my first appointment for February 6th. I was excited, yet at the same time uncertain. I knew that breast implants were performed regularly, but I had a very unsettling feeling about my own procedures.

That night I managed to fall asleep after taking one of the pain pills, but I was awakened by searing pain coursing over, under and throughout my chest. I tried to sit up to get a pain pill but that only intensified the agony. I cried out, not wanting to wake anyone, but I just couldn't help myself.

With her back turned to me Kelly yelled, "Take a goddamn pain pill and shut the fuck up! I need to sleep!" She didn't bother to look at me, couldn't take the time to come around the bed and help me. I could hear her heaving sighs of exasperation. I finally managed to sit up enough to get a pain pill and a drink of water.

Three days after I was discharged from the hospital Annie received a phone call from her oldest daughter. Apparently Annie's aunt was in her final days. She was dying from stage four cancer. Annie didn't know what to do, but I told her she must go to her aunt, and that Kelly would drive her to Eloy that evening.

I phoned Kelly at work and told her about Annie's aunt and let her know that she would need to drive Annie home that evening. She vacillated, but I insisted that it had to be done. Annie needed to be there for her family. She told me that she would do it, but that she was not happy about it.

Annie had prepared a beautiful dinner out of the meals I had gotten ready the week before my hospitalization. She wanted to make sure that I had a

611

good meal before she had to leave. Kelly got home just in time to enjoy the food. I was already resting when she arrived, but rest was not meant for me that night.

Kelly stormed into the bedroom and demanded that I get out of bed, that I was going to go with her to take Annie home. I protested. I told her that I had been given orders by both of my doctors for two weeks of complete bedrest. She argued that all I would be doing is riding in the car. In the end, rather than fight, I went with her.

It was with great sadness that I rode in the car that night. I didn't trust Kelly to care for me. Annie had been my strength for those first few days after surgery. When we pulled up in front of her house I struggled out of the car and gave her a long hug goodbye. I knew that I would probably never see my friend again.

The drive home was uncomfortable. I was already sad about Annie having to leave, then to add to the misery Kelly began yelling at me and told me that I was lazy staying in bed all day, that she would not be taking care of me like Annie did, and that she would not be able to come to my next appointments.

I sat with my face to the window. I couldn't fathom her reasoning. I relayed to her what Dr. Kassenbrock had told me; that my surgery had been as delicate as open heart surgery, that I had undergone major surgery, and that I would not be able to recover well if I didn't follow his direct orders.

She chuckled, her eyes never leaving the road. "Sure Susan, sure", she said sarcastically. "My mom told me that you would do this." I asked her how much experience her mother had with cancer and mastectomies. "Well, she never had cancer, or lost her breasts, but she read about it and she said you should join a recovery group."

I was astonished by her cavalier attitude. Even more so I was heartbroken. I knew that things were not right between Kelly and myself, not for an exceptionally long time, but I at least thought that she would treat this situation in a humane manner. Instead, she was cold, heartless, and only looking out for herself.

I immediately went back to bed the moment we got home. Kelly stayed out in the kitchen, or garden, or wherever, anywhere but where I was. It took me some time to get to sleep. My heart was burdened. I didn't know how I was going to get through this alone, but I supposed that many others had done that very thing.

The next day Kelly phoned me. She told me that she knew a young woman from work who was in an abusive relationship and that the woman needed a place to stay for a while. I mentioned that we didn't have an extra bed as Terry and Haylie had the other two bedrooms, but Kelly said that would not be a problem.

I suggested that we discuss the issue when she came home that evening, to which she agreed. She knew that I had a soft spot for those who are abused, and that I had taken quite a few people into my home over the years. However, at this point in my recovery I really had to consider the implications of having another guest in our home.

Even though the house was in a bit of disarray I decided to lie down for a while and rest. The pain was beginning to subside a little more each day, and I found that I only had to take a pain pill in the evenings before bedtime. I turned the television on and slowly lowered myself onto the bed.

I had just begun to relax when I heard Kelly's voice. I thought to myself that she was home quite early. Then I heard another woman's voice. I carefully sat up and listened. They were whispering in the kitchen. I gently pushed myself up off of the bed and walked out of the bedroom.

There was a backpack and sleeping bag on the floor of the kitchen. I was confused. I thought that Kelly and I were going to talk about this first. I didn't feel adequately healed from my surgeries to take on another person in the household. I braced myself against the kitchen island waiting for Kelly to speak.

Kelly had a grin on her face. She introduced me to the woman, whose name was Jessica. She was a tall, rather large, homely looking woman with mousy hair and a smug look on her face. I looked at Kelly and asked what was going on. She said that she thought she may as well let Jessica stay the night and that we could all three talk.

I poured myself a glass of iced tea and went outside. I was not in the least bit happy about this situation. I could hear them talking in the kitchen. Kelly opened the door and asked me where the extra house keys were. I asked her why and she said that she was going to give one of them to Jessica.

I held myself back from saying anything that I might regret. I told her that I would be back inside in a few minutes. She laughed and closed the door. They began laughing together, about what I couldn't be sure. I went inside and looked at them. They acted as if they had an inside joke and that the joke was on me.

Rather than argue with Kelly I opened the drawer where I kept the extra house keys and handed one to Jessica. I asked where she planned to sleep and Kelly spoke up. She said that Jessica had brought her sleeping bag and pillow and would be spending the nights in the living room.

Just then, Terry came through the front door. He looked suspiciously at both Kelly and Jessica, and asked if I was doing okay. I told him that I was doing better and that he need not worry. He nodded, then went on to his room. Kelly asked me what was for dinner and I told her that I had not prepared anything.

I said, "Kelly, you know that there are meals in the freezer. All you have to do is put one in the oven." She looked at Jessica and said, "What did I tell you?" Without another word they left the house. I was perplexed to say the least. Kelly knew that I was still recovering but behaved as if it were otherwise.

I went back into the bedroom and sat on the edge of the bed. I had no appetite. I wished that Annie were still there with me. I wished that my children were closer. I wished and wished, and then I began to cry. I couldn't hold back the tears. I was completely heartbroken and didn't know what to do.

I heard a knock on the bedroom door and looked up to see Terry standing there. He asked me if I was okay and I told him no, then I went on to let him know that Kelly was moving Jessica into the house without regard for anyone else. He shook his head. He was uncertain of Kelly, and I could tell that he was suspicious of Jessica.

He asked if I would like to have dinner, and I told him I had truly little appetite. I told him to look in the freezer if he wanted to prepare a meal, and that I would try to eat a bit if he did. He said that he would do so, and that he would like to sit down to eat dinner with me. I told him that I would genuinely enjoy his company.

I could hear him in the kitchen putting food in the oven and setting the table. He popped his head into the bedroom briefly and told me that he needed to run to the store, but that he would be right back. I allowed myself to relax, but the tears were still running down my cheeks. I was hopelessly brokenhearted.

I must have dozed off because the next thing I knew Terry was waking me. He told me that dinner was ready whenever I was. He actually helped me to sit up, and then to stand. The pain was still there but decreasing a little more each day. He walked me out to the kitchen and helped me into a chair.

He had heated up a stroganoff casserole that I had prepared. There was sour cream, a bowl of salad, salad dressing and fresh Italian bread. There was even Tiramisu for dessert. I was overcome with gratitude. It had only been a few days since Annie had left, but this was the first good meal I had eaten since then.

We had just begun to eat when Kelly and Jessica walked through the door. I asked if they would like to join Terry and myself, but Kelly laughed and said that they had already eaten. Even though I had food in front of me I was a bit baffled that they had not brought anything back for me to eat.

In fact, Kelly had not done a single thing for me since my surgeries. She refused to help me to empty the surgical drain bulbs. She told me that was my problem and that she would not touch anything so gross. She became incensed when I showed any reaction to the pain I was having. In other words, she was derelict as far as support went.

She took Jessica by the arm and led her out the back door and into the meditation garden. Terry and I looked at each other. I hung my head, as if in shame, although I had nothing to be ashamed of. Terry sighed and told me that everything was going to be okay, not to worry about those two.

He let me know that he would be out of town for the next week and half on a work project, but that he would be available by phone or online if I needed anything. I thanked him for that as well as the dinner, and choking back tears I took my plate, which was still half full, to the sink, and went into the bedroom to cry alone.

I listened while Terry cleared the table. He even washed the dishes and put them away. He poked his head into my bedroom and said goodnight, telling me that he hoped I felt better in the morning. I thanked him for the wonderful dinner and wished him the same. I lay back on my pillows, pulled my comforter up, and drifted off to sleep.

When I awoke the next morning Kelly was not in bed. I had no idea whether or not she had actually slept in the bedroom or not. I carefully sat up and went into the bathroom to wash up. The binding on my chest was beginning to irritate me, but I didn't know when I should take it off.

The house was quiet. Terry was already gone for his job out of town, and Hailey was spending time with her boyfriend. I started the coffee and looked around the house. Kelly and Jessica were nowhere to be seen. I went out to the garage and saw that my car was gone. My heart dropped. I began to suspect that something was not quite right.

My pain was elevated, so I decided to take a pain pill. I opened the coffee cabinet where I had stored them and reached behind the canister for the bottle. I was astonished to discover that there were only a couple of pills left. I looked at the Xanax and Percocet bottles and they were both empty. Someone had been taking the pills.

I was highly disappointed, but I knew that something like this might happen. After all, Kelly was an addict, and I had a feeling that Jessica was as well. I would have to call Dr. Kassenbrock and try to get a refill on the pain medication prescription, but the possibility was that he would tell me that I would need to wait.

I poured a cup of coffee, and taking the phone with me went out to the meditation garden. The sun was just cresting on the horizon, and it was quite chilly. I pulled my robe tightly around my body. I listened to the early morning songs of the birds as they perched on the fence and in the trees. Hearing them lifted my spirits just a bit.

I was grateful that Terry had tidied the kitchen the night before. I was not in any condition to wash dishes or clean. I knew that I still had to backwash the pool pump, but that would have to be later in the day, and I would need to take my time doing it. That would be my only chore for the day.

Around eight a.m. the phone rang. A pleasant voice greeted me. She introduced herself as Dorothea and informed me that she was my visiting nurse. She asked if she could drop by the house around ten a.m. to check on me. I told her that would be very welcome since I would not be seeing any doctor until the following week.

I wanted to dress for the visit but didn't have the energy, plus I felt that in doing so I would aggravate my chest, and I certainly didn't want the elevated pain. I went into the bathroom and made sure that my hair, which I had gotten cut short the day before surgery, was at least presentable for the visit with Dorothea.

There was still no sign of Kelly or Jessica. I didn't even know if Kelly had the day off from work. She was being very secretive and extremely neglectful. I didn't bother phoning her. I supposed that eventually I would hear from her. I went back outside to wait for Dorothea to stop by.

Soon I heard the doorbell ring. I slowly made my way through the living room and opened the front door. I saw a charming, older Black woman standing there. She asked if I was Susan and I said yes. She introduced herself and I invited her in. She told me that she wanted to start by doing an assessment of my current condition.

I suggested that we sit out on the patio. I asked if she would like a refreshment, coffee or tea, and she asked for a cup of tea. I put the kettle on the stove, poured myself another cup of coffee, and led her outside to the meditation garden. She carried with her large bag filled with an assortment of medical supplies.

She began by asking if I was getting adequate rest. I explained to her that I did have someone to help me when I was first discharged, but that she had to return home to be near her dying aunt. Since then, I had not been able to actually stay in bed as much as I had been instructed to.

I heard the tea kettle whistling. I asked if she took cream or sugar, and she replied that she liked her tea with just a bit of sugar, so I went back inside to prepare a cup of tea for her. When I went back outside I saw that she had wandered to the vegetable garden and was admiring the variety of vegetables.

Dorothea saw that I had come outside and walked over to me, taking the cup of tea from my hands. She pulled a clipboard out of her bag and asked me more questions about my daily routines. She began writing on a piece of paper, a look of concern on her face as I told her that I had to do everything around the house myself.

She mentioned that she had been informed that I had a fiancée. I lowered my head and told her that Kelly was uncomfortable around me and refused to assist. Dorothea sighed. She asked if I had taken my binder off and showered yet and I told her no, I had only taken sponge baths so far.

She asked if she could take a look at my surgical wounds and I replied that of course she could. We went inside the house and into my bathroom. She helped me to remove my robe, then she gently lifted my pajama top off of me. She carefully pulled the Velcro apart on the binder and exposed the wounds.

She took some antiseptic wash out of her bag and carefully cleansed the wounds. She then placed an antibiotic ointment on both of them. When she was finished she wrapped gauze completely around my body and over my chest area. Dorothea replaced the binder and helped me with my pajama top and robe.

"Susan, you can start taking full showers now. It is particularly important that you keep the surgical sites clean and dry." I told her that I would start that afternoon. She then checked the surgical drains and asked me if I was having a problem keeping the bulbs emptied. I told her that I was doing the best that I could.

"Your drain sites are inflamed" she said. She cleansed them and then put antibiotic ointment on them. Dorothea told me to keep them clean and dry as well, and to watch out for any inflammation or infection. When she was finished we went out into the kitchen to talk some more, giving her the opportunity to instruct me further.

"You must find a way to get bedrest Susan. Your doctors ordered two weeks for you." I laughed and told her that it was senseless trying to do so. She shook her head, dismayed by my circumstance. I was sure that she must have seen similar instances in her time as a nurse. I said, "I am smiling through the pain and laughing through the tears."

She smiled when I said it, and I am sure that she understood what I meant. She mentioned that the right side of my chest concerned her. It was almost black, which I thought was from the surgery, simply bruising. She told me that I needed to bring it to Dr. Jacobsen's attention when I saw him the following week.

I promised her that I would. She pulled two boxes of gauze pads out of her bag, along with a bottle of antiseptic wash and a tube of antibiotic ointment. "After your shower wash your chest with the antiseptic and then apply the ointment to both wounds. You can use some of the ointment on your drain sites."

I mentioned the missing pain medication to her, and she said that might be a problem for me. Doctors didn't like to double up on prescriptions, especially for pain medication. She told me to call my surgeon and talk to him, which I had already planned on doing. But now I was worried.

She stood up, ready to leave. She gave me a gentle hug and told me that she would be back on Friday the 31st and asked if she could come at the same time in the morning. I told her that would be fine. I walked her to the front door and watched her get into her car. I waved to her as she drove away.

I closed the front door behind me, sighing heavily. I assumed that Kelly was at work, perhaps Jessica as well. I thought about phoning Kelly but decided against it. I pulled a pork roast out of the freezer and prepped it for roasting. I added some carrots, onions and potatoes to the pan and placed it in the oven to slow roast.

I decided to phone Dr. Kassenbrock and talk to him about the medication. The receptionist told me that he was with a patient and took my number, promising me that he would phone me as soon as was possible. I told her why I was calling and asked that she forward the message to the doctor.

I was five days post-surgery, but still experiencing elevated pain. I supposed that was due to the fact that I was not able to stay in bed, but perhaps that was my fault. I could have just stayed in bed and let everything in the house go, went hungry, allowed the pool pump to build up gunk, but my conscience would not allow me to do so.

I was tired and needed to rest, but I wanted to talk to Dr. Kassenbrock first. I poured myself a glass of iced tea, got the phone, and went outside to the meditation garden. It was still early in the day, not even noon yet. The visit with Dorothea was short, but I was so grateful to have met her and have her expert knowledge and support.
About ten minutes later the phone rang. It was Dr. Kassenbrock. He was quite unhappy about my pain medication situation. I assured him that I

had not taken all of the pills, but he was reluctant to issue another prescription, and told me that I could take Ibuprofen or Tylenol for pain. I thanked him and hung up the phone.

Now I had a real dilemma. Because I had previously had Hepatitis C I was unable to take either of the drugs he had recommended. I supposed that I could take aspirin. The initial high degree of pain had subsided quite a bit, so I determined to power through and face the situation as far as the pain was concerned.

I was tired, so I went back inside and into my bedroom. The house was pleasantly quiet. Kudos followed me and jumped up on the bed, cuddling with me as I relaxed. I turned on the television. I wanted to distract myself, so I watched Seinfeld. It was always entertaining and a comedy that I really enjoyed.

I must have dozed off because the next thing I knew I was startled awake by the raucous and irritating laughter of Kelly and Jessica. I sat up, careful not to put any strain on my chest. I put a smile on my face and went into the kitchen. They were sitting opposite one another at the dining room table, each with a laptop computer.

I walked over to Kelly and gave her a kiss. Jessica smirked when she saw that. I noticed that she was using my personal laptop computer. I questioned her as to why she had not asked my permission, and she said that Kelly thought that it would be okay with me. I shrugged my shoulders and smiled, not saying another word to her.

I told Kelly that I had a roast in the oven for dinner, and that it would be ready by five p.m. She didn't bother to reply to me. I poured myself a glass of ice water and went outside. They were both very full of themselves, lacking in kindness and compassion. I was, to say the least, quite exasperated.

Kelly followed me outside. She asked how I was doing and I told her that I was as well as I could possibly be at this point. She lit a cigarette and looked at me, not saying anything. Jessica came outside a few minutes later and sat next to Kelly, almost snuggling up to her. For some reason this made me extremely uncomfortable.

I sat sipping my water, smoking a cigarette, and watching them whisper in each other's ears. I felt like screaming, but I controlled myself. Kelly said that she had to use the toilet and went inside the house. Jessica looked at her, then at me, but she didn't follow Kelly. Instead, she stayed outside with me.

She cleared her throat, looked at me, and asked "Why are you and Kelly still together? She doesn't love you." I was shocked. I asked her what

business it was of hers and she chuckled. "I guess that you'll find out."
She told me that Kelly had warned her against helping me because I
would take advantage of her.

I was shocked. Kelly had actually told me that Jessica would be able to
help me, and I relayed that to Jessica. I told her that I would never take
advantage of anyone. She smirked at me and said as far as she was
concerned I was on my own. She abruptly got up and went back into the
house, leaving me with a rather peculiar feeling.

The days that followed gave me the reason for what Jessica had said to
me, that I would "find out". One day, when coming out of my bedroom, I
saw them emerge from the guest bathroom only wearing towels. Kelly
had a tray with several scented candles on it and Jessica was carrying my
laptop.

I asked them what they were doing and Kelly replied that they were
steaming themselves. I suspected otherwise. I began to become very
agitated with the situation. Kelly was not sleeping in our bed, and I could
only imagine that she was probably lying with Jessica in the living room
at night.

One day, while they were both at work, I took my laptop and hid it. I
didn't want Jessica using it any longer, especially with her disrespect,

and the way that she carried it, balancing it carelessly on one of her hands, throughout the house, into the guest bathroom and outside into the meditation garden. I took back what was mine.

When they came home that evening the first thing that Jessica did was look for my laptop. She asked me where it was and I told her that it was somewhere that she would never find it. Kelly started shouting at me, calling me a cunt, a whore, and telling me that I was worthless. I smiled at both of them and went into my bedroom.

Later that evening Kelly brought a plate of food into the bedroom. She said, "Here's your dinner". Instead of waiting for me to sit up she simply tossed it onto the bed, spilling the food everywhere. I was actually shocked. I got out of bed, put all of the food back on the plate, and got a wet towel to clean the comforter off.

I was becoming increasingly weaker as the days passed, but I attributed that to still recovering from the surgeries. I was taking my vitamins regularly, and they contained plenty of iron, but still I was beginning to feel somewhat anemic. I tried not to worry about it. This was something to discuss with my doctors.

The days passed. Dorothea paid me two visits before my appointment with Dr. Jacobsen, each time more pleased with my recovery, but still concerned with the right side of my chest. She told me to make sure that I mentioned it to Dr. Jacobsen. I promised her that I would the very next day at my appointment with him.

When Kelly and Jessica came home that evening Kelly told me that she would drive me to my doctor's appointment. I was a bit skeptical, but I thanked her and told her that would be fine. Jessica suspiciously lurked about the shadows of the house, trying to avoid me. I asked Kelly what was wrong and she strongly suggested I not bother her.

I went to bed wondering what that meant exactly. Was Jessica an angry person, or hiding something? Kelly came to bed with me that night, the first time in a week and a half, but kept her back turned to me the entire night. I fell asleep with conflicting thoughts about Kelly, Jessica, and the change in the dynamics of my home.

I awoke early the next morning. The pain of the surgeries was diminishing, and it was becoming easier to sit up and get out of bed. I started the coffee, then went into the bedroom, got my clothing ready, and took a shower. The coffee was ready for me when I was finished. I went out to the meditation garden to think about the day ahead.

Kelly was still asleep, and that was fine. My appointment was not until ten that morning. I had not seen Jessica since the night before. I was sure that she was hiding from me, rolled up tightly in her sleeping bag in the living room. There was something not quite right about the woman, and I planned to find out exactly what that was.

The drive to the doctor's office was filled with palpable tension. As we drove Kelly told me that she was not going to be signing the lease renewal, and that she was going to find a place for Jessica and herself. She said that I was welcome to live with them. My heart began pounding, and I could feel my blood pressure rising.

"What do you mean?", I asked. Kelly refused to answer me. She turned the volume up on the stereo, making it impossible to have a conversation. I should have expected this, but I had not allowed myself to believe that this was really happening, and from the very moment Kelly had brought Jessica into our home, if not before.

We arrived at the doctor's office very close to my appointment time. Stressed from what Kelly had said, I walked slowly from the car to the elevator. Inside the office I checked in with Rani and I was told that I would be the next patient. Kelly and I sat in chairs next to each other, but we may as well have been worlds apart.

It was not long before Rani called my name. Kelly followed behind me as Rani led me back to an examination room. She asked me to put on one of the robes and said that Dr. Jacobsen would be with me shortly. I turned my back to Kelly, removed my blouse and put on one of the long silk robes.

Kelly sat in a chair in the corner of the room leafing through a magazine. She never once spoke to me, nor did she lift her eyes to look at me. I sat on top of the exam table, gazing out of the windows. I suddenly had the shattering realization that it was over between Kelly and myself. My mind began racing for a solution.

There was a soft knock on the door and Dr. Jacobsen came into the room. He patted me on the shoulder and said hello to Kelly. She nodded her head. He asked me how I was doing and I replied that I had been feeling better of late, but unexpectedly weak. He asked if he could examine my chest and I said of course he could.

I had taken my binder off a few days before, so when Dr. Jacobsen opened the robe my chest was in full view. He took a look and exclaimed "Oh no!" and took a few steps back from me. "Susan, you have to get to the hospital now! You're hemorrhaging internally!" He told me that he had to perform surgery to stop the bleeding.

Kelly finally spoke up. "I can't take you to the hospital. I have to pick Jessica up from work." Dr. Jacobsen looked at her, then at me. I sighed

632

and said that was fine. I asked her to take me home and from there I would take a taxi to the hospital. Dr. Jacobsen said whatever it took, but that I needed to get there right away.

I must have gone into shock. I barely noticed that I was in the car, that Kelly was driving, or where we were going. I faintly saw Jessica on the side of the road, Kelly picking her up, and then going through a fast-food drive-through buying food for herself and Jessica. Eventually she took me to the emergency room at Banner Hospital.

From that point on everything at the hospital became surreal. I vaguely remember the triage, the blood work, being told that my Hemoglobin level was at 3.4, which was life threatening, and being given an emergency blood transfusion. I don't remember being taken into surgery. Where Kelly and Jessica went to I never knew.

What I was told after the fact is that the muscle expander on my right side had been ripped away from my chest wall, which is what caused the hemorrhage. Dr. Jacobsen had to open the wound, remove the muscle expander, and replace it with a new one. In so doing more of my skin and flesh was cut away.

I remember waking up in recovery and wondering what happened. A nurse was by my side taking my vital signs. She told me that she would be taking me to my room soon. I closed my eyes, hoping that this was all just an unbelievably bad dream. But realization suddenly set in when I was wheeled into my room.

As I was wheeled through the door I saw two exceptionally large security guards rifling through the room. The nurse was helping me out of the wheelchair and to the bed when they told me to stop where I was. I asked what was going on and one of them told me a narcotic pill had been found in my bed.

He wanted to know where the rest of "my" drugs were. I was flabbergasted! I told him that I had not even been in the room yet, that I had just undergone an emergency blood transfusion and surgery, and that I had no drugs. He looked at me as if I were a suspect while the other security guard continued to search the room.

My adrenaline kicked in and I became enraged. I looked around the room and saw my fanny pack on a shelf, the only thing, besides the clothing I had worn, that I had brought into the hospital. I pointed to the fanny pack and told the security guards to search it and they would see that I didn't have any narcotics, or any other drug, with me.

They looked at me as if I were speaking in a foreign language. The nurse who had wheeled me into the room was speechless. I stood up, wobbling, and walked to my fanny pack. I opened it and poured the contents onto the bed. "Look! There are NO pills in here!" I was absolutely fuming.

I said, "Strip the bed, check the towel dispenser, soap dispenser, and toilet. While you are at it, why not stick your hands into the hazardous waste container and search around? Strip the entire room!". I turned to the nurse and told her to bring my discharge paperwork, that I was going to go home.

She said that the doctor had not discharged me yet, but I insisted. I told her that I would walk out the door without any paperwork if she did comply. I put my belongings back into my fanny pack, got the phone, and sat down in a chair and waited. The security guards left the room, both giving me wary glances as they walked out the door.

The anesthetic from my surgery was beginning to wear off. I still felt weak, but I was determined to leave the hospital as soon as possible. I tried phoning Kelly, but as usual it went to voicemail. I was going to get home one way or another, so instead of waiting for Kelly I decided to phone for a taxi.

A few minutes later the nurse returned with Dr. Jacobsen following close behind. He told me that I shouldn't be going home yet, but if I insisted that he would discharge me. He had prepared my discharge paperwork, along with an appointment with Oncologist. He said that my blood work had come back with elevated tumor markers.

He also said that Rani had made a follow-up post-surgical appointment at his office for February 27th, and that if I had any complications or questions at all that I should phone his immediately. He asked where my fiancée was, and I told him that I had not seen Kelly since she had dropped me off at the emergency room.

More medical drama for me to deal with. I wondered if I was ever going to get past all of this. I told him that I did want to go home and promised to try to rest as much as possible. He went over the paperwork with me himself, making sure that I understood all of the instructions he had given me, including complete bedrest.

I looked the discharge paperwork over, noting the date of the appointment with him and the Oncologist, which was two days away. Realizing that Kelly had severed our relationship I knew that I was going to have to find a way to get there myself. I was determined to find my own way to the best of my ability.

I thanked both the nurse and Dr. Jacobsen, then phoned for a taxi. The nurse remained behind long enough to help me get into my clothing. She wheeled me out to the front of the hospital but told me that she was going to have to go back inside with the wheelchair. I stood up, wobbling a bit, and took a seat on one of the benches.

I began feeling disoriented, dizzy and nauseated. I could barely keep myself in an upright condition. I looked towards Thunderbird Road, watching for the taxi. I didn't want to miss it, so I unsteadily stood up and made my way closer to the main road. I found a power pole to lean on and that is where I waited until the taxi arrived.

It felt like an eternity passed before the taxi pulled up at the curb. The driver got out of the car and helped me into the back seat. I gave him my address and he started driving. He glanced at me several times through the rearview mirror, and inquired if I was okay. I told him that I had just had surgery, but that I was going to be fine.

He pulled up in front of my house, got out of the car, and helped me to the front door. I thanked him, got my keys from my fanny pack, and unlocked the door. I went inside. The house was dark and quiet. Kudos came out from the bedroom and rubbed against my legs. I tried to bend over to pet him and almost passed out.

I made my way to my bedroom and collapsed on the bed. The new surgical wound was throbbing, but I had no pain pills left. I was concerned that Dr. Jacobsen had not prescribed any. I turned on the television, lay back on the pillows, and tried to relax. Eventually I was able to doze off into a very uneasy and pain filled sleep.

Home And Hearth Once More

I was abruptly awakened by the front door slamming. I heard Kelly and Jessica giggling loudly as they walked into the house. I got out of the bed and went into the kitchen. They were shocked when they saw me. Kelly asked loudly "What the fuck are you doing here?" I didn't answer her. Instead, I walked past them and went outside.

She followed after me, angry words spewing from her lips. Jessica stayed in the house, and I was incredibly happy that she did. I told Kelly what had happened at the hospital, with the security guards finding a narcotic pill in the bed in my room. She looked down at the cement, purposely avoiding my gaze.

Kelly said, "Susan, I am moving into a place with Jessica and I won't be paying any rent for March." I was not in the least bit surprised. I told her that was fine, that I would find a way to pay the extra money for the rent. She told me that I was the reason for everything bad happening to me and that she would be glad to be gone.

I replied that I would be glad for both of them to gone as well. I couldn't handle any further abuses, neglect and poor treatment from either one of them. I told her that I was not angry, and that I wished her well, but I also told her that I didn't care in the least bit for Jessica, that I thought there was something terribly wrong with her.

"I brought home food. You might as well eat." I told her that I was not feeling too well, but that I could eat a little food. I went inside and saw bags of fast-food on the island in the kitchen. I asked what I could have and she said "whatever". I got a hamburger and some fries and went into my bedroom to eat.

The rest of the evening was spent listening to their loud conversations, their laughter and jokes. I pulled my pillow over my ears trying to shut the noise out. I finally was able to fall asleep and didn't awaken until the next morning, but my night was filled with troubled dreams, almost nightmarish and quite troubling.

The next morning I awoke much later than usual. I attributed that to the anesthesia from my surgery the day before. The right side of my chest was very sore, and I still had the surgical drains dangling from each side, but I knew that I was going to make it through this. I walked into the kitchen, poured a cup of coffee, and went outside.

Suddenly, I became dizzy and disoriented, so I went back inside to lie down on my bed. Jessica was in the kitchen scrounging around in the refrigerator, helping herself to the food that I had bought. She said "Sup" as I walked by. I didn't reply. I just kept on walking past her and into my bedroom.

I listened to Jessica making food for herself. I was curious about what she was doing, so I watched her from my bedroom door. She sat at the dining room table stuffing her face as fast as she could. When she was finished she threw the plate into the sink, with food still on it. She didn't even bother to rinse it off.

I had had enough. I knew that she and Kelly would not be here much longer, but I had to talk to her about the rules of hospitality and being a guest in someone else's home. I asked if she would join me out in the meditation garden. I told her that I wanted to discuss a few things with her.

She followed me outside and sat on a folding chair across from where I sat. I spoke with her for about forty-five minutes. I began by telling her that my first irrational thought was to have her arrested for trespassing, but that I realized I really couldn't do that to her. She didn't say a word and refused to look at me.

I asked if she knew what hospitality was and she said no. I defined it for her, as well as what it meant to be a guest in my home. I addressed the manner in which she was taking my hospitality for granted, and all she could do was stare off into the distance. I knew that she wasn't listening to me, but I continued with what I had to say.

When I finished speaking I asked if she had anything to say, and she replied, "Nope", and went back into the house. I sat on the patio wondering about her. When I went back into the house I saw that she was packing her few belongings. I asked her if she was packing to leave, and she replied 'Yep'.

I had not asked her to leave, only to respect the rules of hospitality. In my life I had helped countless people, having them in my home, allowing them to stay as long as they needed in order to get their lives together. There were only a handful who were as ungrateful as this woman, and those I actually did ask to leave.

When she had all of her belongings gathered I asked her to return the house key to me. I didn't want her to have access to the house. I didn't trust her, I knew that she had somehow manipulated her way into Kelly's heart, and I had a feeling that she was either a drug addict, criminal, or both. I was glad that she left.

Jessica had been gone less than an hour when the phone rang. It was Kelly. She was enraged and began spewing every profanity that she could think of at me. She told me that Jessica had nowhere to go, that she had a warrant for her arrest from New York State, and that what I had done was evil.

All that I could do was laugh. I felt as if a ton of bricks had been lifted off of me. Kelly told me that she was on her way home to sort things out, but I replied that Jessica was not welcome in my home, ever, no matter what. This only served to anger Kelly even more, but I no longer cared.

Soon after, Kelly flew through the front door and confronted me in the kitchen. She was screaming at the top of her lungs, her face purple, and tears streaming down her face. I didn't care what she said. I was finished. I told her that I needed my car for an appointment the next day, and she said fine, she would find her own way to work.

She went into the bedroom and began shoving some of her clothing and toiletries into a backpack. She said that she would be back for the rest of her belongings and warned me not to try and throw them away. I replied that I had no such intention. In fact, I told her she could have the bed, nightstands, and whatever else furniture that she wanted.

She looked at me and began violently cursing, using every imaginable guttural word that she could conjure. Cunt, whore, slut, bitch, fucker, jackass, and on and on she went. I simply listened to her. Of course, the words did hurt my feelings, but they hardly pierced my heart. I had heard them far too many times for that to happen.

I reminded her about the car and she slammed the keys on the kitchen counter, told me to go to hell, that she would be back, and walked out the front door, banging it behind her. My heart was breaking, but deep inside I knew that this was for the best, a new beginning for me, and that somehow I would come out victorious despite all of the setbacks.

From that moment on time accelerated almost to the point of blurring. I phoned my son and told him that I was coming back to California and that I would let him know what my plans were. I phoned my landlord and let him know that I would not be renewing the lease after all and that I would be forwarding a thirty day notice to vacate.

That evening I asked Terry and Haylie to join me outside in the meditation garden. They already knew that things were not right between Kelly and me. I told them that I was not going to be able to keep the house, that Kelly was moving in with Jessica, and that I planned on returning to California to be near my family.

Tears were streaming down my face. I loved both of them and wanted to provide them with a safe and comfortable home. Terry took one of my hands in his, gently patting it and said "It's okay Miss Susan. I already found another place to live. I couldn't stay here the way that Kelly is acting, and I didn't trust that Jessica."

I told them both that I was so deeply sorry. Haylie said that she was pretty much already moved in with her boyfriend, she was just waiting for an opportunity to tell me. I let them know that they needn't pay for March, but they both told me that they were going to pay their portion of the rent anyway.

I thanked them for their understanding. Terry said that he would be moving out by March 1st and asked when I planned to leave. I told him that I thought by March 31st, but it could be sooner than that. I still had to research renting a moving truck and get the house packed, and that would take time.

Terry said that he didn't want me being alone and that he was going to have one of his Army buddies come and stay with me until I was gone. I hugged him and thanked him for the kindness. I didn't want to be alone with Kelly and Jessica potentially lurking about. Kelly still had a key to the house and might come in while I was sleeping.

That night I slept like a baby, even though I was in a pain. I took aspirin before going to sleep, and that helped to abate some of the discomfort. Haylie was gone to her boyfriend's house, but Terry was in his room, keeping a watch over everything. I couldn't have asked for a better

645

friend.

The next day, February 10th, was my Oncology appointment. The office was only a few miles from my house and the drive there was easy. I checked in with the receptionist and waited for my name to be called. When the nurse called my name I got up and followed her to the back of the offices and into an examination room.

Soon after the doctor came in. For the life of me I cannot remember his name. He said that my tumor markers were slightly elevated, and that they were going to draw more blood and run a battery of tests. I asked him to check my chart to make sure that I was given Type O Negative during my transfusion, and he reassured me that I was.

I let him know that this would be the only time that we met as I was moving back to California to be with my children and grandchildren. He told me that all of the test results would be made available to my new Oncologist once I had become established as a patient in California. He shook my hand, wished me luck, and I drove home.

The next week was a flurry of activity for me. Kelly returned several times to pick up her belongings. She told me that she would be taking Kudos. I argued that I had been caring for him for almost five and a half years and we were quite attached to one another. She said "I don't give a fuck! I own him, he is mine, and I'm taking him!"

I knew that I would get through this. I had no choice but to. I phoned Rani to let her know that I would be leaving Arizona and that I would need all of my patient records to take with me. She told me that was not a problem, that she would have everything ready for me at the appointment.

A few days later, while I was sitting in the meditation garden, I heard a noise inside the house. I got up and gingerly opened the back door. I saw Kelly rummaging through the kitchen drawers. I asked her what she was doing and she said she needed to use my car, but she would bring it back when she was finished. That was a lie.

Now I had no car. I would have to take a taxi to my appointment with Dr. Jacobsen. I was fine with that. Suddenly, I got a very strange feeling and went into the bedroom to check my wallet. My food stamp card was missing! I had almost no food in the house, truly little money, and now I would not be able to buy groceries.

This was the final straw, a black mark on the name of Kelly that would remain for all eternity, never to be erased. No matter what, no matter how low she fell in life, her name would forever be as dung upon my lips. I cared not whether I ever saw or heard from her again, either her or her

647

consort Jessica.

I was completely finished with everything to do with Kelly. The more that I thought about it the more I wanted out of Arizona, and way sooner than the end of March. I called David and told him that I was going to rent a moving truck and drive it myself, and that I planned to leave on or before March 7th.

I heard him sigh, then he said "I refuse to let you drive seven hundred miles by yourself. You just underwent three surgeries in the past month. Mom, let me look at some things here and I'll call you back in about an hour." I insisted that I could do it but told him that I would wait for him to call me back.

In the meantime I began calling the utility companies as well as my phone service. I told them that I was moving on or before March 7th and asked them to disconnect everything in the house on March 31st. I looked up rental moving trucks online and found a Home Depot close by that rented Penske trucks.

David phoned less than an hour later. He had booked a flight from San Jose to Sky Harbor International for the early morning of March 7th. He told me that he would do all of the driving from the airport, that all I had to do was get the truck there. I was filled with such relief. I had not really wanted to drive those seven hundred miles.

When I got off of the phone with David I booked an online reservation with Home Depot for their largest moving truck for March 6th. I didn't know how I was going to pick it up, but I knew that I would be able to figure it out. I no longer wanted my car, so I decided that I would sign the title over to Kelly.

She could do with it what she wished. I was sure that was something that would make her happy. There was still a small place in my heart for her, but it was dwindling by the second. There had been too much abuse, neglect, and unfaithfulness during the five and half years I had been with her, and soon that small place would close forever.

My last appointment with Dr. Jacobsen was only two days away, so I phoned and booked a taxi for the morning of February 27th. I knew that my funds were dwindling, but I had to keep that appointment to have my sutures and surgical drains removed, and make sure that I was well enough to travel.

Terry was getting ready to move out, and Haylie had already moved in with her boyfriend. Terry told me that he was leaving before March 1st but reassured me that I would be well taken care of. He had been kind to bring dinners home for me since Kelly and Jessica had taken most of the food from the house, plus my food stamp card.

At least I knew that I would not be alone in the house for the remainder of my time there. The night before my last appointment with Dr. Jacobsen, Terry brought his friend Ryan to the house to introduce us. Ryan knew about my situation, and he told me that I would have nothing to worry about while he was there.

I woke up excited the morning of February 27th. I was a bit sad that Dr. Jacobsen wouldn't be completing my restoration surgeries, but I was so looking forward to having the sutures from the first and second surgeries removed, and oh so happy to know that I would no longer have the surgical drains dangling from my sides.

I was ready to go an hour before the taxi was due to pick me up. I sat in the meditation garden for a while, looking at my watch every few minutes. When it was fifteen minutes before the reservation I got my purse and went outside in the front yard to wait. The taxi arrived shortly after and we made the drive to Scottsdale.

On the way there I decided that I would stop at the bank on the way home, close both of my accounts, and then open new ones. I had added Kelly to my accounts, once again, the year before. I had never given her the debit card, but I wanted to make sure that she would never have access to my money.

I arrived at the doctor's office fifteen minutes early, with plenty of time to check in and relax for a bit. Rani was cordial, as usual, but she had a strange look on her face. I confirmed that she had all of my paperwork ready and she handed me a manila envelope. She told me that everything that I needed for my new doctors was inside.

Rani called my name and led me to an examination room. She asked me to take off my blouse and put on a robe and told me that the doctor would be in shortly. I changed into a robe and sat in one of the chairs. I pulled the paperwork out of the manila envelope and glanced at it. I noticed that my birthdate was incorrect, but that was fine.

Soon Dr. Jacobsen came through the door. He patted me on the shoulder and asked how I was feeling. I replied that I was doing so much better. He wondered why I was leaving Arizona and I briefly told him about some of the drama, and that I needed to be close to my children and grandchildren.

He asked me to lie back on the exam table so that he could take a look at my surgical wounds. He said that they both looked fine and were healing well. He removed all of the sutures, which took a good five minutes. Then he gently pulled on the surgical drains and removed them. I heaved a sigh of relief.

"I bet that feels better", he said, to which I replied it was the difference between night and day. He told me to connect with another restoration surgeon as soon as I was settled in California and told me not to hesitate to contact him if I had any questions or was in need of his support. I shook his hand, thanked him, and told him goodbye.

I stopped at the reception desk long enough to phone for a taxi, told Rani goodbye, and walked out the door. I was actually exhilarated, feeling true freedom for the first time in so many years. I would be glad to be shut of all this, and home with my family, in the love, safety and comfort of their embraces.

As I waited for the taxi I decided to look over my records more deeply. On the third page I read with amazement the following notation:

"According to her fiancée, she has had difficulty with narcotics and apparently has a narcotic addiction problem which is managed by her family doctor. The result is that I have given her no further narcotic medications. She is here at the hospital for emergency surgery with her female fiancée who states that she was mixing Xanax with her Norco medication. As a result, I won't manage her pain medication and I will contact her family doctor who is prescribing this for her."

Kelly had lied, once again, and this time to my doctor. At that very moment I put two and two together and realized that it was Kelly, and most likely Jessica as well, who put the narcotic pill in my bed while I was undergoing the emergency transfusion and surgery three weeks before, the same day that she suggested these things to him.

I was hurt and humiliated! I could feel my blood pressure rising and a silent rage building. I wanted to go immediately back into Dr. Jacobsen's' office, but I couldn't as my taxi had arrived. All the way home I thought about what I had read. I had the taxi stop at the bank and wait for me while I closed my bank accounts.

When I arrived home I sat down at my computer and drafted the following email:

"Dear Dr. Jacobsen,

After my appointment with you, and while I was awaiting my taxi just earlier, I pulled the medical and consultation reports for further review. I am MORTIFIED with the words you wrote in the second paragraph of the consultation report. I am not now, nor have I EVER been a narcotics addict.

I had not taken Xanax or Norco before Dr. Bitza prescribed these a week before my first surgery. I didn't ABUSE the medications, as it was implied by my former fiancée Kelly. In fact, all of those medications mysteriously disappeared from where I had hidden them, and I deeply suspect that Kelly and her lover stole them from me.

Please, I do not want this in my permanent medical records. Please, remove this paragraph from my medical records. PLEASE! Let me know that you will do this, and please forward a new copy of that consultation report to my email address. I appreciate all that you have done for me and will follow up with my new doctor in the Bay Area.

I plan to keep you informed of my progress.

The Very Best,

Susan Isabella Sheehan"

I then phoned my children who knew that I have never had a drug addiction and read the words in the report to them. They all knew that I had dabbled with Meth, and had allowed alcohol into my life, but they also knew beyond any reasonable doubt that I was not a narcotics addict.

All three of my children told me the same thing: don't worry about it, that I would be home soon, and if I wanted to pursue this issue then that I would have plenty of time. All that I needed to do was concentrate on packing and getting ready for my day of freedom, and I could hardly wait.

Terry moved out and Ryan moved into Terry's room, taking his place as guardian and protector of the house. He was charming and kind, and brought dinner for me every evening, for which I was incredibly grateful. He was gone during the day, but once he was home he stayed there watching over me.

Ryan drove me to the store to purchase moving boxes, tape and a padlock for the moving truck. I did all of the packing myself. I phoned Kelly and told her that she could stop by on the afternoon of March 4th to pick up Kudos, the rest of the furniture, and the title to my car. She said that was fine and that she would see me then.

As I packed I moved all of the boxes into the living room to stage my move. I tried to be careful when lifting them, especially the boxes with books and cookware, but I could feel pulling on my chest muscle wall. I didn't allow that to stop me. I knew that I would be fine and I had to get the packing done and over with.

When I emptied the cabinets, cupboards and drawers I cleaned and disinfected them. I took everything that I was not keeping into the garage. I called the thrift store where Kelly worked and requested a pickup of donations. The pile was quite large, but I didn't want the memories associated with many of the items.

I cleaned the meditation garden, the patio, and hauled all of the trash that was in the back yard out to the curb in front of the house, putting most of it in the dumpsters. I pushed the lawnmower out to the curb and put a "free" sign on it. I did the same thing with my beautiful dining room table and chairs, which Kelly said that she didn't want.

I carried all of my plants that were in containers through the house and found a place for them in the living room. I had nurtured and cared for them, grown them with love, and I didn't plan on leaving them behind to die. I looked at the garden, which was flourishing, and saddened at the thought of it becoming derelict.

Haylie stopped by to pick up a few of her belongings and I asked her if she wanted my washer and dryer, which were almost new. She was thrilled, and so incredibly grateful. I told her that I would leave them for her, and that she had until the end of March to move the remainder of her belongings out of the house.

Two days before my move I phoned Home Depot to talk about picking up the moving truck. I spoke with the manager, Donna. I let her know that I had been diagnosed with breast cancer in early January and had undergone three surgeries since then. I also told her that I didn't have transportation.

I asked if there was a possibility that someone could drop the truck off for me, and that I would be happy to drive the person back to Home Depot. She said that she had to look into a few things and would call me back. The phone rang almost immediately. Donna told me to expect someone with the truck by nine a.m. the next morning.

I was all finished with packing. I slept in my bed that night, the last time ever. When I awoke the next morning I stripped it completely, washed and folded the sheets, blanket and comforter, and put those in the living room with my pillows. I absolutely refused to give them to Kelly, and especially not to the interloper Jessica.

I awoke early to wait for the associate from Home Depot to arrive with the truck. At nine a.m. on the dot there was a knock on the front door. I made my way through the maze of boxes and bags and opened the door. Standing there was Donna, the manager, with five of her associates. I asked her why there were so many people with her.

She smiled and said "Susan, we're going to load the truck for you. You need not lift a finger." I must have looked like I had gone into shock because Donna took a hold of my shoulders, steadying me. She said "Just find a place to relax. Is this everything that you want loaded into the truck?"

I led her into the garage and showed her my small chest freezer and said that I wanted to take that with me. She called two of the associates into the garage and pointed to the freezer. "Make sure that you load this as well." I told her that I couldn't believe she was doing this and she said it was her style of customer service.

I filled my mug with water from the sink faucet. There was no ice since I had already packed my ice trays, but I was fine with what I had. I went outside to the now emptied meditation garden and sat on the old folding chair that I was leaving behind. I thought about how truly blessed I was to have all of this help.

It took them less than an hour to pack the truck. Donna came and got me to show me what they had done. The back of the twenty-six foot truck was packed full, and everything was secured. They had done an impressive job. I told Donna that I would never be able to thank her enough. She told me that it was her pleasure to have done it.

I gave her a warm hug and thanked her associates. I watched as they drove away, then went into the house to get the padlock. I was not going to take any chances on someone stealing any of my belongings. I heaved a great sigh of relief. There was nothing else to do except face Kelly that afternoon, and it couldn't come soon enough.

Kudos was confused, the poor baby. He roamed through the almost empty house mewling loudly. I hoped that Kelly would bring a carrier for him, and that she would care for him the way that I had. I checked his dishes to make sure that he had plenty of food and water. I had already brought his litter box and cat tree into the kitchen for Kelly.

For some reason my heart was heavy. I went outside and sat down on the old folding chair. I looked around at the emptiness of what was once a beautiful and serene space that I had created with my own hands. I looked at where the bird feeders had been and watched as confused birds milled about looking for food that was not there.

I heard a knock at the front door and knew that it was Kelly. I wanted to get this done and over with. I walked through the empty house and opened the door. She stood there with a man that I didn't know. The first thing she asked, pointing to the moving truck, was "What the fuck it that?" I calmly reminded her that I was leaving the next day.

There was a pickup truck parked at the curb. Someone was standing on the other side of the truck just out of sight. I suspected that it was Jessica. I let Kelly and the man inside. Kelly went through the door to the garage and opened the garage door. As the door opened I saw Jessica standing there.

I said, "You aren't permitted on my property, and if you don't leave immediately I will phone the police." She nearly fell trying to run off of the property. Kelly began yelling at me, telling me it was not my place to do that, but I reminded her that even she was not on the lease and I could have her arrested for trespassing.

"Kelly" I said, "just get everything out of here. Did you bring a carrier for Kudos?" Without looking at me she nodded and went back outside to the truck and brought the carrier inside. She took the man into my bedroom and started taking the bed apart. "Where's the bedding", she asked. I told her that I was keeping it.

I told her that I had purchased everything that she was taking, the bed, the television, the nightstands, everything but her clothing and toiletries. "Just be glad that I'm giving you these items." While they loaded the truck I asked if she had transferred the car into her name, and she told me not yet.

I got a screwdriver and went outside to the car. I removed the license plates and brought them inside. I said, "Now you're going to have to transfer the title." She called me a bitch and whore. I just smiled. I was almost free of her. I suggested that she also get car insurance as I had cancelled my policy.

She asked, "Are you trying to make things hard for me?" I laughed and told her that she didn't know the meaning of hard. I said, "Please, finish and leave." She asked me if I knew how strange she had felt when she saw 'our' belongings at her place of work. I reminded her that they were mine, not hers, and that I really didn't care anyway.

It took some time for them to load everything into the truck. The last thing that Kelly did was put Kudos into the carrier. I petted him, gave him a kiss, and said goodbye. I knew that I would never see him again. My heart was broken. She walked out of the front door with him and I shut it, locking it tightly behind myself.

I took a deep breath and exhaled slowly. I was so relieved. I stood in the empty kitchen and sipped on my water. All that I had left to load into the moving truck was my luggage and laptop computer. It was late afternoon and Ryan would be there soon. There was nothing for me to do inside so I sat in the empty garden and waited for him.

Haylie knew that I would not have a bed for my last night in Arizona, and since she was staying at her boyfriend's house she offered me her bed for the night. I was worried about not having my bed, and I was incredibly pleased that my old bones would not have to rest on a bare floor that night with no pillows or blanket.

The afternoon quickly turned into evening and Ryan came in from work. He brought a complete feast of Chinese food with him. There was an enormous amount of food, so much that it would have been impossible for both of us to finish it, but it was delicious and filling. I suggested that he store the leftovers in the refrigerator for himself.

I knew that he had been having trouble finding a room or apartment to rent, so I gave him permission to stay in Terry's old room until the end of March. He didn't even know me when he agreed to take over the responsibility of watching over me, and I wanted to be able to pay him back, even in a small way, his kindness in doing so.

I went outside to smoke a cigarette and Ryan joined me. He was a genuinely nice young man, had seen so many atrocities in the battles he had been a part of, and had risen above those. He finished his cigarette first and told me that he had to get up early in the morning and needed to get to bed.

I stood up from the old folding chair that I had been sitting on and gave him a warm, motherly hug. I thanked him for his kindness and generosity, for watching over me and making sure that I had at least one good meal a day. He told me that it was his duty, and that he had been happy to do all of it.

It was getting late for me as well. David's flight landed at ten a.m., and I had to navigate the thirteen ton truck down several freeways in order to get to Sky Harbor International. My heart began to pound in anticipation. It had been years since I had driven such a big truck, but drive it I would, and safely.

I filled my mug with water and went into Haylie's room. It was neat and tidy, and the bed was made. I was so happy that she had a television. I could watch something, anything, with the volume on low, and allow the droning sounds to lull me to sleep. I watched television for only a while before drifting off the dreamland.

Ryan was already gone for the day by the time I woke up. I made Haylie's bed and went out to the kitchen to heat up water in the microwave for coffee. I had kept a jar of instant coffee and some powdered creamer to use during my last few days in Arizona. It was not my first choice, but it certainly had plenty of caffeine.

I sat outside, drinking my coffee and waking up. All that I had to do was get dressed and load my luggage and laptop into the moving truck. I was getting more excited by the minute. It was close to eight a.m., and I planned on leaving by nine, so I took some clothes out of my luggage and got dressed.

I checked my laptop for any messages, and there were several from my children, but not a single one from Kelly. I had not really expected one, nor did I expect an apology from one who was so immature, selfish and shallow. I would have appreciated hearing something from her, anything to aid in closing this chapter in my life.

Time was moving by very slowly. Nine o'clock couldn't come soon enough for me. I loaded my luggage and laptop into passengers side of the cab of the truck, locking the door behind me. I went back into the house and began pacing, looking at my watch every few minutes. I smoked another cigarette and it was finally time to leave.

I went into the house and did a last walk-through. My room, bathroom, the kitchen, dining room and living room were all emptied and clean. I wasn't concerned with Haylie and Terry's rooms as I trusted that they would make certain that their rooms, as well as the guest bath, were emptied and clean.

I picked up my purse and the truck keys and walked out the front door for the very last time. I said goodbye to what I thought was going to be a life filled with love and laughter, a relationship that would blossom into something wonderful, as well as all of the dreadful events that I had experienced at the hands of Kelly and my brothers.

Unlocking the driver's side door of the truck, I climbed up the steps and pulled myself into the cab. My heart began to race and I found that I needed to take deep breaths to calm myself down. I put the keys in the ignition and started the engine. I sat there for a moment, just breathing, finally put it gear, and pulled out of the driveway.

The truck was amazingly easy to drive. I made it down Glendale Avenue to Interstate 17, merging seamlessly with the heavy traffic. I drove on Interstate 17 to Buckeye Road, which only took about half an hour. Once I was on Buckeye Road it was a straight shot to the airport.

I effortlessly maneuvered the large truck through the many lanes leading into Sky Harbor International and found the arrivals area. As I pulled up to the curb I saw David standing just outside the doors of the airport lighting a cigarette. I could barely contain myself. I jumped out of the truck without regard to my wounds and ran to him.

I literally fell into his arms. He held me for a moment, then said "Let's go!" I handed him the truck keys and pulled myself into the passenger side of the cab. He started the engine and drove away from the airport, heading towards Interstate 10 to California. I couldn't believe this was actually happening. I took his hand in mine and thanked him.

We had a seven hour drive ahead of us. David had made reservations for the night at a Best Western in San Bernadino. I watched as my once beloved desert, which was in full Springtime bloom, slowly disappeared behind us, but I was only saddened a little. I knew that I was now moving towards a future that would be filled with love.

Just under three hours into our drive we were approaching the California state line. David stopped at a truck stop for fuel and to purchase some drinks and snacks. I only left the truck to use the restroom, then returned to wait for David. I still was not confident enough about my appearance to be out in public.

David returned to the truck laden with goodies. He climbed into the cab and handed me a large cup filled with ice and soda and told me that there were sandwiches and snacks in the bag that he had put on the seat between us. He started the engine and maneuvered the truck back onto the Interstate and drove towards the state line.

I watched through the side view mirror as Arizona receded into the background. Any sadness that I had felt melted away. David had rescued me, as he had predicted a year before, and even though I had come close to death I was still alive, and heading towards my beloved family, and back to my home and hearth once more!

Epilogue

Kelly was my Svengali. All that she need do was whisper, and I would dissolve into a useless puddle of the woman I once was. It took years, and sheer determination, to break the spell that she had cast over me when we first met, to learn to become the woman I once was, and to have the strength and fortitude to know when to say enough is enough.

While writing the final paragraphs of this book, I received word that Kelly had succumbed to her demons and addictions. On February 29th, 2024, she took her life by hanging herself in her bedroom. Her father found her the next day. I literally stepped away from the keyboard at that very moment and couldn't bring myself to write again for over a month.

Kelly was not the only one to lose her life as a result of addiction. Dallas, Victor, and several other friends from the Camp also lost their battles to those same demons. They all depended on the teachings/philosophies of AA/NA and all of the other A's to heal them from their afflictions, but regretfully that very dependence was futile, hopeless, and deadly.

I often wondered if Kelly was born the way she was, or if life molded her into what she became. During the five and a half years that I knew her I was one "who has loved not wisely, but too well". I was hurt, I grieved, yet I learned through all of this, the chaos, the violence and the abandonment, that each one of the betrayals were a blessing.

As for me, I am, as of this date, a ten year cancer survivor. I am still happily single, living my life free from any substance that might dim my visions and dreams, no thanks to AA, and enjoying my precious children and grandchildren on a daily basis. I have, gratefully, never had another suicidal thought.

About the Author

Susan is the author of five non-fiction books with more to come!

She also creates unique 460 page daily planners and journals every year. These planners offer daily quotes from around the world, different spiritualities, and throughout time. Be on the lookout for her newest daily planners and journals!

Her interests are expansive, and that is evident in her writings. Susan is a lover of life and all that it has to offer, and has traveled extensively across the United States, Mexico, Ireland and Europe.

She is a mother of three and grandmother of seven. Her use of words in poetry and prose will change how you perceive your surroundings, love and life itself, and will take you on journeys that you might otherwise not ever be able to experience.

When she is not writing, Susan enjoys her children and grandchildren, traveling, gardening, baking, and caring for her female pups: Orion's Nebula, who is a Bosti-HuaHua, and Cassiopeia, who is a Shih Tzu-HuaHua.

Be sure to follow Susan for news about upcoming books and publications!

Made in the USA
Las Vegas, NV
06 July 2024

91689020R10367